W9-AZK-995

Knitting for Children

Knitting for Children

Louise Daniels

Hamlyn

London · New York · Sydney · Toronto

Shown in photograph on front cover:
his and hers trouser suits (see page 86).

Shown in photograph on back cover:
left, girl's ribbed suit (see page 78)
and boy's striped suit (see page 73);
top right, pink and white layette (see
page 30); bottom right, pink dress (see
page 125).

Shown in photograph inside front flap of
cover: pink and white trouser outfit
(see page 84).

Photographs on pages 94, 95, 101, 114, 129, 131,
132, 136, 138, 149, 155, 157, 163, 165, 167 and
210 by courtesy of Chessington Zoo, Surrey

Published by the Hamlyn Publishing Group Limited
London · New York · Sydney · Toronto
Hamlyn House, Feltham, Middlesex, England

Printed in Hong Kong by
Lee Fung Printing Company

Contents

Introduction

Knitting has always been a useful craft and a pleasant hobby, and knitting for children brings special rewards of its own. There is the satisfaction that comes from making something yourself, there is the convenience of choosing exactly the style, size and colour you require, and there is the ease and simplicity of making fairly small size garments. Also, even when you use top-quality materials, a home-knitted garment will cost far less than a comparable ready-made one. This, where growing children are concerned and the life of a garment must necessarily be short, is an important factor indeed.

The knitted look has become top-fashion. There was a time not so long ago when knitting was used only for sweaters, socks and baby garments. Now the picture is quite different, for virtually every garment from delicate lacy-patterned party dresses to sturdy top coats can be successfully knitted. Added to this, knitted fabrics are particularly suitable for today's soft, casual styles – cardigan and trouser suits, sweater dresses and tunics.

Moreover the development of synthetic yarns in an extensive range of weights and types gives considerable practical benefits. These yarns are relatively stable (that is, they hold their shape) and so they are easy and quick to wash. A thick chunky coat made in a white synthetic yarn, for instance, can be washed frequently and will keep its shape and whiteness almost indefinitely. It may even dry overnight and require little pressing.

I have carefully selected the patterns in this book to give a good balance between the fashion outfits that today's children and teenagers like to wear, and the classic favourites – the twin sets, cardigans, socks and sweaters – that are invaluable for every day and school wear. There is also a chapter of simple accessories and household items for the children to make themselves.

Knitting is one of the easiest of handicrafts, for it needs no expensive equipment and can be done almost anywhere: experienced workers can knit while they read or watch television. As a soothing, relaxing and creative hobby it has no equal. I wish you all many happy hours of knitting.

LOUISE DANIELS

Chapter 1

All about Knitting

THE EQUIPMENT YOU WILL NEED

Knitting equipment is both simple and cheap. The only real essentials in fact are knitting needles, a tape measure – and, of course, a suitable yarn for the item you wish to make. The following list however includes other small items which are useful to have as they will help to save you time and trouble.

Needles. Good knitting needles are light, smooth and have well-defined but not too sharp points. They are usually made of either lightweight coated metal or of plastic – it is immaterial which you use provided they are in good condition, smooth and scratchfree. Extra thick needles are also made in wood for knitting loose, open-work patterns. Needles are graded from very fine through to thick by a numbered system (see chart on page 26), and each size is usually available in a choice of two or three different lengths. The length you choose depends on the item you are making – and on personal preference. Some people find long needles unwieldy, but for a large piece of work of course they are essential. Very small needles on the other hand – sometimes sold as children's needles – are convenient for making an edging, perhaps only a few stitches wide, or any other small item. The sensible procedure is gradually to build up a stock of needles so that you have a range of sizes and lengths to suit different purposes.

Needles are available in pairs, and in sets of four. Sets of four have points at both ends of each needle. These are used for knitting in continuous rounds, which produces a seamless tube. The four-needle method is used for such items as socks, gloves and polo necklines. Circular knitting can also be achieved with a very long, flexible needle with a point at each end. This can be used for dresses, sweaters or other fairly large garments. The great advantage in circular knitting is that you avoid side seams.

Ideally, knitting needles should be kept all together, in a stout box, so that they do not get bent. Usually needles are individually marked with their size number but, if you have an unmarked pair or set, twist an elastic band round the pair or set and slip in a piece of paper with the size marked. Never use a needle if you are uncertain of its size – tension problems will occur if you do (see note on tension, page 15).

Cable needles. In cable designs (cable looks like twisted rope) a short needle pointed at each end is used to take stitches to the front or back of the work as the cable is worked. It is helpful if these needles are the same size as those being used for the body of the work; if the exact size is not available then use the one nearest to it. Cable needles are usually packed in sets of assorted sizes, but are available separately too.

Stitch holder. Frequently there comes a point where certain stitches in your work are left unworked and then picked up again at a later stage (perhaps in the centre of a neckline or at the top of a sleeve). Leaving these stitches on a spare needle, as many patterns direct, is risky, as the stitches can easily slip off the needle. A small number of stitches can be left on a large safety pin, but for a large number of stitches it is best to use a proper stitch holder. These are available in different shapes: some look like an outsize safety pin, others have a flexible wire section fixed to a rigid needle. Both types are equally efficient, and it is well worth investing in at least one.

Row counter. This is usually a small numbered cylinder which slips on to the needle itself, and can be adjusted to change the numbers shown on the face and so keep a record of the progress of your work. For instance if a complicated pattern is being worked, or if decreasing or increasing has to be done at regular intervals (such as on every sixth row), the marker is useful for keeping a tally as you go along.

Needle gauge. There are various gadgets available with slots or holes by which you can test the size of a needle if you are in doubt. Some are combined with a 1-in. slot which is useful for checking tension.

Tape measure. A rigid metal measure is best, as there is then no danger of its stretching, and it is easier to use for exact measuring over small distances, such as between buttonholes.

Cloths. As knitting grows on the needle, it dangles against the body or into the lap, and the constant movement against your clothes can make the knitting grubby. For pale colours particularly, it is important to keep a light cloth spread over your lap, and always wrap work up in it, or in a polythene bag, when you are not knitting. An old clean pillowcase is ideal for this. Hands should, of course, be perfectly clean before you start to knit. Nails and skin should also be as smooth as possible to avoid snagging the yarn – this is especially important if you are working with a synthetic yarn.

Crochet hook. A fairly fine crochet hook (International Standard Size 3·00) is a useful accessory. It can be used for picking up dropped stitches and picking up stitches round a neckline and also for making decorative edgings.

You will also need – rustless steel dressmaking pins and safety pins, several sizes of large-eyed, blunt-pointed sewing needles (for making-up) and a good pair of scissors. For pressing and blocking, you will need a few clean cotton cloths, an iron and ironing board.

HOW TO BEGIN

Knitting is the action of building up a fabric out of a series of interlaced loops or stitches, working one row of stitches on top of the other. The work is held in the left hand and transferred each row stitch by stitch on to a needle held in the right hand. When the row is completed the work is reversed, and the filled needle put once more into the left hand.

Holding the work

It is customary for non-continental knitters to hold the yarn in the right hand and to pass it between the two needles to make a stitch. If the yarn is controlled so that it is paid out evenly, this method produces knitting with a smooth, regular texture, and experienced knitters can work very quickly indeed. In continental knitting the yarn is held in the left hand and the right-hand needle is twisted round the yarn to make each stitch. It is sometimes claimed that this method is much quicker but, when dealing with designs for the English-speaking market, it is safer to learn the "English" way first.

During work the left-hand needle is held with the hand above the needle, so that the needle is held gently but firmly by fingers and thumb against the palm (see diagram 1). The right-hand needle rests on the division between thumb and forefinger, and is held between the tips of the thumb and the first two fingers (see diagram 2). Usually, the yarn is passed round the little finger of the right hand, under the third and middle fingers, and over the index finger (see diagram 3). This ensures that the yarn slips through the fingers easily, but is controlled. However, there is no hard and fast rule about the method of holding the yarn, and most knitters work out their own individual style. The important thing is that the method chosen should be comfortable and should produce a regular, even flow of yarn.

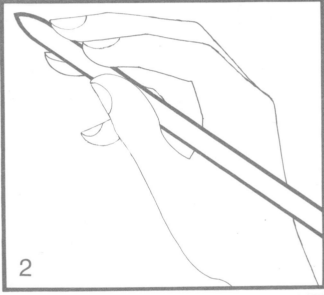

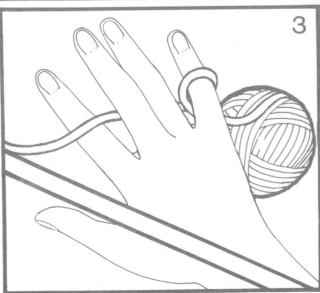

Casting on

Putting the first row of stitches on to the needle is called casting on, and there are several methods of doing this.

Every method, however, begins with a slip loop, which forms the first stitch. To make a slip loop, hold the yarn firmly between forefinger and thumb of the left hand. Taking the yarn in the right hand, make a loop round the first two fingers of the left hand in a clockwise direction. Hold the loop thus formed firmly with the left thumb (see diagram 4). Now take a needle in the right hand, slip it through the loop and with it draw the length of yarn from the ball through the loop, forming a loop on the needle (see diagram 5). Pull firmly on the yarn ends to form a slip loop on the needle (see diagram 6). This forms the first stitch and you are ready to cast on by any of the following methods.

Thumb method. This method, which uses only one needle, is generally recommended since it gives a firm yet fairly springy edge. Undo a length of yarn from the ball (about three times the width required for the item you are making). Make a loop near the ball as described left. Put the needle with the loop into the right hand with the yarn coming from the ball at the back. Take the other length of yarn in the left hand and make a loop round the left thumb in a clockwise direction. This is most easily done by holding the yarn into the palm with the last three fingers and twisting your thumb round the yarn (see diagram 7). Slip the point of the needle into the loop thus formed, from front to back, and with the right hand wrap the main yarn from the ball round the point of the needle, from back to front (see diagram 8). Draw yarn through loop leaving stitch on the needle. Slip off the loop on your thumb. Pull the yarn gently to make a taut stitch. Continue in this way, to make as many stitches as required.

If you use this method of casting on you can begin the pattern at once, instead of working a foundation row first. If the shorter length of yarn is too long or unwieldy after you have cast on, trim it about 5 in. from the knitting.

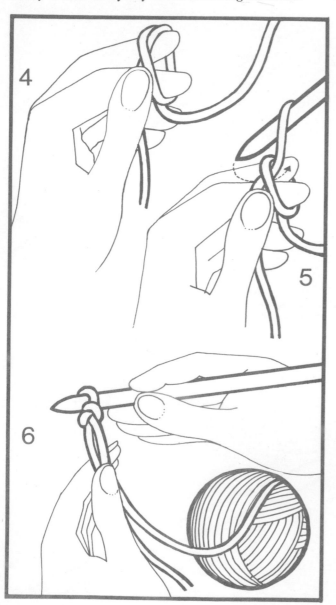

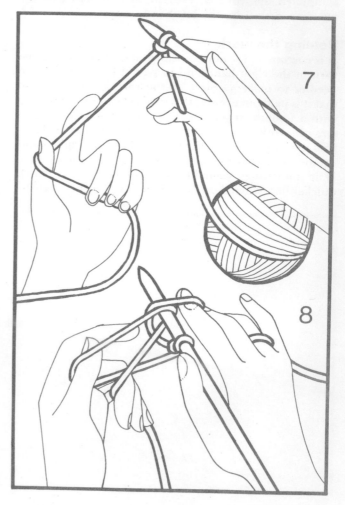

Two-needle method. This gives a stretchy edging with pronounced loops, and is useful for patterns where you will later pick up those loops, perhaps to make a hem. Make a slip loop on the needle as described on page 10, at least 3 in. from the end of yarn. Put the needle in the left hand. Insert the point of the right-hand needle through the stitch, working from front to back and wrap the yarn from the back round between the needles and over the right-hand needle (see diagram 9). With the point of the right-hand needle draw the yarn through the loop to make a stitch. Transfer this to the left-hand needle so yarn is at the front (see diagram 10). You now have 2 stitches on the left-hand needle. Put the right-hand needle into the second stitch formed and make a third in the same way; continue thus until the required number of stitches are cast on. If you want to use this method and also to have a firm edging, then work the first row into the back of the cast-on stitches to give the necessary taut edge, before beginning the pattern. In most cases, however, this type of casting-on is best used for designs which require an edge with well-defined loops, and most patterns will specify when such an edge is required.

Between-stitch method. This gives a twisted edge to the work and is springy and suitable for most purposes, especially knitting worked in the round. Make a slip loop and first stitch, as described for the Two-needle method. Transfer stitch to left-hand needle, then put the right-hand needle *between* the two stitches on left-hand needle, and bring the yarn forward and round the point of right-hand needle (diagrams 11A and B). Draw yarn through space between stitches, and transfer stitch thus formed to the left-hand needle (see diagram 12). Continue in this way to make as many stitches as required.

This is a neat way of casting on during work if the design widens, and so requires extra stitches to be added.

NOTE. *If you are a tight knitter, or need a very flexible edge to a garment, cast on using a needle or needles one or two sizes larger than that to be used for the main part of the garment.*

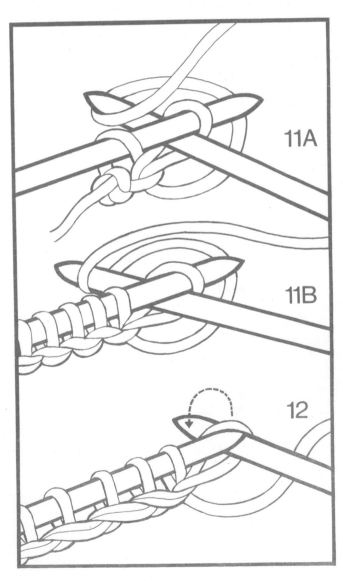

THE STITCHES YOU WILL USE

With casting on complete, you are ready to begin work properly. There are only two basic stitches used in knitting: the knit stitch and the purl stitch. Every pattern – however fancy or complicated – is created out of different combinations and permutations of these two simple basic stitches, so it is essential to be able to work both quickly and smoothly. Concentrate first on knitting; when you have mastered this go on to purling.

The knit stitch

This stitch is worked with the yarn kept at the back of the work and brought forward for each stitch. Cast on as many stitches as you need and put the needle with the stitches into your left hand. Take the second needle in your right. Put the point of this needle into the front of the first stitch on the left-hand needle, from left to right. Wrap the yarn round the point of the right-hand needle, bringing it from the back of the work between the two needles (see diagram 13). Turn the right-hand needle slightly towards you and with it draw the yarn through to form a loop on the needle (see diagram 14). Let the loop on the left-hand needle drop. Continue in this way until all the stitches have been transferred from the left needle to the right needle. The row is now worked. Turn the work round, put the needle with the stitches on it into your left hand and work the next row in a similar way.

The purl stitch

The yarn is kept at the front of the work for this stitch. Cast on required number of stitches and hold the needle with the stitches in your left hand. Keeping the yarn at the front of the work, slip the point of the right-hand needle into the front of the first stitch on the left-hand needle in a *right to left* direction, then wrap the yarn in a clockwise direction round the point of the right-hand needle (see diagram 15), keeping it at the front when you have finished. Turn the right-hand needle slightly away from you and with the point draw yarn through to form a loop on the needle (see diagram 16). Let the loop on the left-hand needle drop. The stitch has now been purled; continue in this way all along the row.

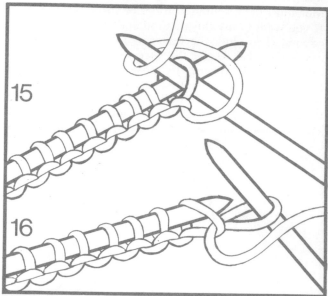

CASTING OFF

Casting off is the name given to the last row of knitting when the stitches are finally worked off the needle to make a firm edge which will not undo. Knit the first 2 stitches from the left-hand needle on to the right-hand needle. With the point of the left-hand needle draw the first stitch knitted over the second (see diagram 17), and let it drop. Knit the next stitch. There are now 2 stitches again on the right-hand needle. Draw the first over the second as before, and let it drop. Continue in this way all along the row until only 1 stitch is left. Cut the yarn, slip the needle out of the stitch, pulling at it gently to enlarge it first, pass the free end of the yarn through the loop and draw it up securely (see diagram 18). This end will be sewn in when the making-up is done.

If you are casting off while working a pattern, then you should keep to the pattern for the casting-off row, i.e. knit the knit stitches and purl the purl stitches. They can be taken over each other just as easily as if they were all worked in the same way, and the continuity of the design will not be broken.

It is essential that cast-off edges should not be too tight. If they are, they can distort the shape of the

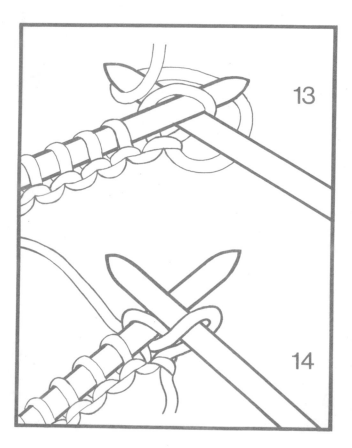

finished garment, and they may also break in use. For instance, the edging of a neckline or a polo collar must have enough "give" in it to accommodate the head as it is pulled over. So be sure to keep the knitting loose when you cast off. It is sometimes easier to use a needle one or two sizes larger for this last row.

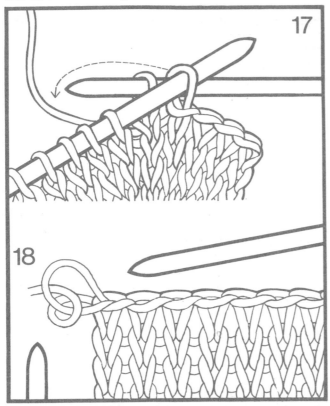

WORKING WITH FOUR NEEDLES

If you are making a sock, glove or polo collar, you will probably be working with four needles. It is easiest to cast *all* the stitches on to one needle only and perhaps work one row straight using two needles, to form a foundation. Then divide the stitches as directed (usually equally among three needles). Then begin by knitting the first stitch of the first needle, working this one rather tightly, to close the gap between the third and first needles. Casting off can be done needle by needle, taking care to work extra tightly at the dividing stitches between needles.

INCREASING

To "shape" a piece of knitting, it is usually necessary in the course of work to add to the number of stitches originally cast on. There are several methods of doing this.

1. Working twice into a stitch. When you have knitted or purled the stitch, do not slip it off the left-hand needle, but put the point of the right-hand needle into the back of the stitch and knit or purl into it again (see diagram 19). Now drop the original stitch off the left-hand needle.

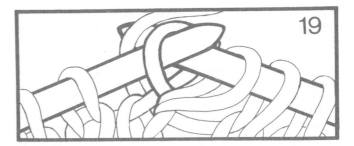

2. Picking up a loop between stitches. Put the right-hand needle into the fabric between 2 stitches, pick up a loop, and slip loop on to the left-hand needle (see diagram 20). Knit into the back of loop and draw off the stitch thus formed.

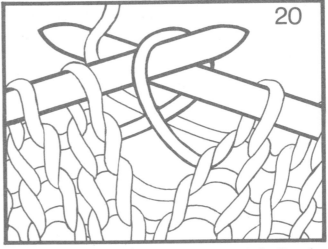

3. Knitting into the base of the next stitch. Put the right-hand needle into the fabric *below* the next stitch, pick up a loop (see diagram 21A), transfer loop on to left-hand needle and knit it (see diagram 21B).

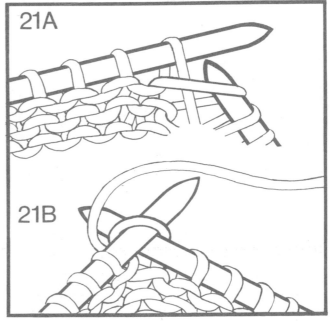

13

4. Putting yarn over the needle. This makes a hole in the fabric and is deliberately used in lacy patterns. Between 2 knit stitches the yarn is brought forward, and wrapped round needle (see diagram 22), then the next stitch is worked in. This is called wool (or yarn) forward. If you are working a purl row, then the yarn is wound over and round the needle in a complete turn to make an extra stitch (see diagram 23). This is called wool (or yarn) round needle. If the extra stitch is to be made after a knit and before a purl stitch, or after a purl and before a knit stitch, then the yarn is taken under and round needle before next stitch is made (diagram 24). This is called wool (or yarn) on needle.

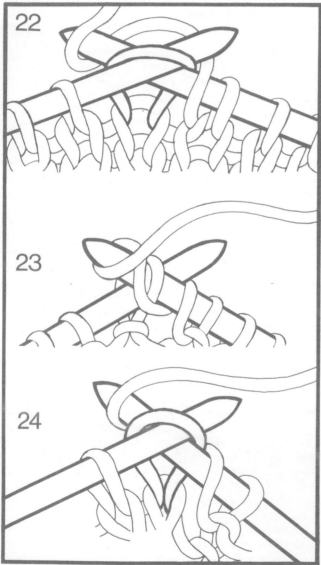

5. By casting on. If you have to cast on a given number of stitches at the end of a row, you can use the Between-stitches method (see page 11), or the Two-needle method (see page 11). In both cases, it is wise to work the first row on these new stitches into the back of each stitch.

DECREASING

As with increasing, there are several ways of reducing – or "decreasing" – the number of stitches originally cast on.

1. Working 2 stitches together. This consists simply of putting the needle through 2 stitches (sometimes 3) instead of 1, and knitting or purling them together (see diagram 25). Sometimes this is worked through the back of the loops.

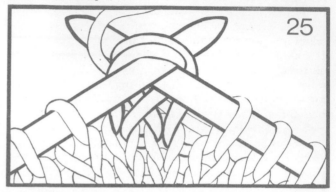

2. Passing slipped stitch over. Slip the first stitch on to right-hand needle, without working it (26A), knit the next, then pass slipped stitch over the knitted one (using the point of the left-hand needle as in casting off) and drop it (see diagram 26B).

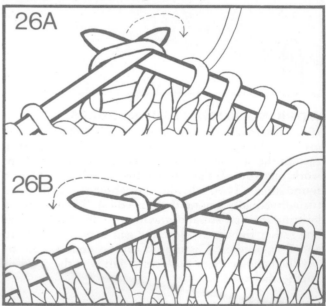

3. Group decreasing. If a block of stitches has to be taken off (for instance when a shoulder or armhole is shaped) then this is done as for casting off, but keeping the continuity of the pattern, i.e. knitting the knit stitches and purling the purl stitches during the casting off.

NOTE. *All increasing or decreasing techniques can be worked with knit or purl stitches, the action of the work being carried out knitwise or purlwise as the pattern dictates.*

JOINING IN NEW YARN

Yarn should always be joined at the end of a row whenever possible. If you are in doubt about whether the amount of yarn left is sufficient to work a whole row, measure it against the width of your work. If the yarn is equal to at least four times the width of your work, it will probably last out. If not, break it fairly near the work and join in a new ball of yarn. This is done by making a loose knot close to the fabric. The knot can be undone later if you wish, and the ends either worked into the back of the knitting with a darning needle, or taken into the seam during finishing.

If you have to join in the middle of a row (for instance on tubular knitting, where there is no side seam), you must "splice" the yarn. To do this, unravel the yarn for a few inches at the end of the old ball and at the beginning of the new, and cut away a few strands of each (see diagram 27). Twist the two ends together (they should now be equal to one thickness of the basic yarn) for a few inches (see diagram 28) and knit this yarn in. Any loose ends can be carefully cut away later.

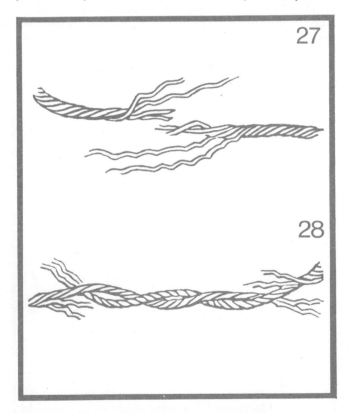

27

28

PICKING UP DROPPED STITCHES

If you drop a stitch, it can be usually picked up easily with the right-hand needle, or better still, with a fine crochet hook. Slip the hook into the stitch and take it up the fabric looping it through each row as if it had been knitting. Similarly, if you see that you have made a mistake in the knitting, drop the stitch above the mistake down to the wrong part, and use the crochet hook to "knit" the stitch up again correctly.

PICKING UP ALONG AN EDGE

Very often stitches have to be picked up in fabric already made – for instance, round a neckline to form a collar, or round armholes. To do this, use a fine knitting needle (sometimes slightly smaller than the one you are going to knit with) or a crochet hook. Put the needle or hook through a stitch along edge of the fabric, wrap the yarn round it and draw it through (see diagram 29). This makes a stitch. If you are using a

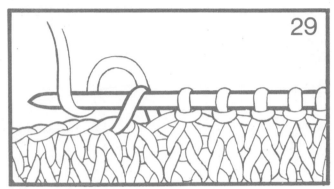

29

crochet hook, transfer the stitch to a knitting needle. Always pick the stitches up at regular intervals. For example, if you have to pick up eighty stitches along an edge, begin by marking the halfway point on the edge with a pin. Then mark the midway point of each half, and then the midway point of each quarter, so the edge is sectioned into eight equal divisions. You should now find it comparatively easy to pick up ten stitches in each division, and to space them equally.

THE IMPORTANCE OF TENSION

The word "tension" in knitting as in crochet refers to the number of stitches and rows worked to each square inch of fabric. This measurement is a result of the combination of a particular weight and type of yarn with a suitable needle size, and can be varied by altering the yarn and/or needle used. For instance, by using a No. 8 knitting needle and double knitting yarn, the usual tension is $5\frac{1}{2}$ stitches to 1 in. With a finer needle there would be a greater number of stitches to 1 in.

From this it follows that tension is the determining factor in the size of a garment. All knitting patterns quote the correct tension required, and for a successful result, it is essential that your work achieves this measurement exactly. For instance, suppose you are knitting a child's cardigan to fit a size 20 in. chest, you are using No. 8 needles and double knitting yarn, and pattern instructs you to cast on 55 stitches. If your tension is correct you will produce a piece of work 10 in. wide, but if you knit tightly and knit a fabric which has 6 stitches to 1 in., then your 55 stitches will measure only 9 in. This means that your completed cardigan will fit only an 18-in. chest. And if a discrepancy of only half a stitch to a small garment makes such a difference, you can see why it is essential to test your tension before you start work on any pattern. To check your tension, knit a square of about 3 or 4 in., using the yarn and needle size recommended in your pattern, and the particular stitch pattern given. Press the square lightly and give it time to settle back to its natural size. Now, lay it on a flat surface and in the centre, mark off a 2-in. square with pins (see diagram 30). If the pattern says that your tension should be

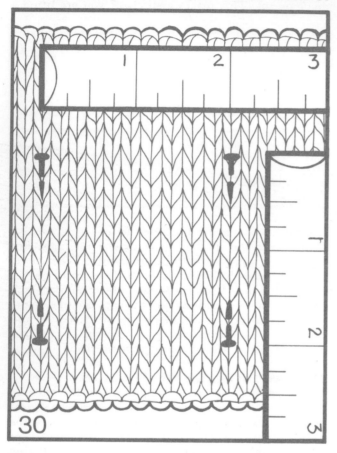

7 stitches and 9 rows to 1 in., from the top left-hand pin mark count across 14 stitches and put a pin in at this point and then count 18 rows down from top left-hand pin and mark this point with a pin. If these last two pins coincide exactly with your original pinned square your tension is correct and you can go ahead. If the second pins are inside your original pinned square, you are working too tightly – make another sample, trying thicker needles. Alternatively, if the second pins are outside the original pinned square, you are working too loosely, and should try again using finer needles. Keep on making sample squares until you achieve the correct tension.

If you cannot get both stitch and row counts correct (and this happens very rarely) then aim for an accurate stitch count. In this way the width of the garment will be correct, and adjustment to the length can be made fairly easily. Most designs are based on measurement by inches rather than an exact row count, so a slight

deviation from the norm in the row count will not matter too much.

FINISHING DETAILS

Time and trouble spent on correct pressing and making-up are never wasted, for you will be rewarded with a neat, well-fitting, professional-looking garment. So – even if you are anxious to see the results of your efforts as quickly as possible – try never to rush the finishing details.

Pressing

It is important to read any specific pressing instructions given in a pattern, as different yarns need different treatments. Acrylic fibres, for instance, do not require pressing at all. If, however, pressing is recommended, this should be carried out before making up, in the following way: each individual piece of your work should be pinned out to the correct shape and size, right side downwards, on a thick pressing blanket, care being taken to keep stitches and rows running in straight lines. Do not stretch ribbed sections such as welts, cuffs and collars. Plenty of pins should be used, and these should be inserted from the outer edge towards the centre of the work; the closer the pins are, the straighter the pressed edge will be (see diagram 31). This process is called *"blocking"*. When you

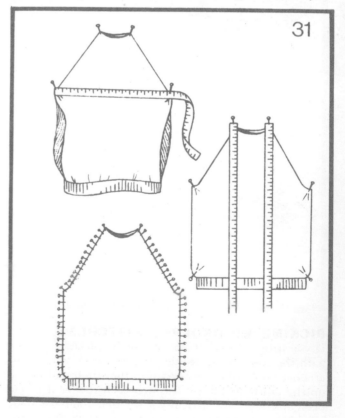

Opposite: smocked jacket, bonnet and bootees – instructions are on page 46

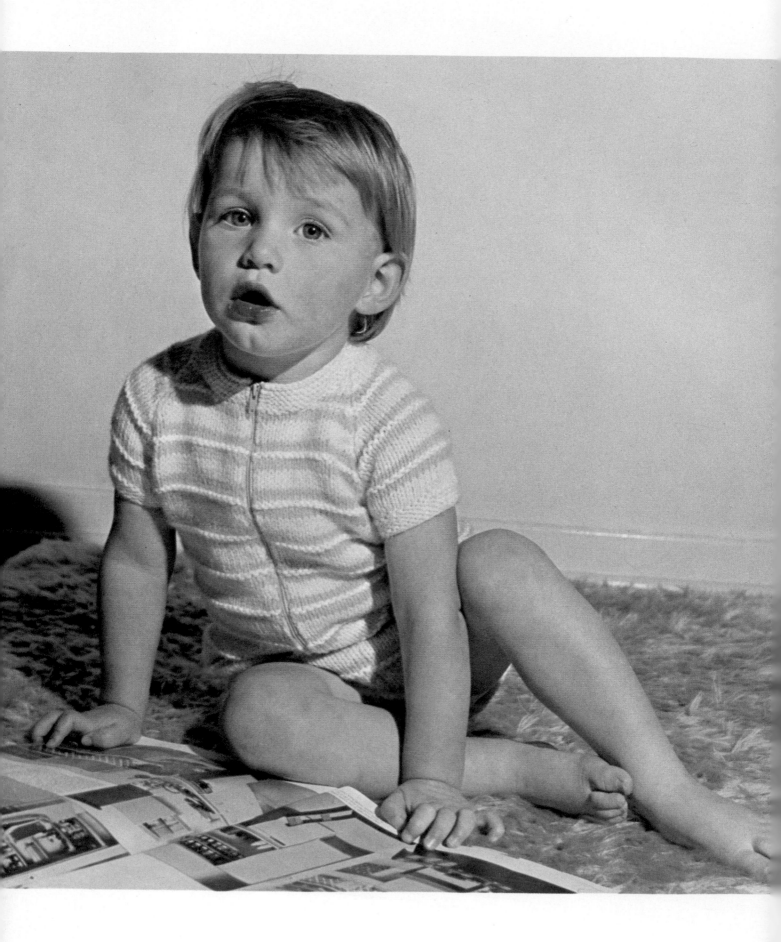

are satisfied you have a piece pinned sufficiently, to the right size, press the main part of the work using a warm iron over a damp cloth. Wait a few minutes until the steam has settled then remove the pins. Care should be taken not to overpress the main part of the work, especially when a fancy pattern has been used. A garment that is completely worked in rib, for instance, should not be pressed as much as one in a flat design. Although many man-made fibres should not be pressed, in order to ensure a perfect fit they should still be blocked. Pin out in a similar way as described above, then lay a damp cloth over the fabric, leaving until the cloth is completely dry.

Making-up
After the individual pieces of your work have been blocked and pressed they are stitched together. First make sure all loose ends are neatly darned in to the work, and then using the same yarn as you used for knitting the item (or if it is too heavy, one that matches exactly), stitch pieces together with either of the two following seams:

1 Flat seam. Use this seam for putting on edgings. With right sides facing, place the 2 pieces of work together, edge to edge. Place your forefinger of your left hand just between these edges. Using an overcasting stitch draw the edges together over your finger (see diagram 32). Move finger along as work proceeds.

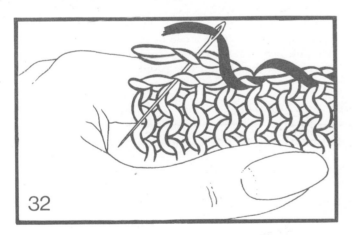

Opposite: zip-up play suit, striped in three pastel colours – see page 62

2 Backstitch seam. This seam should be used for edges where there will be extra pull or strain, such as side, shoulder and sleeve seams. With right sides of work together, backstitch seam as close to the edges as possible (see diagram 33).

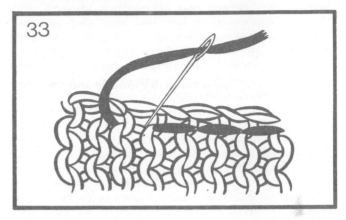

Press all seams flat to finish.
Seams should, ideally, be stitched in the following order: shoulders; set in sleeves; sleeve and sides all in one. Edgings, pockets and so on are stitched on last of all.

After-care
Never allow knitted garments to get too dirty before washing. Careful washing – no matter how frequent – will never harm wool or man-made fibres.
Wool. Wash woollen items gently in lukewarm soapy water; rinse thoroughly in at least three changes of warm water. Always support a woollen garment with both hands while it is wet or it will stretch out of shape from its own weight. Gently squeeze the garment after its final rinse, and roll it in a clean dry white towel without twisting. Better still, if you have a spin drier, spin the excess moisture out. Leave to dry flat on a clean towel, away from direct sunlight or strong artificial heat. Ease it into its correct shape and size. When the garment is dry, press lightly on the wrong side with a medium hot iron over a damp cloth.
Man-made fibres. Wash as for wool, press with a warm iron over a dry cloth.
NOTE. *No pressing at all is required for Courtelle, Acrilan, Tricel or Orlon yarns.*

YARNS USED IN KNITTING
Yarns can be natural (wool, cotton) or man-made (nylon, acrylics). All types of yarn are made in varying weights and, in the case of wool in different qualities to suit the purpose for which it is to be used. Botany wool is fine and soft and ideal for baby wear and underclothes. Crossbred yarns are stronger and less soft to the touch. Cashmere, finest and softest of all, is the most expensive but, as it is so light, an ounce goes a long way so that the cost is balanced by the small quantity used.

Man-made yarns are marketed under trade names such as Orlon, Courtelle, Acrilan. There are also various firms which produce large ranges of nylon yarns. These yarns knit up into strong, stable fabrics which keep their shape well in wear and wash. They are easy to launder, dry quickly and, when dyed, produce clear sharp colours which are fast. Like wool, such yarns are available in different thicknesses. Some firms produce blends of natural and synthetic fibres – notably wool and nylon – which combine the natural softness and comfort of wool with the strength and washing qualities of the synthetic. Such yarns dry quickly and are especially useful for school knitwear, socks and other articles which need frequent washing and take a lot of wear. Yarns are marked as 2-ply, 3-ply, 4-ply or as heavier weights such as double knitting. The term "ply" means the number of threads twisted together to make a yarn – while 2-ply is normally a fine yarn, it need not necessarily be so, since two heavy threads could be twisted together to produce a very bulky yarn. In general terms, 2-ply yarn is used for the finest underwear and shawls, 3-ply and 4-ply for more serviceable items in everyday use and double knitting yarn (about twice the weight of 3-ply) for heavier jerseys, cardigans, sweaters, dresses, suits and coats. Very heavy yarns are occasionally available which are especially good for coats and knit up very rapidly.

Crêpe yarns are available in wool and synthetics. These will knit to the same weight as a comparable flat yarn – i.e. a 4-ply crêpe will be roughly equal to an ordinary 4-ply. The difference is that crêpe yarns are twisted in a special way in the spinning so as to produce a fabric which has a slightly crinkled surface and which is flatter than that knitted from other types of yarn.

Buying yarn

Spinners dye their yarn in lots, and the lots are numbered (you will find the number on the band round the yarn). Unfortunately, it is inevitable that very small discrepancies occur between one dye lot and another and such discrepancies, which may be virtually unnoticeable when the yarn is on the counter, may show only too plainly when the garment is knitted up, and this applies as much to white and black yarn as it does to a colour. So if you want to avoid a patchy-looking garment, it is best always to buy the total quantity of yarn required for a particular pattern at one time. If you do not want to take it all at once, most stores and shops have a lay-by system whereby you can complete your purchase within a specified time.

Comparative weights of yarns

All the knitting patterns in this book quote specific brand names and weights of wools and yarns, and for the best results it is recommended that these are used. However, in some countries a particular yarn may not be readily available, but a direct equivalent known by a different brand name is. Where no direct equivalent exists then a standard alternative can often be used. The following chart lists the direct and standard equivalents for the yarns quoted in this book. If a yarn does not appear on the chart it can be assumed it is generally available in South Africa, Australia, Canada and U.S.A. as well as in the United Kingdom.

UNITED KINGDOM	SOUTH AFRICA	AUSTRALIA	CANADA	U.S.A.
EMU YARNS	Often available in all countries but in cases of difficulty use the following:			
Bri-Nylon 2-ply	standard 2-ply	standard 2-ply	standard 2-ply	standard 2-ply
Bri-Nylon 3-ply	standard 3-ply	standard 3-ply	standard 3-ply	standard 3-ply
Bri-Nylon 4-ply	standard 4-ply	standard 4-ply	standard 4-ply	standard 4-ply
Scotch 4-ply	''	''	''	''
Super Crêpe	''	''	''	''
Double Crêpe	standard d.k.	standard d.k.	standard d.k.	standard d.k.
Scotch Double Knitting	''	''	''	''
Bri-Nylon Double Knitting	''	''	''	''
Quickerknit Bri-Nylon	''	''	''	''
Tripleknit	standard triple knitting	standard triple knitting	standard triple knitting	standard triple knitting

HAYFIELD YARNS All yarns quoted in this book should be available in the United Kingdom, South Africa and Canada. In cases of difficulty in South Africa, contact Messrs. Union Spinning Mills (Pty.) Ltd., P.O. Box 4032, Berwick Street, Neave Township, Port Elizabeth. In cases of difficulty in Canada, contact M. Steiner Corporation, 410 St. Francois

UNITED KINGDOM	SOUTH AFRICA	AUSTRALIA	CANADA	U.S.A.
		Xavison Street, Montreal, 1, Quebec. Australia and U.S.A. equivalents are listed below.		
Jewel	—	standard 3-ply	—	standard 3-ply
Courtier Super Crimp Bri-Nylon 3-ply	—	"	—	"
Beaulon 4-ply	—	standard 4-ply	—	standard 4-ply
Crêpe or Gold Medal 4-ply	—	"	—	"
Gaylon Double Knitting	—	standard d.k.	—	standard d.k.
Brig	—	"	—	"

IRISH YARNS

Should be generally available but in cases of difficulty use the following standard equivalents. (NOTE *It is particularly important in the case of Aran knitting yarns that tension is carefully and accurately checked before you begin work.*)

Mahoney's Blarney Bainin	any Aran yarn or standard triple knit	any Aran yarn or standard triple knit	any Aran yarn or standard triple knit	any Aran yarn or standard triple knit
3-ply Bainin	standard 3-ply	standard 3-ply	standard 3-ply	standard 3-ply
Regency Bainin	standard d.k.	standard d.k.	standard d.k.	standard d.k.
Maggie	standard triple knitting	standard triple knitting	standard triple knitting	standard triple knitting

LEE TARGET YARNS

Should be readily available in United Kingdom, South Africa, Australia, Canada and U.S.A., but in cases of difficulty use the following:

Cherub 4-ply Bri-Nylon	standard 4-ply	standard 4-ply	standard 4-ply	standard 4-ply
Motoravia D.K.	standard d.k.	standard d.k.	standard d.k.	standard d.k.

LISTER YARNS

All yarns quoted in this book should be readily available in the United Kingdom, South Africa, Australia, Canada and U.S.A., but in cases of difficulty use the following:

Lavenda 4-ply	standard 4-ply	standard 4-ply	standard 4-ply	standard 4-ply
Lavenda Crisp Crêpe 4-ply	"	"	"	"
Nursery Time Baby D.K. Bri-Nylon	standard baby d.k.	standard baby d.k.	standard baby d.k.	standard baby d.k.
Lavenda Double Six	standard triple knitting	standard triple knitting	standard triple knitting	standard triple knitting
Fun Fur Knit	There is no standard equivalent for this yarn. In cases of difficulty a postal service is operated by the Knitting Dept., Dickins and Jones Ltd., Regent Street, London W.1. The service is available to overseas customers as well as those in the U.K.			

PATONS YARNS

Fuzzy Wuzzy	as U.K.	as U.K.	Fuzzy Wuzzy or Beehive Angora	any Angora yarn
School Knitting 4-ply	standard 4-ply	standard 4-ply	standard 4-ply	standard 4-ply
Moorland D.K.	standard d.k.	standard d.k.	standard d.k.	standard d.k.

UNITED KINGDOM	SOUTH AFRICA	AUSTRALIA	CANADA	U.S.A.
Capstan	as U.K.	"	"	"
Courtelle 101 Crêpe D.K.	as U.K.	"	"	"
Brilliante Quickerknit	as U.K.			
Totem D.K.	as U.K.	Totem (Patonised)	"	"
Courtelle 101 D.K.	as U.K.	Bonny Courtelle	"	"
Ninepin	standard double d.k.	standard double d.k.	standard double d.k.	standard double d.k.

ROBIN YARNS	Often available in all countries but in cases of difficulty use the following:			
Vogue 4-ply	standard 4-ply	standard 4-ply	standard 4-ply	standard 4-ply
Tricel-Nylon Boucle	standard d.k.	standard d.k.	standard d.k.	standard d.k.
Vogue D.K.	"	"	"	"
Orlon/Antron Baby D.K.	"	"	"	"
Aran	any Aran yarn or standard triple knit	any Aran yarn or standard triple knit	any Aran yarn or standard triple knit	any Aran yarn or standard triple knit

SIRDAR YARNS				
Baby Courtelle 4-ply	as U.K.	as U.K.	standard baby 4-ply	standard baby 4-ply
Fontein Crêpe 4-ply	as U.K.	as U.K.	standard 4-ply crêpe	standard 4-ply crêpe
Double Knitting	as U.K.	Double Crêpe	standard d.k.	standard d.k.
Courtelle Crêpe D.K.	Double Crêpe	"	"	"
Double Crêpe	"	"	"	"
Sportswool	D.K. or Candytwist	as U.K.	"	"
Pullman	as U.K.	as U.K.	standard double d.k.	standard double d.k.

TWILLEY YARNS	All Twilley yarns quoted in this book should be readily available in the United Kingdom, South Africa, Australia, Canada and U.S.A.

WENDY YARNS				
Nylonised 4-ply	as U.K.	standard 4-ply	standard 4-ply	standard 4-ply
Courtelle Crêpe 4-ply	as U.K.	"	as U.K.	"
Peter Pan Baby Bri-Nylon 4-ply	as U.K.	"	as U.K.	"
Peter Pan Bri-Nylon 4-ply	as U.K.	"	as U.K.	"
Tricel/Nylon D.K.	as U.K.	standard d.k.	standard d.k.	standard d.k.
Courtelle Double Crêpe	as U.K.	"	as U.K.	"
Fashionflake D.K.	as U.K.	"	standard d.k.	"
Nylonised D.K.	as U.K.	"	"	"

IMPORTANT NOTE Where the exact yarn given in a pattern is not available an equivalent may not work up to precisely the same measurements, therefore it is doubly important to make a tension check before beginning (see page 15). Yardage also varies with different yarns and you may find you need either more or less than the quantity specified in the pattern.

CHOOSING A PATTERN

If you are a beginner, your first pattern should be for something small and simple in stitch. This does *not* mean in plain knitting. In fact, simple plain knitting shows every flaw and is usually worked really well only by an experienced knitter. Choose something with a small, easy pattern which has little variation and gives an all-over surface effect, rather than a complex pattern.

When making a garment for a child, choose a pattern size closest to the chest size desired, since other measurements (length of sleeve, legging, dress and so on) can easily be adjusted as you work.

SOME BASIC STITCH PATTERNS

There are, as already explained, only two basic stitches in knitting, but they can be combined in an unlimited number of ways to form different stitch patterns. Some simple combinations are in constant use, however, and should be mastered by the beginner.

Garter stitch. Every row is worked in knit stitches. This gives a fabric with well defined ridges (2 rows per ridge).

Stocking stitch. One row all knit stitches, the next all purl stitches, the rows worked alternately. The knit side forms the right side of the work, except when reversed stocking stitch is specified; in this case, the purl side is the right side. This stitch gives a smooth, plain surface.

Rib. 1 stitch knit, 1 stitch purl, alternately all along the row, using an even number of stitches. Every row is worked in the same way. This gives a close, springy fabric (much smaller than a flat stitch worked over the same number of stitches) and is therefore ideal for welts, cuffs and collars, where clinging qualities are necessary. Ribs can be varied in many ways – 2 stitches knit, 2 purl, for instance, or a few rows with ribs going one way followed by a group of rows with ribs going in a different way. If the total number of stitches is a multiple of the number of repeated stitches, then every row is worked the same, as knit stitches are purled when the work is reversed. For example, if you are working knit 2, purl 2 rib, total number of stitches should be divisible by 4.

Moss stitch. Worked as for rib, but with uneven number of stitches, so that the knit and purl stitches on the first row are knitted and purled again on the second – and so on. If the pattern demands an even number of stitches, then the second row should start with a purl stitch so you maintain the "uneven" ribbing. Moss stitch gives a flat fabric with a most attractive textured surface. Again, this stitch can be worked double, with 2 purl stitches followed by 2 knit stitches.

Cables. These are groups of stitches which are crossed over each other to give a twisted, rope-like effect. They look complex but are really simple to do if you follow the design correctly. Cables are always worked on knit stitches.

COLOUR KNITTING

Any type of knitting which involves the use of more than one colour of yarn is termed "colour knitting". This refers to simple stripe patterns as well as to more complicated Fair Isle and chequered designs. Usually colour pattern work is done in stocking stitch.

Although the technique is a little more difficult than for one-colour knitting, with practice the art of working with two or more yarns at the same time can soon be mastered. The important thing is to learn to regulate the tension of the different yarns, so that neither pulls too tightly or remains too slack. Before starting any colour pattern, try working small samples so you can get used to the manipulation of the yarns.

Holding your wool

Even in Fair Isle designs where several different yarns are used, it is unusual to have to work with more than 2 colours of yarn at any one time. The simplest way to hold your work is to have one colour in your left hand, the other in your right, as in diagram 34.

Yarn is always carried across the back of your work, and there are two methods of doing this: stranding or weaving.

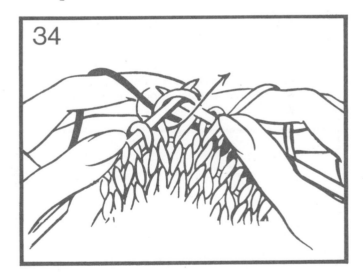
34

Stranding

In this method, you simply take the wool not in use across the back of the knitting, and pick it up when required (see diagram 35). The important thing here is not to pull the yarn too tightly: there should be enough slackness to allow for stretching when the garment is worn, but on the other hand not so much slackness that the yarn forms loops at the back of the work.

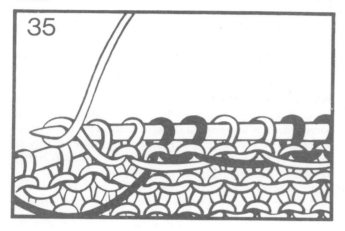

Weaving

This method is a little more complicated than stranding but gives a neater and more professional looking finish. The principle here is to weave the colour not in use under the colour in use. The diagram 36 shows the woven strands as they appear at the back of the knitted fabric.

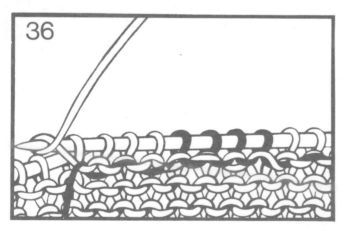

Reading colour charts

Very often with a Fair Isle or fairly complex design, the colour pattern is given in the form of a chart (for example, see pattern on page 195). Every square on a chart represents either one stitch (reading across) or one row (reading up). Normally you work in stocking stitch, reading the odd rows (knitted) from right to left, the even rows (purl) from left to right. If you are working in rounds, every round is knitted and the chart is read from right to left.

USING CROCHET FOR EDGINGS

A crochet edging can often give an attractive and neat finish to a knitted garment – lacy borders, for instance, can be added round hem, cuff or neck edges, or an edging in a contrast coloured yarn added to a garment. Also if a cord or drawstring is required for a fastening, this can be more effectively worked in a crochet chain, rather than knitted strip. It is therefore an advantage to be able to work a few basic crochet stitches. The following simple diagrams and instructions show how to do these.

How to begin

Make a slip loop as for knitting (see page 10), but use crochet hook instead of knitting needle to draw yarn through loop. Pull the short end of yarn and the ball thread in opposite directions to bring the loop close round the hook (see diagram 37).

Holding the work

Loop the long thread round the little finger of your left hand, across the palm and behind the forefinger.

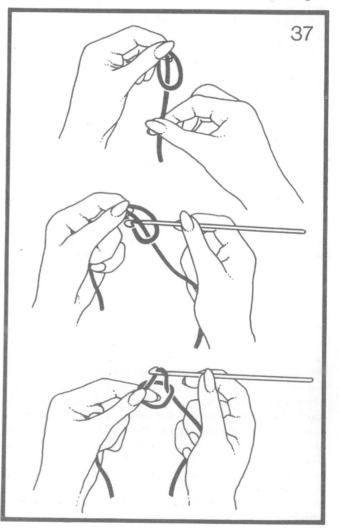

This should keep the tension of your work even. Catch the knot of the loop on the hook between the thumb and forefinger of left hand (as your work grows you will still continue to steady it by holding in this position). Hold the bar of the hook between thumb and forefinger of the right hand, as you would a pencil, and place the tip of the middle finger on head of hook to guide it (see diagram 38).

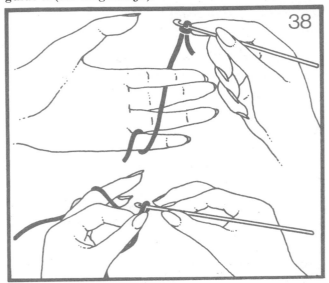

Chain stitch

This is the foundation of all crochet work. With the yarn in position, and the first loop on hook, pass hook under the yarn held between left hand forefinger and hook, catch yarn with hook (diagram 39). Draw yarn and head of hook through loop already on hook (diagram 40). Each time you pull yarn through loop on hook counts as 1 chain. Continue until required number of chains are formed.

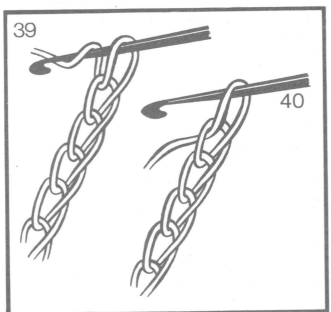

Slip stitch

Insert the hook into the stitch to the left of the hook (or into a stitch along edge of knitting), catch the long thread and draw it through the stitch and the loop already on the hook (see diagram 41). This forms a flat chain and is sometimes called single crochet.

Treble

Pass the hook under yarn which is held in left hand, insert the hook into the stitch to the left of the hook (or into a stitch along edge of knitting) and draw yarn through. You now have 3 loops on the hook. Put the yarn over the hook again (diagram 42) and pull it through the first 2 loops on the hook, leaving 2 loops on the hook (diagram 43). Put the yarn over the hook once more and draw through the last 2 loops, leaving you with 1 loop on the hook (diagram 44).

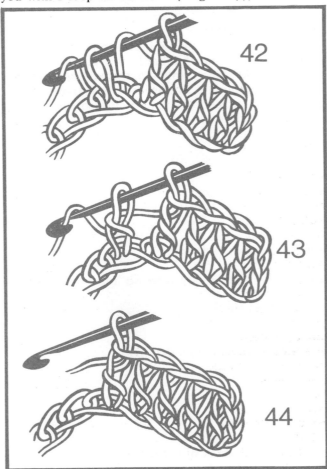

Double crochet

This stitch is frequently used for edging purposes. Insert the hook into the stitch to the left of the hook (or into a stitch along edge of knitting) and catch yarn with hook (diagram 45). Draw yarn through stitch. You now have 2 loops on the hook (diagram 46). Put the yarn over the hook and draw it through the 2 loops. This leaves 1 loop on the hook (diagram 47).

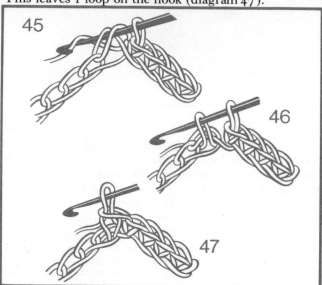

ABBREVIATIONS

The following are the abbreviations used in the patterns throughout this book. If a pattern involves a complicated stitch formation, this will be described and the appropriate abbreviation given within the pattern. Colour abbreviations will also be given in individual patterns.

alt., alternate
beg., beginning
ch., chain
cont., continue
d.c., double crochet
dec., decrease(e) (ed) (ing)
foll., following
in., inch(es)
inc., increase(e) (ed) (ing)
k., knit
m.1, make 1 stitch (by working into front and back of stitch)
m.st., moss stitch
p., purl
patt., pattern
p.s.s.o., pass slipped stitch over
rem., remain(ing)
rep., repeat
sl., slip
s.s., slip stitch
st(s)., stitch(es)
st.st., stocking stitch
t.b.l., through back of loop(s)
tog., together

tr., treble
y.b., yarn back
y.fwd., yarn forward
y.o.n., yarn on needle
y.r.n., yarn round needle

Size Note

Instructions in every pattern are given in size order, with larger sizes in brackets. Where only one set of figures occurs this refers to all sizes.

USEFUL FACTS AND FIGURES

Imperial Standard measurements are used throughout this book. If it is wished to convert these into the appropriate metric equivalents, follow the simple conversion tables below.

Weights

1 oz. = 28·35 grammes
4 oz. = 113·4 grammes
8 oz. = 226·8 grammes
1 lb. = 454 grammes
2 lb. 3 oz. (approx.) = 1 kilogramme

N.B. When buying knitting yarn, a 25-gramme ball of yarn will very approximately equal a 1-oz. ball. But as 1 oz. equals slightly over 25 grammes for larger quantities increase the number of gramme balls, e.g. if 12 oz. yarn is required, buy fourteen 25-gramme balls, and if 20 oz. is required, buy twenty-three 25-gramme balls.

Linear measures

1 inch = 2·54 centimetres
6 inches = 15·2 centimetres
1 foot (12 inches) = 30·48 centimetres
1 yard = 0·914 metre (just over 91 centimetres)
1 yard 4 in. (approximately) = 1 metre

COMPARATIVE SIZES OF KNITTING NEEDLES

British	Continental	American
14	2	0
13	—	—
12	2·50	1
11	3·00	2
10	3·25	3
—	3·50	4
9	4·00	5
8	4·50	6
7	4·75	7
6	5·00	8
5	5·50	9
4	6·00	10
3	7·00	10½
2	8·00	11
1	9·25	13

The Patterns

95 easy-to-follow patterns
using the knitting stitches and
techniques described in the
previous chapter.

Chapter 2

Babies' Clothes

Baby's trousseau

(photographed in colour on page 35)

MATERIALS
4 balls Emu Bri-Nylon 3-ply for short dress (see note on wools and yarns, page 20), 8 balls for long dress, 14 balls for shawl; one pair each Nos. 10 and 11 knitting needles, and one pair of long No. 10 knitting needles for the shawl (see page 26); 3 small buttons for each dress.

MEASUREMENTS
To fit chest size 19 (20) in.; length at centre back 14¾ (15) in. (short dress), 23½ (23¾) in. (long dress); sleeve seam 2 in.; measurement of shawl 45 in. square.

TENSION
8 sts. and 11 rows to 1 in. over patt.; 8 sts. and 10½ rows to 1 in. over st.st. (see note on tension, page 15).

ABBREVIATIONS
See page 26.

SHORT DRESS
BACK
**With No. 10 needles, cast on 133 (141) sts. and work 4 rows in st.st.
Next row (make picot hemline): k.2, *y.fwd., k.2 tog.; rep. from * to last st., k.1. Work 5 rows in st.st. Begin. patt.:
1st row (right side): p.
2nd row: p.
3rd row: k.1, *y.fwd., sl.1, k.2 tog., p.s.s.o., y.fwd., k.1; rep. from * to end.
4th row: p.
5th row: k.1, *y.fwd., sl.1, k.2 tog., p.s.s.o., y.fwd., k.5; rep. from * to last 4 sts., y.fwd., sl.1, k.2 tog., p.s.s.o., y.fwd., k.1.
6th row: p.

7th row: as 5th row.
8th row: p.
9th row: k.1, *k.3, y.fwd., sl.1, k.1, p.s.s.o., k.1, k.2 tog., y.fwd.; rep. from * to last 4 sts., k.4.
10th row: p.
11th row: as 3rd row.
12th, 13th and 14th rows: p.
15th row: k.
16th row: p.
Rep. the last 2 rows twice more.
These 20 rows form the patt.
Commence Shaping. Rep. rows 1 to 16 inclusive.
17th row: k.9 (6), (sl.1, k.1, p.s.s.o., k.5 (6)) 7 times, sl.1, k.1, p.s.s.o., k.13 (13), k.2 tog., (k.5 (6), k.2 tog.) 7 times, k.9 (6): 117 (125) sts.
18th row: p.
19th row: k.
20th row: p.
Rep. rows 1 to 16 inclusive.
17th row: k.9 (6), (sl.1, k.1, p.s.s.o., k.4 (5)) 7 times, sl.1, k.1, p.s.s.o., k.11 (11), k.2 tog., (k.4 (5), k.2 tog.) 7 times, k.9 (6): 101 (109) sts.
18th row: p.
19th row: k.
20th row: p.
Rep rows 1 to 16 inclusive.
17th row: k.9 (6), (sl.1, k.1, p.s.s.o., k.3 (4)) 7 times, sl.1, k.1, p.s.s.o., k.9 (9), k.2 tog., (k.3 (4), k.2 tog.) 7 times, k.9 (6): 85 (93) sts.
18th row: p.
19th row: k.
20th row: p.
Rep. the 20 patt. rows once, then rows 1 to 16 inclusive.
17th row: k.11 (9), (sl.1, k.1, p.s.s.o., k.11 (6)) 2 (4) times, sl.1, k.1, p.s.s.o., k.7 (7), k.2 tog., (k.11 (6), k.2 tog.) 2 (4) times, k.11 (9): 79 (83) sts.
18th row: p.
Change to st.st.

Shape Armholes. Cast off 4 sts. at the beg. of the next 2 rows. Dec. 1 st. at each end of the next and every foll. alt. row until 65 (67) sts. rem. **

Cont. without further shaping until work measures 1¼ (1½) in. from beg. of armhole shaping, ending with a p. row.

Divide for Back Opening. Next row: k.35 (36) sts. and turn, leaving rem. sts. on a stitch holder.

Next row: k.5, p. to end.

Buttonhole row: k. to last 3 sts., y.fwd., k.2 tog., k.1.

Next row: k.5, p. to end.

Next row: k.

Rep. the last 2 rows until work measures 3¼ (3½) in. from beg. of armhole shaping, ending at armhole edge, *at the same time* make another buttonhole 1¼ in. from base of previous buttonhole.

Shape shoulder. Cast off 7 sts. at the beg. of the next and foll. alt. row and 6 sts. on the next alt. row. Work 1 row. Leave the rem. 15 (16) sts. on a stitch holder.

Join in yarn at neck edge to rem. sts., cast on 5 sts., k. to end.

Next row: p. to last 5 sts., k.5.

Complete to match first side, reversing all shapings and omitting buttonholes.

FRONT

Work as for Back from ** to **.

Cont. without further shaping until work measures 1½ (1¾) in. from beg. of armhole shaping, ending with a p. row.

Shape Neck. Next row: k.27 sts. and turn, leaving rem. sts. on a stitch holder. Dec. 1 st. at neck edge on the next 7 rows. Cont. without further shaping until work measures the same as Back to shoulder, ending at armhole edge.

Shape Shoulder. Cast off 7 sts. at the beg. of the next and foll. alt. row. Work 1 row. Cast off the rem. 6 sts. Slip the centre 11 (13) sts. on to a stitch holder. Join in yarn at neck edge to rem. sts., k to end. Complete to match first side of neck.

SLEEVES (make 2 alike)

With No. 11 needles cast on 44 (44) sts. and work ½ in. in k.1, p.1 rib, ending with a right-side row.

Next row: rib 6, *work twice into next st., rib 3; rep. from * to last 6 sts., work twice into next st., rib 5: 53 (53) sts.

Change to No. 10 needles and work patt. rows 1 to 14 inclusive as given for Back of Dress.

Next row: k.5 (4), *k. twice into next st., k.5 (4); rep. from * to last 6 (4) sts., k. twice into next st., k.5 (3): 61 (63) sts.

Cont. in st.st. Beg. with a p. row, work 3 rows.

Shape Top. Cast off 4 sts. at the beg. of the next 2 rows. Dec. 1 st. at each end of the next and every foll. alt. row until 43 sts. rem., then 1 st. at each end of every row until 17 sts. rem. Cast off.

NECKBAND

Join shoulder seams. With right side of work facing and No. 11 needles, k. across the 15 (16) sts. on left side of back neck, pick up and k.17 (17) sts. down left side of front neck, k. across the 11 (13) sts. at centre, pick up and k.17 (17) sts. up right side of front neck, then k. across the 15 (16) sts. on right side of back neck: 75 (79) sts.

Next row: k.5, * p.1, k.1; rep. from * to last 6 sts., p.1, k.5.

Next row: k.6, * p.1, k.1; rep. from * to last 5 sts., k.5.

Rep. these 2 rows for ½ in., working a third buttonhole 1¼ in. from base of previous buttonhole.

Cast off, casting off in rib over the rib section.

TO COMPLETE

Join side and sleeve seams. Set sleeves into armholes. Catch down lower edge of back neck underlap. Sew on buttons opposite buttonholes. Turn in hem at picot hemline, and slipstitch in place on to wrong side.

LONG DRESS

Work as for Short Dress, but work 6 complete patt. (120 rows) before beg. shaping.

SHAWL
TO MAKE

With long No. 10 needles, cast on 361 sts. K. 17 rows. Beg. patt.:

1st row (right side): k.

2nd row: k.10, p. to last 10 sts., k.10.

Rep. these 2 rows twice more.

7th row: as 2nd row.

8th row: as 2nd row.

9th row: k.11, *y.fwd., sl.1, k.2 tog., p.s.s.o., y.fwd., k.1; rep. from * to last 10 sts., k.10.

10th row: as 2nd row.

11th row: k.11, *y.fwd., sl.1, k.2 tog., p.s.s.o., y.fwd., k.5; rep. from * to last 14 sts., y.fwd., sl.1, k.2 tog., p.s.s.o., y.fwd., k.11.

12th row: as 2nd row.

13th row: as 11th row.

14th row: as 2nd row.

15th row: k.11, *k.3, y.fwd., sl.1, k.1, p.s.s.o., k.1, k.2 tog., y.fwd; rep. from * to last 14 sts., k.14.

16th row: as 2nd row.

17th row: as 9th row.

18th, 19th and 20th rows: as 2nd row.

Rep. these 20 rows 22 times more, then rows 1 to 5 inclusive once.

K. 17 rows.

Cast off.

Carrying cape

(photographed in black and white opposite)

MATERIALS
14 oz. Sirdar Baby Courtelle 4-ply (see note on wools and yarns, page 20); one pair each Nos. 7 and 10 knitting needles (see page 26); a ½-in. button.

MEASUREMENTS
Length at centre back (excluding hood) 23 in.

TENSION
5 sts. and 7 rows to 1 in. on No. 7 needles (see note on tension, page 15).

ABBREVIATIONS
See page 26.

MAIN SECTION

With No. 7 needles cast on 200 sts. K.13 rows.
14th row: k.8, p. to last 8 sts., k.8.
15th row: k.
Rep. last 2 rows 4 times then 14th row once.
25th row: k.16, *p.1, k.1; rep. from * to last 16 sts., k.16.
26th row: k.8, p.8, *k.1, p.1; rep. from * to last 16 sts., p.8, k.8.
Rep. last 2 rows 4 times.
35th row: k.16, (p.1, k.1) 3 times, p.1, k. to last 23 sts., (k.1, p.1) 3 times, k.17.
36th row: k.8, p.8, (k.1, p.1) 3 times, k.1, p. to last 23 sts., (p.1, k.1) 3 times, p.9, k.8.
Rep. last 2 rows until work measures 20 in., ending with a wrong-side row. Cont. thus:
1st row: k.10, *k.1, k.2 tog. t.b.l., k.6, k.2 tog., k.1; rep. from * 15 times, k.10: 170 sts.
2nd row: k.8, p. to last 8 sts., k.8.
3rd row: k.
4th row: as 2nd row.
5th row: k.

6th row: as 2nd row.
7th row: k.10, *k.1, k.2 tog. t.b.l., k.4, k.2 tog., k.1; rep. from * 15 times, k.10: 140 sts.
8th – 12th rows: as 2nd – 6th rows.
13th row: k.10, *k.1, k.2 tog. t.b.l., k.2, k.2 tog., k.1; rep. from * 15 times, k. 10: 110 sts.
14th – 16th rows: as 2nd – 4th rows.
17th row: k.10, *k.1, k.2 tog. t.b.l., k.2 tog., k.1; rep. from * 15 times, k.10: 80 sts.
18th – 20th rows: as 2nd – 4th rows.
21st row: k.10, *k.1, k.2 tog., k.1; rep. from * 15 times, k.10: 65 sts.
Change to No. 10 needles.
Next row: *p.1, k.1; rep. from * to last st., p.1.
Next row: *k.1, p.1; rep. from * to last st., k.1.
Rep. last 2 rows once then the first of the 2 rows again.
Next row: (k.1, p.1) 3 times, k.1, *m.1, sl.1, k.1, p.s.s.o.; rep. from * to last 8 sts., rib 8.
Now rib for 4 more rows, then cast off 8 sts. at beg. of next 2 rows: 49 sts. Change to No. 7 needles.

HOOD
1st and alt. rows: k.4, p. to last 4, k.4.
2nd row: k.23, inc. in next st., k.1, inc. in next st., k.23.
4th and 6th rows: k.
8th row: k.24, inc. in next st., k.1, inc. in next st., k.24.
Cont. in st.st., keeping garter st. border of 4 sts. at each end of work and inc. 1 st. at each side of centre st. every 6th row until hood is 7 in. Cast off.

TO COMPLETE
Fold hood in half and sew seam at top, make rouleau loop for button at neck of cape. Sew button to opposite edge. Make a plaited, crocheted or twisted cord about 1 yd. long and thread through holes at neck.

Pink and white layette

(photographed in colour on the back cover and in black and white on pages 32 and 33)

MATERIALS
3 (3, 4) balls Hayfield Beaulon 4-ply in pink, 6 (7, 7) in white (see note on wools and yarns, page 20); one pair each Nos. 9, 10, 11 and 12 knitting needles (see page 26); 3 small white buttons; 3 medium white buttons; 2 yards white ribbon, ⅜ in. wide.

MEASUREMENTS
To fit chest size 18 (20, 22) in.; length of dress at centre back 12 (13½, 15) in.

TENSION
5½ sts. and 12 rows to 1 in. on No. 10 needles over patt. (see note on tension, page 15).

Hooded carrying cape is worked in stocking stitch with a patterned edging

ABBREVIATIONS

See page 26; P., pink; W., white.

DRESS
FRONT

With No. 11 needles and W., cast on 66 (74, 84) sts. K.8 rows.

Change to No. 9 needles and work in patt. thus:

1st and 2nd rows: k. in W. Join in P.

3rd row: work in P., *k. into loop of st. below next st., k.1; rep. from * to end.

4th row: k. in P.

5th row: work in W., *k.1, k. into loop of st. below next st.; rep. from * to end.

6th row: k. in W.

These 6 rows form patt. Rep. them, taking 2 tog. at each end of 10th and every foll. 12th row until there are 54 (60, 66) sts.

Change to No. 10 needles and cont. in patt. until work is 8½ (9¾, 11) in., ending after a 6th patt. row.

Shape Armholes. Cast off 2 sts. at beg. of next 2 rows and take 2 tog. at each end of next 3 (4, 5) rows and of foll. alt. row. Work in patt. on rem. 42 (46, 50) sts. until armhole is 2½ (2¾, 3) in., ending after a wrong-side row.

Shape Neck. Patt. 15 (16, 17); turn.

Patt. another 7 rows on these sts., taking 2 tog. at neck edge on next and foll. alt. rows: 11 (12, 13) sts.

Shape Shoulders. Cast off 3 (4, 4) sts. at beg. of next and foll. alt. row. Work 1 row. Cast off.

Slip centre 12 (14, 16) sts. on to a stitch holder and complete other side to match first reversing shapings.

BACK

Work as for Front until armhole shaping is reached.

Shape Armhole. 1st row: cast off 2 sts., patt. to end.

2nd row: cast off 2 sts., patt. 22 (25, 28); turn. Work on these 23 (26, 29) sts. only. Keeping centre edge straight, cont. in patt. taking 2 tog. at side edge on next 3 (4, 5) rows and on foll. alt. row. Work on rem. 19 (21, 23) sts. until Back measures the same as the Front to shoulders.

Shape Shoulder. Cast off 3 (4, 4) sts. at beg. of next and foll. alt. row and 5 (4, 5) at beg. of next alt. row. Leave rem. 8 (9, 10) sts. on a stitch holder.

Button Band. With No. 12 needles and W., cast on 4 sts. and work in garter st. (see page 23) until band, slightly stretched, will fit from lower edge of back opening to stitch holder with 8 (9, 10) sts. at neck. Cast off 2 sts. at beg. of final right-side row, add rem. 2 sts. to stitch holder and sew side of band to side of back opening.

With pins, mark positions for 3 buttons on this band, one at the top of the band, another about ½ in. up from lower edge of band, and the third halfway between. Returning to sts. on needle, slip first 4 sts. on to a safety pin, and complete 2nd side of back to

match first, reversing shapings.

Buttonhole Band. With No. 12 needles and W., pick up 4 sts. from safety pin and work in garter st. making buttonholes to correspond with button markers thus:

Buttonhole row (side edge): k.1, y.fwd., k.2 tog., k.1.

Complete band as for Button Band, casting off 2 sts. at beg. of last wrong-side row. Add rem. sts. to those on stitch holder (right back) and sew band in position.

SLEEVES (make 2 alike)

With No. 12 needles and W., cast on 30 (34, 38) sts. K. 8 rows.

Change to No. 10 needles, join in P. and work 2 reps. of the 6-row colour patt., as given for Front.

Shape Top. Cast off 2 sts. at beg. of next 2 rows, then take 2 tog. at beg. of next 10 rows and cast off 2 sts. at beg. of foll. 8 (10,12) rows. ** Cast off.

NECKBAND

Sew shoulder seams. With right side of work facing, No. 12 needles and W., k. across sts. at left back, pick up and k. 6 sts. down left side of neck, k. across 12 (14, 16) sts. at centre front, pick up and k. 6 sts. up other side of neck and k. across sts. at right back: 44 (48, 52) sts.

K. 6 rows and cast off.

Four-piece layette consists of jacket, bonnet, bootees and short-sleeved dress

COAT

LEFT FRONT

With No. 11 needles and W., cast on 36 (40, 44) sts. K. 7 rows.

8th row: k.6, leave these sts. on safety pin or stitch holder, k. to end.

Change to No. 9 needles, join in P. and cont. in 6-row colour patt. as given for Dress Front, taking 2 tog. at side edge on 9th and every foll. 12th row until there are 27 (30, 33) sts. Change to No. 10 needles and cont. until work is 4 (5¼, 6½) in., ending at side edge.

Shape Armhole. Cast off 3 sts. at beg. of next row and take 2 tog. at side edge on next 3 (4, 5) rows and foll. alt. row. Work on rem. 20 (22, 24) sts. in patt. until armhole is 3 (3¼, 3½) in., ending at side edge.

Shape Neck. Patt. 16 (17, 18) sts.; turn. Leave rem. sts. on a safety pin or stitch holder. Patt. for 7 rows, taking 2 tog. at neck edge on next and foll. alt. rows.

Shape Shoulder. Cast off 4 sts. at beg. of next and foll. alt. rows. Work 1 row. Cast off.

Button Band. With No. 12 needles and W., pick up the 6 sts. from safety pin near lower edge and work in garter st. until band, slightly stretched, will fit centre edge as far as safety pin holding 4 (5, 6) sts. Add 6 sts. to pin and sew band in position. With pins, mark positions for 2 buttons on this band, the lower being just below armhole shaping, the 2nd being about 2 in., above, and allowing for a 3rd button at beg. of neckband.

RIGHT FRONT

Work as for Left Front but reverse all shapings and working buttonholes to correspond with button markers in band thus:

Buttonhole row (side edge): k.2, cast off 2 sts., k.2.

Next row: k.2, cast on 2, k.2.

BACK

With No. 11 needles and W., cast on 66 (74, 82) sts. and k. 8 rows.

Change to No. 9 needles, join in P. and cont. in 6-row colour patt. taking 2 tog. at each end of 9th and every foll. 12th row until 60 (66, 72) sts. rem. Change to No. 10 needles and work until Back matches Fronts to beg. of armhole shaping.

Shape Armholes. Cast off 3 sts. at beg. of next

2 rows, then take 2 tog. at each end of next 3 (4, 5) rows and foll. alt. row. Work on 46 (50, 54) sts. until Back matches Fronts to beg. of shoulder.

Shape Shoulders. Cast off 4 sts. at beg. of next 4 rows and 4 (5, 6) sts. at beg. of foll. 2 rows. Leave 22 (24, 26) sts. on a stitch holder.

SLEEVES (make 2 alike)

With No. 12 needles and W., cast on 30 (34, 38) sts. Work 11 rows in k.1, p.1 rib, inc. at each end of last row.

12th row: k.

Change to No. 10 needles, join in P. and cont. in 6-row colour patt., inc. at each end of 9th and 21st rows.

Work on 36 (40, 44) sts. until sleeve is 5 (6, 7) in., ending with a wrong-side row.

Shape Top. Work as for top of dress sleeve as far as **. Cast off 2 sts. at beg. of next 2 rows. Cast off.

NECKBAND

Sew shoulder seams. With right side of work facing, No. 12 needles and W., pick up and k. sts. from safety pin at Right Front, pick up and k. 6 sts. up right side of neck, k. across sts. on stitch holder at Back, pick up and k. 6 sts. down left side of front, and pick up and k. sts. from safety pin at Left Front: 54 (58, 62) sts. Work 6 rows garter st., making another buttonhole on the 3rd row, as given for buttonhole band of Right Front. Cast off.

BONNET
MAIN PIECE

With No. 12 needles and W., cast on 66 (72, 78) sts. K. 8 rows.

Next 2 rows: k. 4 sts. and leave these on a safety pin; k. to end.

Change to No. 10 needles, join in P. and cont. in 6-row colour patt. on rem. 58 (64, 70) sts., until work is 4 (4½, 5) in., ending with a wrong-side row.

Next 2 rows: cast off 20 (22, 24), patt. to end. ***

Cont. in patt. on these 18 (20, 22) sts. until work measures 3¾ (4, 4¼) in. from ***. Cast off.

EDGING

Sew seam on each side of back of head. With No. 12 needles and W., pick up each set of 4 sts. from safety pins. Work on each set of sts. separately in garter st. until they both, slightly stretched, will meet on line of seam at left side of back of head. Cast off.

BOOTEES
TO MAKE (2 alike)

With No. 12 needles and W., cast on 42 (42, 50) sts. Work 8 rows in k.1, p.1 rib.

9th row: rib 2, *y.fwd., k.2 tog., rib 2; rep. from * to end.

Work another 5 rows in rib, inc. at end of last row.

Top of Foot. Rib 29 (29, 33); turn.

Next row: k. 15; turn. Join in P.

Next row: work in P., k.1, *k. into loop of st. below next st., k.1; rep. from * to end.

Next row: k. in P.

Next row: work in W., k.2, * k. into loop of st. below next st., k.1; rep. from * to last st., k.1.

Next 3 rows: k. in W.

Rep. these last 6 rows 3 (4, 4) times more.

Patt. 5 rows, taking 2 tog. at each end of every row. Leave 5 sts. on a stitch holder or safety pin.

Sides of Foot. With right side of work facing and No. 12 needles join in W. in front of the 14 (14, 18) sts. on right-hand needle and cont. the k.1, p.1 rib from these sts., pick up and rib 25 (27, 27) sts. along side of top of foot, the 5 sts. from stitch holder or safety pin, 25 (27,27) sts. from other side of top of foot, and rem. 14 (14, 18) sts.: 83 (87, 95) sts. Work 5 rows in k.1, p.1 rib. Cast off.

TO COMPLETE
DRESS

Sew in sleeves and sew side and sleeve seams. Sew on the 3 small buttons, where marked.

COAT

Sew in sleeves, sew side and sleeve seams. Sew on the 3 medium buttons, where marked.

BONNET

Stitch short edges of edging together. Sew edging in position to bonnet. Cut ribbon into 4 equal lengths; tie a small bow at one end of each of 2 lengths. Stitch through the bows to each side of bonnet front, to form ties.

BOOTEES

Sew seam under sole and at back of heel. Thread remaining lengths of ribbon through holes at ankle to tie in a bow at the front of each bootee.

Opposite: baby's trousseau (instructions on page 28). Overleaf: pink and white trouser outfit (instructions on page 84)

Vest and pants

(photographed in black and white on page 40)

MATERIALS

4 (4, 5) oz. Lister Lavenda 4-ply (see note on wools and yarns, page 20); one pair each Nos. 10 and 12 knitting needles (see page 26); 2 yards baby ribbon.

MEASUREMENTS

To fit chest size 16 (18, 20) in.; length of vest at centre back 10 (11, 12) in.; length of pants from front waist to crutch 6 (6½, 7) in.

TENSION

10 sts. and 8 rows to 1 in. on No. 10 needles over patt. (see note on tension, page 15).

ABBREVIATIONS

See page 26.

VEST
FRONT

With No. 10 needles cast on 62 (67, 72) sts.
1st row: p.2, *k.3, p.2; rep. from * to end.
2nd row: k.2, *p.3, k.2; rep. from * to end.
Rep. these 2 rows once more.
Inc. row: p.2, *(k.1, y.fwd.) twice, k.1, p.2; rep. from * to end: 86 (93, 100) sts.
Next row: k.2, *p.5, k.2; rep. from * to end.
Next row: p.2, *k.2 tog., y.fwd., k.1, y.fwd., sl.1, k.1, p.s.s.o., p.2; rep. from * to end. Rep. these last 2 rows until work measures 6½ (7, 7½) in. from beg., ending with a wrong-side row. (If more length is needed adjust here.)
Shape Armholes. Keeping patt. correct cast off 3 sts. at beg. of next 2 rows, then take 2 tog. at each end of next 4 (6, 6) rows and of next 3 alt. rows: 66 (69, 76) sts.
Cont. straight on these sts. till work measures 9 (10, 11) in. from beg., ending with a wrong-side row.
Shape Neck. Patt. 16 (17, 20); turn.
Work a further 3 rows on these sts. taking 2 tog. at neck edge on next and foll. alt. row.
Shape Shoulder. Cast off 4 (4, 5) sts.; patt to end.
Next row: take 2 tog., patt. to end.
Rep. these 2 rows once more, then cast off rem. 4 (5, 6) sts. Slip 34 (35, 36) sts. from those still on

Opposite: navy and lime dress for a toddler (instructions on page 88). On previous page: ribbon-trimmed dress and matching coat (instructions on page 71)

needle on to a stitch holder and complete second shoulder to match first, reversing shapings.

BACK

Work exactly as for Front.

NECK RIBBING

Sew right shoulder seam. With right side of work facing and No. 12 needles, start at left front shoulder and pick up 10 sts. along side of neck, work across 34 (35, 36) centre front sts. on stitch holder, pick up 10 sts. along other side of neck as far as shoulder seam, pick up 10 (9, 8) sts. from side of back of neck, work across centre back 34 (35, 36) sts. from stitch holder, pick up 10 (9, 8) sts. from rem. side of neck: 108 sts.
1st row: k.1, p.1, k.1, *k.2 tog., p.1; rep. from * to end: 73 sts.
2nd row: *k.1, y.fwd., k.2 tog., p.1, y.fwd., p.2 tog.; rep. from * to last st., p.1.
Work 2 rows in k.1, p.1 rib. Cast off loosely in rib.

ARMHOLE EDGINGS

Sew up left shoulder seam, joining sides of neck ribbing. With right side of work facing and No. 12 needles pick up 58 (66, 72) sts. round first armhole and work 3 rows in k.1, p.1 rib. Cast off loosely in rib. Work the other armhole edging in the same way.

PANTS
FRONT

With No. 12 needles cast on 72 (77, 82) sts.
Work 4 rows in rib as for beg. of Vest.
5th row: p.2, *k.1, y.fwd., k.2 tog., p.2; rep. from * to end.
Work another 5 rows in rib.
Change to No. 10 needles and work inc. row as for Vest: 100 (107, 114) sts.
Cont. on these sts. till work is 4¼ (4½, 4¾) in. from beg., ending with a wrong-side row. (If more length is needed adjust here.)
Shape Legs. Next 2 rows: work to last 7 sts.; turn and work back.
Next 2 rows: patt. to last 14 sts.; turn.
Next 2 rows: patt. to last 21 sts.; turn.
Next 2 rows: patt. to last 28 sts.; turn.
Next 2 rows: patt. to last 35 sts.; turn.
Next 2 rows: patt. to last 42 sts.; turn.
18 in. and 20 in. sizes only. Next 2 rows: work to last 46 (49) sts.; turn.
All sizes. This leaves 16 (15, 16) sts. unworked in centre. Patt. 3 (3, 5) rows on these sts. only and then cast them off.
Leave rem. sts. at each side on a stitch holder.

Vest and pants are in an unusual rib pattern, ribbon trimmed at neck and waist

BACK

With No. 12 needles cast on 72 (77, 82) sts.
Work first 9 rows as for Front.
Next 2 rows: rib until last 5 sts.; turn.
Next 2 rows: rib to last 15 sts.; turn.
Next 2 rows: rib to last 25 sts.; turn. Rib to end of row.
Change to No. 10 needles and complete as for Front.

LEG RIBBINGS

Sew seam at crutch. With right side of work facing and No. 12 needles pick up one set of 42 (46, 49) sts. at Front of Pants, pick up and k. 8 (8, 10) sts. along straight edge of crutch and work across 42 (46, 49) sts. at Back of Pants on the same leg: 92 (100, 108) sts.

1st row: *k.2 tog., p.1, k.1, p.2 tog., k.1, p.1; rep. from * to last 4 sts., k. 2 tog., p.1, k.1.
2nd row: k.2 tog., p.1, *k.1, p.1; rep. from * to end. Work 1 more row in k.1, p.1 rib, and cast off.
Work second leg ribbing in the same way.

TO COMPLETE
VEST

Sew side seams. Press lightly. Thread 1 yard of ribbon through eyelet holes at neck and tie in bow at centre front.

PANTS

Sew side seams. Press lightly. Thread remaining 1 yard of ribbon through eyelet holes at waist and tie in a bow at the front.

Pram set

– in double knitting or quickerknit yarn
(photographed in black and white on page 42)

MATERIALS
For version 1: 7 balls Emu Scotch Double Knitting or Double Crêpe or Bri-Nylon Double Knitting (see note on wools and yarns, page 20) for coat, 6 balls for leggings, 2 balls for bonnet, 2 balls for beret; one pair each Nos. 8 and 10 knitting needles (see page 26).
For version 2: 5 balls Emu Quickerknit Bri-Nylon (see note on wools and yarns, page 20) for coat, 4 balls for leggings, 1 ball for bonnet, 1 ball for beret; one pair each Nos. 7 and 9 knitting needles (see page 26).
For both versions: 3 medium buttons; a waist length of narrow elastic plus 8 in.; 1½ yd. of ribbon, 1 in. wide.

MEASUREMENTS
To fit chest size 20 (21, 22) in.; length of coat at centre back 12 (12¾, 13½) in.; sleeve seam 5½ (6, 6½) in.

TENSION
Both versions: 6½ sts. and 8 rows to 1 in. over patt.; 5½ sts. and 8 rows to 1 in. over st.st. (see note on tension, page 15).

ABBREVIATIONS
See page 26.

Version 1: in Double Knitting Yarn

COAT
BACK
With No. 10 needles, cast on 95 (103, 107) sts. Work in garter st. (see page 23) for 1 in., ending with a wrong-side row.
Change to No. 8 needles and work in patt. thus:
1st row (right side): k.24 (28, 30), p.1, k.45, p.1, k. to end.
2nd row: p.24 (28, 30), k.47, p. to end.
3rd row: k.24 (28, 30), p.1, (k.3 tog. and leave sts. on left-hand needle, k. the first of these 3 sts. again, k.2 tog. the 2nd and 3rd sts.) 15 times, p.1, k. to end.
4th row: p.24 (28, 30), k.1, p.45, k.1, p. to end.
These 4 rows form the patt.
Cont. in patt. until work measures 5½ (6, 6½) in. from beg., ending with a wrong-side row.
Next row: (k.2 tog.) 12 (14, 15) times, patt. to last 24 (28, 30) sts., (k.2 tog.) 12 (14, 15) times: 71 (75, 77) sts.
Mark each end of last row with a coloured thread.

Cont. in patt. until work measures 1 in. from coloured thread, ending with a wrong-side row.
Next row: k.1 (1, 2), (k.2 tog.) 5 (6, 6) times, k.1, p.1, patt. to last 13 (15, 16) sts., p.1, k.1, (k.2 tog.) 5 (6, 6) times, k.1 (1, 2): 61 (63, 65) sts.
Cont. in patt. until work measures 7½ (8, 8½) in. from beg. ending with a wrong-side row.
Shape Raglan Armholes. Keeping patt. correct, cast off 4 (3, 3) sts. at the beg. of next 2 rows. Dec. 1 st. at each end of the next and every foll. alt. row until 19 (21, 21) sts. rem., ending with a wrong-side row.
Leave these sts. on a stitch holder.

LEFT FRONT
With No. 10 needles, cast on 53 (57, 59) sts. and work in garter st. for 1 in., ending with a wrong-side row.
Change to No. 8 needles and work in patt. thus:
1st row: k.24 (28, 30), p.1, k.21, p.1, k. to end.
2nd row: k.29, p. to end.
3rd row: k.24 (28, 30), p.1, (k.3 tog. and leave sts. on left-hand needle, k. the first of these 3 sts. again, k.2 tog. the 2nd and 3rd sts.) 7 times, p.1, k. to end.
4th row: k.7, p.21, k.1, p. to end.
Cont. in patt. until work measures 5½ (6, 6½) in. from the beg., ending with a wrong-side row.
Next row: (k.2 tog.) 12 (14, 15) times, patt. to last 6 sts., k.6: 41 (43, 44) sts.
Mark side edge with a coloured thread. Cont. in patt. until work measures 1 in. from coloured thread, ending at side edge.
1st and 2nd sizes only. Next row: (k.2 tog.) 6 (7) times, patt. to last 6 sts., k.6: 35 (36) sts.
3rd size only. Next row: k.1, (k.2 tog.) 7 times, patt. to last 6 sts., k.6: 37 sts.
All sizes. Cont. in patt. until work measures the same as Back to armhole, ending at side edge.
Shape Raglan Armhole. Cast off 4 (3, 3) sts., patt. to end.
Next row: patt. to end.
Dec. 1 st. at the beg. of next and every foll. alt. row until 20 (21, 22) sts. rem. ending at front edge.
Shape Neck. Next row: k. across the first 6 sts. and slip them on to a safety pin., patt. to end. Cont. to dec. at armhole edge as before, dec. 1 st. at neck edge on every row until 3 (3, 4) sts. rem. Keeping neck edge straight, dec. at armhole edge as before until 1 st. remains. Fasten off.

RIGHT FRONT
With No. 10 needles, cast on 53 (57, 59) sts. Work in garter st. for 1 in. ending with a wrong-side

Snug for winter – pram set has a choice of bonnet or pompon beret for headwear

row.
Change to No. 8 needles and work in patt. thus:
1st row: k.6, p.1, k.21, p.1, k. to end.
2nd row: p.24 (28, 30), k. to end.
3rd row: k.6, p.1, (k.3 tog. and leave sts. on left-hand needle, k. the first of these 3 sts. again, k.2 tog. the 2nd and 3rd sts.) 7 times, p.1, k. to end.
4th row: p.24 (28, 30), k.1, p.21, k.1, k. to end.
Cont. in patt. until work measures 5½ (6, 6½) in. from the beg., ending with a wrong-side row.
Next row: k.6, patt. to last 24 (28, 30) sts., (k.2 tog.) 12 (14, 15) times: 41 (43, 44) sts. Mark side edge with a coloured thread. Cont. in patt. until work measures 1 in. from coloured thread, ending at front edge.

1st and 2nd sizes only. Next row: k.6, patt. to last 12 (14) sts., (k.2 tog.) 6 (7) times: 35 (36) sts.
3rd size only. Next row: k.6, patt. to last 15 sts., (k.2 tog.) 7 times, k.1: 37 sts.
All sizes. Next row: patt. to end.
Next row (buttonhole row): k.2, cast off 2, k.2 including st. used in casting off, patt. to end.
Next row: patt. to end, casting on 2 sts. over cast-off sts. in previous row.
Complete to match Left Front, reversing all shapings, *at the same time* make another buttonhole 1¾ in. from base of previous buttonhole.

SLEEVES (make 2 alike)
With No. 10 needles cast on 29 (31, 33) sts. and

work in garter st. for 1 in., ending with a wrong-side row.

Change to No. 8 needles and work in st.st. (see page 23), inc. 1 st. at each end of the 3rd and every foll. 4th (4th, 5th) row until there are 41 (45, 47) sts. on the needle.

Cont. without further shaping until work measures 5½ (6, 6½) in. from the beg. ending with a p. row.

Shape Raglan Top. Cast off 4 (3, 3) sts. at the beg. of the next 2 rows. Dec. 1 st. at each end of the next and every foll. 4th row until 25 (33, 35) sts. rem., ending with a p. row.

Now dec. 1 st. at each end of the next and every foll. alt. row until 5 (7, 7) sts. rem., ending with a p. row. Leave these sts. on a safety pin.

NECKBAND

Join raglan seams. With No. 10 needles and right side of work facing, slip the 6 sts. at front neck on to the needle. Join in yarn, pick up and k.10 (12, 12) sts. up right side of neck, k. across the 5 (7, 7) sts. on top of right sleeve, 19 (21, 21) sts. on back neck, 5 (7, 7) sts. on top of left sleeve, pick up and k.10 (12, 12) sts. down left side of neck, k. across the 6 sts. at front neck: 61 (71, 71) sts.

Work in garter st. for 1 in. making buttonhole 1¾ in. from base of previous buttonhole, as given for right front.

LEGGINGS
RIGHT LEG

With No. 10 needles, cast on 54 (56, 58) sts.
Work in k.1, p.1 rib for ½ in.

Next row: rib 2 (1, 2), y.fwd., k.2 tog., *rib 2, y.fwd., k.2 tog.; rep. from * to last 2 (1, 2) sts., rib 2 (1, 2).

Work a further ½ in. in rib. Change to No. 8 needles.

Shape Top. 1st row: k.9 (10, 11) sts.; turn.
2nd and all wrong side rows: p.
3rd row: k.18 (19, 20) sts.; turn.
Cont. in this way, working 9 extra sts. on every k. row until 9 (10, 11) sts. rem. to be knitted. Turn and p. back. Cont. in st.st. working across all sts. for 12 (16, 16) rows. Inc. 1 st. at each end of the next and every foll. 5th row until there are 72 (74, 78) sts. on the needle. Inc. 1 st. at each end of the next 3 rows: 78 (80, 84) sts.

Shape Leg. Dec. 1 st. at each end of every row until 64 (66, 70) sts. rem. then 1 st. at each end of every foll. alt. row until 50 (52, 54) sts. rem. then 1 st. at each end of every foll. 3rd row until 26 (28, 30) sts. rem. Cont. without further shaping until work measures 8½ (9, 10) in. from the beg. of leg shaping, ending with a p. row.

Shape Instep. Next row: k.21 (22, 23) sts.; turn.
Next row: p.10 sts.; turn.
Work on these 10 sts. for 1½ (1¾, 2) in., ending with a p. row. Break off yarn and join it to the 11 (12, 13)

sts. already knitted, pick up and k. 10 (11, 12) sts. along side of instep, k. across the 10 toe sts., pick up and k.10 (11, 12) sts. along the other side of instep and k. remaining 5 (6, 7) sts.: 46 (50, 54) sts.
K. 7 rows.
Cast off.

LEFT LEG

Work as for Right Leg, reversing all shapings by reading p. for k. and k. for p. throughout.

BONNET
TO MAKE

With No. 10 needles, cast on 79 (85, 91) sts.
K. 4 rows.
Change to st.st. and work 1 in. ending with a wrong-side row.
P. 1 row to mark folding line. Change to No. 8 needles and work in patt. thus:

1st row (right side): k.
2nd row: k.
3rd row: k.2, *k.3 tog. and leave sts. on left-hand needle, k. the first of these 3 sts. again, k. tog. the 2nd and 3rd sts.; rep. from * to last 2 sts., k.2.
4th row: k.2, p. to last 2 sts., k.2.
Cont. in patt. until work measures 4½ (4¾, 5) in. from folding line, ending with a wrong-side row.

Shape Back. 1st row: k.2 (2, 3), *sl.1, k.1, p.s.s.o., k.11 (12, 13). k.2 tog.; rep. from * 4 times more, k.2 (3, 3): 69 (75, 81) sts.
2nd and alt. rows: p.
3rd row: k.2 (2, 3), *sl.1, k.1, p.s.s.o., k.9 (10, 11), k.2 tog.; rep. from * 4 times more, k.2 (3, 3): 59 (65, 71) sts.
5th row: k.2 (2, 3), *sl.1, k.1, p.s.s.o., k.7 (8, 9), k.2 tog., rep. from * 4 times more, k.2 (3, 3): 49 (55, 61) sts.
7th row: k.2 (2, 3), *sl.1, k.1, p.s.s.o., k.5 (6, 7), k.2 tog.; rep. from * 4 times more, k.2 (3, 3): 39 (45, 51) sts.
9th row: k.2 (2, 3), *sl.1, k.1, p.s.s.o., k.3 (4, 5), k.2 tog., rep. from * 4 times more, k.2 (3, 3): 29 (35, 41) sts.
11th row: k.2 (2, 3), *sl.1, k.1, p.s.s.o., k.1 (2, 3), k.2 tog.: rep. from * 4 times more, k.2 (3, 3): 19 (25, 31) sts.
13th row: k.2 tog. to last st., k.1.
Break off yarn, thread through rem. sts., draw up and fasten off.

BERET
TO MAKE

With No. 10 needles, cast on 106 (110, 114) sts.
Work 11 rows in k.1, p.1 rib.
Next row: rib 9 (11, 13), *work twice into next st., rib 2; rep. from * to last 10 (12, 14) sts., work twice into next st., rib 9 (11,13): 136 (140, 144) sts.
Change to No. 8 needles and work 16 (18, 20) rows

in st.st.

Shape Crown. 1st dec. row: k.1 (7, 6), *k.2 tog., k.7 (5, 4); rep. from * to end: 121 sts.
Work 3 rows straight.

2nd dec. row: *k.9, k.3 tog.: rep. from * to last st., k.1: 101 sts.
Work 3 rows straight.

3rd dec. row: *k.7, k.3 tog.; rep. from * to last st., k.1: 81 sts.
Work 3 rows straight.

4th dec. row: *k.5, k.3 tog., rep. from * to last st., k.1: 61 sts.
Work 3 rows straight.

5th dec. row: *k.3, k.3 tog., rep. from * to last st., k.1: 41 sts.
Work 3 rows straight.

6th dec. row: *k.1, k.3 tog., rep. from * to last st., k.1: 21 sts. Work 3 rows straight.

Next row: *k.2 tog., rep. from * to last st., k.1. Break off yarn, thread through rem. sts., draw up and fasten off.

TO COMPLETE
COAT
Join side and sleeve seams. Sew on buttons opposite buttonholes.

LEGGINGS
Join back, front and leg seams. Cut a waist length of elastic and thread through eyelet holes at waist, stitching short ends of elastic together. Cut remaining elastic into two 4-in. lengths. Sew a length to side of each instep.

BONNET
Join back seam for 3 in. Turn back brim at folding line and catch down on each side. Cut ribbon in half, and sew on a length to each side of bonnet front to form ties. Cut ribbon ends into points if wished.

BERET
Join seam. Make a pompon, following instructions on page 82, but with card circles each 3 in., and centre hole $\frac{3}{4}$ in.
Sew pompon to top of beret.

Version 2: in Quickerknit Yarn
Work exactly as for Version 1, but use No. 9 needles instead of No. 10; and No. 7 needles instead of No. 8.

Ribbed jumper and bonnet

MATERIALS
5 (6) oz. Twilley's Lyscordet (see note on wools and yarns, page 20); one pair each Nos. 11 and 12 knitting needles (see page 26); eight $\frac{5}{8}$-in. buttons; a fine crochet hook.

MEASUREMENTS
To fit chest size 18 (20) in.

TENSION
7 sts. and 16 rows to 1 in. over rib on No. 11 needles (see note on tension, page 15).

ABBREVIATIONS
See page 26.

JUMPER
BACK
With No. 12 needles cast on 71 (79) sts. Work 16 rows in k.1, p.1 rib. Change to No. 11 needles and work in patt. thus:

1st row (right side): k.1, *y.fwd., sl.1, k.1; rep. from * to end.

2nd row: *k.1, k. sl.st. and loop st. tog., p.1; rep. from * to last 2 sts., k. sl.st. and loop st. tog., k.1.
These 2 rows form brioche rib. Rep. them until work is 6 (7) in., ending with a 2nd row.

Raglan Shaping. Cast off 2 sts. at beg. of next 2 rows.

Next row: k.1, y.fwd., sl.1, k.3 tog., *y.fwd., sl.1, k.1; rep. from * to last 6 sts., y.fwd., sl.1, k.3 tog., y.fwd., sl.1, k.1.
Work 5 rows.
Rep. last 6 rows until 27 (31) sts. rem. Work 5 more rows and leave sts. on a stitch holder.

FRONT
Work as for Back until 35 (39) sts. rem.
Neck shaping (wrong side). Patt. 12; turn. Work on these sts. taking 2 tog. at neck edge on every alt. row, at the same time shaping raglan as before on 5th row (8 sts.). Now take 2 tog. at neck edge only at end of next and foll. 6 alt. rows. Fasten off. Slip centre 11 (15) sts. on a stitch holder and complete second side to match, reversing shapings.

SLEEVES (make 2 alike)
With No. 12 needles cast on 37 (41) sts. Work 20 rows in k.1, p.1 rib.
Change to No. 11 needles and patt. as for Back, inc. at each end of every 10th row until there are 53 (57) sts.

*Jumper fastens along each raglan edge
with four small buttons*

Cont. till work is 7 (8) in., ending with a 2nd row. Shape raglan as for Back until there are 9 (9) sts. Work 5 rows. Leave sts. on a stitch holder.

NECKBANDS

Join back and sleeve raglan shapings. With right side of work facing and No. 12 needles, k. across sts. of right sleeve, k. across sts. of Back and then of left sleeve: 45 (49) sts. Work in k.1, p.1 rib for 2½ in., then cast off loosely in rib.

With right side of work facing pick up and k. 15 sts. down left side of front neck, k.11 (15) centre sts. and pick up and k.15 sts. up other side of neck: 41 (45) sts.

Work in k.1, p.1 rib for 2½ in. Cast off loosely in rib.

TO COMPLETE

Join front raglan seams for 1 (2) in. at lower edge. Fold neckband in half to wrong side and slipstitch down, then join sides. Join side and sleeve seams. With a fine crochet hook work 24 d.c. down one side of front raglan opening (see page 26). Work 1 row in d.c.

Buttonhole row: 2 d.c., *make 2 ch., miss 2 d.c., 4 d.c.; rep. from * 3 times in all, make 2 ch., miss 2 d.c., 2 d.c.

Work 2 more rows d.c. and fasten off.
Work other side to match. Sew 4 buttons to each side of raglan, opposite buttonholes.

BONNET
TO MAKE

With No. 11 needles, cast on 51 (55) sts. Work 6 rows in patt. as for Back.
Next row: (k.1, y.fwd., sl.1) twice, k.3 tog., *y.fwd., sl.1, k.1; rep. from * to end.
Work 7 rows in patt.
Rep. last 8 rows until 41 (45) sts. rem.
Work 15 (17) rows.
Next row: (k.1, y.fwd., sl.1) twice, work (k.1, p.1, k.1) into next st., *y.fwd., sl.1, k.1; rep. from * to end.
Work 7 rows.
Rep. first 8 rows until there are 51 (55) sts.**
Work 7 rows.
Now rep. from ** to **. Work 5 rows straight.
Cast off in rib.

TO COMPLETE

Join back seam. With crochet hook work 2 rows d.c. along lower edge of bonnet. Fasten off. Make 2 crochet chains, each 11 in., and sew one to each front corner of bonnet to form ties.

Smocked jacket, bonnet and bootees
(photographed in colour on page 17)

MATERIALS

7 (8, 9) balls Lee Target Cherub 4-ply Bri-Nylon (see note on wools and yarns, page 20); one pair each Nos. 10 and 12 knitting needles (see page 26); 2 yd. baby ribbon ⅜ in. wide; 2 buttons, ½ in. in diameter.

MEASUREMENTS

Jacket: to fit chest size 18 (20, 22) in.; length of jacket at centre back 9 (10½, 12) in.; sleeve seam 5 (6, 7) in.
Bonnet: to fit an average-sized head.
Bootees: length of foot from back of heel to toe 4½ (5, 5½) in.

TENSION

10 sts. and 10 rows to 1 in. over smocking patt. on No. 10 needles (see note on tension, page 15).

ABBREVIATIONS

See page 26; sm.6 (smock 6), insert right-hand needle between 6th and 7th sts. on left-hand needle as though to knit, pull through a loop and place this on left-hand needle, k. this loop tog. with next st., then k.1, p.2, k.2.

JACKET
BACK

With No. 10 needles cast on 98 (106, 114) sts.
1st row (wrong side): k.2, *p.2, k.2; rep. from * to end.
2nd row: k.
Rep. these 2 rows till work is 6 (7, 8) in. from beg., ending with a wrong-side row.
Shape Armholes and Beg. Smocking Patt. 1st row: cast off 4, p.1, *k.2, p.2; rep. from * to end.
2nd row: cast off 4, k.1, *p.2, k.2; rep. from * to end.
3rd row: p.2 tog., *sm.6 (see Abbreviations), p.2; rep. from * to last 8 sts., sm. 6, p.2 tog.
4th row: p.2 tog., p.1, rib until last 3 sts., p.1, p.2 tog.
5th row: k.2 tog., rib to last 2 sts., k.2 tog.
6th row: k.2 tog., rib to last 2 sts., k.2 tog. Rep. these last 4 rows 6 (7, 8) times more, then 3rd and 4th rows once.
Leave rem. 30 sts. on a stitch holder.

RIGHT FRONT

With No. 10 needles cast on 50 (54, 58) sts. Work as for Back until Front measures the same as Back to beg. of armhole shaping, ending at inner edge.

Shape Armhole. 1st row: k.2, *k.2, p.2; rep. from * to end.

2nd row: cast off 4, k.1, *p.2, k.2; rep. from * to end.

3rd row: patt. 6 (2, 6), *sm.6, p.2; rep. from * to last 8 sts., sm.6, p.2 tog.

Keeping 2 garter sts. at inner edge correct, rib 3 rows, dec. 1 st. at side edge on every row.

7th row: patt. 2 (6, 2), *sm.6, p. 2; rep. from * to last 8 sts., sm.6, p.2 tog.

Keeping the 2 garter sts. at inner edge correct, rib 3 rows, dec. 1 st. at side edge on every row.

Cont. to work as for the last 8 rows until 26 sts. rem. ending at inner edge.

Shape Neck. Next row: patt. 11 and leave these sts. on a stitch holder, then cont. in smocking patt. to last 2 sts., take 2 tog.

Cont. in patt., dec. at side edge on every row and at neck edge on next and every alt. row until there are 2 sts. K.2 tog. Fasten off.

LEFT FRONT

Work as for Right Front, reversing all shapings and reversing instructions for patt., i.e. first smocking row should read: p.2 tog., *sm.6, p.2; rep. from * to last 12 (8, 12) sts., sm.6, patt. 6 (2, 6).

SLEEVES (make 2 alike)

With No. 12 needles cast on 46 (49, 52) sts.

1st row: p.1, *k.2, p.1, rep. from * to end.

2nd row: k.1, *p.2, k.1; rep. from * to end. Rep. these 2 rows 3 times more.

9th row: p. twice in first st., *k.2, p. twice in next st.; rep. from * to end: 62 (66, 70) sts.

Change to No. 10 needles.

Next row (wrong side): k.2, *p.2, k.2; rep. from * to end.

Next row: k.

Cont. in this patt., inc. 1 st. at each end of 3rd and every foll. 5th row until there are 74 (82, 90) sts.

Cont. till work is 5 (6, 7) in., ending with a wrong-side row.

To Shape Top. Work as for armhole shaping and smocking on the Back. Leave rem. 6 sts. on a safety pin or stitch holder.

NECKBAND

Sew sleeves to Fronts and Back. With right side of work facing and No. 12 needles work across 11 sts. on Right Front thus: k.2, (k.2, p.2) twice, k.1, then pick up and cont. to work in the k.2, p.2 rib 9 sts. up side of neck, 6 sts. on safety pin at top of sleeve, the 30 sts. of Back, 6 sts. of other sleeve, pick up 9 sts. down left side of neck and across 11 sts. on Left Front, ending with 2 k. sts.

Keeping 2 garter sts. at each end, work another 5 rows in rib. Cast off in rib.

BONNET
TO MAKE

With No. 12 needles cast on 122 (130, 138) sts.

1st row: k.2, *k.2, p.2; rep. from * to last 4 sts., k.4.

2nd row: k.2, *p.2, k.2; rep. from * to end.

3rd row: k.2, *sm.6, p.2; rep. from * to last 8 sts., sm.6, k.2.

4th and 6th rows: as 2nd row.

5th row: as first row.

7th row: patt.6, *sm.6, p.2; rep. from * to last 6 sts., patt.6.

8th row: as 2nd row. Change to No. 10 needles and work 1 row k.

Next row: as 2nd row.

Rep. these 2 rows until work is 4 (4½, 5) in. from beg.

Working in patt. cast off 41 (45, 45) sts. at beg. of next 2 rows then cont. in patt. on rem. 40 (40, 48) sts. for 4 (4½, 4½) in.

Keeping patt. correct, work 4 rows in k.2, p.2 rib. Cast off in rib.

BOOTEES
TO MAKE (2 alike)

With No. 12 needles cast on 42 (42, 50) sts.

1st row: p.2, *k.2, p.2; rep. from * to end.

2nd row: k.2, *p.2, k.2; rep. from * to end.

Rep. these 2 rows 3 times more, then the first row again.

10th row: k.2, *y.r.n., p.2 tog., k.2; rep. from * to end. Rep. first and 2nd rows 3 times more.

Top of Foot. Rib 29 (29, 33); turn. Now rib 16; turn. Rib 4 more rows on these 16 sts.

1st and 2nd sizes. Rib 5, sm.6, rib 5. Rib 3 rows.

Next row: p.1, sm.6, p.2, sm.6, p.1. Rib 3 rows.

3rd size. P.1, sm.6, p.2, sm.6, p.1. Rib 3 rows.

Next row: rib 5, sm.6, rib 5. Rib 3 rows.

All sizes. Cont. in smocking patt. as worked in the last 8 rows to complete in all 30 (34, 38) rows from beg. of top of foot.

Next row: p.1, k.2 tog., p.2 tog., sm.6, p.2 tog., k.2 tog. t.b.l., p.1.

Next row: k.1, p.1, k.1, p.2 tog. t.b.l., k.2, p.2 tog., k.1, p.1, k.1.

Next row: (k.2 tog.) twice, p.2, (k.2 tog.) twice. Leave these 6 sts. on a safety pin or stitch holder.

Foot. With right side of work facing and No. 12 needles, join yarn in front of the 13 (13, 17) sts. on right-hand needle then pick up and, starting with 1 p. st., work in k.2, p.2 rib 33 (37, 41) sts. along side of top of foot, the 6 sts. from safety pin at toe, 33 (37, 41) sts. along other side of top of foot and rem. 13 (13, 17) sts.: 98 (106, 122) sts.

Work 10 rows in k.2, p.2 rib on No. 10 needles, and then 3 rows on No. 12 needles. Cast off.

TO COMPLETE

JACKET

Sew side and sleeve seams. Sew a button to each side of centre front opening at lower edge of neckband. Make a rouleau loop, big enough to go over button. Stitch ends of loop beside one button. Fasten by putting loop over opposite button.

BONNET

Sew seam at each side of head. Cut two 18-in. lengths of ribbon, tie one end of each length into a small bow and stitch to each side of bonnet front through the bows, to form ties.

BOOTEES

Sew seam at back of heel and seam under sole on each bootee. Cut remaining ribbon in half, and thread each length through eyelet holes at ankle of each bootee.

Tie in a bow at the front.

Matinée jacket

MATERIALS

6 oz. Lister Nursery Time Baby Double Knitting Bri-Nylon (see note on wools and yarns, page 20); one pair No. 8 knitting needles (see page 26); 2 buttons; ¾ yd. narrow ribbon.

MEASUREMENTS

To fit chest size 19 in.; length at centre back 9 in.; sleeve seam 5¾ in.

TENSION

11½ sts. and 24 rows to 2 in. over garter st. (see note on tension, page 15).

ABBREVIATIONS

See page 26.

MAIN SECTION

Cast on 137 sts. and work in garter st. (see page 23) for 6 rows. Now patt. thus:

1st row: k.
2nd row: k.5, p. to last 5 sts., k.5.
3rd row: k.5, *y.fwd., k.2 tog., k.1; rep. from * to last 6 sts., y.fwd., k.2 tog., k.4.
4th row: as 3rd row.
Rep. these 4 rows 11 times more.
Next row: k.
Next row: k.5, p.3, *p.2 tog., p.4; rep. from * to last 9 sts., p.2 tog., p.2, k.5: 116 sts. Work 2 rows in garter st., ending with a wrong-side row.
Divide for Fronts and Back. K.27, cast off 4, k.54, cast off 4, k. to end. Work on last group of sts. in garter st. thus:
Next row: k.
Cont. taking 2 tog. at raglan edge on next and alt. rows until 13 sts. rem. ending at front edge.
Shape Neck. Cast off 4 sts. at beg. of next row. Take 2 tog. at beg. of next 7 rows. K.2 tog. Fasten off.
Complete Back. Rejoin yarn to inner group of 54 sts.

1st row: k. Now take 2 tog. at each end of next and alt. rows until there are 18 sts. Slip sts. on to a stitch holder.
Complete Second Front. Rejoin yarn to rem. sts.
Next row: k. Now, taking 2 tog. at raglan edge on next and alt. rows, work 2 rows garter st.
Next row (buttonhole row): k.2, y.fwd., k.2 tog., k. to last 2 sts., k.2 tog.
Cont. shaping at raglan edge as before making a second buttonhole on the 14th row from the first. Complete to match first front.

SLEEVES (make 2 alike)

Cast on 29 sts. and work 12 rows garter st. Now inc. at each end of the next and every foll. 12 rows until there are 39 sts. Cont. till work measures 5¾ in. from beg.
Shape Raglan. Cast off 2 sts. at beg. of next 2 rows. Work 1 row. Take 2 tog. at beg. of every row until 13 sts. rem. and then at each end of alt. rows until 7 sts. rem. Leave sts. on a stitch holder.

NECKBAND

Join sleeves to Back and Fronts. With right side of work facing, pick up and k. 8 sts. up right front, k. across 7 sts. of sleeve, k. across 8 of back sts., k.2 tog. and k. across rem. 8, k. across 7 sts. of second sleeve and pick up and k. 8 sts. down left front: 47 sts.
Next row: k.
Next row: k.2, *y.fwd., k.2 tog., k.1; rep. from * to last 3 sts., y.fwd., k.2 tog., k.1. Work 3 rows garter st. and cast off.

TO COMPLETE

Join side and sleeve seams. Sew on buttons opposite buttonholes and thread ribbon through holes at neckband.

Jacket is worked mainly in garter stitch with a patterned skirt section

Button-up cardigan

MATERIALS

4 (5) oz. Hayfield Courtier Super Crimp Bri-Nylon 3-ply (see note on wools and yarns, page 20); one pair each Nos. 11 (10) and 12 (11) knitting needles (see page 26); 5 small buttons.

MEASUREMENTS

To fit chest size 21 (22) in.; sleeve seam 6½ (7½) in.

TENSION

8 sts. to 1 in. on No. 11 needles and 23 sts. to 3 in. on No. 10 needles, both over st.st. (see note on tension, page 15).

ABBREVIATIONS

See page 26.

BACK

With No. 12 (11) needles cast on 84 sts. K.6 (10) rows.
Change to No. 11 (10) needles and patt. as follows:
1st row: k.
2nd and 4th rows: p.
3rd row: k.5, *p.4, k.10; rep. from * ending last rep. with k.5.

5th-12th rows: rep. 3rd and 4th rows 4 times.
13th and 14th rows: as first and 2nd rows.
15th row: p.2, *k.10, p.4; rep. from * ending last rep. p.2.
16th row: p.
17th-24th rows: rep. 15th and 16th rows 4 times. These 24 rows form patt.; rep. them once then the first 18 rows again.
Raglan Shaping. Cast off 4 sts. at beg. of next 2 rows.
Next row: k.1, p.2 tog., patt. to last 4 sts., p.2 tog., k.1.
Next row: p.
Rep. the last 2 rows until 28 sts. rem. Cast off.

RIGHT FRONT

With No. 12 (11) needles cast on 46 sts. K.6 (10) rows.
Next row: k.6, slip these sts. on to a safety pin or stitch holder.
Change to No. 11 (10) needles and patt. thus:
1st and 2nd rows: work as for first and 2nd rows of Back.
3rd row: k.3, *p.4, k.10; rep. from * once, p.4, k.5.
4th row: p.
Rep. 3rd and 4th rows 4 times.
13th and 14th rows: as first and 2nd rows.
15th row: *k.10, p.4; rep. from * once, k.10, p.2.
16th row: p.
17th-24th rows: rep. 15th and 16th rows 4 times. Rep. these 24 rows once, then the first 19 rows again.**
Raglan Shaping. Cast off 4 sts., p. to end.
2nd row: patt. to last 3 sts., p.2 tog., k.1.
3rd row: p.
Rep. last 2 rows until 18 sts. rem.
Shape Neck. 1st row: cast off 5 sts., k. to last 3 sts., p.2 tog., k.1.
2nd row: p.
3rd row: k.2 tog., k. to last 3 sts., p.2 tog., k.1.
Rep. last 2 rows 3 times, then 2nd row again.
Next row: p.3 tog., k.1, p.2 tog., and fasten off.

LEFT FRONT

Work first 6 (10) rows as for Right Front.
Next row: k. to last 6 sts., leave these on a safety pin or stitch holder.
2nd row: p.
3rd row: k.5, *p.4, k.10; rep. from * once, p.4, k.3.
Now work in patt. on these sts. as set as for Right

Cardigan can serve as matinee jacket when baby is small, as a cover-up with a summer dress when she gets older

Front, but ending at ** by working first 18 rows again.

Shape Raglan. Cast off 4 sts., patt. to end. Now cont. as for Right Front, keeping patt. correct and reversing shapings.

SLEEVES (make 2 alike)

With No. 12 (11) needles cast on 42 sts. and k.6 (10) rows.

Change to No. 11 (10) needles and work in patt. thus:

1st and 2nd rows: work as for first and 2nd rows of Back.

3rd row: p.2, *k.10, p.4; rep. from * ending p. 2.

4th row: p.

Rep. 3rd and 4th rows once. Cont. in patt. as set inc. at each end of next and every foll. 6th row until the 11th inc. row has been worked. On 64 sts. patt. for 11 rows.

Shape Top. Work as for Back raglan shaping until there are 8 sts. Cast off.

FRONT BANDS

Left Band. Rejoin yarn to 6 sts. left on safety pin or stitch holder, and with No. 12 (11) needles k.100 rows. Leave sts. on a stitch holder and sew band to front edge.

Right Band. Rejoin yarn to inside edge on wrong side of work and work as for Left Band. Do not break off yarn.

NECKBAND

Sew Back to sleeves and sleeves to Fronts. With right side of work facing and No. 12 (11) needles, k. across 6 sts. from right front band, pick up and k.12 sts. up right side of neck, 6 sts. at top of sleeve, 22 sts. at centre back, 6 sts. at top of second sleeve, 12 sts. down left side of neck and k. across 6 sts. of left band: 70 sts.

K.5 rows and cast off.

TO COMPLETE

Sew side and sleeve seams. With pins, mark positions for buttons down left front at 2-in. intervals, and make holes in right front band thus: using a very thick needle push through 4th st. from outside edge and oversew round it.

Sew on buttons where marked.

Bow-patterned dress

MATERIALS

5 (5, 6) oz. Wendy Nylonised 4-ply yarn (see note on wools and yarns, page 20); one pair each Nos. 9, 10 and 12 knitting needles (see page 26); three $\frac{5}{8}$-in. buttons.

MEASUREMENTS

To fit chest size 18 (20, 22) in.

TENSION

7 sts. and 9 rows to 1 in. on No. 10 needles (see note on tension, page 15).

ABBREVIATIONS

See page 26; m.b. (make bow), insert right-hand needle into st. 8 rows below next st. on left-hand needle, pull through loop as if to k. Place this loop on left-hand needle and k. tog. this loop and next st.

FRONT

With No. 12 needles cast on 99 sts. (for all sizes), and k. 10 rows.

Change to No. 9 needles and work in st.st. (see page 23) for 2 rows.

Beg. patt. thus:

1st row: k.9, (p.9, k.9) 5 times.

2nd row: p.9, (k.9, p.9) 5 times.

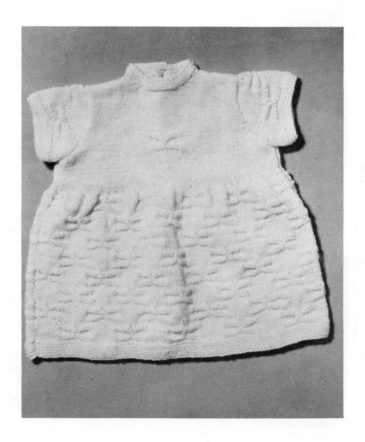

The·unusual bow effect in the pattern of this summer dress is easy to work

3rd row: k.

4th row: p.

5th row: as 3rd row.

6th row: as 4th row.

7th row: as first row.

8th row: as 2nd row.

9th row: k.9, *k.4, m.b. (see Abbreviations), k.13; rep from * to end.

10th row: p.

11th row: as 2nd patt. row.

12th row: as first patt. row.

Rep. 3rd and 4th patt. rows twice.

17th row: as 2nd patt. row.

18th row: as first patt. row.

19th row: k.4, * m.b., k.17; rep. from * to last 5 sts., m.b., k.4.

20th row: p.

These 20 rows form patt. Rep. them until 70 (80, 90) patt. rows in all have been worked. Change to No. 12 needles.

Next row: k.0 (9, 18), (k.2 tog., k.1) 15 (12, 9) times, k.9, (k.1, k.2 tog. t.b.l.) 15 (12. 9) times, k.0 (9, 18): 69 (75, 81) sts.

Beg. with a p. row, work 3 rows st.st.

Change to No. 10 needles.

Now cont. in st.st. until work is 8½ (9½, 10½) in. from beg., ending with a p. row.

Shape Armholes. Cast off 3 sts. at beg. of next 2 rows.

Next row: k.2 tog., k.25 (28, 31), p.9, k. 25 (28, 31), k.2 tog.

Completing one rep. of the 10-row bow patt. on sts. as now set, complete armhole shaping by taking 2 tog. at each end of next 3 (4, 5) rows and of foll. 2 alt. rows.

Cont. on rem. 51 (55, 59) sts. until work is 2½ (3, 3½) in. from beg. of armhole shaping, ending with a p. row.

Working in st.st. cont. thus:

Shape Neck. K.19 (20, 21), k.2 tog.; turn.

Work another 3 rows, taking 2 tog. at neck edge on every row: 17 (18, 19) sts.

Shape Shoulder. Cast off 5 sts. at beg. of next row, k. to end.

Next row: p.2 tog., p. to end.

Rep. these last 2 rows once more.

Cast off.

Slip 9 (11, 13) centre sts. on to a stitch holder and complete second half to match, reversing shapings.

BACK

Work as for Front to beg. of armhole shaping.

Shape Armhole and Make Button Band. Cast off 3 sts., k. to end.

Next row: cast off 3 sts., p.28 (31, 34), cast on 5; turn: 34 (37, 40) sts.

Next row: k. to last 2 sts., k.2 tog.

Next row: p. 2 tog., p. to last 5 sts., k.5. Keeping 5

garter st. border correct, complete armhole shaping by taking 2 tog. at side edge on next 2 (3, 4) rows and on foll. 2 alt. rows. Cont on rem. 28 (30, 32) sts. until work is as long as Front to beg. of shoulder shaping, ending at side edge.

Shape Shoulder. Cast off 5 sts. at beg. of next and foll. alt. row and 5 (6, 7) sts. at beg. of next alt. row. Leave 13 (14, 15) sts. on a stitch holder. With pins, mark positions for 2 buttons on this band, the first 1¼ in. from lower edge of band, the second 1¼ in. up from this point. Allow for a third button at top of band. Rejoin yarn to sts. at other side and work thus:

Next row (wrong side): k.5, p. to end: 34 (37, 40) sts. Cont. and complete this side to match first, reversing shapings and working 2 buttonholes to correspond with marked button positions thus:

1st buttonhole row (side edge): work to last 4 sts., cast off 2, k.1.

2nd buttonhole row: k.1, cast on 2, patt. to end of row.

SLEEVES (make 2 alike)

With No. 12 needles cast on 41 (47, 53) sts. and work 6 rows garter st., inc. at each end of last row. Change to No. 9 needles and work 2 rows st.st.

Next row: k.8 (11, 14), p.9, k.9, p.9, k.8 (11, 14). Keeping bows correct on sts. as now set, work another 5 rows.

Shape Top. Keeping patt. correct, cast off 3 sts. at beg. of next 2 rows, then take 2 tog. at beg. of next 2 rows: 35 (41, 47) sts.

Next row: k.2 tog., k.11 (14, 17), p.9, k.13 (16, 19).

Completing bow on sts. as now set, take 2 tog. at beg. of next 5 rows, and cast off 2 sts. at beg. of foll. 6 (8, 10) rows.

Cast off.

NECKBAND

Sew shoulder seams. With right side of work facing, and No. 12 needles, k. across 13 (14, 15) sts. of left back neck, pick up and k.10 sts. down side of neck, k. across centre 9 (11, 13) sts., pick up and k. 10 sts. up other side of neck and k. across 13 (14, 15) sts. of right back: 55 (59, 63) sts.

Making a buttonhole as before on 2nd row, work 6 rows garter st. Cast off.

TO COMPLETE

Set in sleeves and sew sleeve and side seams. Catch lower edge of button band in place. Sew on buttons where marked.

Opposite: lime green sun dress and scarf, edged with white (see page 67). Overleaf: orange two-piece, for beach or garden wear (see page 64)

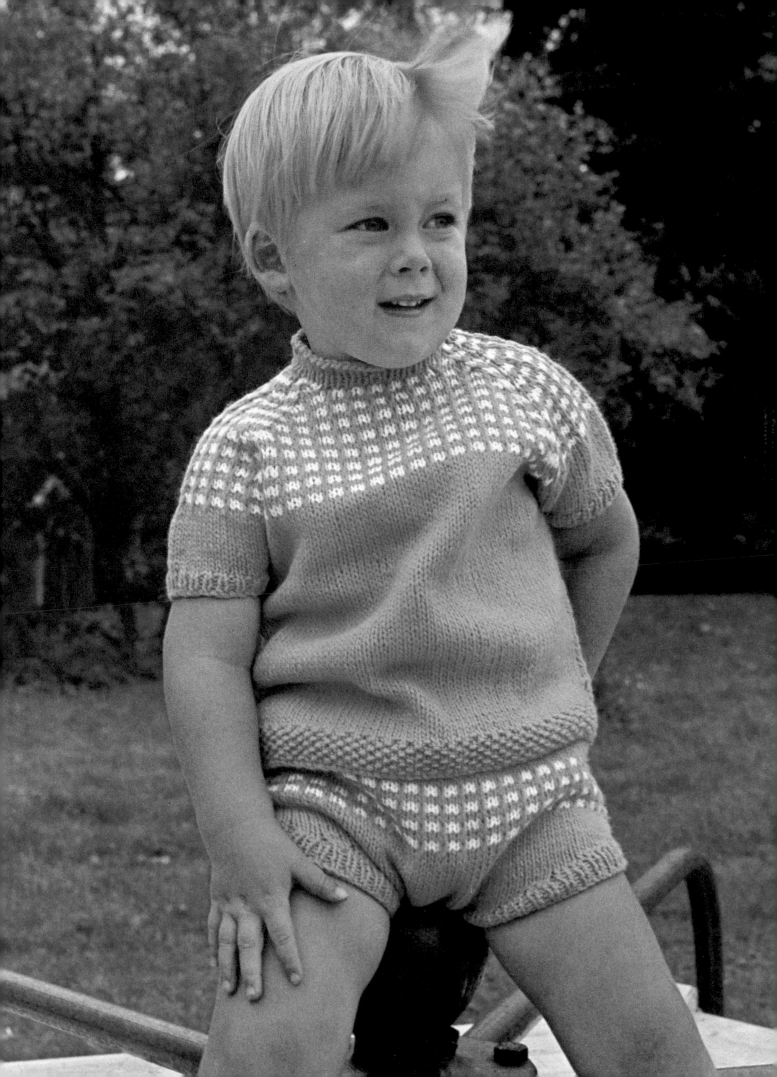

Cotton two-piece

(photographed in black and white on page 60)

MATERIALS

2 balls (2-oz.) Twilley's Stalite for the cardigan, 2 balls for the pants (see note on wools and yarns, page 20); one pair each Nos. 10 and 12 knitting needles (see page 26); seven ½-in. buttons; approx. 1 yd. narrow elastic.

MEASUREMENTS

To fit chest size 18 (20) in.; length of cardigan at centre back 9 (10½) in.; length of pants at side 5 (6) in.

TENSION

6½ sts. and 8 rows to 1 in. over st.st. on No. 10 needles (see note on tension, page 15).

ABBREVIATIONS

See page 26.

CARDIGAN

BACK

With No. 12 needles cast on 63 (69) sts. Work 10 rows in k.1, p.1 rib.
Change to No. 10 needles and work in patt. thus:
1st row (right side): k.27 (30), y.fwd., sl.1, k.1, p.s.s.o., k.5, k.2 tog., y.fwd., k. to end.
2nd and alt. rows: p.
3rd row: k.28 (31), y.fwd., sl.1, k.1, p.s.s.o., k.3, k.2 tog., y.fwd., k. to end.
5th row: k.29 (32), y.fwd., sl.1, k.1, p.s.s.o., k.1, k.2 tog., y.fwd., k.29 (32).
7th row: k.30 (33), y.fwd., sl.1, k.2 tog., p.s.s.o., y.fwd., k. to end.
8th row: p.
These 8 rows form patt. Cont. in patt. until work is 5 (6) in., ending with a wrong-side row.
Raglan Shaping. Keeping centre panel correct, cast off 4 sts. at beg. of next 2 rows.
Next row: k.1, sl.1, k.1, p.s.s.o., patt. to last 3 sts., k.2 tog., k.1.
Next row: p.
Rep. these last 2 rows until there are 23 (25) sts. Leave these on a stitch holder.

RIGHT FRONT

With No. 12 needles cast on 31 (35) sts. Work 10 rows in k.1, p.1 rib.
Change to No. 10 needles and work in patt. thus:

Opposite: gaily-striped jersey and pinafore set (instructions on page 97). On previous page: blue and white play suit for a little boy (see page 83)

1st row (right side): k.11 (13), y.fwd., sl.1, k.1, p.s.s.o., k.5, k.2 tog., y.fwd., k. to end.
2nd and alt. rows: p.
3rd row: k.12 (14), y.fwd., sl.1, k.1, p.s.s.o., k.3, k.2 tog., y.fwd., k. to end.
5th row: k.13 (15), y.fwd., sl.1, k.1, p.s.s.o., k.1, k.2 tog., y.fwd., k. to end.
7th row: k.14 (16), y.fwd., sl.1, k.2 tog., p.s.s.o., y.fwd., k. to end.
8th row: p.
These 8 rows form patt. Rep. them until work is 5 (6) in., ending with a right-side row.
Raglan Shaping. Keeping centre panel correct as far as dec. will allow, cast off 4 sts. at beg. of next row.
Next row: patt. to last 3 sts., k.2 tog., k.1.
Next row: p.
Rep. the last 2 rows until there are 15 (17) sts. Work 1 row p.
Neck Shaping. Shaping raglan as before, cast off 3 (5) sts. at beg. of next row and then take 2 tog. at neck edge on every row until all sts. are worked off.

LEFT FRONT

Work as for Right Front, reversing all shapings and working sl.1, k.1, p.s.s.o. for k.2 tog. on raglan shaping.

SLEEVES (make 2 alike)

With No. 12 needles cast on 37 (39) sts. Work 16 rows in k.1, p.1 rib.
Change to No. 10 needles and work in patt. thus:
1st row: k.14 (15), y.fwd., sl.1, k.1, p.s.s.o., k.5, k.2 tog., y.fwd., k. to end.
Place centre panel in this way and cont. in patt. as for Back, inc. at each end of every 6th row until there are 49 (53) sts.
Cont. straight until work is 7 (8) in., ending with a p. row.
Raglan Shaping. Work as for Back until there are 9 sts. Work 1 row p. and leave sts. on a stitch holder.

NECKBAND

Join raglan seams. With No. 12 needles pick up and k.12 (14) sts. up right side of neck, k.9 sts from right sleeve, k. across 23 (25) sts. of back, k. across 9 sts. of second sleeve and pick up and k.12 (14) sts. down left side of front neck: 65 (71) sts.
Work 7 rows of k.1, p.1 rib on these sts., cast off in rib.

FRONT BANDS

With No. 12 needles cast on 7 sts. and work 4 rows

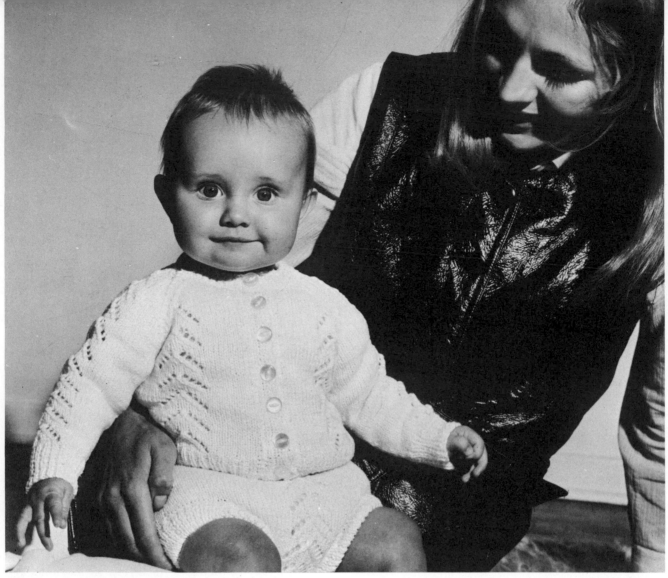

Made in a cotton yarn, this little suit is light and cool for summer wear

in p.1, k.1 rib, beg. 2nd row k.1.

Buttonhole row: p.1, k.1, p.1, y.r.n., p.2 tog., k.1, p.1.

Cont. in rib making 6 more buttonholes 1¼ (1½) in. apart. Rib 2 more rows. Cast off in rib. Work a second band in the same way, omitting buttonholes.

TO COMPLETE

Join side and sleeve seams. Sew on bands; buttonhole band to right front if the garment is for a girl, to the left front if it is for a boy. Sew on buttons opposite buttonholes.

PANTS

MAIN PART

With No. 12 needles cast on 63 (69) sts. Work 2 in. in k.1, p.1 rib.

Change to No. 10 needles and shape back thus:
Next row: k.38 (44); turn. **Next row:** p.13 (19); turn. **Next row:** k.19 (25); turn. **Next row:** p.25 (31); turn. **Next row:** k.31 (37); turn. **Next row:** p.37 (43); turn. **Next row:** k.43 (49); turn. **Next row:** p.49 (55); turn. **Next row:** k. to end.
Work 1 row p.

Now work first to 8th patt. rows as for Back of Cardigan and cont. in patt. until work is 5½ (6½) in., measured at side edges.

Cast off 5 (6) sts. at beg. of next 2 rows then take 2 tog. at each end of every alt. row until 23 (23) sts. rem.

Work 16 rows, then inc. at each end of next and every alt. row until there are 37 (41) sts. then cast on 13 (14) sts. at beg. of next 2 rows: 63 (69) sts. Cont. for a further 3½ (4½) in., ending with an 8th patt. row.

Change to No. 12 needles and work 2 in. in k.1, p.1 rib.

Cast off in rib.

LEG BANDS

With No. 12 needles pick up and k. 84 (94) sts. round one leg edge and work in k.1, p.1 rib for 1½ in. Cast off in rib.

Work other leg band to match.

TO COMPLETE

Join side and leg band seams. Cut lengths of elastic to fit waist and leg tops and join into rings. Fold waist and leg band ribbings in half to wrong side and slipstitch down, enclosing elastic.

Zip-up cat suit

MATERIALS

7 (8) oz. Paton's Brilliante Quickerknit Baby Nylon (see note on wools and yarns, page 20); one pair each Nos. 10 and 12 knitting needles (see page 26); a 12 (14)-in. zip; approx. 1 yard shirring elastic.

MEASUREMENTS

To fit chest size 18 (20) in.

TENSION

7 sts. and 9 rows to 1 in. on No. 8 needles (see note on tension, page 15).

ABBREVIATIONS

See page 26.

MAIN SECTION

*With No. 10 needles cast on 10 (12) sts. for left foot.
Working in st.st. (see page 23), inc. at each end of every alt. row until there are 22 (26) sts.
Cont. until work is 3 (3½) in., ending with a p. row.*

Warm for playtime — in stocking stitch with a garter stitch centre front band

Leave sts. on a stitch holder.

With No. 10 needles cast on 4 (8) sts. for back of work and work 8 rows st.st., beg. with a k. row and inc. at each end of every row.

Next row: k.20 (24), k.22 (26) from stitch holder. Work 1 row p. **Change to No. 12 needles and work 6 rows in k.1, p.1 rib.

Change to No. 10 needles and cont. in st.st. inc. at each end of every 6th row until there are 62 (70) sts. Cont. till work is 7 (8) in. from lower edge of rib ending with a p. row.** Leave sts. on a stitch holder and rep. from * to * for right foot, but ending with a k. row. Leave sts. on a stitch holder and work the back of the foot as for right foot but working 1 row k. on 20 (24) sts.

Next row: p. 20 (24), p.22 (26) from stitch holder and work as for left leg from ** to **.

Joining row: cast on 8 sts., k.62 (70), cast on 8 sts., k.62 (70) from stitch holder, cast on 8: 148 (164) sts.

Next row: k.8, p. to last 8 sts., k.8. Cont. in st.st. with 8 sts. each end in garter st. for 7 (8) in., ending with a p. row.

Next row: k.42 (46), (k.1, p.1) 32 (36) times, k. to end.

Next row: k.8, p.34 (38), (k.1, p.1) 32 (36) times, p.34 (38), k.8.

Rep. last 2 rows twice more, then cont. in st.st. with garter st. borders as before until work is 10 (11½) in. from joining row, ending with a p. row.

Armhole Division. K.37 (41), cast off 4, k.66 (74), cast off 4, k.37 (41).

Work on last set of sts. for left front thus:

Next row: k.8, p. to last st., k.1.

Next row: k.1, sl.1, k.1, p.s.s.o., k. to end. Rep. last 2 rows until 25 (26) sts. rem.

Neck Shaping. K.9 (10) sts. and leave on a stitch holder or safety pin, p. to last st., k.1. Shaping raglan as before, take 2 tog. at neck edge on every alt. row until all sts. are worked off.

Rejoin yarn to centre 66 (74) sts. for back and work:

Next row: k.1, p. to last st., k.1.

Next row: k.1, sl.1, k.1, p.s.s.o., k. to last 3 sts., k.2 tog., k.1.

Rep. last 2 rows until there are 26 (28) sts. Work 1 row and leave sts. on a stitch holder. Rejoin yarn to wrong side of rem. sts. for right front and work thus:

Next row: k.1, p. to last 8 sts., k.8.

Next row: k. to last 3 sts., k.2 tog., k.1. Complete to match first front, reversing neck shaping.

SLEEVES (make 2 alike)

With No. 12 needles cast on 38 (42) sts. Work in k.1, p.1 rib for 16 rows.

Change to No. 10 needles and work in st.st. inc. at each end of every 6th row until there are 52 (58) sts.

Cont. until work is 6 (7) in., ending with a p. row.

Shape Raglan. Cast off 2 sts. at beg. of next 2 rows, then work as for raglan shaping of Back until there are 8 sts. Work 1 row. Leave sts. on a stitch holder.

NECKBAND

Join all raglan seams. Place 9 (10) sts. at right front edge on a No. 12 needle then pick up and k.14 sts. up right side of neck, k. sts. of right sleeve, k. across sts. of back and left sleeve, pick up and k. 14 sts. down left side of neck and k. across 9 (10) sts. of left front: 88 (92) sts.

Work 9 rows in k.1, p.1 rib, keeping 8 sts. in garter st. at each end of row.

Cast off 8 sts. at beg. of next 2 rows.

Work 8 more rows in rib. Cast off in rib.

FOOT SOLES (make 2 alike)

With No. 10 needles cast on 6 (8) sts. Work in st.st., inc. at each end of every row until there are 20 (24) sts. Now take 2 tog. at each end of every 4th row until 6 (8) sts. rem. Cast off.

TO COMPLETE

Join sleeve seams. Fold 4 sts. at front edges to wrong side and slipstitch in place. Join inside leg seams, ending at lower edge of ankle rib. Sew in soles, placing cast-on edge at back. Sew in zip at centre front. Fold 8 rows rib on neckband to wrong side and slipstitch in place. Thread a double row of shirring elastic through wrong side of back waist rib and ankle ribs.

Striped play suit

(photographed in colour on page 18)

MATERIALS

3 oz. Robin Orlon/Antron Baby Double Knitting in pink, 2 oz. in blue and 1 oz. in yellow (see note on wools and yarns, page 20); one pair each Nos. 9 and 11 knitting needles (see page 26); a 12-in. zip.

MEASUREMENTS

To fit chest size 18/20 in.

TENSION

5½ sts. to 1 in. on No. 9 needles (see note on tension,

page 15).

ABBREVIATIONS
See page 26; P., pink; B., blue; Y., yellow.

RIGHT FRONT
With No. 9 needles and P., cast on 6 sts. The whole suit is worked in st.st. (see page 23), in the foll. 10-row striped patt.:
1st-4th rows: P.
5th and 6th rows: B.
7th and 8th rows: work both these rows k. in Y.
9th and 10th rows: as 5th and 6th rows.
Now work 8 rows, inc. at end of next (9th) row and then at this end of every row until there are 16 sts. Cast on 3 sts. at end of next and alt. rows: 22 sts., then cast on 4 sts. at end of next and alt. rows: 30 sts. Leave these sts. on a stitch holder.

CENTRE SECTION (back of suit)
With No. 9 needles and P., cast on 12 sts. Work 8 rows in striped patt., inc. at each end of next and every row until there are 32 sts. Then cast on 3 sts. at beg. of every row till there are 44 sts. and then cast on 4 sts. at beg. of every row until there are 60 sts. Leave sts. on a stitch holder.

LEFT FRONT
Work as for Right Front, reversing shapings.

MAIN SECTION (Back and Front worked in 1 piece)
Next row: work across all sts. from stitch holders (120) and cont. in striped patt. until work is 10 in. from this first row, ending with a wrong-side row.
Next row: k.29, cast off 2, k.58, cast off 2, k. to end.
Now on this last group of sts. (Left Front) work in patt. taking 2 tog. at inner edge (raglan shaping) on next 6 rows and then on alt. rows until there are 15 sts., ending with a right-side row.
Next row: work 5 sts., put these on a safety pin.
Cont. to take 2 tog. at armhole edge every alt. row as

before and *at the same time* take 2 tog. at neck edge on every row for 5 rows.
Cont. to dec. at armhole edge only until all sts. are worked off.
Rejoin yarn to centre section (back of suit) and work in patt. taking 2 tog. at each end of every row for 6 rows and then at each end of every alt. row until there are 20 sts. Leave these sts. on a stitch holder. Rejoin yarn to rem. sts. (Right Front) and work as for first group (Left Front), reversing shapings.

SLEEVES (make 2 alike)
With No. 11 needles and P. cast on 32 sts. Work in garter st. (see page 23) for ¾ in. Change to No. 9 needles and work in st.st. and stripe patt., inc. at each end of every 5th row until there are 38 sts.
Cont. till work is 1½ in., ending at the same row of striping as at armhole shaping on main section and finishing with a wrong-side row. Now take 2 tog. at each end of every alt. row until there are 6 sts. Leave these on a safety pin.

NECKBAND
Join raglan seams. With right side of work facing, No. 11 needles and P., k. across 5 sts. of Right Front, pick up and k.12 sts. up side of neck, k. across 6 sts. of sleeve, 20 sts. of Back and 6 sts. of other sleeve, pick up and k. 12 sts. down side of neck and k. across 5 sts. of Left Front: 66 sts.
Work in garter st. on these sts. for 1 in.
Cast off.

LEG EDGINGS
With No. 11 needles and P., pick up 72 sts. round one leg and work in garter st. for ¾ in. Cast off. Work edging round other leg in the same way.

TO COMPLETE
Join crutch seam. Join centre front seam for 5 in. up from crutch seam. Sew in zip to centre front opening.

Chapter 3

Toddlers' Togs

Orange beach suit

(photographed in colour on page 56)

MATERIALS

5 (5, 6) balls Wendy Courtelle Crêpe 4-ply (see note on wools and yarns, page 20); one pair each Nos. 7, 8, 9, 10 and 12 knitting needles (see page 26); a waist length of elastic $\frac{1}{4}$ in. wide.

MEASUREMENTS

To fit chest size 20 (22, 24) in.

TENSION

6 sts. to 1 in. over patt. on No. 10 needles (see note on tension, page 15).

ABBREVIATIONS

See page 26.

TOP

BACK AND FRONT (make 2 pieces alike)

With No. 7 needles cast on 63 (69, 75) sts. Work edging patt. thus:

1st row: *k.1, y.fwd., k.2 tog.; rep. from * to end. Rep. this row 5 times more.

Now start main patt. thus:

1st row: k.

2nd row: p.

3rd and 4th rows: as for first row of edging patt. These 4 rows form main patt.

Cont. in main patt. changing to No. 8 needles when work measures $2\frac{1}{2}$ (3, $3\frac{1}{2}$) in., then to No. 9 needles when work measures $4\frac{1}{2}$ ($5\frac{1}{2}$, $6\frac{1}{2}$) in., and to No. 10 needles when work measures 6 ($7\frac{1}{2}$, 9) in. from beg. Cont. until work measures $6\frac{1}{2}$ (8, $9\frac{1}{2}$) in. ending with a 4th patt. row.

Armhole Edgings. 1st row: k.1, y.fwd., k.2 tog., k. to last 3 sts., k.1, y.fwd., k.2 tog.

2nd row: k.1, y.fwd., p. to last 3 sts., k.1, y.fwd., k.2 tog.

3rd and 4th rows: work in patt.

5th row: (k.1, y.fwd., k.2 tog.) twice, k. to last 6 sts., (k.1, y.fwd., k.2 tog.) twice.

6th row: (k.1, y.fwd., k.2 tog.) twice, p. to last 6 sts., (k.1, y.fwd., k.2 tog.) twice.

Shape Armholes. 1st row: (k.1, y.fwd., k.2 tog.) twice, k.2 tog., k.1, patt. to last 9 sts., k.1, k.2 tog., (k.1, y.fwd., k.2 tog.) twice.

2nd row: patt. 6, k.2 tog., patt. to last 8 sts., k.2 tog., patt. 6.

3rd row: patt. 6, k.2 tog., k. to last 8 sts., k.2 tog., patt. 6.

4th row: patt. 6, p.2 tog., p. to last 8 sts., p.2 tog., patt. 6.

Keeping 6 sts. at each end correct in edging patt., cont. to dec. by 2 sts. in the same way on each row until there are 51 (51, 57) sts.

Cont. on these sts. keeping edging correct, until a 2nd patt. row has been worked, where necessary.

Neck Edging. Work 5 rows in edging patt. on all sts.

Shape Neck. Patt. 12, cast off 27 (27, 33) sts., patt. to end.

Now cont. in edging patt. on each set of 12 sts. separately until work measures 11 (13, 15) in. from beg., ending at side edge. Cast off 6 sts.

Work 1 row. Cast off.

PANTS

FRONT

With No. 12 needles cast on 60 (66, 72) sts.

Work 8 rows in k.1, p.1 rib.

Change to No. 10 needles, and work 16 rows in the 4-row main patt.

Change to No. 9 needles and cont. in patt. until work measures $5\frac{1}{2}$ (6, 6) in., ending after a wrong-side row.

Cont. in patt. shaping thus:

1st row: patt. 30 (33, 36), m.1 (by picking up thread between next 2 sts. and k. t.b.l.), patt. 24 (27, 30); turn.

2nd row: patt. 24 (27, 30), p. twice in next st., patt. 24 (27, 30); turn.

3rd row: patt. 24 (27, 30), k.1, m.1, k.1, patt. 18 (21, 24); turn.

4th row: patt. 18 (21, 24), p.3, patt. 18 (21, 24); turn.

5th row: patt. 18 (21, 24), k.1, (m.1, k.1) twice, patt. 12 (15, 18); turn.

6th row: patt. 12 (15, 18), p.5, patt. 12 (15, 18); turn.

7th row: patt. 12 (15, 18), k.1, m.1, k.3, m.1, k.1, patt. 6 (9, 12); turn.

8th row: patt. 6 (9, 12), p.7, patt. 6 (9, 12); turn.

Size 24 in. only. Next row: patt. 12, k.1, m.1, k.5, m.1, k.1, patt. 6; turn.

Next row: patt. 6, p.9, patt. 6; turn.

All sizes: patt. 6 (9, 6), cast off 7(7, 9).

This leaves 2 sets of 30 (33, 36) sts., one for each leg.

With No. 12 needles work 5 rows in the edging patt. on one set of leg sts. Cast off, and work other leg edging in the same way.

BACK

With No. 12 needles cast on 60 (66, 72) sts. and work first 7 rows as for Front.

8th row: rib 54 (57, 60); turn. **Next row:** rib 48; turn. **Next row:** rib 42; turn. **Next row:** rib 36; turn. **Next row:** rib 30; turn. **Next row:** rib 24; turn. **Next row:** rib 18; turn. **Next row:** rib 12; turn. **Next row:** rib to end.

Change to No. 10 needles and work as for Front checking measurements at side edge.

TO COMPLETE

TOP

Join side and shoulder seams.

PANTS

Sew side and inner leg and crutch seams. Join elastic into a ring and attach to inside of waistband with herring-boning.

Cable-patterned two-piece

(photographed in black and white on page 66)

MATERIALS

16 (17, 18) balls Wendy Tricel/Nylon Double Knitting (see note on wools and yarns, page 20); one pair each Nos. 8 and 10 knitting needles (see page 26); one cable needle; a 10 (12, 12)-in. open-ended zip fastener; waist length elastic $\frac{3}{4}$ in. wide.

MEASUREMENTS

To fit chest size 20 (22, 24) in.; length of jacket 12 (13, 14) in.; jacket sleeve seam 9 (9½, 10) in.; inside leg measurement 12 (13, 14) in.

TENSION

6 sts. and 8 rows to 1 in. over patt. with No. 8 needles (see note on tension, page 15).

ABBREVIATIONS

See page 26.

JACKET

BACK

With No. 10 needles cast on 71 (79, 87) sts. and work 12 rows in k.1, p.1 rib.

Change to No. 8 needles and patt. thus:

1st row: *k.3, p.1; rep. from * to last 3 sts., k.3.

2nd row: k.1, *p.1, k.3; rep from * to last 2 sts., p.1, k.1.

Rep. these 2 rows until work measures 8½ (9, 9½) in., ending with a 2nd row.

Shape Armholes. Cast off 7 sts. at beg. of next 2 rows.

Cont. straight until work measures 12 (13, 14) in. from beg., ending with a 2nd row.

Cast off in patt. 16 (20, 23) sts. at beg. of next 2 rows. Leave remaining 25 (25, 27) sts. on stitch holder.

LEFT FRONT

With No. 10 needles cast on 35 (39, 43) sts. and work 12 rows in k.1, p.1 rib.

Change to No. 8 needles and patt. thus:

1st row: (k.3, p.1) 3 (4, 5) times, (k. into front of 2nd st. on left-hand needle, then k. into front of first st., slip both off needle tog.: tw.2f.), p.2, k.4, p.2, tw.2f., (k. into back of 2nd st., then into front of first st., slip both off needle tog.: tw. 2b.), p.2, k.4, p.3.

2nd row: k.3, p.4, k.2, p.4, k.2, p.4, k.2, p.2, k.2, (p.1, k.3) 2 (3, 4) times, p.1, k.1.

3rd row: (k.3, p.1) 3 (4, 5) times, tw.2f., p.2, (put next 2 sts. on to cable needle and put to front of work, k. next 2 sts., then k. sts. from cable needle: c.4f.), p.2, tw.2f., tw.2b., p.2, (put next 2 sts. on to cable needle and put to back of work, k. next 2 sts., then k. sts. from cable needle: c.4b.), p.3.

4th row: as 2nd row.

Rep. these 4 rows until work measures 8⅛ (9, 9½) in., ending with a wrong-side row.

Shape Armhole. Next row: cast off 7 sts., patt. to end.

Keeping patt. correct, cont. straight until work measures 11 (12, 13) in. from beg., ending with a right-side row.

Next row: patt. 6 (8, 10) sts., slip them on to a safety pin, work 2 sts. tog., patt. to end. Cont. working 2 sts. tog. at neck edge on every row until 16 (20, 23) sts. remain, then work straight until Front measures 12, (13, 14) in. Cast off.

RIGHT FRONT
Cast on and work ribbing as for Left Front.
Change to No. 8 needles and patt. thus:
1st row: p.3, k.4, p.2, tw.2f., tw.2b., p.2, k.4, p.2, tw.2b., (p.1, k.3) 3 (4, 5) times.
2nd row: k.1, (p.1, k.3) 2 (3, 4) times, p.1, k.2, p.2, k.2, p.4, k.2, p.4, k.2, p.4, k.3.
3rd row: p.3, c.4b., p.2, tw.2f., tw.2b., p.2, c.4f., p.2, tw.2b., (p.1, k.3) 3 (4, 5) times. Cont. as Left Front on these sts., reversing shapings.

SLEEVES (make 2 alike)
With No. 10 needles cast on 35 (39, 43) sts. and work 12 rows in k.1, p.1 rib.
Change to No. 8 needles and work in patt. as for Back, inc. 1 st. at each end of next and every foll. 6th row until there are 57 (63, 67) sts.
Cont. straight until work measures 10 (10½, 11) in. from beg.
Shape Top. Cast off 10 (11, 12) sts. at beg. of next 4 rows.**
Cont. straight on remaining sts. until sleeve measures the same from point ** as the cast-off shoulder seam of Back. Leave sts. on stitch holder.

COLLAR
Sew shoulder seams. With right side facing and No. 10 needles, k.6 (8, 10) sts. on safety pin at front edge of Right Front, pick up and k.9 (10, 11) sts. round Right Front neck, k. across 17 (19, 19) sts. at top of Right Sleeve, k. across 25 (25, 27) sts. of back neck, k. 17 (19, 19) sts. at top of Left Sleeve, pick up

and k. 9 (10, 11) sts. round Left Front neck, and k. 6 (8, 10) sts. at front edge of Left Front: 89 (99, 107) sts. Work 3 in. in k.1, p.1, rib.
Cast off in rib.

TO COMPLETE
Set sleeves into armholes, sewing cast-off edges of sleeves down straight edges of armholes, then sewing a further 1 in. of sleeve across cast-off edges of armholes, so sleeves fit squarely into armholes. Join remainder of sleeve seams and side seams. Sew zip fastener down centre front.

TROUSERS
LEFT LEG
With No. 10 needles, cast on 43 (47, 51) sts. and work 12 rows in k.1, p.1 rib.
Change to No. 8 needles and patt. as for Back, inc. 1 st. at each end of every 6th row until there are 67 (73, 77) sts.
Cont. straight until work measures 12 (13, 14) in. Now inc. 1 st. at each end of every alt. row 4 times. Work 10 rows straight.
Now work 2 sts. tog. at each end of the next and every foll. 6th row until 6 decs. have been worked.
Cont. straight until work measures 17 (19, 20) in., ending with a wrong-side row.***
Next row: patt. 20; turn and work back.
Next row: patt. 10; turn and work back. Change to No. 10 needles and work in k.1, p.1 rib over all sts. for 1 in. Cast off in rib.

RIGHT LEG
Work as Left Leg, except that at *** end with a right-side row.

TO COMPLETE
Join back and front seams and leg seams. Join elastic in a circle of desired size. Put inside top ribbing and work herringbone-stitch over it to keep it in place.

Beach dress and scarf
(photographed in colour on page 55)

MATERIALS
7 (8) oz. Robin Vogue Double Knitting in lime green, 1 oz. Robin Vogue 4-ply in white (see note on wools and yarns, page 20): one pair No. 8 knitting needles (see page 26); one crochet hook International Standard Size 3·50.

Cable-patterned two-piece (see page 65) has a zip-up jacket, long trousers

MEASUREMENTS
To fit chest size 22 (24) in.; length of dress at centre back 17 (19) in.

TENSION
5½ sts. and 7½ rows to 1 in. (see note on tension, page 15).

ABBREVIATIONS
See page 26; L., lime green; W., white.

DRESS
BACK AND FRONT (make 2 pieces alike)
With L., cast on 84 (90) sts. Work 5 rows st.st. (see page 23).

Next row: k. (this makes ridge for hem). Cont. in st.st. till work measures $4\frac{1}{4}$ in., ending with a p. row.

Next row: k.2 tog., k.23 (25), k.2 tog., k.1 (centre st.), k.2 tog., k. 24 (26), k.2 tog., k.1 (centre st.), k.2 tog., k. to last 2 sts., k.2 tog.

Cont. in st.st., working a dec. row as the last one (i.e. taking 2 tog. at each end of the row and on each side of the 2 centre sts.) every 3 in. from the last until there are 66 (72) sts. Cont. till work measures $11\frac{3}{4}$ ($13\frac{1}{2}$) in., ending with a p. row.

Shape Armholes. Cast off 3 sts. at beg. of next 2 rows, then take 2 tog. at each end of every k. row until there are 56 (58) sts. Cont. till armhole is $2\frac{1}{2}$ ($2\frac{1}{2}$) in. ending with a p. row.

Shape Neckline. K.19 (19), k.2 tog.; turn. Work on these sts. taking 2 tog. at neck edge on every row until there are 12 (13) sts.

Cont. till armhole is $5\frac{1}{4}$ ($5\frac{1}{2}$) in., ending with a p. row. Cast off. Rejoin yarn to rem. sts., cast off 14 (16), and complete other side to match, reversing shapings.

POCKETS (make 2 alike)
With L., cast on 8 sts. Work 2 rows st.st.
Now inc. at each end of every k. row until there are 16 sts. Cont. till pocket measures 3 ($3\frac{1}{2}$) in. from beg. Cast off.

HEAD SCARF
MAIN PIECE
With L., cast on 100 sts. Work in st.st. taking 2 tog. at each end of every k. row until there are 4 sts. Cast off.

TIES (make 2 alike)
With L., cast on 8 sts. Work in k.1, p.1 rib until the tie is 6 in. long. Cast off.

TO COMPLETE
DRESS
Join side and shoulder seams. With crochet hook and W., work edging (see page 24) round neck, armholes and pockets thus:

1st round: work d.c. all along edges.

2nd round: d.c.

3rd round: 4 tr. into 2nd d.c. from hook, * miss 2 d.c., 1 d.c. into next d.c., miss 2 d.c., work 4 tr. into next d.c.; rep. from * all round.
Fasten off.

Stitch pockets in position to dress front, positioning them about $3\frac{1}{2}$ in. up from lower edge, as in photograph on page 55. Turn up hem at lower edge of dress and slipstitch in place.

HEAD SCARF
Work crochet edging in W., as for dress, right round edges of scarf. Sew on tie to each end of longest edge of the triangle.

Yoked dress

MATERIALS
4 (5, 5) oz. Twilley's Bubbly in main shade, 1 oz. Stalite in contrast shade (see note on wools and yarns, page 20); one pair each Nos. 9, 11 and 12 knitting needles (see page 26); 3 small buttons.

MEASUREMENTS
To fit chest size 24 (25, 26) in.; length at centre back $15\frac{1}{2}$ ($15\frac{3}{4}$, 16) in.

TENSION
$6\frac{1}{2}$ sts. to 1 in. on No. 9 needles over st.st. (see note on tension, page 15).

ABBREVIATIONS
See page 26; M., main shade; C., contrast shade.

BACK AND FRONT (make 2 pieces alike)
With No. 9 needles and M. cast on 106 (110, 114) sts. Beg. with p. row (right side), work in st.st. (see page 23), taking 2 tog. at each end of 9th and every foll. 8th row until there are 84 (88, 92) sts.

Cont. straight till work measures 13 ($13\frac{1}{4}$, $13\frac{1}{2}$) in. ending with a k. row.

Shape Armholes. Cast off 4 (5, 6) sts. at beg. of next 2 rows, 2 at beg. of next 2 rows then 1 at beg. of next 2 rows: 70 (72, 74) sts.

Shape For Yoke. P.2 tog., p.27 (28, 29); turn. Cont. to work on these sts. only.

Next row: ** cast off 3, work to end.

Next row: take 2 tog., work to end. Rep. last 2 rows once. Now keeping side edge straight cast off 3 sts. at beg. of next 2 neck edge rows, 2 at beg. of foll. neck edge row and then take 2 tog. at beg. of every foll. alt. row 10 times.

Next row. First size: p.2 tog. **Second size:** p.3 tog. **Third size:** p.2 tog. twice, p.2 tog.

All sizes: fasten off.

The lacy-patterned yoke and sleeve edgings are in a contrast shade to rest of dress

Now with right side of work facing rejoin yarn to rem. 41 (43, 45) sts. Cast off 12, p. to end.
Next row: k.2 tog., k. to end. Complete to match first side from **.

FRONT YOKE

With right side of Front facing, No. 11 needles, and C., pick up and k.80 sts. evenly round shaped yoke line.

1st row (wrong side): k.
2nd row: p. Rep. these 2 rows once more then the first row again.
6th row: k.2, *y.r.n., k.2 tog.; rep. from * to last 2 sts., k.2.
7th row: k.
8th row: k.1, p.1, *p.2 tog., p.4; rep. from * to end: 67 sts.
9th row: k.
10th row: p.
11th row: k.
12th row: as 6th row but end k.1, instead of k.2.
13th row: k.
14th row: k.1, p.1, *p.2 tog., p.4; rep. from * to last 5 sts., p.2 tog., p.3: 53 sts.
15th-17th rows: as 9th-11th rows.
18th row: as 6th row.
19th row: k.
20th row: as 8th row: 47 sts.
21st-23rd rows: as 9th-11th rows.
24th row: as 6th row, but end k.1.
25th row: k.
26th row: k.1 p.1, *p.2 tog., p.4; rep. from * to last 3 sts., p.2 tog., p.1: 39 sts.
27th-29th rows: as 9th-11th rows.
Change to No. 12 needles and, beg. with a k. row, work 3 rows st.st.
Cast off very loosely.

BACK YOKE

With right side of work facing, No. 11 needles and C., pick up and k. 42 sts. evenly to centre, then 42 sts. up other side.

1st row: k.
2nd row: p.40, cast off 2, k.2; turn and work on these sts.
3rd row: k.2, cast on 2, k. to end.
4th row: p. to last 4 sts., k.4.
5th row: k.
6th row: k.2, *y.r.n., k.2 tog.; rep from * to last 6 sts., k.6.
7th row: k.

8th row: k.1, p.1, *p.2 tog., p.4; rep. from * to last 6 sts., k.6: 38 sts.
9th row: k.
10th row: p.
11th row: k.
12th row: as 6th row.
13th row: k.
14th row: k.1, p.1, *p.2 tog., p.4; rep. from * to last 6 sts., p.2 tog., cast off 2, k.2: 32 sts.
15th-17th rows: as 9th-11th rows, but cast on 2 sts. over those cast off in previous row.
18th row: as 6th row.
19th row: k.
20th row: k.1, p.1, *p.2 tog., p.4; rep. from * to last 6 sts., k.6: 28 sts.
21st-23rd rows: as 9th-11th rows.
24th row: as 6th row.
25th row: k.
26th row: k.1, p.1, *p.2 tog., p.4; rep. from * to last 8 sts., p.2 tog., p.2, cast off 2, k.2.
27th-29th rows: as 9th-11th rows, but cast on 2 sts. over those cast off in previous row. Change to No. 12 needles and beg. with a k. row, work 3 rows st.st.
Next row: k., casting on 2 sts. over those cast off in previous row. Cast off very loosely.
With No. 11 needles and C., cast on 4 sts., then on to end of same needle and with right side of work facing, p. across 40 sts. of other side and work as follows:
Next row: k.
Work in patt. to match first side, beg. with a 4th row, omitting buttonholes and reversing shaping by reading all rows from end to beg.

ARMBANDS (make 2 alike)

Join shoulder seams of yoke and main piece of garment above armhole. With right side of work facing, No. 12 needles and C., pick up and k.58 sts. round armhole. Work 5 rows st.st., beg. with a k. row. Beg. again with a k. row and work 3 rows st.st. Cast off loosely.

TO COMPLETE

Join side seams and ends of armbands. Turn last 3 rows of st.st. at neck edge and sleeve edges to wrong side and slipstitch in place. Turn up a narrow hem at lower edge of skirt and slipstitch in place. Sew lower edge of button band to edge of yoke; sew on buttons opposite buttonholes.

Ribbon-trimmed dress and coat

(photographed in colour on page 37 and in black and white on page 72)

MATERIALS

12 (13) oz. Peter Pan Bri-Nylon 4-ply (see note on wools and yarns, page 20); one pair each Nos. 10 and 12 knitting needles (see page 26); 6 small buttons; 3 yards narrow ribbon in colour to contrast or tone with yarn.

MEASUREMENTS

To fit chest size 20 (22) in.; length of dress at centre back: 16 (17) in.; sleeve seam of coat 8 (8½) in.

TENSION

8 sts. and 10½ rows to 1 in. on No. 10 needles (see note on tension, page 15).

ABBREVIATIONS

See page 26.

DRESS

BACK

With No. 10 needles cast on 104 (110) sts.

1st row: p.2, y.fwd., *sl.1, k.1, p.s.s.o., k.2 tog., y.r.n., p.2; rep. from * to end.

2nd row: p.

These 2 rows form patt. Rep. them 8 times more then work first patt. row again.

20th row: p.7 (10), (p.2 tog., p.8) 9 times, p.2 tog., p. to end: 94 (100) sts.

Cont. in st.st. (see page 23) until work is 11½ (12¼) in., ending with a k. row.

Next row: p.10 (13), (p.2 tog., p.7) 8 times, p.2 tog., p. to end: 85 (91) sts.

Shape Armholes. Cast off 4 sts. at beg. of next 2 rows.

Next row: p.5 (8), y.fwd., (sl.1, k.1, p.s.s.o., k.2 tog., y.r.n., p.2) 6 times.

Turn and work on these 41 (44) sts.

Next row: p. to last 2 sts., p.2 tog. Keeping patt. correct, take 2 tog. at side edge on every row until there are 36 (39) sts. Cont. on these sts. till work is 16 (17) in., ending at neck edge.

Shape Shoulders. Work to last 8 (9) sts., turn and work back.

Next row: work to last 16 (18) sts., turn and work back.

Next row: work to last 22 (25) sts., turn and work back. Sl. these 22 (25) sts. on to a stitch holder and the rem. 14 sts. on to another stitch holder. Return to rem. sts. and with right side of work facing, cast on 5 sts. at beg. of row.

1st row: p.5, (y.fwd., sl.1, k.1, p.s.s.o., k.2 tog., y.r.n., p.2) 5 times, p. to end.

2nd row: p.2 tog., p. to end. Complete to match first side.

FRONT

Work as for Back as far as armhole shaping, ending with a k. row.

Next row: p.5 (8), (p.2 tog., p.7) 9 times, p.2 tog., p. to end: 84 (90) sts.

Shape Armholes. Cast off 4 sts. at beg. of next 2 rows.

Next row: p.3 (6), y.fwd., *sl.1, k.1, p.s.s.o., k.2 tog., y.r.n., p.2; rep. from * to last 1 (4) sts., p. to end. Keeping patt. correct take 2 tog. at each end of every row until there are 68 (74) sts. and cont. on these sts. until work is 14¾ (16) in. ending with a wrong-side row.

Next row: work 25 (28) sts.; turn. Work on these sts., taking 2 tog. at neck edge on every row until there are 22 (25) sts., then cont. until work is 16 (16½) in.

Work shoulder shaping exactly as for Back. Slip centre 18 sts. on a stitch holder and complete other side of Front to match, reversing shapings.

Place sts. of Back and Front shoulders together and cast off together, to make a seam.

NECKBAND

With No. 12 needles and right side of work facing, k. across 14 sts. of right back neck, pick up and k. 9 sts. down side of right neck, k. across centre front 18 sts., pick up 9 sts. at other side of neck and k. across rem. 14 sts. at back: 64 sts.

Work 1 row p.

Work 2 rows in st.st.

Next row: k.2, *y.fwd., k.2 tog.; rep. from * to end. Now beg. with a p. row, work 3 rows st.st.

Cast off.

ARMBANDS (make 2 alike)

With No. 12 needles pick up 76 sts. round armhole and work as for Neckband.

COAT

BACK

With No. 10 needles cast on 106 (112) sts. Work 12 rows in garter st. (see page 23), then cont. in st.st. until work is 12 (12½) in., ending with a k. row.

Next row: p.0 (3) sts., (p.2 tog., p.3) 20 times, p.2 tog., p. to last 2 sts., p.2 tog.: 84 (90) sts.

Shape Armholes. Work as for Front of dress until there are 68 (74) sts.

Work on these until Back is 16¼ (17¼) in.

Shape Shoulders. 1st and 2nd rows: work to last 8 (9) sts.; turn.

3rd and 4th rows: work to last 16 (18) sts.; turn.

5th and 6th rows: work to last 22 (25) sts.; turn. Slip shoulder and neck sts. on to stitch holder.

LEFT FRONT

With No. 10 needles, cast on 59 (65) sts. Work 13 rows in garter st.

Next row: k.9, p. to end. Now cont. in st.st., keeping 9-st. garter st. border until work is 12 (12½) in., ending with a k. row.

Next row: k.9, (p.2 tog., p.3) 9 times, p.2 tog., p. to end: 49 (55) sts.

Shape Armholes. Cast off 4 sts., *p.2, sl.1, k.1, p.s.s.o., p.2 tog., y.r.n.; rep. from * to last 9 sts., k.9. Keeping patt. correct, take 2 tog. at armholes until there are 42 (45) sts.

Cont. on these sts. until work is 14¾ (16¼) in.

Slip 20 sts. from neck edge on to stitch holder and cont. on rem. sts. until work is 16¼ (17¼) in.

Shape Shoulders. Work as for Back of Coat.

RIGHT FRONT

Work as for Left Front, reversing shapings and working garter st. border at beg. of row. Make a buttonhole in first row of yoke patt. in the garter st. border, thus:

Buttonhole row: k.3, y.fwd., k.2 tog., k.4.

Work 2 more buttonholes, the first on 23rd row, the second on 45th row.

Placing sts. of Fronts tog. with those of Back shoulders cast off tog.

SLEEVES (make 2 alike)

With No. 10 needles cast on 44 sts. Work in patt. as for dress hem, inc. at each end of every 12th row until there are 52 (56) sts., working the extra sts. in p. throughout.

Cont. until sleeve is 8 (8½) in.

Shape Top. Cast off 4 sts. at beg. of next 2 rows then take 2 tog. at each end of every alt. row until there are 36 sts., then take 2 tog. at each end of every row until there are 18 sts. Cast off 6 sts. at beg. of next 2 rows.

Cast off rem. sts.

NECKBAND

With right side of work facing and No. 12 needles, k.20 sts. of Right Front, pick up 12 sts. up right side of neck, k.24 sts. of Back neck, pick up 12 sts. down left side of Front and k. across 20 sts. of Left Front: 88 sts. Complete as for Neckband of dress.

TO COMPLETE

DRESS

Sew side seams, turn in neck and armhole facings and slipstitch in place. Thread ribbon through yoke holes, and st. ends tog. Thread ribbon through hem holes, break ribbon in 2 places, and tie in bows, as in photograph opposite. Sew 3 buttons to left back opening, the first at neck edge, the other two below at 1¾-in. intervals. Use holes in lacy patt. (just beyond garter st. border) on right back opening as buttonholes.

COAT

Sew in sleeves and join side and sleeve seams. Turn neck facing inside and slipstitch in place.

Thread ribbon through yoke holes and st. ends to inside of coat at centre front edges. To prevent pulling under arms, ribbon can be broken and ends stitched to inside of coat at either side of armholes. Sew on 3 buttons to left front opposite buttonholes.

Boy's striped suit

(photographed in colour on back cover and in black and white on page 77)

MATERIALS

6 (6, 7) oz. Paton's Ninepin in navy, 1 (2, 2) oz. in red (see note on wools and yarns, page 20); one pair each Nos. 9 and 10 knitting needles (see page 26); 7 small buttons; 1 medium crochet hook; a waist length of elastic, 1 in. wide.

MEASUREMENTS

To fit chest size 20 (22, 24) in.

TENSION

5½ sts. to 1 in. on No. 9 needles (see note on tension, page 15).

The ribbon-trimmed dress is sleeveless with a patterned yoke and hemband

ABBREVIATIONS

See page 26; N., navy; R., red.

TOP

FRONT

With No. 9 needles and N., cast on 72 (78, 84) sts. Work 7 rows st.st. (see page 23).

Next row: k. (to make hem ridge).

Work 6 rows st.st. and then join in R. Cont. to work in stripes of 2 rows in each colour, taking 2 tog. at each end of 3rd and every foll. 8th row until there are 60 (66, 72) sts. Cont. until work is 6½ (7, 7½) in. from hem ridge.

Shape Armholes. Keeping stripes correct, cast off 3 (3, 4) sts. at beg. of next 2 rows, then take 2 tog. at each end of next and every alt. row until there are

48 (54, 58) sts. Cont. until armhole is 2 (2, 2¼) in.

Shape Neck. K.18 (20, 22), sl. next 12 (14, 14) sts. on to a stitch holder and work on rem. sts., taking 2 tog. at neck edge on next and alt. rows until there are 13 (15, 17) sts. Cont. until armhole is 3½ (3¾, 4) in., ending at armhole edge.

Shape Shoulder. Cast off 7 (8, 9) sts. at beg. of next row. Work 1 row and cast off. Rejoin yarn to rem. sts., and work other side in the same way, reversing shapings.

RIGHT BACK

With No. 9 needles and N., cast on 36 (39, 42) sts. Work 7 rows st.st., inc. 1 st. at end of every k. row.

Next row: k. (for hem ridge). Now work 6 rows st.st., inc. at end of every k. row. Join in R. and working in 2-row stripes as before, inc. at end of first row: 43 (46, 49) sts.

Now cont. taking 2 tog. at beg. of 3rd and every 8th row until work is 2½ (3, 3½) in. from hem ridge, ending with a p. row.

Next row (buttonhole row): k. to last 7 sts., cast off 2, k.2, cast off 2, k.1.

Next row: p.1, cast on 2, p.2, cast on 2, p. to end. Now cont. in st.st., dec. at beg. of every 8th row, until there are 37 (40, 43) sts., at the same time making buttonholes at intervals of 2 in. until work measures 6½ (7, 7½) in. from hem ridge, ending with a p. row.

Shape Armholes. Cast off 3 (3, 4) sts. at beg. of next 2 rows, then take 2 tog. at beg. of next k. row and every alt. row until there are 30 (33, 35) sts. Cont. until armhole is 3½ (3¾, 4) in., ending at the armhole edge. Work 4th buttonhole 2 in. from previous one.

Shape Shoulder. Cast off 7 (8, 9) sts. at beg. of next row. Work 1 row and cast off 6 (7, 8) sts. at beg. of next row. Leave rem. 17 (18, 18) sts. on stitch holder.

LEFT BACK

Work as for Right Back but omit buttonholes and reverse all shapings, i.e. inc. and dec. at end of row instead of beg. and vice versa.

SLEEVES (make 2 alike)

With No. 9 needles and N., cast on 40 (44, 48) sts. Work 4 rows garter st. (see page 23).
Change to st.st. and inc. at each end of 5th and every foll. 8th row until there are 52 (54, 56) sts. Cont. till sleeve is 7 (8, 9) in. from beg.

Shape Top. Cast off 3 (3, 4) sts. at beg. of next 2 rows, then take 2 tog. at beg. of next and every alt. row until there are 38 (40, 40) sts. Cast off 3 sts. at beg. of next 6 rows. Cast off.

POCKETS (make 2 alike)

With No. 9 needles and N., cast on 12 sts.
Work 2 rows st.st.
Cont. in st.st., inc. at each end of every k. row 3 (3, 4) times ending with a p. row.

Work 5 rows.

Next row: k. (to form hem ridge). Beg. with a k. row, work 4 rows st.st. Cast off.

NECKBAND

Join shoulder seams. With right side of work facing, No. 10 needles and N., beg. with sts. on stitch holder at left side of back, cast off first 4 sts. then k.13 (14, 14), pick up and k.10 (11,12) sts. down side of neck, k.12 (14, 14) across centre front, pick up and k.10 (11, 12) up right side of neck, k.17 (18, 18) on stitch holder across right side of back.

Next row: cast off 4, work in k.1, p.1 rib to end. Rib for 2 rows.

Next row (buttonhole row): rib to last 3 sts., cast off 2, k.1.

Next row: k.1, cast on 2, rib to end. Work 2 more rows rib and cast off.

TROUSERS
LEFT LEG

With No. 9 needles and N. cast on 64 (70, 76) sts. and work in st.st. for 5 rows.

Next row: k. (to make hem ridge).

Next row: k. 15 (17, 18), sl.1, k.32 (34, 38), sl.1, k.15 (17, 18).

Next row: p.
Rep. last 2 rows once then the first row again.

Next row: *p. tog. 1 st. of next row with 1 st. of cast-on edge; rep. from * to end of row.

Now work as follows:

1st row: k.5 (6, 7); turn.

2nd and 4th rows: p.

3rd row: k.10 (12, 14); turn.

5th row: k.15 (17, 18), sl.1, k.32 (34, 38), sl.1, k.15 (17,18).

6th row: p.5 (6, 7); turn.

7th row: k.

8th row: p.10 (12, 14); turn.

9th row: k.

10th row: p.

Keeping sl. st. to mark crease edge cont. in st.st. inc. at beg. of 19th and every 6th row until 68 (74, 80) sts. Cont. until work is 6½ (7, 7½) in. at centre, ending with a p. row.**

Next row: k.18 (21, 24); turn.

Next and alt. rows: p.

Next row: k.12 (14, 16); turn.

Next row: k.6 (7, 8); turn.

Next row: p.

Work 7 rows st.st.

Next row: k.

Opposite: white, blue and navy long-sleeved dress (instructions on page 99)

74

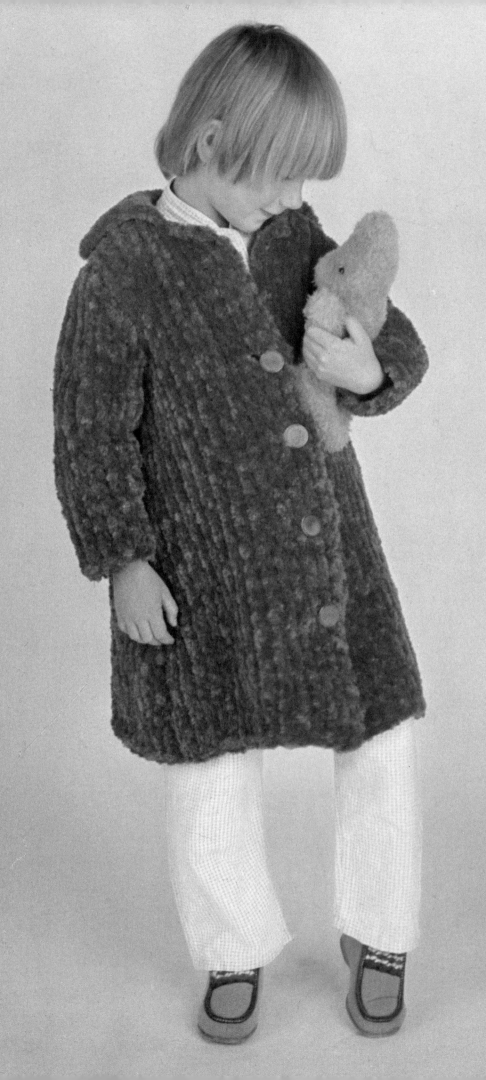

Little boy's suit has a striped top, plain coloured matching trousers

Work 6 rows st.st. Cast off.

RIGHT LEG

Work as for Left Leg to ** but working inc. at end of row and finishing with a k. row.

Next row: p. 18 (21, 24); turn.
Next row: k.
Next row: p.12 (14, 16); turn.
Next row: k.
Next row: p.6 (7, 8); turn.
Work 8 rows st.st.
Next row: k.
Work 6 rows st.st. Cast off.

GUSSET

With No. 9 needles and N., cast on 16 (18, 20) sts. and work 18 (20, 22) rows st.st. Cast off.

Opposite: dressing-gown worked in a yarn that looks just like fur (see page 108)

TO COMPLETE
TOP

Set in sleeves, and join side and sleeve seams. Mitre corners of centre back facings and of lower hem, fold back and slipstitch in place. Neaten buttonholes and sew on buttons to left back opposite buttonholes. Fold back top hem on each pocket, slipstitch in place. With crochet hook, work d.c. round side and lower edges of pockets (not hem edge). Sew pockets in place to front of jersey positioning them about $1\frac{1}{2}$ in. up from lower edge, as in photograph above. Stitch one button to the front of each pocket, midway along top edge, stitching to jersey at the same time.

TROUSERS

Stitch each leg seam for about 1 in. Join centre back and centre front seams for about 6 in. from waist edge. Stitch gusset in along rem. open edges. Turn in waistband along ridge row and hem on inside, leaving a gap for inserting elastic. Thread elastic through and stitch ends together. Stitch hem closed.

Girl's ribbed suit

(photographed in colour on back cover and in black and white on right)

MATERIALS

8 (9, 10) oz. Wendy Peter Pan Baby Bri-Nylon 4-ply (see note on wools and yarns, page 20); one pair each Nos. 10 and 12 knitting needles (see page 26); a waist length of narrow elastic.

MEASUREMENTS

To fit chest size 20 (22, 24) in.; skirt length 7 (8, 9) in.

TENSION

$7\frac{1}{2}$ sts. and 10 rows to 1 in. on No. 10 needles over st.st. (see note on tension, page 15).

ABBREVIATIONS

See page 26.

SKIRT (back and front worked alike)

With No. 12 needles cast on 83 (88, 93) sts. and work 9 rows in st.st. (see page 23).

Next row: k. (for hem ridge). Beg. with a k. row and inc. at each end of the first row, work 10 rows in st.st. Change to No. 10 needles.

1st row: (p.1, k.1) in first st., * k.4, m.1 purlwise by picking up thread between sts. and purling it t.b.l., k.1; rep. from * to last 4 sts., k.3, (k.1, p.1) in last st.: 103 (109, 115) sts.

2nd row: k.1, *p.5, k.1; rep. from * to end. Cont. on these sts. in rib patt. as set, until work is $2\frac{1}{2}$ in. from hem ridge, ending after a right-side row.

Next row: k. twice into first st., *p.5, k. twice in next st.; rep. from * to end: 121 (128, 135) sts.

Next row: p.2, *k.5, p.2; rep. from * to end. Cont. in this rib patt. until work is 4 in. from hem ridge, ending after a right-side row.

Next row: k.2, *p.5, k. twice in next st., k.1; rep. from * to last 7 sts., p.5, k.2.

Next row: p.2, *k.5, p.3; rep. from * to last 7 sts., k.5, p.2.

Cont. in this rib patt. until work is $5\frac{1}{2}$ (6, $6\frac{1}{2}$) in. from hem ridge, ending with a right-side row.

Next row: k. twice into first st., k.1, *p.5, k. twice in next st., k.2; rep. from * to last 7 sts., p.5, k.1, k. twice in last st.

Next row: p.3, *k.5, p.4; rep. from * to last 8 sts., k.5, p.3.

Cont. in this rib patt. until work is 7 (8, 9) in. from hem ridge. Cast off in patt.

JERSEY FRONT

With No. 12 needles cast on 97 (105, 113) sts.

1st row: p.1, *p.1, k.5, p.2; rep. from * to end.

2nd row: k.1, *k.1, p.5, k.2; rep. from * to end.

Rep. these 2 rows until work is $3\frac{1}{2}$ (4, $4\frac{1}{2}$) in. ending

Ribbing gives a pleated effect to skirt

after a wrong-side row. Change to No. 10 needles.

Next row: k.31, rib 35 (43, 51) as before, k.31.

Next row: p.31, rib 35 (43, 51) as before, p.31. Rep. these 2 rows until work is $8\frac{1}{2}$ (9, $9\frac{1}{2}$) in., ending after a wrong-side row.

Shape Armholes. Cast off 4 sts. at beg. of next 2 rows then take 2 tog. at each end of next 5 (6, 7) rows and of foll. 3 alt. rows: 73 (79, 85) sts.

Cont. until 16 (20, 24) rows from beg. of armholes have been worked.

Next row: k.19 (18, 17), (p.2 tog., p.1, k.5) 4 (5, 6) times, p.1, p.2 tog., k. to end.

Next row: p.19 (18, 17), (k.2, p.5) 4 (5, 6) times, k.2, p. to end.

Next row: k.19 (18, 17), (p.2 tog., k.5) 4 (5, 6) times, p.2 tog., k. to end.

Next row: p.19 (18, 17), (k.1, p.5) 4 (5, 6) times, k.1, p. to end: 63 (67, 71) sts.

Cont. on these sts. in st.st. until armholes measure $2\frac{1}{2}$ (3, $3\frac{1}{2}$) in. ending after a wrong-side row.

Shape Front Neck. K.21 (22, 23); turn. Work 7 rows on these sts. taking 2 tog. on next and foll. alt. rows: 17 (18, 19) sts.

Shape Shoulder. Cast off 5 (5, 6) sts., k. to end. Take 2 tog. at beg. of next row then cast off 5 (6, 6) sts. at beg. of next row. Work 1 row. Cast off. Slip 21 (23, 25) sts. on stitch holder and work other side to match, reversing shapings.

JERSEY BACK

With No. 12 needles cast on 97 (105, 113) sts. and work 3½ (4, 4½) in. of ribbing as for Front. Change to No. 10 needles.

Next row: k.7 (9, 1), *k.2 tog., k.7 (6, 6); rep. from * to end: 87 (93, 99) sts.

Beg. with a p. row, cont. in st.st. until work measures as for Front as far as armhole shaping.

Shape Armholes. Cont. in st.st., cast off 4 sts. at beg. of next 2 rows then take 2 tog. at each end of next 5 (6, 7) rows and of foll. 3 alt. rows. Work on rem. 63 (67, 71) sts. until Back measures as for Front as far as shoulder shaping.

Shape Shoulders. Cast off 5 (5, 6) sts. at beg. of next 2 rows and 5 (6, 6) at beg. of next 2 rows, then 6 sts. at beg. of next 2 rows. Leave rem. 31 (33, 35) sts. on stitch holder.

SLEEVES (make 2 alike)

With No. 12 needles cast on 43 (49, 55) sts.

1st row: p.1, * k.2, p.1; rep. from * to end.

2nd row: k.1, * p.2, k.1; rep. from * to end.

Rep. these 2 rows until work is 1 in., ending after a wrong-side row. Change to No. 10 needles.

Next row: p.1, *k.5, p.1; rep. from * to end.

Next row: k.1, *p.5, k.1; rep. from * to end.

Cont. in this rib patt. until work is 2½ in., ending after a right-side row.

Next row: k. twice in first st., *p.5, k. twice in next st.; rep. from * to end: 51 (58, 65) sts.

Next row: p.2, *k.5, p.2; rep. from * to end.

Cont. in this rib patt. until work is 4 (4½, 4½) in. ending after a right-side row.

Next row: k.2, *p.5, k. twice in next st., k.1; rep. from * to last 7 sts., p.5, k.2: 57 (65, 73) sts.

Next row: p.2, *k.5, p.3; rep. from * to last 7 sts., k.5, p.2.

Cont. in this rib patt. until work is 5½ (6, 6½) in.,

ending after a right-side row.

Next row: k.2, *p.5, k. twice in next st., k.2; rep. from * to last 7 sts., p.5, k.2: 63 (72, 81) sts.

Next row: p.2, *k.5, p.4; rep. from * to last 7 sts., k.5, p.2.

Cont. in this rib patt. until work is 7 (8, 9) in., ending with a wrong-side row.

Shape Top. Cast off 4 sts. at beg. of next 2 rows and 2 sts. at beg. of foll. 18 (22, 26) rows.

Cast off.

POLO COLLAR

Join right shoulder seam of jersey. With right side of work facing and No. 12 needles pick up 13 sts. from left side of neck, k. across 21 (23, 25) sts. from centre front, pick up 12 sts. up other side of neck and work across 31 (33, 35) sts. of Back: 77 (81, 85) sts.

1st row: p.1, *k.3, p.1; rep. from * to end.

2nd row: k.1, *p.3., k.1; rep. from * to end.

In this rib patt. work 8 rows on No. 12 needles and 9 rows on No. 10 needles.

Next row: k. twice in first st., *p.3, k. twice in next st.; rep. from * to end.

Next row: p.2, *k.3, p.2; rep. from * to end. Work 8 rows in this patt.

Next row: k.2, *p.3, k. twice in next st., k.1; rep. from * to last 5 sts., p.3, k.2.

Next row: p.2, *k.3, p.3; rep. from * to last 5 sts., k.3, p.2. Work 5 rows in this rib patt.

Cast off loosely.

TO COMPLETE

Skirt. Sew side seams. Turn in waistband at ridge row and hem on inside, leaving a gap for inserting elastic. Thread elastic through and stitch ends together. Stitch hem closed.

Jersey. Sew left shoulder seam and collar seam. Set in sleeves and join side and sleeve seams.

Three-piece Aran outfit

(photographed in black and white on page 80)

MATERIALS

12 (14, 16) oz. of Mahoney's 3-ply Bainin Yarn (see note on wools and yarns, page 20) for sweater, 12 (14, 16) for trousers, 4 oz. for hat; one pair each Nos. 7 and 10 knitting needles (see page 26); a waist length of elastic, ½ in. wide.

MEASUREMENTS

Sweater: to fit chest size 22 (24, 26) in.; length at centre back 14 (15½, 17) in.; sleeve seam 9½ (11, 12½) in. **Trousers:** inside leg length 14½ (17, 19½) in.;

length at side to centre of waistband 22 (25, 28) in.
Hat: to fit average-size head.

TENSION

6 sts. and 6 rows to 1 in. on No. 7 needles over patt. (see note on tension, page 15).

ABBREVIATIONS

See page 26; cr.3 (cross 3), sl.1 knitwise, then k.1, y.f. (to make a st.), k.1, lift the sl. st. over these 3 sts. and drop it off needle; tw.2l. (twist 2 left), p. into back of

2nd st. on needle then k. first st. in usual way, slipping both sts. off needle tog.; tw.2r. (twist 2 right), k. 2nd st. on needle, then p. first st., slipping both off needle at the same time; sl. marker, make a sl. knot in a short length of contrasting coloured yarn and place on needle where indicated. On the foll. rows sl. the marker from one needle to the other until the patt. is established and the marker no longer required.

SWEATER
BACK
With No. 10 needles cast on 66 (70, 74) sts.
1st row: p.2, *k.2, p.2; rep. from * to end.
2nd row: k.2, *p.2, k.2; rep. from * to end.
Rep. these 2 rows 3 times more, then work first row again.
Next row: (k.2, inc. in next st., p.1) twice, rib 14 sts., (inc. in next st., p. 1, k.2) 5 (6, 7) times, inc. in next st., p.1, rib 14 sts., (inc. in next st., p.1, k.2) twice: 76 (81, 86) sts.
Change to No. 7 needles and work 4 foundation rows thus:
1st row (right side): (p.2, cr.3) twice, * sl. marker (see Abbreviations), p.1, k.1, p.2, k.1, p.4, k.1, p.2, k.1, p.1, sl. marker *, cr.3, (p.2, cr.3) 5 (6, 7) times; rep. from * to *, (cr.3, p.2) twice.
2nd row: (k.2, p.3) twice, *k.1, p.1, k.2, p.1, k.4, p.1, k.2, p.1, k.1*, p.3, (k.2, p.3) 5 (6, 7) times; rep. from * to *, (p.3, k.2) twice.
Rep. the last 2 rows once more.
Begin Pattern. Cont. to work the cr.3 rib patt. on the centre 28 (33, 38) sts. and on the 10 sts. at each end of row, now beg. the patt. as foll. on the 14 sts. between each pair of markers:
1st row: p.1, k.1, p.2, tw.2l., p.2, tw.2r., p.2, k.1, p.1.
2nd row: k.1, p.1, k.3, p.1, k.2, p.1, k.3, p.1, k.1.
3rd row: p.1, k.1, p.3, tw.2l., tw. 2r., p.3, k.1, p.1.
4th row: k.1, p.1, k.4, purl 2nd st. on needle then purl first st. slipping both off needle tog. (called cross 2 purl), k.4, p.1, k.1.
5th row: p.1, (tw.2l., p.2, tw.2r.) twice, p.1.
6th row: (k.2, p.1) 4 times, k.2.
7th row: (p.2, tw.2l., tw.2r.) twice, p.2.
8th row: k.3, cross 2 purl, k.4, cross 2 purl, k.3.
9th row: p.2, (tw.2r., tw.2l., p.2) twice.
10th row: as 6th row.
11th row: p.1, (tw.2r., p.2, tw.2l.) twice, p.1.
12th to 19th rows: rep. the 4th to 11th rows.
20th row: as 4th row.
21st row: p.1, k.1, p.3, tw.2r., tw.2l., p.3, k.1, p.1.
22nd row: as 2nd row.

Matching sweater, trousers and pompon hat are all in a traditional Aran pattern

23rd row: p.1, k.1, p.2, tw.2r., p.2, tw.2l., p.2, k.1, p.1.
24th row: k.1, p.1, k.2, p.1, k.4, p.1, k.2, p.1, k.1.
25th row: p.1, k.1, p.2, k.1, p.4, k.1, p.2, k.1, p.1.
Rep. the last 2 rows twice.
30th row: as 24th row.
These 30 rows form the patt.
Cont. in patt. and cr.3 rib until Back measures 8½ (9½, 10½) in. ending with a wrong-side row.
Shape Armholes. Cast off 3 sts. at beg. of next 2 rows. Dec. 1 st. at each end of next 6 rows: 58 (63, 68) sts. rem. Work straight until armholes measure 4½ (5, 5½) in. measured straight and ending with a wrong-side row.
Shape Shoulders. Cast off 6 sts. at beg. of next 4 rows.
Next row: cast off 5 (6, 7) sts., work to end.
Next row: cast off 5 (6, 7) sts., work to end.
Sl. rem. 24 (27, 30) sts. on to a stitch holder.

FRONT
Work as given for Back until Front is 8 rows shorter than Back to start of shoulder shaping, thus ending with a wrong-side row.
Shape Neck. 1st row: work 22 (23, 24) sts., turn and complete this side first leaving rem. sts. on stitch holder.
** Dec. 1 st. at neck edge of next 3 rows then every alt. row twice, thus ending at armhole edge: 17 (18, 19) sts. rem.
Shape Shoulder. Cast off 6 sts. at beg. of next row and following alt. row. Work 1 row. Cast off rem. 5 (6, 7) sts.** Sl. next 14 (17, 20) sts. on to a stitch holder. With right side of work facing rejoin yarn to rem. sts. and complete as first side from ** to **.

SLEEVES (make 2 alike)
With No. 10 needles cast on 30 (30, 34) sts.
Work 9 rows in rib as given for Back.
Next row: k.2, * inc. in next st. p.1, k.2; rep. from * to end: 37 (37, 42) sts.
Change to No. 7 needles and beg patt.:
1st row: p.2, *cr.3, p.2; rep. from * to end.
2nd row: k.2, *p.3, k.2; rep. from * to end.
Bringing new sts. into cr.3 rib patt. inc. 1 st. at each end of next and every foll. 6th row until there are 53 (55, 62) sts. Work straight until sleeve measures 9½ (11, 12½) in. (or required seam length), ending with a wrong-side row.
Shape Top. Cast off 3 sts. at beg. of next 2 rows. Dec. 1 st. at each end of next 10 (11, 12) rows. Cast off 3 sts. at beg. of next 2 rows. Cast off.

COLLAR
Join right shoulder seam. With right side facing and No. 10 needles pick up and k.8 sts. down left front slope, k. across sts. on holder at centre front, pick up and k.8 sts. up right front slope and k. across sts.

on holder at back neck: 54 (60, 66) sts. Work 6 (8, 10) rows in k.1, p.1 rib.

Next row: inc. in each st. to last 22 (26, 30) sts., rib to end. Work in p.2, k.2 rib as given for beg. of Back until Collar measures 3½ (3¾, 4) in. Cast off loosely in rib.

TROUSERS
RIGHT LEG
With No. 10 needles cast on 42 sts. for all sizes and work 2½ in. in k.1, p.1 rib.

Next row: rib 2, (inc. in next st., rib 3) 3 times, rib 4 sts., (inc. in next st., rib 3) twice, rib 4, (inc. in next st., rib 3) 3 times: 50 sts.

Change to No. 7 needles and work 2 foundation rows thus:

1st row (right side): p.2, cr.3, *sl. marker (see Abbreviations), p.1, k.1, p.2, k.1, p.4, k.1, p.2, k.1, p.1, sl. marker*, (cr.3) 4 times; rep. from * to *, cr.3, p.2.

2nd row: k.2, p.3, *k.1, p.1, k.2, p.1, k.4, p.1, k.2, p.1, k.1 *, p.12; rep. from * to *, p.3, k.2.

Rep. the last 2 rows until leg measures 4½ (4½, 4¾) in. ending with a wrong-side row. Adjust leg length at this point if required.

Shape Seams and Beg. Patt. (Note. Bring increased sts. into patt. of cr.3, p.2 rib.) With right side of work facing, cont. to work cr.3 patt. as set, now work patt. as given for Back on the 14 sts. between each pair of markers and *at the same time* inc. 1 st. at each end of next row, and every foll. 4th row until there are 62 (66, 68) sts.

Next row: work 28 (30, 31) sts., lift the yarn lying between the st. just worked and next st. and knit into back of it (called inc. k.), (p.3, inc. k.) twice, work to end: 65 (69, 71) sts.

With 1 st. in reversed st.st. between cr.3 ribs at centre, work 2 rows, then cont. to inc. 1 st. each end of next and every 4th row until there are 75 (83, 89) sts.

Next row: work 33 (37, 40) sts., (inc. k., k.1, p.3) 3 times, work to end: 78 (86, 92) sts. Working 2 sts. in reversed st.st. between the cr.3 ribs at centre now inc. 1 st. at each end of next row, then every alt. row 8 times, ending with the wrong-side row: 96 (104, 110) sts.

Mark each end of last row for completion of leg seam.

Shape Crutch. Cast off 3 sts. at beg. of next 4 rows. Dec. 1 st. at each end of next 3 rows, then foll. alt. rows 1 (2, 3) times: 76 (82, 86) sts. rem.

Work straight until piece measures 7 (7½, 8) in. from marked row, measured straight, and ending with a right-side row.

Shape Back of Seat. 1st row: work 44 (47, 49) sts.; turn.

2nd row: sl.1, work to end.

3rd row: work 29 (32, 34) sts.; turn.

4th row: sl.1, work to end.

5th row: work 15 (18, 20) sts.; turn.

6th row: sl.1, work to end.

Change to No. 10 needles and work 1 inc. in k.1, p.1 rib across all sts.

Cast off in rib.

LEFT LEG
Work as given for Right Leg, reversing the shaping by ending with a wrong-side row before starting to shape back of seat.

HAT
MAIN PIECE
With No. 10 needles cast on 90 (94, 98) sts. and work 11 rows of rib as given for Back of sweater.

Next row: k.2, *inc. in next st., p.1, k.2; rep. from * to end: 112 (117, 122) sts.

Change to No. 7 needles and beg. patt.:

1st row: p.2, *cr.3, p.2; rep. from * to end.

2nd row: k.2, *p.3, k.2; rep. from * to end. Rep. the last 2 rows until hat measures 6 (6¼, 6½) in. ending with a right-side row.

Shape Top. Next row: k.2 tog. *p.3, k.2 tog.; rep. from * to end.

Next row: p.1, *cr.3, p.1; rep. from * to end. Keeping patt. correct work 2 rows straight.

Next row: *p.2 tog., p.2; rep. from * to last 5 sts., p.2 tog., p.1, p.2 tog.

Next row: *cr.3; rep. from * to end.

Next row: p.

Rep. the last 2 rows once.

Next row: k.3 tog. across the row.

Thread yarn through rem. sts. then draw up firmly and fasten off.

TO COMPLETE
SWEATER
Join left shoulder, collar, side and sleeve seams. Press seams.

TROUSERS
Join front and back seams above markers, and leg seams below markers. Join waist-length of elastic into a ring and sew inside waistband using a herringbone st. to form a casing.

HAT
Sew back seam.

Pompon. Cut 2 circles of card, each 2 in. in diameter. Cut a circle ½ in. in diameter out of the centre of each card. Put the 2 circles tog. and wind yarn over card and out through centre hole, working round card until centre hole is full. Cut through strands round outside edge. Wind a strand of yarn very tightly between cards and tie in a secure knot. Pull off cards and fluff out pompon.
Sew pompon to top of hat.

Boy's play suit

(photographed in colour on page 57)

MATERIALS

6 oz. Paton's Courtelle 101 Crêpe Double Knitting in blue, 1 oz. in white (see note on wools and yarns, page 20); one pair each Nos. 8 and 10 knitting needles (see page 26); 7 medium buttons; a waist length of elastic, $\frac{1}{4}$ in. wide.

MEASUREMENTS

To fit chest size 26 in.

TENSION

$5\frac{1}{2}$ sts. to 1 in. on No. 8 needles (see note on tension, page 15).

ABBREVIATIONS

See page 26; B., blue; W., white.

JERSEY
FRONT

With No. 8 needles and B., cast on 74 sts. and work in moss st. (see page 23) for 9 rows, then in st.st. (see page 23) for 48 rows.

Shape Armholes. Cast off 4 sts. at beg. of next 2 rows, and take 2 tog. at each end of every k. row 4 times in all. Join in W., and cont. to dec. at each end of every k. row, work as follows:

Next row: k.2 tog. W., k.1 W., * sl. next B. st., k.2 W.; rep. from * to last 3 sts., k.1 W., k.2 tog. W.

Next row: *p.2 W., sl. next B. st.; rep. from * to last 2 sts., p.2 W.

Next row: k. in B. (taking 2 tog. at each end of the row).

Next row: p. in B.

These 4 rows form patt. Rep. them keeping B. sts. above each other until 8 W. stripes in all have been worked: 28 sts.

Next row: k.2 tog. W., patt. 6, cast off 12 sts., patt. to last 2 sts., k.2 tog. W.

Cont. on these 7 sts. taking 2 tog. at armhole edge on alt. rows as before, and taking 2 tog. at neck edge on 2nd row, until all sts. are worked off. Rejoin yarn to rem. sts. and complete second side to match, reversing shapings.

RIGHT BACK

With No. 8 needles and B., cast on 38 sts. and work as for Front to armhole shaping, ending with a wrong-side row.

Shape Armhole. Cast off 4 sts. at beg. of next row, and take 2 tog. at armhole edge of every k. row 4 times in all.

Join in W.

Next row: k.2 tog. W., k.1 W., *sl.1 B., k.2 tog. W.;

rep. from * to end of row.

Cont. in patt. as for Front, taking 2 tog. at armhole edge as before, until 10 W. stripes have been worked. Now work 2 rows in B.

Cast off.

LEFT BACK

Work as for Right Back, reversing armhole shaping.

SLEEVES (make 2 alike)

With No. 8 needles and B., cast on 42 sts.

Work in k.1, p.1 rib for 5 rows.

Change to st.st. and inc. at each end of every row for the next 14 rows: 70 sts.

Cast off 4 sts. at beg. of next 2 rows and take 2 tog. at each end of every k. row until 4 such decs. have been worked.

Join in W. and, working in patt. as for Front and taking 2 tog. at each end of every k. row, cont. until 10 W. stripes have been worked. Work 2 rows B. and cast off.

NECKBAND

Join shoulder seams. With right side of work facing, No. 10 needles and B., pick up 62 sts. round neck (including centre 12) and work in k.1, p.1 rib for 7 rows.

Cast off in rib.

RIBBED BANDS

Buttonhole Band. With No. 10 needles and B., cast on 7 sts. and work in moss st., making a buttonhole on every 19th row thus: patt. 2, cast off 2, patt. to end. In next row, cast on 2 sts. over cast-off sts. of previous row. Make 7 buttonholes in all, then cont. till band measures the same as Back edge. Cast off.

Plain Band. Work as for Buttonhole Band, omitting buttonholes.

SHORTS
FRONT

With No. 8 needles and B., cast on 18 sts. Work 2 rows in st.st.

Cont. in st.st., casting on 3 sts. at beg. of every row until 69 sts.

Work 7 rows straight, then join in W., and work in patt. as for Front until 4 W. stripes have been worked.

Cont. in st.st. with B., for 13 more rows, then change to No. 10 needles and work 5 rows in k.1, p.1 rib.

Next row: rib 3, *m.1, k.2 tog., patt. 1; rep. from * to end.

Work 3 more rows in rib and cast off in rib.

BACK

Work as for Front until last striped patt. row, then work 9 rows in st.st. with B.
Next row: work to last 12 sts., turn and work to last 12 sts., turn and work to last 18 sts., turn and work to last 18 sts., turn and work to end of row. Work 2 more rows st.st., then cont. in rib as for Front to end.

LEG EDGINGS (both alike)

Join side seams. With right side of work facing, No. 10 needles and B., pick up 70 sts. round one leg and work in k.1, p.1 rib for 6 rows. Cast off in rib.

TO COMPLETE
JERSEY

Sew in sleeves and join side and sleeve seams. Sew buttonhole band to right back, plain band to left back. Sew buttons to plain band opposite button-holes.

SHORTS

Sew crutch seam. Thread elastic through holes at waist and stitch ends tog.

Pink and white trouser outfit

(the full outfit is photographed in colour on page 36, the coat and cap inside front flap of cover)

MATERIALS

For coat and cap: 10 balls Wendy Courtelle Crêpe 4-ply in white. **For sweater and trousers:** 16 balls Wendy Courtelle Double Crêpe in pink (see note on wools and yarns, page 20). **For whole outfit:** one pair each Nos. 6, 9 and 11 knitting needles (see page 26); a fine crochet hook; a 1-in. button mould; a waist length of elastic, $\frac{7}{8}$ in. wide.

MEASUREMENTS

To fit chest size 24–26 in.

TENSION

4 sts. to 1 in. on looped patt. on No. 6 needles; 6 sts. and $7\frac{1}{2}$ rows over st.st. on No. 9 needles (see note on tension, page 15).

ABBREVIATIONS

See page 26; W., white; P., pink.

COAT
BACK

With No. 6 needles and W., cast on 65 sts. and work in patt. as follows:
1st-3rd rows: st.st. (see page 23), beg. with k. row.
4th row: * needle in first st. knitwise, in opposite direction from knitting wind yarn twice round right needle and two first fingers of left hand, wind yarn over right-hand needle in normal direction and draw 3 loops through st. and place on left-hand needle; k. all 4 sts. tog. Rep. from * to last 2 sts., k.2.
Cont. in patt. for another 17 rows.
K.2 tog. at each end of next and every foll. 2nd row of patt. until there are 57 sts. Cont. in patt. until work is $12\frac{1}{4}$ in., ending on 4th patt. row.
Shape Armholes. Cast off 3 sts. at beg. of next 2 rows and then take 2 tog. at each end of next and foll. 2 alt. rows: 45 sts.

Cont. until work is $16\frac{1}{4}$ in., ending on 4th patt. row.
Shape Shoulders. Cast off 5 sts. at beg. of next 2 rows and 4 sts. at beg. of next 2 rows. Cast off rem. 27 sts.

RIGHT FRONT

With No. 6 needles and W., cast on 35 sts. Work 21 rows in patt. K. 2 tog. at end of next and every foll. 2nd row of patt. 4 times in all: 31 sts.
Cont. in patt. until work measures the same as Back to armhole shaping, ending with a right-side row.
Cast off 3 sts. at beg. of next row. Work 1 row. Take 2 tog. at armhole edge on next and foll. 2 alt. rows; **at the same time** take 2 tog. at front edge on every row until there are 9 sts. Cont in patt. until armhole measures the same as Back to shoulder shaping, ending with a right-side row.
Next row: cast off 5 sts., work in patt. to end. Work 1 row. Cast off.

LEFT FRONT

Work as for Right Front, reversing all shapings, i.e. dec. at beg. of rows for first 4 decs., and read "wrong side" for "right side".

CAP
MAIN PART

With No. 6 needles and W., cast on 65 sts. and work 20 rows in patt. as for Coat. Now take 2 tog. at each end of next and every alt. row until there are 61 sts.
Next row: k.1, *k.2 tog., k.10; rep. from * to end. Work 3 more rows in patt.
Next row: k.1, *k.2 tog., k.9; rep. from * to end. Work 1 row in patt.
Next row: k.1, *k.2 tog., k.8; rep. from * to end. Now cont. to dec. thus, working one st. fewer each time and working 1 row between each dec. row, keeping the patt. correct, until you have worked the

row: k.1, *k.2 tog., k.3; rep. from * to end.
Work 1 row.
Next row: k.1, *k.2 tog.; rep. from * to end of row.
Break yarn, draw through rem. sts. and fasten off.

BAND
With No. 11 needles and W., knit up 66 sts. along cast-on edge of cap and work 3 rows in k.1, p.1 rib. Cast off very loosely.

SWEATER
BACK
With No. 11 needles and P., cast on 72 sts. Work 5 rows in st.st., beg. with a k. row.
Next row: k. (for hem ridge). Change to No. 9 needles and beg. with a k. row, work in st.st. for 8 in. from hem ridge, ending with a p. row.
Cast off 2 sts. at beg. of next 2 rows.
Next row: k.2, k.2 tog., k. to last 4 sts., k.2 tog., k.2. Work 3 rows straight. Rep. these 4 rows once.
Next row: rep. the first of the previous 4 rows.
Next row: p. Rep. these last 2 rows until there are 26 sts. and leave on a stitch holder.

FRONT
With No. 11 needles and P., cast on 72 sts. Work as for Back until there are 44 sts., ending with a p. row.
Next row: k.2, k.2 tog., k.12; turn. Work on these sts. taking 2 tog. on alt. rows at armhole as before; *at the same time* take 2 tog. at neck edge on every row until there are 8 sts. Now dec. only at armhole edge until there are 3 sts. Work these 3 tog. and fasten off. Slip centre 12 sts. on to a safety pin or stitch holder and work other side to match, reversing shapings.

SLEEVES (make 2 alike)
With No. 11 needles and P., cast on 37 sts. and work hem as for Back.
Change to No. 9 needles and beg. with a k. row, work in st.st., inc. at each end of next and every foll. 12th row until there are 51 sts., then cont. until work is 10 in. from hem ridge. Dec. as for back armhole shaping until there are 7 sts., ending with a p. row.
Next row: k.2, k.3 tog., k.2. Work 1 more row and leave rem. 5 sts. on a safety pin or stitch holder.

POLO COLLAR
Sew Front to sleeves and right sleeve to Back. With right side of work facing and No. 11 needles, k. across 5 sts. of left sleeve, pick up and k. 14 sts. down side of front neck, k. across centre 12 sts., pick up and k. 14 sts. up other side of neck, k. across 5 sts. of right sleeve and 26 sts. of Back: 76 sts.

Work in k.1, p.1 rib for 1¾ in., then with right side facing, work 1 row p. Beg. with a k. row, work 2¼ in. in st.st., ending on a k. row. Work 1 row k. for hem ridge, then, beg. with a k. row, work 4 rows st.st. Cast off.

TROUSERS
LEFT LEG
With No. 11 needles and P., cast on 91 sts. and work hem as for Back.
Change to No. 9 needles and, beg. with a k. row, work in st.st., taking 2 tog. at each end of 11th and every foll. 10th row until there are 79 sts. Cont. till work is 12¼ in. from hem ridge, then cast off 2 sts. at beg. of next 2 rows. Take 2 tog. at each end of 9th and every foll. 6th row until there are 65 sts. Cont. until work is 21¼ in. from hem ridge, ending with a p. row.**
Next row: k.34; turn and work back.
Next row: k.27; turn and work back. Cont. thus working 7 sts. fewer each time until you have completed the row: k.13; turn and work back.
Next row: k.
Change to No. 11 needles and work in к.1, p.1 rib for 1 in. Cast off.

RIGHT LEG
Work as for Left Leg but end with a k. row at ** and beg. first shaping row: p.34; turn and work back. Cont. in this way.

TO COMPLETE
COAT
Join shoulder and side seams. With crochet hook and W., work 2 rows d.c. round front edges and neck (see page 26).

CAP
Sew back seam. With crochet hook and P., make 4 ch., sl.st. into a ring, then work in rounds of d.c. till work is deep enough to cover button mould. Fasten off. Use to cover button mould and stitch button to top of cap.

SWEATER
Join shoulder and neck seams, and sleeve and side seams. Turn in hems at neck, sleeve and lower edges, and slipstitch neatly in place.

TROUSERS
Join centre front, centre back and inside leg seams. Turn up hems on trouser bottoms and slipstitch in place. Stitch elastic into a circle and attach to inside of waist ribbing with herringboning.

His and hers trouser suits

(photographed in colour on front cover and in black and white on right)

MATERIALS

For jacket and trousers: 15 oz. Sirdar Double Crêpe in red. **For jumper:** 7 oz. Sirdar Fontein Crêpe in white, 1 oz. Sirdar Fontein Crêpe in red (see note on wools and yarns, page 20). **For both:** one pair each Nos. 9, 10 and 11 knitting needles (see page 26); four ½-in. buttons; a 5-in. zip fastener; 3 press studs; shirring elastic (optional).

MEASUREMENTS

To fit chest size 24 in.

TENSION

6 sts. and 8 rows to 1 in. in Double Crêpe on No. 9 needles; 7 sts. and 9 rows to 1 in. in Fontein Crêpe on No. 10 needles (see note on tension, page 15).

ABBREVIATIONS

See page 26; R., red; W., white.

TROUSERS

RIGHT BACK LEG AND LEFT FRONT LEG (both worked alike)

With No. 10 needles and Double Crêpe yarn, cast on 44 sts.

Beg. with a k. row, work 4 rows st.st. (see page 23). Now work 1 row in p. to make a ridge for hemline. Change to No. 9 needles and beg. with a p. row, work a further 9 rows in st.st., then dec. 1 st. at end of the next and every foll. 8th row until there are 34 sts.

Cont. until work measures 8½ in., ending with a p. row. Now inc. 1 st. at each end of next and every foll. 9th row until there are 46 sts.**

Cont. on these sts. for 9 rows.

*** Cast off 4 sts. at beg. of next row, then dec. 1 st. at same edge on each of next 4 rows, then on 2 foll. alt. rows: 36 sts.

Work 6 rows straight, then dec. 1 st. at the edge opposite to the edge where decs. have been worked so far on the next and every foll. 6th rows until there are 30 sts.***

Change to No. 10 needles and work 1 row k. to make ridge for hemline.

Work another 6 rows in st.st. Cast off.

LEFT BACK LEG AND RIGHT FRONT LEG (both worked alike)

Work as for Right Back Leg and Left Front Leg until ** is reached. On these 46 sts. work 10 rows, then work from *** to ***.

Change to No. 10 needles and work 1 row p. to make ridge for hemline.

Trousers and jacket are red, jumper is white, with the polo collar edged in red

Work another 5 rows in st.st. Cast off.

JACKET

BACK

With No. 10 needles and Double Crêpe yarn, cast on 76 sts. Work in st.st. for 6 rows, then work 1 row p. to make ridge for hemline.

Change to No. 9 needles, and cont. in st.st. until work measures 12 in. from hemline, ending with a p. row.

Shape Armholes. Cast off 4 sts. at beg. of next 2 rows.

Next row: cast on 4 sts., k. these 4 sts., sl.1, k.2 tog. t.b.l., k. to last 3 sts., k.2 tog., k.1.

Next row: cast on 4 sts., p. to end.

Next row: k.4, sl.1, k.2 tog. t.b.l., k. to last 7 sts., k.2 tog., sl.1, k.4.

Next row: p.

Rep. last 2 rows twice: 68 sts. Cont. straight until armhole measures 6 in., ending with a p. row.

Shape Shoulders. Cast off 12 sts. at beg. of next 2 rows, then 6 sts. at beg. of next 4 rows, p. next row to make ridge for hemline, then work 5 rows in st.st. Cast off.

LEFT FRONT

With No. 10 needles and Double Crêpe yarn cast on 40 sts. K. 1 row. Inc. 1 st. at beg. of next row and at the same edge of next 4 rows. Work 1 row p. to make ridge for hemline.

Change to No. 9 needles.

1st row: inc. in first st., p. to end.

2nd row: k. to last 2 sts., sl.1, inc. in next st.

3rd row: as first row.

4th row: k. to last 4 sts., sl.1, k.2, inc. in next st.

5th row: as first row: 50 sts.

Now cont. in st.st. till work measures 11½ in. from hem ridge, ending with a k. row.

Next row: p.6, p.2 tog., p. to end.

Work 2 rows st.st.

Next row: k. to last 8 sts., k.2 tog., sl.1, k. to end.

Work 1 row.

Shape Armhole. Cast off 4 sts., k. to end.

Next row: p.6, p.2 tog., p. to end.

Next row: cast on 4 sts., k. these 4 sts., sl.1, k.2 tog. t.b.l., k. to last 6 sts., sl.1, k. to end.

Next row: p.

Next row: k.4, sl.1, k.2 tog. t.b.l., k. to last 8 sts., k.2 tog., sl.1, k.5.

Next row: p.

Next row: k.4, sl.1, k.2 tog. t.b.l., k. to last 6 sts., sl.1, k. to end.

Cont. in st.st., working sl. sts. on k. rows to mark armhole and front facings and dec. every 3rd row from last dec. on front slope, until 29 sts. rem. Cont. till armhole measures 6 in., ending with a p. row.

Shape Shoulder. Cast off 12 sts. at beg. of next row, work 1 row. Cast off 6 sts. at beg. of next row.

Work 1 row.

Cast off.

RIGHT FRONT

Work as for Left Front, reversing all shapings.

JUMPER

BACK

With No. 11 needles and W., cast on 96 sts. Work in k.1, p.1 rib for 20 rows, inc. at each end of the last row: 98 sts.

Change to No. 10 needles and cont. in st.st. until work measures 9 in. from beg., ending with a p. row.

Shape Armholes. Cast off 6 sts. at beg. of the next 2 rows, then take 2 tog. at each end of next 4 rows and foll. 3 alt. rows: 72 sts.

Cont. until armhole is 5½ in., ending with a p. row.

Shape Shoulders. Cast off 7 sts. at beg. of next 6 rows.

Leave rem. 30 sts. on stitch holder.

FRONT

Work as for Back until armhole is 3½ in., ending with a p. row.

Next row: k.31 and leave these sts. on stitch holder, k.10 and sl. these on a safety pin, k. to end, and cont. on these 31 sts.

Dec. 1 st. at neck edge on next 8 rows and the foll. 2 alt. rows and then work straight until armhole is 5½ in., ending at side edge.

Shape Shoulder. Cast off 7 sts. at beg. of next row and 2 foll. alt. rows.

Rejoin yarn to other group of 31 sts., and complete second side to match first, reversing shapings.

SLEEVES (make 2 alike)

With No. 11 needles and W., cast on 44 sts.

Work 19 rows in k.1, p.1 rib.

Next row: rib 4, * inc. in next st., rib 2, rep. from * to last 4 sts., inc. in next st., rib 3: 57 sts.

Change to No. 10 needles and work in st.st., inc. at each end of every 5th row until there are 81 sts., and then work straight until sleeve is 11 in. from beg., ending with a p. row.

Shape Top. Cast off 6 sts. at beg. of next 2 rows, then take 2 tog. at each end of next and foll. alt. rows until 49 sts. rem.

Now take 2 tog. at each end of every row until 25 sts. rem.

Cast off.

POLO COLLAR

Join left shoulder seam. With right side facing, No. 10 needles and W., k. across 30 sts. of Back, pick up and k. 28 sts. down Left Front, k. across centre 10 sts. on safety pin, pick up and k. 28 sts. up side of Right Front: 96 sts. Work in k.1, p.1 rib on these sts. for 2½ in., ending with a right-side row.

Break off W.

Join in R. Fontein Crêpe and k. 1 row.

Work 1 row in rib and cast off in rib.

TO COMPLETE

TROUSERS

Sew back and leg seams, leave 5 in. opening on front seam for zip. Sew in zip. Turn all hems to wrong side and slipstitch in place. If wished, thread shirring elastic through back of waistband. Make rouleau loop at waist edge of front opening, on right-hand edge for girl's suit, left-hand edge for boy's suit. Sew button opposite.

JACKET

Join shoulder and side seams, turn hems and facings to wrong side and slipstitch in place. Sew on three buttons to right front for girl's suit, left front for boy's suit, positioning first one 3½ in. up from lower edge, the other two at 2½-in. intervals above. Sew press studs under buttons to fasten.

JUMPER

Sew shoulder and collar seam, sew in sleeves and sew side and sleeve seams.

Navy and lime dress

(photographed in colour on page 38)

MATERIALS

4 (4, 5) oz. Lister Lavenda Crisp Crêpe 4-ply in navy, 1 (2, 2) oz. in lime green (see note on wools and yarns, page 20); one pair each of Nos. 10 and 12 knitting needles (see page 26).

MEASUREMENTS

To fit chest size 20 (22, 24) in.; length at centre back 13 (15, 18) in.

TENSION

7½ sts. and 10 rows to 1 in. on No. 10 needles (see note on tension, page 15).

ABBREVIATIONS

See page 26; N., navy; G., green.

FRONT

With No. 12 needles and N. cast on 96 (106, 118) sts.

Work 7 rows in st.st. (see page 23). Work 1 row k. (to make hem ridge).

Change to No. 10 needles and, beg. with a k. row, work 32 (40, 48) rows st.st., taking 2 tog. at each end of 9th and every foll. 12th row.

Cont. to dec. every 12th row until there are 82 (90, 98) sts.

Join in G. and work in patt. as follows:

4 rows st.st. G., 6 rows st.st. N., 20 (24, 28) rows st.st. G., 4 rows st.st. N., 10 rows st.st. G.

Cont. in N. until work measures 9½ (11, 13½) in. from hem ridge, ending with a p. row.

Shape Armholes. Working in N., cast off 4 sts. at beg. of next 2 rows, then take 2 tog. at each end of next 5 (6, 7) rows.

Work 4 rows in G., dec. 1 st. at each end of both alt. rows.

Work 3 (4, 3) rows in N. on these 60 (66, 72) sts.

Cont. in G. until work is 2¼ (2¾, 3¼) in. from beg. of armholes, ending with a p. row.

Work 2 rows st.st. in N.

Shape Neck. Next row: k. 20 (22, 24); turn. Work a further 5 rows on these sts., taking 2 tog. at neck edge on next and alt. rows: 17 (19, 21) sts.

Shape Shoulder. Next row: cast off 5 (5, 6), patt. to end.

Next row: take 2 tog., patt. to end.

Rep. these 2 rows once more than cast off rem. 5 (5, 7) sts.

Slip centre 20 (22, 24) sts. on to a stitch holder and work other side to match reversing shapings.

BACK

Work as for Front, omitting neck shaping and working straight after armhole shaping till Back matches Front to beg. of shoulder shaping.

Shape Shoulders. Cast off 5 (5, 6) sts. at beg. of next 4 rows and 5 (7, 7) sts. at beg. of next 2 rows. Leave rem. 30 (32, 34) sts. on a stitch holder.

NECKBAND

Sew right shoulder seam. With right side facing, No. 12 needles and N., pick up and k. 12 sts. down left side of neck, k. across centre front 20 (22, 24) sts., pick up and k. 12 sts. up other side of neck and k. across 30 (32, 34) sts. of back: 74 (78, 82) sts.

Work 1 row p., then work 5 rows in k.1, p.1 rib.

Next row: k. (to make a ridge for hem). Work another 4 rows in k.1, p.1 rib and cast off loosely, using a No. 10 needle.

ARMHOLE EDGINGS (make 2 alike)

Sew left shoulder seam, joining sides of neck ribbing. With right side facing, No. 12 needles and N., pick up and k. 64 (72, 80) sts. round armhole. Work 1 row p., then work 2 rows in k.1, p.1 rib. Cast off loosely in rib.

TO COMPLETE

Sew side seams, joining armhole edging seams. Turn up hem at lower edge and slipstitch in place; turn in neck ribbing and slipstitch in place.

Dress with short or long sleeves

(photographed in black and white opposite)

MATERIALS

Dress with short sleeves: 6 (7, 8, 9) balls of Emu Scotch 4-ply *or* Emu Super Crêpe *or* Emu Bri-Nylon 4-ply (see note on wools and yarns, page 20).

Dress with long sleeves: 8 (8, 9, 10) balls of any of the above yarns. **For either dress:** one pair each Nos. 9 and 11 knitting needles (see page 26); 3 small buttons.

Pretty for partytime — lacy-patterned dress has a choice of sleeve styles

MEASUREMENTS

To fit chest size 20 (21, 22, 23) in.; length at centre back 15¾ (16, 17¼, 17½) in.; sleeve seam 2 in. (short sleeve), 6 (6, 7, 7) in. (long sleeve).

TENSION

7½ sts. and 10½ rows to 1 in. over patt. (see note on tension, page 15).

ABBREVIATIONS

See page 26.

BACK

**With No. 9 needles, cast on 135 (139, 147, 151) sts. and work 5 rows in garter st. (every row k.). Now beg. patt. as follows:

1st row (right side): p.2, k. to last 2 sts., p.2.
2nd row: k.2, p. to last 2 sts., k.2.
3rd row: p.1, *p.1, k.3; rep. from * to last 2 sts., p.2.
4th row: k.1, *k.1, p.3; rep. from * to last 2 sts., k.2.
5th row: p.1, *p.1, y.o.n., sl.1, k.2 tog., p.s.s.o., y.r.n.; rep. from * to last 2 sts., p. 2.
6th row: k.1, *k.1, p.3; rep. from * to last 2 sts., k.2.
Rep. the last 4 rows once more. These 10 rows form the patt.
Next row: p.2, k.14 (16, 18, 20), sl.1, k.1, p.s.s.o., k.29 (29, 30, 30), sl.1, k.1, p.s.s.o., k.37 (37, 39, 39), k.2 tog., k.29 (29, 30, 30), k.2 tog., k.14 (16, 18, 20), p.2: 131 (135, 143, 147) sts.
Next row: k.2, p. to last 2 sts., k.2.
Work rows 3 to 10 of patt.
Next row: p.2, k.14 (16, 18, 20), sl.1, k.2 tog., p.s.s.o., k.27 (27, 28, 28), sl.1, k.2 tog., p.s.s.o., k.33 (33, 35, 35), k.3 tog., k.27 (27, 28, 28), k.3 tog., k.14 (16, 18, 20), p.2: 123 (127, 135, 139) sts.
Next row: k.2, p. to last 2 sts., k.2.
Work rows 3 to 10 of patt.
Next row: p.2, k.14 (16, 18, 20), sl.1, k.1, p.s.s.o., k.26 (26, 27, 27), sl.1, k.1, p.s.s.o., k.31 (31, 33, 33), k.2 tog., k.26 (26, 27, 27), k.2 tog., k.14 (16, 18, 20), p.2: 119 (123, 131, 135) sts.
Next row: k.2, p. to last 2 sts., k.2.
Work rows 3 to 10 of patt.
Next row: p.2, k.14 (16, 18, 20), sl.1, k.2 tog., p.s.s.o., k.24 (24, 25, 25), sl.1, k.2 tog., p.s.s.o., k.27 (27, 29, 29), k.3 tog., k.24 (24, 25, 25), k.3 tog., k.14 (16, 18, 20), p.2: 111 (115, 123, 127) sts.
Next row: k.2, p. to last 2 sts., k.2.
Work rows 3 to 10 of patt.
Next row: p.2, k.14 (16, 18, 20), sl.1, k.1, p.s.s.o., k.23 (23, 24, 24), sl.1, k.1, p.s.s.o., k.25 (25, 27, 27), k.2 tog., k.23 (23, 24, 24), k.2 tog., k.14 (16, 18, 20), p.2: 107 (111, 119, 123) sts.
Next row: k.2, p. to last 2 sts., k.2.
Work rows 3 to 10 of patt.
Next row: p.2, k.14 (16, 18, 20), sl.1, k.1, p.s.s.o., k.22 (22, 23, 23), sl.1, k.1, p.s.s.o., k.23 (23, 25, 25), k.2 tog., k.22 (22, 23, 23), k.2 tog., k.14 (16, 18, 20),

p.2: 103 (107, 115, 119) sts.
Next row: k.2, p. to last 2 sts., k.2.
Work rows 3 to 10 of patt.
Next row: p.2, k.14 (16, 18, 20), sl.1, k.1, p.s.s.o., k.21 (21, 22, 22), sl.1, k.1, p.s.s.o., k.21 (21, 23, 23), k.2 tog., k.21 (21, 22, 22), k.2 tog., k.14 (16, 18, 20), p.2: 99 (103, 111, 115) sts.
Next row: k.2, p. to last 2 sts., k.2.
Work rows 3 to 10 of patt.
Next row: p.2, k.14 (16, 18, 20), sl.1, k.1, p.s.s.o., k.20 (20, 21, 21), sl.1, k.1, p.s.s.o., k.19 (19, 21, 21), k.2 tog., k.20 (20, 21, 21), k.2 tog., k.14 (16, 18, 20), p.2: 95 (99, 107, 111) sts.
Next row: k.2, p. to last 2 sts., k.2.
Work rows 3 to 10 of patt.
Next row: p.2, k.14 (16, 18, 20), sl.1, k.1, p.s.s.o., k.19 (19, 20, 20), sl.1, k.1, p.s.s.o., k.17 (17, 19, 19), k.2 tog., k.19 (19, 20, 20), k.2 tog., k.14 (16, 18, 20), p.2: 91 (95, 103, 107) sts.
Next row: k.2, p. to last 2 sts., k.2.
Work rows 3 to 10 of patt.
Next row: p.2, k.14 (16, 18, 20), sl.1, k.1, p.s.s.o., k.18 (18, 19, 19), sl.1, k.1, p.s.s.o., k.15 (15, 17, 17), k.2 tog., k.18 (18, 19, 19), k.2 tog., k.14 (16, 18, 20), p.2: 87 (91, 99, 103) sts.
Next row: k.2, p. to last 2 sts., k.2.
Work rows 3 to 10 of patt.
3rd and 4th sizes only. Next row: p.2, k.18 (20), sl.1, k.1, p.s.s.o., k.18, sl.1, k.1, p.s.s.o., k.15, k.2 tog., k.18, k.2 tog., k.18 (20), p.2: 95 (99) sts.
Next row: k.2, p. to last 2 sts., k.2.
Work rows 3 to 10 of patt.
All sizes. Mark each end of last row with a coloured thread.
Shape Raglan Armholes. Next row: work 2 tog., k.14 (16, 18, 20), sl.1, k.1, p.s.s.o., k.17, sl.1, k.1, p.s.s.o., k.13, k.2 tog., k.17, k.2 tog., k.14 (16, 18, 20), work 2 tog.
Keeping patt. correct, work 3 rows straight.
Dec. 1 st. at each end of the next row. Rep. the last 4 rows once more. Work 1 row.
1st and 2nd sizes only. Next row: work 2 tog., k. 11 (13), sl.1, k.1, p.s.s.o., k.16, sl.1, k.1, p.s.s.o., k.11, k.2 tog., k.16, k.2 tog., k.11 (13), work 2 tog.
3rd and 4th sizes only. Next row: k.17 (19), sl. 1, k.1, p.s.s.o., k.16, sl.1, k.1, p.s.s.o., k.11, k.2 tog., k.16, k.2 tog., k.17 (19).
All sizes. Work 1 row. Dec. 1 st. at each end of the next and every foll. alt. row until 63 (67, 73, 77) sts. rem. ending with a wrong-side row.
Next row: work 2 tog., k.6 (8, 11, 13), sl.1, k.1, p.s.s.o., k.15, sl.1, k.1, p.s.s.o., k.9, k.2 tog., k.15, k.2 tog., k.6 (8, 11, 13), work 2 tog.
Work 1 row. Dec. 1 st. at each end of the next and every foll. alt. row ** until 53 (55, 61, 63) sts. rem. ending with a wrong-side row.
Divide for Back Neck Opening. Next row: work 2 tog., patt. 22 (23, 26, 27), k.5; turn, leaving

rem. sts. on a stitch holder.
Next row: k.5, patt. to end.
Next row: work 2 tog., patt. to last 5 sts., k.5.
Next row: k.5, patt. to end.
Next row (buttonhole row): work 2 tog., patt. to last 5 sts., k.2, y.f., k.2 tog., k.1.
Cont. in patt., dec. as before at armhole edge and keeping continuity of garter st. band until 22 (23, 25, 26) sts. rem., ending with a wrong-side row.
Next row (buttonhole row): work 2 tog., patt. to last 5 sts., k.2, y.f., k.2 tog., k.1.
Cont. in patt., dec. as before at armhole edge and keeping continuity of garter st. band until 17 (18, 19, 20) sts. rem., ending with a wrong-side row. Leave these sts. on a stitch holder.
Rejoin yarn to inner edge of rem. sts., cast on 5 sts., k. across these 5 sts., patt. to last 2 sts., work 2 tog. Complete to match other side omitting buttonholes.

FRONT
Work as for Back from ** to ** until 49 (51, 53, 55) sts. rem. ending with a wrong-side row.
Shape Neck. Next row: work 2 tog., patt. 15; turn, leaving rem. sts. on a stitch holder.
Keeping patt. correct, work 1 row. Dec. 1 st. at each end of the next and every foll. alt. row until 4 sts. rem. Keeping neck edge straight, cont. to dec. at armhole edge as before until 1 st. rem. Fasten off. Slip the centre 15 (17, 19, 21) sts. on to a stitch holder. Rejoin yarn to inner edge of rem. sts., patt. to last 2 sts., work 2 tog. Complete to match other side.

LONG SLEEVES (make 2 alike)
With No. 11 needles, cast on 38 (38, 42, 42) sts. and work 12 rows in k.1, p.1 rib, inc. 1 st. at end of last row: 39 (39, 43, 43) sts.
Change to No. 9 needles and work in patt. as given for Back, inc. and work into patt. 1 st. at each end of the 7th (3rd, 9th, 3rd) row and every foll. 4th row until there are 57 (61, 65, 69) sts. on the needle.
Work 11 (7, 11, 9) rows straight, thus ending with a 10th row of patt. Mark each end of the last row with a coloured thread.

Shape Raglan Top. *** Keeping patt. correct, dec. 1 st. at each end of next and foll. alt. row.
Work 1 row.
Next row: work 3 tog., patt. to last 3 sts., work 3 tog.
Work 1 row.
Dec. 1 st. at each end of the next and every foll. alt. row until 5 (7, 7, 9) sts. rem. ending with a wrong-side row. Leave these sts. on a stitch holder ***.

SHORT SLEEVES (make 2 alike)
With No. 11 needles, cast on 56 (60, 64, 68) sts. and work 8 rows in k.1, p.1 rib, inc. 1 st. at end of last row: 57 (61, 65, 69) sts.
Change to No. 9 needles and beg. patt.:
1st row (right side): p.1, k. to last st., p.1.
2nd row: k.1, p. to last st., k.1.
3rd row: *p.1, k.3; rep. from * to last st., p.1.
4th row: *k.1, p.3; rep. from * to last st., k.1.
5th row: *p.1, y.o.n., sl.1, k.2 tog., p.s.s.o., y.r.n.; rep. from * to last st., p.1.
6th row: *k.1, p.3; rep. from * to last st., k.1.
Rep. the last 4 rows once more. Mark each end of last row with a coloured thread.
Shape Raglan Top. Follow instructions for Long Sleeves from *** to ***.

NECKBAND
Join raglan seams. With right side of work facing and No. 11 needles, k. across the 17 (18, 19, 20) sts. on left side of back neck, 5 (7, 7, 9) on top of left sleeve, pick up and k. 18 sts. down left side of front neck, k. across the 15 (17, 19, 21) sts. at centre, pick up and k. 18 sts. up right side of front neck, k. across the 5 (7, 7, 9) sts. on top of right sleeve, and 17 (18, 19, 20) sts. on right side of back neck, working buttonhole as before in band: 95 (103, 107, 115) sts.
Work 5 rows in garter st.
Cast off.

TO COMPLETE
Join side and sleeve seams. Catch down base of button band on wrong side of dress. Sew on buttons opposite buttonholes.

Chapter 4

Early Schooldays

Three-piece beach set

(photographed in colour on page 94 and in black and white on page 95)

MATERIALS
9 (10) oz. Robin Vogue 4-ply in white, 6 (6) oz. Robin Vogue Double Knitting in apricot and 1 oz. Robin Vogue Double Knitting in green (see note on wools and yarns, page 20); one pair each Nos. 8, 10 and 12 knitting needles (see page 26); one crochet hook International Standard Size 3·50; 4 buttons $\frac{1}{2}$ in. in diameter; a waist length of shirring elastic.

MEASUREMENTS
To fit chest size 22 (24) in.; length of jersey $13\frac{1}{4}$ (14) in.; jersey sleeve seam $9\frac{1}{2}$ ($10\frac{1}{2}$) in.; length of slip-over $18\frac{1}{4}$ (20) in.

TENSION
4-ply yarn: 7 sts. and 9 rows to 1 in. with No. 10 needles; **double knitting yarn:** $5\frac{1}{2}$ sts. and $7\frac{1}{2}$ rows to 1 in. with No. 8 needles (see note on tension, page 15).

ABBREVIATIONS
See page 26; W., white; A., apricot; G., green.

BIKINI
FRONT AND BACK TOP (make 2 pieces alike)
With No. 10 needles and W., cast on 78 (84) sts. and work 2 rows in k.1, p.1 rib.
Change to st.st. (see page 23) and work until Top measures $2\frac{1}{2}$ (3) in., ending with a p. row.
Shape Armholes. Cast off 5 sts. at beg. of next 2 rows then work 2 sts. tog. at each end of every k. row until 64 (68) sts. remain.
Cont. straight until armholes measure $2\frac{1}{2}$ in., ending with a p. row.
Shape Neck. Next row: k. 23 (24); turn. Now work on these sts. only, working 2 sts. tog. at neck edge on every row until 15 (16) sts. remain.
Cont. straight until armhole measures $5\frac{1}{4}$ ($5\frac{1}{2}$) in. Cast off.

Slip centre 18 (20) sts. on to a stitch holder.
Work on remaining 23 (24) sts. to match first side.

FRONT AND BACK PANTS (make 2 pieces alike)
With No. 10 needles and W., cast on 12 (14) sts. and work 10 rows in st.st.
Cont. in st.st. inc. 1 st. at beg. of every row until there are 22 (24) sts., then inc. 1 st. at each end of every row until there are 40 (44) sts.
Cast on 6 sts. at beg. of next 4 rows and then 7 (8) sts. at beg. of next 2 rows: 78 (84) sts.
Cont. straight until work measures 4 ($4\frac{1}{2}$) in. from end of shaping.
Work 6 rows in k.1, p.1, rib. Cast off.

TO COMPLETE
Neck Edging. Join right shoulder seam. With right side of work facing, No. 12 needles and W., pick up and k.18 (20) sts. from left side of front neck, k. across 18 (20) centre front neck sts., pick up and k. 18 (20) sts. from right side of front neck, pick up and k. 18 (20) sts. from right side of back neck, k. across 18 (20) centre back neck sts., pick up and k. 18 (20) sts. from left side of back neck: 108 (120) sts.
Work 4 rows in k.1, p.1 rib. Cast off in rib.
Armhole Edgings (both alike). Join left shoulder seam. With right side of work facing, and with No. 12 needles and W., pick up and k. 84 (88) sts. round armhole.
Work 4 rows in k.1, p.1 rib. Cast off.
Border for Lower Edge of Top. Join side seams. With crochet hook and A., and with work towards

Opposite: Mexican-style poncho, with a two-colour fringe (see page 97)

you, work 1 d.c. (see page 26) into each cast-on st. round lower edge. Fasten off.
Join G.

Shell round: 2 ch., *miss 2 d.c., work 4 tr. into next d.c., miss 2 d.c., 1 d.c. into next d.c.; rep. from * to end, omitting last d.c. of last rep., s.s. into 2nd ch. Fasten off:

Leg Edgings (both alike). Join crutch. With right side of work facing, No. 12 needles and W., pick up and k. 84 (90) sts. round leg opening.
Work 4 rows in k.1, p.1 rib. Cast off.

Leg Borders (both alike). Join side seams, including ribbed edging. With crochet hook and A., and with work towards you, work 1 d.c. into each cast-off st. round leg edging. Fasten off. Join G. and work next round as for Top Border. Fasten off.

To Finish. Run shirring elastic through ribbing at waist of Pants.

Opposite: bikini and slipover from beach set. Above: bikini worn on its own. Right: the jersey worn with the bikini pants

JERSEY
BACK
With No. 12 needles and W., cast on 82 (88) sts. and work 2 in. in k.1, p.1 rib.

Cont. in st.st. and work until Back measures 7½ (8) in., ending with a p. row.

Shape Armhole. Cast off 4 sts. at beg. of next 2 rows, then work 2 sts. tog. at each end of every k. row until 70 (74) sts. remain.**

Cont. straight until armholes measure 5¼ (5½) in., ending with a p. row.

Shape Shoulder. Cast off 10 sts. at beg. of next 2 rows, then 9 (10) sts. at beg. of next 2 rows. Leave remaining 32 (34) sts. on stitch holder.

FRONT
Work as Back to **.

Cont. straight until armholes measure 3¾ in., ending with a p. row.

Shape Neck. Next row: k. 25 (26), k.2 tog.; turn. Work on these sts. only, working 2 sts. tog. at neck edge on every row until 19 (20) sts. remain.

Cont. straight until armhole measures 5¼ (5½) in. ending with a p. row.

Shape Shoulder. Cast off 10 sts. at beg. of next row. Work 1 row. Cast off.

Slip centre 16 (18) sts. on to a stitch holder. Work on remaining 27 (28) sts. to match first side, reversing shapings.

SLEEVES (make 2 alike)
With No. 12 needles and W., cast on 40 (44) sts. and work 2 in. in k.1, p.1 rib.

Change to No. 10 needles and st.st., inc. 1 st. at each end of every 6th row until there are 66 (70) sts.

Cont. straight until Sleeve measures 9½ (10½) in., ending with a p. row.

Shape Top. Cast off 4 sts. at beg. of next 2 rows, then work 2 sts. tog. at beg. of every row until 40 sts. remain. Cast off 4 sts. at beg. of next 6 rows. Cast off.

POLO COLLAR
Join right shoulder seam. With right side of work facing and with No. 10 needles and W., pick up and k. 20 (22) sts. down left side of front neck, k. across centre 16 (18) sts., pick up and k. 20 (22) sts. round right side of front neck and k. across 32 (34) sts. of Back: 88 (96) sts.

Work 1 in. in k.1, p.1 rib.

Change to No. 12 needles and work 1 in. in rib.

Change to No. 10 needles and work another 2 in. in rib.

Cast off loosely in rib.

TO COMPLETE
Join left shoulder seam and collar seam. Sew in sleeves and join side and sleeve seams. Fold polo collar in half on to right side.

SLIPOVER
BACK
With No. 8 needles and A., cast on 84 (90) sts. and work in st.st. When work measures 3½ (4½) in. work 2 sts. tog. at each end of next k. row and then at 1-in. intervals until 68 (72) sts. remain.

Cont. straight until work measures 12 (13½) in., ending with a p. row.

Shape Armholes. Cast off 6 sts. at beg. of next 2 rows, then work 2 sts. tog. at each end of every k. row until 52 (56) sts. remain.

Cont. straight until armholes measure 5¾ (6) in., ending with a p. row.

Shape Shoulders. Cast off 7 sts. at beg. of next 2 rows and 6 (7) sts. at beg. of next 2 rows. Cast off remaining sts.

LEFT FRONT
With No. 8 needles and A., cast on 42 (45) sts. and work in st.st. When work measures 3½ (4½) in. work 2 sts. tog. at beg. of next k. row and then at this side edge at 1-in. intervals until 34 (36) sts. remain. Cont. straight until Front measures 12 (13½) in., ending with a p. row.

Shape Armhole and Front Slope. Next row: cast off 6 sts., k. to last 2 sts., k.2 tog. Work 2 sts. tog. at armhole edge on next 2 k. rows and at the same time work 2 sts. tog. at front edge on every 3rd row from first dec. until 13 (14) sts. remain. Cont. straight until armhole measures 5¾ (6) in., ending with a p. row.

Shape Shoulder. Cast off 7 sts. at beg. of next row. Work 1 row. Cast off.

RIGHT FRONT
Work as Left Front, reversing all shapings.

TO COMPLETE
Armhole Edgings (both alike). Join shoulder seams. With right side of work facing, and with No. 10 needles and A., pick up and k. 86 (90) sts. round armhole.

Work 4 rows in k. 1, p.1 rib. Cast off in rib.

Border. Join side seams. With crochet hook and W. yarn double, and with work towards you, start at bottom of side edge of Right Front and work d.c. round hem edge of Right Front up centre edge, across back neck, down Left Front and round hem to beg. Now mark position of buttons on Left Front, placing first one level with beg. of armhole and last one about 2½ in. from hem and others evenly between. Mark places for buttonholes on Right Front to match. With W., work 1 d.c. into each d.c. of first round, but at every buttonhole point work 2 ch., miss 2 d.c., 1 d.c. into next d.c. Fasten off.

Join G. and work shell round as for Bikini Top Borders.

Fasten off. Sew on buttons.

Orange poncho

(photographed in colour on page 93)

MATERIALS
11 oz. Sirdar Double Knitting in orange, 2 oz. in yellow (see note on wools and yarns, page 20); one pair No. 7 knitting needles (see page 26); one crochet hook approx. International Standard Size 4·00.

MEASUREMENTS
Length to front point 16 in.

TENSION
11 sts. and 15 rows to 2 in. over patt. (see note on tension, page 15).

ABBREVIATIONS
See page 26; k.1b., k.1, insert needle through loop below the next st. then k. loop and st. tog.; Or., orange; Y., yellow.

TO MAKE
With Or., cast on 5 sts. and work 2 rows in garter st. (see page 23).
Next row: k.1, (with left-hand needle lift horizontal thread before next st. and k. it t.b.l.: m.1), k. to last st., m.1, k.1.
Next row: k.
Rep. these 2 rows until there are 19 sts.
Next row (right side) k.1, m.1, k.5, (k.1b.) 3 times, k.1, k.5, m.1, k.1.
Next row: k.7, k.1, (with right-hand needle k. the thread of previous row with the st. above it, k.1) 3 times, k.7.
Next row: k.1, m.1, k.5, (k.1, k.1b.) 4 times, k.1, k.5, m.1, k.1.
Next row: k.7, k.1, (with right-hand needle k. the thread of previous row with the st. above it, k.1) 4 times, k.7.
Keeping border of 7 sts. in garter st. and patt. correct, inc. 1 st. at each end of garter-st. border every alt. row until there are 171 sts. finishing with a right-side row.
Next row: k.7, patt. 58, k.41, patt. 58, k.7.
Next row: k.1, m.1, k.5, patt. 59, k.41, patt. 59, k.5, m.1, k.1.
Next row: k.7, patt. 59, k.41, patt. 59, k.7.
Next row: k.1, m.1, k.5, patt. 60, k.41, patt. 60, k.5, m.1, k.1.
Next row: k.7, patt. 60, k.41, patt. 60, k.7.
Next row: k.1, m.1, k.5, patt. 61, k.41, patt. 61, k.5, m.1, k.1: 177 sts.
Next row: k.7, patt. 61, k.8, cast off 28 sts., k.5, patt. 61, k.7.
Next row: k.1, k.2 tog.t.b.l., k.5, patt. 60, k.8, cast on 28 sts., k.5, patt. 60, k.5, k.2 tog., k.1.
Next row: k.7, patt. 60, k.41, patt. 60, k.7.
Next row: k.1, k.2 tog.t.b.l., k.5, patt. 59, k.41, patt. 59, k.5, k.2 tog., k.1.
Next row: k.7, patt. 59, k.41, patt. 59, k.7.
Next row: k.1, k.2 tog.t.b.l., k.5, patt. 58, k.41, patt. 58, k.5, k.2 tog., k.1.
Next row: k.7, patt. 58, k.41, patt. 58, k.7.
Keeping continuity of patt. as above, dec. 1 st. at each end of each border until 19 sts. remain, ending at front of work. **Next row:** k.
Next row: k.1, k.2 tog.t.b.l., k. to last 3 sts., k.2 tog., k.1.
Rep. these 2 rows until 5 sts. remain. Work 2 rows in garter st. Cast off.

TO COMPLETE
Fringe. Cut Or. and Y. yarn into 7-in. lengths. Take 6 strands of yarn together and double them. Insert crochet hook into edge of poncho and draw through looped end of yarn. Pull ends of yarn through loop and draw up tightly. Work all round edge of poncho, using Or. and Y. yarn alternately.

Jersey and pinafore

(photographed in colour on page 58)

MATERIALS
For jersey: 3 (3) balls Sirdar Fontein Crêpe 4-ply in blue, 3 (3) balls in white and 1 ball in red (see note on wools and yarns, page 20); one pair each Nos. 10, 11 and 12 and set of four No. 12 knitting needles (see page 26); an 8-in. white zip fastener.
For pinafore: 6 (8) balls Sirdar Fontein Crêpe 4-ply in white and 2 balls in red (see note on wools and yarns, page 20); one pair each Nos. 10 and 11 knitting needles (see page 26); one crochet hook International Standard Size 3·50.

MEASUREMENTS
To fit chest size 24 (26) in.; length of jersey 14½ (15½) in.; length of pinafore 18½ (22) in.

TENSION
7½ sts. and 9 rows to 1 in. with No. 10 needles (see note on tension, page 15).

ABBREVIATIONS
See page 26; B., blue; W., white; R., red.

JERSEY
BACK
With No. 12 needles and B., cast on 96 (102) sts. and work 8 rows in k.1, p.1 rib.

Change to W., p. 1 row, rib another 9 rows, then p. another row.

Change to No. 10 needles and, beg. with B. and a k. row, work in st.st. (see page 23) in stripes of 8 rows B., 10 rows W.

Work until Back measures 8½ (9) in., ending with a p. row. Cont. working in stripes.

Divide for Opening. Next row: k.48 (51); turn and work on these sts. only.

Next row: k.2, p. to end.

Shape Armhole. Next row: cast off 6 sts., k. to end. Now cont. working 2 sts. in garter st. at centre edge and remainder in st.st., work 2 sts. tog. at side edge on every k. row until 38 (40) sts. remain. Cont. straight until Back measures 14¼ (15¼) in., ending with a p. row.

Shape Shoulder. Cast off 8 (8) sts. at beg. of next and foll. alt. row. Work 1 row. Cast off 8 (9) sts. at beg. of next row, work to end. Cast off remaining 14 (15) sts.

Rejoin yarn to 48 (51) sts. on other side of opening and complete to match first side reversing shapings.

FRONT
Work as Back until the same number of rows have been worked to beg. of armhole shaping.

Shape Armhole. Cast off 6 sts. at beg. of next 2 rows, then work 2 sts. tog. at each end of every k. row until 76 (80) sts. remain. Work straight until armholes measure 4 (4½) in. ending with a p. row.

Shape Neck. K. 32 (33); turn.

Work 2 sts. tog. at neck edge on next 8 rows. Cont. straight on remaining 24 (25) sts. until work measures same as Back to shoulder shaping, ending with a p. row.

Shape Shoulder. Cast off 8 sts. at beg. of next and foll. alt. row. Work 1 row. Cast off.

Rejoin yarn to remaining sts., cast off 12 (14) sts., then work on remaining 32 (33) sts. to match first side, reversing shapings.

SLEEVES (make 2 alike)
With No. 12 needles and B., cast on 62 (68) sts. and work 4 rows in rib. Work 4 rows in st.st. Change to No. 10 needles and W., then work in st.st. stripes of 10 rows W., and 8 rows B., inc. 1 st. at each end of every 3rd row until there are 72 (78) sts.

Cont. straight until Sleeve measures 2½ (3) in., ending with same row of same coloured stripe as Back at beg. of armhole shaping (so stripes match at this point) and ending with a p. row.

Shape Top. Work 2 sts. tog. at each end of every row until 16 (18) sts. remain. Cast off.

NECKBAND
Join shoulder seams. With right side of work facing, and with set of four No. 12 needles and W., pick up and k. 11 (12) sts. across left side of back neck, pick up and k. 52 (54) sts. round front neck and 11 (12) sts. across right side of back neck: 74 (78) sts.

Join R. and p.1 row (wrong side). Now work 2 in. in k.1, p.1 rib. Cast off in rib.

TO COMPLETE
Sew in sleeves. Join side and sleeve seams. Fold neckband in half on to wrong side and slipstitch in place. Sew zip fastener down centre back opening.

PINAFORE
FRONT AND BACK (make 2 pieces alike)
With No. 10 needles and W., cast on 132 (144) sts. Change to No. 11 needles and, beg. with a k. row, work 8 rows in st.st. Join R.

1st row: with R., k.
2nd row: with R., k.
3rd row: with W., k.
4th row: with W., p.
5th row: with W., k.
6th row: with W., p.

These 6 rows form patt. Cont. in patt., working 2 sts. tog. at each end of 11th row and every following 8th row until 98 (104) sts. remain. Cont. straight until work measures 13 (15) in. from end of first R. stripe.

Shape Armhole. Cast off 4 (5) sts. at beg. of next 2 rows, then work 2 sts. tog. at each end of every row until 48 (56) sts. remain.

Cont. straight until armhole measures 3 (4½) in., ending with R. stripe.

Break off R. and join W. Work 6 rows in st.st.

Change to No. 12 needles and work 8 rows in st.st.

Change to No. 11 needles and work 6 rows in st.st. Cast off.

ARMHOLE EDGINGS (both alike)
Fold W. st.st. neck border in half to wrong side and sew down cast-off edge.

With No. 11 needles and W., pick up and k. 40 (48) sts. from bottom of armhole to top of double edge of neck border, cast on 44 (52) sts., pick up and k. 40 (48) sts. down other side of armhole.

Work 6 rows in st.st., working 2 sts. tog. at beg. of every row.

Change to No. 12 needles and work 4 rows, still dec. on each row, then work 3 rows, inc. 1 st. at beg. of every row. Change to No. 11 needles and work 6 rows, inc. 1 st. at beg. of every row. Cast off.

TO COMPLETE
Join mitred edges of armhole edgings, fold edgings

in half on to wrong side and sew down. Turn up hem on first R. stripe and slipstitch in place. Join side seams.

With crochet hook and R., work d.c. (see page 26) along doubled edge of neck border and the inner edges of straps, inserting hook through both cast-on sts. and cast-off sts. of straps.

Then, with wrong side facing, and with No. 11 needles, pick up and k. the top loop of each d.c. Cast off.

White, blue and navy dress

(photographed in colour on page 75)

MATERIALS
4 (4, 5) oz. Wendy Nylonised 4-ply in white, 2 (3, 3) oz. in light blue and 3 (3, 4) oz. in navy (see note on wools and yarns, page 20); one pair each Nos. 10 and 12 knitting needles (see page 26).

MEASUREMENTS
To fit chest size 24 (26, 28) in.; length 18 (21, 24) in.; sleeve seam 9 (10, 11) in.

TENSION
$7\frac{1}{2}$ sts. and $9\frac{1}{2}$ rows to 1 in. with No. 10 needles (see note on tension, page 15).

ABBREVIATIONS
See page 26; W., white; B., blue; N., navy.

FRONT
With No. 12 needles and N., cast on 114 (126, 138) sts. and work 7 rows in st.st.
Next row (hem ridge): k.
Change to No. 10 needles. Beg. with a k. row, work 18 rows in st.st. Cont. in st.st., dec. 1 st. at each end of next and every foll. 10th row until 60 (70, 80) rows from hem ridge have been worked: 104 (114, 124) sts.
Join B.
1st row: with N. k.2 (3, 4), *with B. k.4, with N. k.4; rep. from * to last 6 (7, 8) sts., with B. k.4, with N. k.2 (3, 4).
2nd row: with N. p.2 (3, 4), *with B. p.4, with N. p.4; rep. from * to last 6 (7, 8) sts., with B. p.4, with N. p.2 (3, 4).
Rep. these 2 rows once.
5th row: with B. k.2 (3, 4), *with N. k.4, with B. k.4; rep. from * to last 6 (7, 8) sts., with N. k.4, with B. k.2 (3, 4).
6th row: with B. p.2 (3, 4), *with N. p.4, with B. p.4; rep. from * to last 6 (7, 8) sts., with N. p.4, with B. p.2 (3, 4).
Rep. these 2 rows once.
Cont. with B. in st.st., working 2 sts. tog. at each end of next and every foll. 10th row until 96 (104, 112) sts. remain.
Work straight until 114 (130, 148) rows have been worked from hem ridge. Join W.

1st row: with B. k.2, *with W. k.2, with B. k.2; rep. from * to end.
2nd row: with B. p.2, *with W. p.2, with B. p.2; rep. from * to end.
Rep. these 2 rows once.
5th row: with W. k.2, *with B. k.2, with W. k.2; rep. from * to end.
6th row: with W. p.2, *with B. p.2, with W. p.2; rep. from * to end.
Rep. these 2 rows once.
Cont. with W. in st.st. until work measures 13 (15½, 18) in. from hem ridge, ending with a p. row. Cont. in W.
Shape Armholes. Cast off 4 sts. at beg. of next 2 rows, then work 2 sts. tog. at each end of next 6 (7, 8) rows and then at each end of foll. 2 alt. rows. Cont. straight on remaining sts. until armholes measure 4 (4½, 5) in., ending with a p. row.
Shape Neck. K.24 (26, 28); turn.
Work on these sts. only for another 5 rows, working 2 sts. tog. at neck edge on next and every alt. row: 21 (23, 25) sts.
Shape Shoulder. Next row: cast off 6 (7, 7) sts., k. to end.
Next row: p.2 tog., p. to end.
Rep. these 2 rows once. Cast off.
Slip centre 24 (26, 28) sts. on to a stitch holder. Work on remaining 24 (26, 28) sts. to match first side of neck, reversing shapings.

BACK
Work as Front to end of armhole shaping then cont. straight until work measures same as Front to shoulder shaping.
Shape Shoulders. Cast off 6 (7, 7) sts. at beg. of next 4 rows and 7 (7, 9) sts. at beg. of next 2 rows. Leave remaining 34 (36, 38) sts. on stitch holder.

SLEEVES (make 2 alike)
With No. 12 needles and W., cast on 42 (46, 50) sts. and work 2 in. in k.1, p.1 rib., inc. 1 st. at each end of last row.
Change to No. 10 needles and work in st.st., inc. 1 st. at each end of the 3rd and every foll. 5th row until there are 64 (70, 76) sts.
Cont. straight until work measures 9 (10, 11) in.,

ending with a p. row.

Shape Top. Cast off 4 sts. at beg. of next 2 rows, then work 2 sts. tog. at beg. of next 6 rows. Cast off 2 sts. at beg. of next 16 (18, 20) rows. Cast off.

NECKBAND

Sew right shoulder seam. With right side of work facing, No. 12 needles and W., pick up and k. 11 sts. down left side of front neck, k. across centre 24 (26, 28) sts., pick up and k. 11 sts. from right side of front neck and k. across 34 (36, 38) sts. of back neck: 80 (84, 88) sts. Work 10 rows in k.1, p.1 rib, then k. 1 row (to form ridge). Work a further 8 rows in rib and cast off loosely in rib.

TO COMPLETE

Sew left shoulder seam, and join sides of neckband. Set in sleeves and sew sleeve and side seams. Fold neckband in half on to wrong side and turn up hem of skirt. Slipstitch both in place.

Striped sweater dress

MATERIALS

9 (10, 11, 12) oz. Lee Target Motoravia Double Knitting in main shade and 3 (3, 4, 4) oz. in contrast (see note on wools and yarns, page 20); one pair each Nos. 9 and 11 knitting needles (see page 26) or two No. 9 needles with points at both ends can be used instead of the pair to avoid breaking yarn when working stripes (see below).

MEASUREMENTS

To fit chest size 22 (24, 26, 28) in.; length 15 (17, 20, 23) in.; length of sleeve seam 8¼ (9¾, 11¼, 12¾) in.

TENSION

6 sts. and 8 rows to 1 in. over st.st. with No. 9 needles (see note on tension, page 15).

ABBREVIATIONS

See page 26; M., main shade; C., contrast.

BACK

With No. 11 needles and M., cast on 82 (90, 100, 110) sts. and work 7 rows in st.st.

Next row (hem ridge): k.

Now work 8 rows in st.st., beg. with a k. row. Change to No. 9 needles.

** Join C. and work 2 rows in st.st.

With M., k. 3 rows.

With C., p. 3 rows.

With M., k. 3 rows.

With C., p. 1 row and k. 1 row.**

(**Note.** To avoid breaking and rejoining yarn when working stripes of 3 rows, needles with points at both ends may be used. In this case work from ** to ** as follows: work first 5 rows as given, then start next row from same end as previous row, with C. k. 3 rows, with M. p. 3 rows, start next row from same end as previous row, with C. p. 1 row, k. 1 row.)

Change back to M. and, starting with a p. row cont. in st.st., working 2 sts. tog. at each end of 4th and every foll. 8th row until 70 (76, 82, 88) sts. remain. Work straight until Back measures 9½ (10¾, 13, 15¼) in. from hem ridge, ending with a p. row. Now work from ** to ** once.

Starting with a p. row, work 1 (3, 5, 7) rows with M. in st.st.

Shape Armholes. Still working with M., and in st.st. cast off 3 sts. at beg. of next 2 rows.

3rd row: with C., k.2 tog., k. to last 2 sts., k.2 tog.

4th row: with C., p.

5th row: with M., k.2 tog., k. to last 2 sts., k.2 tog.

6th row: with M., k.

7th row: as 5th row.

8th row: with C., p.

9th row: with C., p.2 tog., p. to last 2 sts., p.2 tog.

10th row: with C., p. 56 (62, 68, 74) sts. With M., rep. 5th, 6th and 7th rows.

14th row: with C., p.

15th row: as 3rd row.

With M., and starting with a p. row, work 3 (5, 7, 9) rows in st.st. working 2 sts. tog. at each end of every k. row: 48 (52, 56, 60) sts.

Rep. from 3rd row: 32 (34, 36, 38) sts. Leave these sts. on a stitch holder.

FRONT

Work as Back, working armhole shaping until 42 (44, 46, 48) sts. remain ending after a wrong-side row.

Shape Neck. Next row: keeping patt. correct and still dec. for armhole shaping as given for Back, patt. 10; turn.

Cont. to patt. and dec. as given for Back at armhole edge and at the same time work 2 sts. tog. at neck edge on next and alt. rows until all sts. are worked off.

Slip centre 22 (24, 26, 28) sts. on to stitch holder.

In simple stocking stitch — this two-colour dress is easy enough for a beginner to make

Rejoin yarn to remaining 10 sts. and work to match first side of neck, reversing shapings.

SLEEVES (make 2 alike)

With No. 11 needles and M., cast on 30 (32, 34, 36) sts. and work 2 in. in k.1, p.1 rib, inc. 1 st. at each end of last row.

Change to No. 9 needles and work in st.st. with M., inc. 1 st at each end of 3rd and every foll. 5th row until there are 44 (48, 52, 56) sts.

Cont. straight until work measures $6\frac{1}{2}$ ($7\frac{3}{4}$, 9, $10\frac{1}{4}$) in. from beg., ending after a p. row.

Work stripe patt. from ** to ** of Back once.

Starting with a p. row, work 1 (3, 5, 7) rows with M. in st.st.

Shape Top. Work as Back armhole shaping until 6 sts. remain. Leave these on safety pin.

NECKBAND

Sew raglan seams, leaving left back seam open.

With right side facing and with No. 11 needles and M., k. across 6 sts. of Left Sleeve, pick up and k. 8 sts. down left side of front neck, k. across centre 22 (24, 26, 28) sts., pick up and k. 8 sts. up right side of front neck, k. across 6 sts. of Right Sleeve and k. across 32 (34, 36, 38) sts. of Back.

Work 12 rows in k.1, p.1 rib, k.1 row (to make ridge) then work 11 rows in rib.

Cast off in rib.

TO COMPLETE

Sew left back raglan seam and Neckband seam. Join side and sleeve seams. Turn up hem and slip-stitch in place. Fold Neckband in half to wrong side and slipstitch down.

Two-colour tunic top

MATERIALS

7 (8, 9) oz. Lister Lavenda Double Six in main shade and 3 (3, 3) oz. in contrast (see note on wools and yarns, page 20); one pair each Nos. 6 and 8 knitting needles (see page 26); 5 buttons $\frac{1}{2}$ in. in diameter.

MEASUREMENTS

To fit chest size 24 (26, 28) in.; length 16 (18, 20) in.; sleeve seam 10 (11, 12) in.

TENSION

9 rows and 11 sts. to 2 in. with No. 6 needles (see note on tension, page 15).

ABBREVIATIONS

See page 26; M., main shade; C., contrast.

BACK

With No. 8 needles and M., cast on 58 (62, 66) sts. and work 5 rows in st.st. (see page 23), beg. with a k. row.

Next row (hem ridge): k.

Change to No. 6 needles and beg. with a k. row work 2 rows in st.st.

Change to C., and work 2 rows in st.st.

Change to M., and work 2 rows in st.st.

Rep. last 4 rows until work measures 4 in. from hem ridge, ending with a p. row.

Next row: k.8, sl.1, k.1, p.s.s.o., k. to last 10 sts., k.2 tog., k.8.

Work in patt. until Back measures 6 in. from hem ridge.

Next row: k.7, sl.1, k.1, p.s.s.o., k. to last 9 sts., k.2 tog., k.7.

Cont. in patt. until work measures $9\frac{1}{2}$ (11, $12\frac{1}{2}$) in.

from hem ridge, ending with a p. row.

Shape Raglan. Cast off 1 st. at beg. of next 2 rows. Now work 2 sts. tog. at each end of every k. row until 18 (20, 22) sts. remain. Leave sts. on stitch holder.

FRONT

Cast on and work first 6 rows as for Back.

Change to No. 6 needles.

1st row: with M., k.

2nd row: with M., p.26 (28, 30), k.2, p.2, k.2, p. to end.

Join C.

3rd row: with C., k.

4th row: with C., p. 26 (28, 30), k.2, p.2, k.2, p. to end.

Rep. last 4 rows until work measures 4 in. from hem ridge, ending with right side facing.

Next row: k.8, sl.1, k.1, p.s.s.o., k. to last 10 sts., k.2 tog., k.8.

Next row: p.25 (27, 29), k.2, p.2, k.2, p. to end.

Cont. in patt. until work measures 6 in. from hem ridge, ending with right side facing.

Next row: k.7, sl.1, k.1, p.s.s.o., k. to last 9 sts., k.2 tog., k.7.

Next row: p.24 (26, 28), k.2, p.2, k.2, p. to end.

Now cont. as for Back, ending before raglan shaping on the same colour and same row as Back at this point, then shape raglan as Back until 30 (32, 34) sts. remain.

Shape Neck. Next row: k.2 tog., k.10; turn. Cont. on these sts. only, working 2 sts. tog. at armhole

This smart striped top looks equally good teamed with trousers or a skirt

edge as before and at the same time k. 2 sts. tog. at neck edge on k. rows until all sts. are worked off.
Slip centre 6 (8, 10) sts. on to a stitch holder.
Rejoin yarn to remaining 12 sts. and complete to match first side, reversing shapings and working sl.1, k.1, p.s.s.o in place of k.2 tog. for neck edge dec.

SLEEVES (make 2 alike)
With No. 8 needles and M., cast on 24 (28, 32) sts. and work 5 rows in st.st.
Next row (hem ridge): k.
Change to No. 6 needles and work in st.st. beg with a k. row, and inc. 1 st. at each end of 5th and every foll. 6th row until there are 40 (42, 44) sts.
Cont. straight until work measures 10 (11, 12) in. from hem ridge.
Shape raglan as for Back until 4 sts. remain.
Leave these sts. on safety pin.

NECKBAND
Join Front to Sleeves and Right Sleeve to Back.
With right side of work facing and with No. 8 needles and M., k. across 4 sts. of Left Sleeve, pick up and k. 10 sts. on left side of front neck, k. across centre 6 (8, 10) sts., pick up and k. 10 sts. on right side of front neck, k. across 4 sts. of Right Sleeve and 18 (20, 22) sts. of Back: 52 (56, 60) sts.
Work 4 rows in k.1, p.1 rib.
Cast off in rib.

TO COMPLETE
Join Left Sleeve to Back and join side and sleeve seams. Turn under hems of skirt and sleeves and slipstitch in place. Sew buttons down centre st.st. panel, the first immediately below Neckband, and last 3½ in. from hem and the others evenly between them.

Patterned twin set
(photographed in colour on page 111)

MATERIALS
12 (12, 14, 14, 16, 17) oz. Emu Scotch Double Knitting *or* Double Crêpe *or* Bri-Nylon Double Knitting (see note on wools and yarns, page 20); one pair each Nos. 8 and 10 knitting needles (see page 26); a 4-in. zip fastener; 6 buttons $\frac{5}{8}$ in. in diameter.

MEASUREMENTS
To fit chest size 20 (21, 22, 23, 24, 25) in.; length of jumper 11¾ (12½, 13½, 14¼, 15¼, 16) in.; jumper sleeve seam 2 (2, 2½, 2½, 2½, 2½) in.; length of cardigan 12¼ (13, 14, 14¾, 15¾, 16½) in.; cardigan sleeve seam 9 (9½, 10½, 11½, 12½, 13½) in.

TENSION
5½ sts. and 8 rows to 1 in. over st.st. with No. 8 needles (see note on tension, page 15).

ABBREVIATIONS
See page 26.

JUMPER
BACK
With No. 10 needles, cast on 60 (64, 66, 70, 72, 74) sts. and work 2 in. in k.1, p.1 rib, ending with a wrong-side row.
Change to No. 8 needles and st.st. (see page 23).
Cont. until work measures 6½ (7, 7½, 8, 8½, 9) in. from beg. ending with a p. row.
Shape Raglan Armholes. For sizes 20 in. and 23 in. Dec. 1 st. at each end of next row. Work 3 rows.
For sizes 22 in., 24 in. and 25 in. Dec. 1 st. at each end of the next and every foll. 4th row until 60 (64, 66) sts. remain, ending with a p. row.
For all sizes. Dec. 1 st. at each end of the next and every foll. alt. row until 20 (20, 22, 22, 24, 24) sts. remain, ending with a p. row. Leave these sts. on a stitch holder.

FRONT
With No. 10 needles, cast on 60 (64, 66, 70, 72, 74) sts. and work 2 in. in k.1, p.1 rib, ending with a wrong-side row.
Change to No. 8 needles and patt.:
1st row: k.22 (24, 25, 27, 28, 29), p.2, k.5, p.2, k.5, p.2, k.22 (24, 25, 27, 28, 29).
2nd row: p.22 (24, 25, 27, 28, 29), k.2, p.5, k.2, p.5, k.2, p.22 (24, 25, 27, 28, 29).
3rd row: k.22 (24, 25, 27, 28, 29), p.2, y.o.n., k.2 tog. t.b.l., k.1, k.2 tog., y.r.n., p.2, y.o.n., k.2 tog. t.b.l., k.1, k.2 tog., y.r.n., p.2, k.22 (24, 25, 27, 28, 29).
4th row: p.22 (24, 25, 27, 28, 29), k.2, k.1 t.b.l., p.3, k.1 t.b.l., k.2, k.1 t.b.l., p.3, k.1 t.b.l., k.2, p.22 (24, 25, 27, 28, 29).
5th row: k.22 (24, 25, 27, 28, 29), p.3, y.o.n., sl.1, k.2, p.s.s.o., y.r.n., p.4, y.o.n., sl.1, k.2, p.s.s.o., y.r.n., p.3, k.22 (24, 25, 27, 28, 29).
6th row: p.22 (24, 25, 27, 28, 29), k.3, k.1 t.b.l., p.2, k.1 t.b.l., k.4, k.1 t.b.l., p.2, k.1 t.b.l., k.3, p.22 (24, 25, 27, 28, 29).
7th row: k.22 (24, 25, 27, 28, 29), p.3, k.2 tog., y.fwd., k.2 tog. t.b.l., p.4, k.2 tog., y.fwd., k.2 tog.

t.b.l., p.3, k.22 (24, 25, 27, 28, 29).

8th row: p.22 (24, 25, 27, 28, 29), k.2, p.2 tog. t.b.l., y.r.n., p.1, y.r.n., p.2 tog., k.2, p.2 tog. t.b.l., y.r.n., p.1, y.r.n., p.2 tog., k.2, p.22 (24, 25, 27, 28, 29).

These 8 rows form patt.

Cont. in patt. until work measures same as Back to beg. of armhole, ending with a wrong-side row.

Shape Raglan Armholes. For sizes 20 in. and 23 in. Dec. 1 st. at each end of the next row. Work 3 rows.

For sizes 22 in., 24 in. and 25 in. Dec. 1 st. at each end of the next and every foll. 4th row until 60 (64, 66) sts. remain, ending with a p. row.

For all sizes. Dec. 1 st. at each end of the next and every foll. alt. row until 32 (32, 34, 34, 36, 36) sts. remain, excluding the 2 made sts. where work ends with the 6th row of patt., and ending with a wrong-side row.

Shape Neck. Next row: k.2 tog., work 9 (9, 9, 9, 10, 10) sts.; turn and leave remaining sts. on a stitch holder.

Still dec. at armhole edge as before, dec. 1 st. at neck edge on the next 4 (4, 4, 4, 5, 5) rows.

Keeping neck edge straight, cont. to dec. at armhole edge until 1 st. remains. Fasten off.

Slip the centre 10 (10, 12, 12, 12, 12) sts. on to a stitch holder.

Join yarn at neck edge to remaining sts., patt. to last 2 sts., k.2 tog. Complete to match first side of neck.

SHORT SLEEVES (make 2 alike)

With No. 10 needles, cast on 40 (42, 44, 46, 48, 50) sts. and work ½ in. in k.1, p.1 rib, ending with a wrong-side row.

Change to No. 8 needles and st.st.

Inc. 1 st. at each end of the next and every foll. alt. row until there are 44 (48, 50, 52, 56, 58) sts. on the needle.

Cont. without further shaping until work measures 2 (2, 2½, 2½, 2½, 2½) in. from beg., ending with a p. row.

Shape Raglan Top. For sizes 20 in. and 21 in. Dec. 1 st. at each end of the next row. Work 3 rows.

For sizes 22 in., 23 in., 24 in. and 25 in. Dec. 1 st. at each end of the next and every foll. 4th row until 44 (46, 48, 50) sts. remain, ending with a p. row.

For all sizes. Dec. 1 st. at each end of the next and every foll. alt. row until 4 (6, 6, 6, 8, 8) sts. remain, ending with a p. row. Leave these sts. on a stitch holder.

NECKBAND

Using backstitch, join raglan seams, leaving left back raglan seam open.

With right side of work facing and No. 10 needles, k.

across the 4 (6, 6, 6, 8, 8) sts. on top of Left Sleeve, pick up and k. 10 sts. down left side of front neck, k. across the 10 (10, 12, 12, 12, 12) sts. at centre front, pick up and k. 10 sts. up right side of neck, k. across the 4 (6, 6, 6, 8, 8) sts. on top of Right Sleeve and the 20 (20, 22, 22, 24, 24) sts. on back neck: 58 (62, 66, 66, 72, 72) sts.

Work 1 in. in k.1, p.1 rib. Cast off loosely in rib.

TO COMPLETE

Using backstitch join side and sleeve seams.

Sew zip fastener to Neckband seam and top of left back raglan seam, then join remainder of seam.

CARDIGAN

BACK

With No 10 needles, cast on 60 (64, 66, 70, 72, 74) sts. and work 2 in. in k.1, p.1 rib, ending with a wrong-side row.

Change to No. 8 needles and st.st. (see page 23).

Cont. until work measures 7 (7½, 8, 8½, 9, 9½) in. from the beg., ending with a p. row.

Shape Raglan Armholes. For sizes 20 in. and 23 in. Dec. 1 st. at each end of the next row. Work 3 rows.

For sizes 22 in., 24 in. and 25 in. Dec. 1 st. at each end of the next and every foll. 4th row until 60 (64, 66) sts. remain, ending with a p. row.

For all sizes. Dec. 1 st. at each end of the next and every foll. alt. row until 20 (20, 22, 22, 24, 24) sts. remain, ending with a p. row. Cast off.

LEFT FRONT

With No. 10 needles, cast on 30 (32, 32, 34, 36, 36) sts. and work for 2 in. in k.1, p.1 rib, ending with a wrong-side row.

For sizes 22 in., 23 in. and 25 in. Inc. 1 st. at end of last row: 30 (32, 33, 35, 36, 37) sts.

For all sizes. Change to No. 8 needles and patt.:

1st row: k.21 (23, 24, 26, 27, 28), p.2, k.5, p.2.

2nd row: k.2, p.5, k.2, p.21 (23, 24, 26, 27, 28).

3rd row: k.21 (23, 24, 26, 27, 28), p.2, y.o.n., k.2 tog. t.b.l., k.1, k.2 tog., y.r.n., p.2.

4th row: k.2, k.1 t.b.l., p.3, k.1 t.b.l., k.2, p.21 (23, 24, 26, 27, 28).

5th row: k.21 (23, 24, 26, 27, 28), p.3, y.o.n., sl.1, k.2, p.s.s.o., y.r.n., p.3.

6th row: k.3, k.1 t.b.l., p.2, k.1 t.b.l., k.3, p.21 (23, 24, 26, 27, 28).

7th row: k.21 (23, 24, 26, 27, 28), p.3, k.2 tog., y.fwd., k.2 tog. t.b.l., p.3.

8th row: k.2, p.2 tog. t.b.l., y.r.n., p.1, y.r.n., p.2 tog., k.2, p.21 (23, 24, 26, 27, 28).

These 8 rows form patt. Cont. in patt. until work measures same as Back to beg. of armhole, ending with a wrong-side row.

Shape Raglan Armhole. For sizes 20 in. and 23 in. Dec. 1 st. at beg. of next row and then work 3 rows.

For sizes 22 in., 24 in. and 25 in. Dec. 1 st. at beg. of next row and at same edge every foll. 4th row until 30 (32, 33) sts. remain, ending with a wrong-side row.

For all sizes. Dec. 1 st. at the beg. of next row and at this same edge on every foll. alt. row until 16 (16, 17, 17, 18, 18) sts. remain, excluding the made st. where work ends with the 5th row of patt., and ending at front edge.

Shape Neck. Next row: cast off 5 (5, 6, 6, 6, 6) sts., work to end. Still dec. at armhole edge as before, dec. 1 st. at neck edge on the next 4 (4, 4, 4, 5, 5) rows.

Keeping neck edge straight, continue to dec. at armhole edge until 1 st. remains. Fasten off.

RIGHT FRONT

With No. 10 needles, cast on 30 (32, 32, 34, 36, 36) sts. and work 2 in. in k.1, p.1 rib.

For sizes 22 in., 23 in. and 25 in. Inc. 1 st. at beg. of last row. End with a wrong-side row: 30 (32, 33, 35, 36, 37) sts.

For all sizes. Change to No. 8 needles and patt.:

1st row: p.2, k.5, p.2, k.21 (23, 24, 26, 27, 28).

2nd row: p. 21 (23, 24, 26, 27, 28), k.2, p.5, k.2.

3rd row: p.2, y.o.n., k.2 tog. t.b.l., k.1, k.2 tog., y.r.n., p.2, k.21 (23, 24, 26, 27, 28).

4th row: p.21 (23, 24, 26, 27, 28), k.2, k.1 t.b.l., p.3, k.1 t.b.l., k.2.

5th row: p.3, y.o.n., sl.1, k.2, p.s.s.o., y.r.n.., p.3, k.21 (23, 24, 26, 27, 28).

6th row: p.21 (23, 24, 26, 27, 28), k.3, k.1 t.b.l., p.2, k.1 t.b.l., k.3.

7th row: p.3, k.2 tog., y.fwd., k.2 tog. t.b.l., p.3, k.21 (23, 24, 26, 27, 28).

8th row: p.21 (23, 24, 26, 27, 28), k.2, p.2 tog. t.b.l., y.r.n., p.1, y.r.n., p.2 tog., k.2.

Complete to match Left Front, reversing all shapings.

LONG SLEEVES (make 2 alike)

With No. 10 needles, cast on 34 (34, 36, 36, 38, 38) sts. and work 2 in. in k.1, p.1 rib, ending with a wrong-side row.

Change to No. 8 needles and st.st.

Inc. 1 st. at each end of the next and every foll. 10th

(8th, 9th, 9th, 9th, 9th) row until there are 44 (48, 50, 52, 56, 58) sts. on the needle.

Cont. without further shaping until work measures 9 (9½, 10½, 11½, 12½, 13½) in. from beg., ending with a p. row.

Shape Raglan Top. For sizes 20 in. and 21 in. Dec. 1 st. at each end of the next row. Work 3 rows.

For sizes 22 in., 23 in., 24 in. and 25 in. Dec. 1 st. at each end of the next and every foll. 4th row until 44 (46, 48, 50) sts. remain, ending with a p. row.

For all sizes. Dec. 1 st. at each end of the next and every foll. alt. row until 4 (6, 6, 6, 8, 8) sts. remain, ending with a p. row. Cast off.

BUTTONHOLE BAND

With No. 10 needles, cast on 9 sts.

1st row: *k.1, p.1; rep. from * to last st., k.1.

2nd row: *p.1, k.1; rep. from * to last st., p.1.

Rep. these 2 rows for ¼ (¾, ½, ¼, ¾, ½) in.

1st buttonhole row: rib 3, cast off 3, rib to end.

2nd buttonhole row: rib, casting on over cast-off sts. in previous row.

Cont. in rib making 5 more buttonholes at intervals of 1¾ (1¼, 2, 2¼, 2¼, 2½) in. measured from base of previous buttonhole.

Work a further ½ in. in rib. Cast off in rib.

BUTTON BAND

Work to match Buttonhole Band, omitting buttonholes.

COLLAR

With No. 10 needles, cast on 77 (83, 87, 87, 95, 95) sts.

1st row: *k.1, p.1; rep. from * to last st., k.1.

2nd row: *p.1, k.1; rep. from * to last st., p.1.

Rep. these 2 rows for ¾ in.

Change to No. 8 needles and cont. in rib until work measures 2½ in. Cast off loosely in rib.

TO COMPLETE

Using backstitch join raglan, side and sleeve seams. Sew Buttonhole Band to Right Front and Button Band to Left Front. Sew Collar in position starting and ending in centre of Front Bands. Sew on buttons to Left Front to match buttonholes.

Chequered sweater

(photographed in black and white opposite)

MATERIALS

6 (6, 7) oz. of Paton's 101 Courtelle Double Knitting in main shade and 4 (5, 6) oz. in contrast (see note on wools and yarns, page 20); one pair each Nos. 8

Ribbed yoke, lower band and cuffs are in main shade, pompon tie round neck is worked in a contrast coloured yarn

and 10 knitting needles (see page 26).

MEASUREMENTS
To fit chest size 26 (28, 30) in.; length 14 (15, 16) in.; sleeve seam $11\frac{1}{2}$ ($13\frac{1}{2}$, $15\frac{1}{2}$) in.

TENSION
17 sts. and 36 rows to 3 in. over patt. with No. 8 needles (see note on tension, page 15).

ABBREVIATIONS
See page 26; M., main shade; C., contrast.

BACK AND FRONT (make 2 pieces alike)
With No. 10 needles and M., cast on 76 (80, 88) sts. and work $1\frac{1}{2}$ in. in k.2, p.2 rib.

For sizes 26 and 30 only: inc. 1 st. at end of last row: 77 (89) sts.

For size 28 only: inc. 1 st. in first, 40th and last sts. of last row: 83 sts.

For all sizes: change to No. 8 needles, join C. and patt. thus:

1st row: with C., sl.1, *k.1, sl.1; rep. from * to end.
2nd row: with C., k.
3rd row: with M., k.1, *sl.1, k.1; rep. from * to end.
4th row: with M., k.
These 4 rows form patt. Rep. patt. until work measures 10 ($10\frac{1}{2}$, 11) in. from beg., ending with a k. row.

Shape Raglan. Keeping patt. correct, work 2 sts. tog. at each end of next and every alt. row until 59 (61, 65) sts. remain, ending with a right-side row.

Shape Neck. Next row: k.20; turn.
** Working on these sts. only, cont. raglan shaping as before and at the same time work 2 sts. tog. at neck edge on every row until 2 sts. remain. Cast off.
Slip centre 19 (21, 25) sts. on to a stitch holder.
Rejoin yarn to remaining 20 sts. and k. 1 row.
Now complete to match first side from **.

SLEEVES (make 2 alike)
With No. 10 needles and M., cast on 36 (40, 44) sts. and work $1\frac{1}{2}$ in. in k.2, p.2 rib, inc. 1 st. at end of last row.
Change to No. 8 needles and patt. as for Back. inc. 1 st. at each end of 9th and every foll. 10th row

until there are 57 (61, 65) sts.
Cont. straight until Sleeve measures $11\frac{1}{2}$ ($13\frac{1}{2}$, $15\frac{1}{2}$) in., ending with same patt. row and same colour as Back at beg. of raglan shaping.
Shape Raglan. Work 2 sts. tog. at each end of next and every alt. row until 27 (27, 29) sts. remain, ending with a k. row. Leave sts. on a stitch holder.

YOKE
Join Sleeves to Front and Right Sleeve to Back. With right side facing, and with No. 10 needles and M., k. across 27 (27, 29) of Left Sleeve, pick up and k. 21 (22, 23) sts. down left side of front neck, k. across centre 19 (21, 25) sts., pick up and k. 21 (22, 23) up right side of front neck, k. across 27 (27, 29) of Right Sleeve, pick up and k. 21 (22, 23) sts. down right side of back neck, k. across centre 19 (21, 25) sts., and pick up and k. 21 (22, 23) up left side of back neck: 176 (184, 200) sts.

1st row (wrong side): *p.2, k.6; rep. from * to end.
2nd row: *p.6, k.2; rep. from * to end.
Rep. last 2 rows 4 (5, 6) times.
Dec. row (wrong side): *p.2, k.2 tog., k.2, k.2 tog.; rep. from * to end: 132 (138, 150) sts.
Next row: *p.4, k.2; rep. from * to end.
Next row: *p.2, k.4; rep. from * to end.
Rep. last 2 rows 4 (5, 6) times, then first row again.
Dec. row: *p.2, (k.2 tog.) twice; rep. from * to end: 88 (92, 100) sts.
Next row: *p.2, k.2; rep. from * to end.
Rep. this row 3 times.
Next (slot) row: *k.2 tog., y.fwd.; rep. from * to last 2 sts., k.1, y.fwd., k.1.
Next row: p.2 tog., rib. to end.
Work 2 rows in rib; cast off.

TO COMPLETE
Join Left Sleeve to Back and join side and sleeve seams.
Cord. Cut 4 strands of C., each 100 in. long, twist tightly, then fold in half, knot ends tog. and allow yarn to twist itself into a cord. Make 2 pompons (see page 82) in C., with card circles $1\frac{1}{2}$ in. in diameter. Thread cord through slots at neck, then sew one pompon to each end.

Furry dressing-gown
(photographed in colour on page 76)

MATERIALS
8 (9, 10) balls Lister Fun Fur Knit (see note on wools and yarns, page 20); one pair No. 00 knitting needles (see page 26); 4 buttons 1 in. in diameter.

MEASUREMENTS
To fit chest size 24 (26, 28) in.

TENSION
4 sts. and $6\frac{1}{2}$ rows to 2 in. over st.st. (see page 15).

ABBREVIATIONS
See page 26.

RIGHT FRONT
Using thumb method (see page 10), cast on 17 (18, 19) sts. and work 14 (16, 18) rows in st.st. (adjust length here if required).
Next (buttonhole and dec.) row: k.2, y.fwd., k.2 tog., k. to last 2 sts., k.2 tog.
Starting with a p. row work 9 rows in st.st.
Rep. last 10 rows twice, then work the first row again, then work 1 row in p.: 13 (14, 15) sts.
Shape Armhole. Work 1 row in k. Cast off 1 st. at beg. of next row, then work 2 sts. tog. at side edge on next 1 (1, 2) rows and on foll. alt. row.
Work in st.st. on remaining 10 (11, 11) sts. until 12 (14, 16) rows have been worked from beg. of armhole shaping, ending at centre edge.
Shape Revers. Next row: cast off 4 sts., k. to end. Work 2 more rows, working 2 sts. tog. at neck edge on each row: 4 (5, 5) sts.
Shape Shoulder. Cast off 2 sts. at beg. of next row. Work 1 row. Cast off.

LEFT FRONT
Work as Right Front, omitting buttonholes and reversing shapings.

BACK
Cast on 30 (32, 34) sts. and work in st.st. until Back matches Fronts to beg. of side dec. (and first buttonhole on Right Front). Work 2 sts. tog. at each end of next and every foll. 10th row until 22 (24, 26) sts. remain. Work until Back matches Fronts to beg. of armhole shaping.
Shape Armholes. Cast off 1 st. at beg. of next 2 rows, then work 2 sts. tog. at each end of next 1 (1, 2) rows and at each end of foll. alt. row.
Work in st.st. on remaining 16 (18, 18) sts. until Back measures same as Fronts to shoulder shaping.
Shape Shoulders. Cast off 2 sts. at beg. of next 2 rows and 2 (3, 3) sts. at beg. of next 2 rows. Cast off remaining sts.

SLEEVES (make 2 alike)
Cast on 13 (14, 15) sts. and work in st.st. When work measures 3 in., inc. 1 st. at each end of next row then at 2-in. intervals until there are 17 (20, 23) sts.
Cont. straight until work measures 9 (10, 11) in. (or required length) from beg., ending with a p. row.
Shape Top. Cast off 1 st. at beg. of next 6 rows, then 2 sts. at beg. of foll. 2 (2, 4) rows. Cast off.

COLLAR
Sew shoulder seams. With right side of work facing, start at top of Right Front and pick up the cast-off loop of the innermost of the 4 sts. cast off to shape revers, then pick up 3 sts. from side of neck, then 8 cast-off sts. at top of Back, 3 sts. from other side of neck and, as before, the innermost of the 4 sts. cast off to complete revers at top of Left Front: 16 sts.
1st row (right side of collar): k.
2nd row: p.
3rd row: k.2, y.fwd., k. to last 2 sts., y.fwd., k.2.
4th row: p.
Rep. the last 4 rows once.
9th row: k.
10th row: p.
Cast off.

TO COMPLETE
Set in sleeves and sew side and sleeve seams.
Sew buttons on Left Front to match buttonholes.

Red cape
(photographed in colour on page 112)

MATERIALS
11 (12, 13, 14) oz. Twilley's Cortina Super Crochet Wool (see note on wools and yarns, page 20); one pair each Nos. 9, 10 and 11 knitting needles (see page 26); 2 buttons $\frac{5}{8}$ in. in diameter.

MEASUREMENTS
To fit chest size 22 (24, 26, 28) in.; length 18 (20, 22, 24) in.

TENSION
8 sts. and 9 rows to 1 in. with No. 9 needles (see note on tension, page 15).

ABBREVIATIONS
See page 26.

BACK
With No. 10 needles cast on 184 (192, 200, 208) sts. and work 7 rows in st.st. (see page 23).
Next row (hem ridge): k.
Change to No. 9 needles.
1st patt. row: k.
2nd, 4th and 6th patt. rows: p.
3rd patt. row: k.1. *sl.1, k.1, y.r.n., p.s.s.o.; rep. from * to last st., k.1.
5th patt. row: as 3rd row.

These 6 rows form patt. Rep. patt. until work measures 10½ (12½, 14½, 16½) in. from hem ridge, ending with a 6th patt. row.

Next patt. row: (k.5, k.3 tog.) 3 times, patt. to last 24 sts., (k.3 tog., k.5) 3 times.

Work 5 rows in patt.

Rep. last 6 rows until 52 (60, 68, 76) sts. remain.

Work 5 rows in patt. from last dec. row.

Next row: k.4 (4, 8, 4), *k.2 tog., k.4 (2, 1, 1); rep. from * to end: 44 (46, 48, 52) sts.

Work 1 p. row, then leave sts. on stitch holder.

RIGHT FRONT

With No. 10 needles cast on 92 (96, 100, 104) sts. and work 7 rows in st.st.

Next row (hem ridge): k. to end, cast on 4 sts.

Change to No. 9 needles and patt. as for Back.

Work until front measures 5 in. from hem ridge, ending with a 6th patt. row.

Divide for Hand Opening. Next row: k.40, cast on 8 sts.; turn. Work on these sts. only.

1st row: k.1, (p.1, k.1) 4 times, p. to end.

2nd row: k.1, patt. to last 9 sts., p.1, (k.1, p.1) 4 times.

Cont. in this way, keeping border of 9 ribbed sts., until work measures 9 in. from hem ridge ending with a 6th patt. row.

Next row: k.40, cast off 8 sts.

Leave sts. on stitch holder.

Rejoin yarn to remaining 56 (60, 64, 68) sts. and patt. on these sts., beg. with a first patt. row, until work measures 9 in. from hem ridge, ending with a first patt. row.

Next row: p. to end, p. 40 sts. from stitch holder. Cont. in patt. on all sts. until work measures 10½ (12½, 14½, 16½) in. from hem ridge, ending with a 6th patt. row.

Next row: k. to last 24 sts., (k.3 tog., k.5) 3 times. Patt. 5 rows.

Rep. last 6 rows until 42 (46, 50, 54) sts. remain.

Work 5 rows in patt. after last dec. row.

Shape Neck. Next row: cast off 11 (15, 19, 23) sts., k.7, (k.3 tog., k.5) 3 times: 25 sts.

** Work 5 rows in patt. working 2 sts. tog. at neck edge on every row.

Next row: k.2, (k.2 tog., k.1) 6 times: 14 sts.

Work 5 rows in patt., working 2 sts. tog. at neck edge on every row.

Next row: k.3 tog. 3 times.

Next row: p.3 tog. Fasten off.

LEFT FRONT

Cast on as for Right Front and work 7 rows in st.st.

Next row (hem ridge): cast on 4 sts., k. to end.

Work as for Right Front until dividing row is reached.

Divide for Hand Opening. Next row: k.56 (60, 64, 68); turn.

Work on these sts. only in patt. until work measures

9 in. from hem ridge, ending with a first patt. row. Leave sts. on stitch holder. Rejoin yarn to remaining 40 sts.

Next row: cast on 8 sts. and work (p.1, k.1) 4 times on these sts., p.1, k.39.

Next row: p.39, k.1, (p.1, k.1) 4 times.

Cont. in patt. with 8 sts. in rib at inner edge until work measures 9 in. from hem ridge, ending with a 6th patt. row.

Next row: cast off 8 sts., k. to end.

Next row: p. to end, p.56 (60, 64, 68) from stitch holder.

Cont. in patt. on all sts. until work measures 10½ (12½, 14½, 16½) in. from hem ridge, ending with a 6th patt. row.

Next row: (k.5, k.3 tog) 3 times, k. to end.

Work 5 rows in patt.

Rep. last 6 rows until 42 (46, 50, 54) sts. remain.

Work 4 rows in patt. after last dec. row.

Shape Neck. Next row: cast off 11 (15, 19, 23) sts., p. to end.

Next row: (k.5, k.3 tog.) 3 times, k.7.

Now complete as Right Front from **.

NECKBAND

Join side seams.

With right side of work facing, and with No. 11 needles, beg. 5 sts. in from Right Front centre edge and pick up and k. 24 (26, 28, 30) sts. round front neck, k.44 (46, 48, 52) sts. from back of neck, then pick up and k.24 (26, 28, 30) sts. round left front neck to within 5 sts. of edge: 92 (98, 104, 112) sts.

Work 5 rows in k.1, p.1 rib.

Next row: k.2, *y.fwd., k.2 tog.; rep. from * to end.

Work another 5 rows in rib. Cast off in rib.

HOOD

With No. 11 needles cast on 134 (140, 144, 150) sts. and work 10 rows in k.1, p.1 rib.

Change to No. 9 needles and patt. as for Back until work measures 5½ (5¾, 6, 6¼) in. from beg., ending with a wrong-side row.

Next row: cast off 52 (54, 56, 58) sts., patt. 30 (32, 32, 34), cast off remaining sts.

Rejoin yarn to centre panel and cont. in patt., working 2 sts. tog. at each end of every 8th row until 18 (20, 20, 22) sts. remain.

Cont. in patt. until work measures 6½ (6¾, 7, 7¼) in. from start of centre panel. Cast off.

TO COMPLETE

Sew side edges of centre panel of hood to two cast-off edges, then sew hood to neckband, beg. and

Continued on page 115

Opposite: patterned twin set (see page 104). Overleaf: red cape (see page 109)

ending 8 sts. in from each front edge of neckband.
Sew down top and lower edges of ribbed borders of
hand openings.

Turn under a 5-st. border on each front edge, and
slipstitch in place.

Fold hem at lower edge to wrong side and slipstitch
in place.

Twist 6 strands of yarn, each 100 in. long, until they
twist back on themselves, double strands and allow
cord to twist itself. Knot cord at each end and trim.
Thread cord through neckband holes.

Sew a button each side of neck just below neckband.
Either crochet a length of chain or plait three strands
of yarn tog. so finished length is $2\frac{1}{2}$ in. Fold into
loop, sew in front of right button and use to fasten
left button.

Lacy jumper
– in 3 yarn weights, with long or short sleeves
(photographed in black and white on page 116)

MATERIALS
For version 1: 6 (7, 8, 9, 10, 11) balls Emu Bri-
Nylon 3-ply (see note on wools and yarns, page 20)
for long-sleeved jumper, 5 (6, 7, 7, 8, 9) balls for
short-sleeved jumper; one pair each Nos. 11 and 13
knitting needles (see page 26).

For version 2: 9 (10, 11, 11, 12, 13) balls Emu
Scotch 4-ply, Super Crêpe *or* Bri-Nylon 4-ply (see
note on wools and yarns, page 20) for long-sleeved
jumper, 7 (8, 9, 9, 10, 11) balls for short-sleeved
jumper; one pair each Nos. 10 and 12 knitting
needles (see page 26).

For version 3: 11 (12, 14, 15, 16, 17) balls Emu
Scotch Double Knitting *or* Double Crêpe *or* Bri-
Nylon Double Knitting (see note on wools and
yarns, page 20) for long-sleeved jumper, 8 (9, 10,
11, 12, 13) balls for short-sleeved jumper; one pair
each Nos. 8 and 10 knitting needles (see page 26).

MEASUREMENTS
To fit chest size 24 (26, 28, 30, 32, 34) in.; length
$16\frac{1}{2}$ (18, $19\frac{1}{2}$, $20\frac{1}{2}$, $21\frac{1}{2}$, $22\frac{1}{2}$) in.; long sleeve seam
11 (12, $13\frac{1}{2}$, 15, 16, 17) in.; short sleeve seam $2\frac{1}{2}$
($2\frac{1}{2}$, $2\frac{1}{2}$, 3, 3, 3) in.

TENSION
3-ply: $8\frac{1}{2}$ sts. and 11 rows to 1 in. over st.st. with
No. 11 needles; **4-ply:** $7\frac{1}{2}$ sts. and $9\frac{1}{2}$ rows to 1 in.
over st.st. with No. 10 needles; **double knitting:**
$5\frac{1}{2}$ sts. and 8 rows to 1 in. over st.st. with No. 8
needles (see note on tension, page 15).

ABBREVIATIONS
See page 26.

Version 1: in 3-Ply Yarn
BACK
With No. 13 needles, cast on 100 (108, 114, 124,

*Opposite: green and yellow dress and
jacket (see page 126). On previous page:
pastel-striped dress (see page 124)*

130, 138) sts. and work $1\frac{1}{2}$ in. in k.1, p.1 rib, ending
with a right-side row.

Next row: rib 5 (9, 9, 8, 9, 6), * work twice into
next st., rib 8 (8, 7, 8, 7, 8); rep. from * to last 5 (9,
9, 8, 9, 6) sts., work twice into next st., rib 4 (8,
8, 7, 8, 5): 111 (119, 127, 137, 145, 153) sts. **.
Change to No. 11 needles and st.st. (see page 23).
Cont. until work measures $9\frac{1}{2}$ ($10\frac{1}{2}$, $11\frac{1}{2}$, 12, $12\frac{1}{2}$,
13) in. from beg. ending with a p. row.

Shape Raglan Armholes. Cast off 1 (1, 1, 2, 2, 2)
sts. at beg. of next 2 rows.

For sizes 24, 26 and 28 only. Next row: k.2 tog.,
k. to last 2 sts., k.2 tog.

Work 3 rows straight.

For all sizes. Dec. 1 st. at each end of the next
and every foll. alt. row until 37 (39, 41, 43, 45, 47)
sts. remain ending with a p. row.

Leave these sts. on a stitch holder.

FRONT
Work as for Back to **.

Change to No. 11 needles and patt.

1st row: k.29 (33, 37, 42, 46, 50), *p.2, sl.1, k.1,
p.s.s.o., y.fwd., k.3, y.fwd., k.2 tog., p.2, k.10; rep.
from * twice, k.19 (23, 27, 32, 36, 40).

2nd row: p. 29 (33, 37, 42, 46, 50), *k.2, p.7, k.2,
p.10; rep. from * twice, p.19 (23, 27, 32, 36, 40).

3rd row: k.29 (33, 37, 42, 46, 50), *p.2, k.2, y.fwd.,
sl.1, k.2 tog., p.s.s.o., y.fwd., k.2, p.2, k.10; rep.
from * twice, k.19 (23, 27, 32, 36, 40).

4th row: as 2nd row.

These 4 rows form patt. Cont. in patt. until work
measures $9\frac{1}{2}$ ($10\frac{1}{2}$, $11\frac{1}{2}$, 12, $12\frac{1}{2}$, 13) in. from beg.
ending with a wrong-side row.

Shape Raglan Armholes. Cast off 1 (1, 1, 2, 2, 2)
sts. at the beg. of next 2 rows.

For sizes 24, 26 and 28 only. Next row: k.2 tog.,
patt. to last 2 sts., k.2 tog.

Work 3 rows straight.

For all sizes. Dec. 1 st. at each end of the next and
every foll. alt. row until 63 (65, 67, 69, 75, 77) sts.
remain ending with a wrong-side row.

Shape Neck. Next row: k.2 tog., patt. 21 (21, 22,

22, 25, 25) sts.; turn and leave remaining sts. on a stitch holder. Dec. 1 st. at each end of every alt. row until 6 (6, 5, 5, 6, 6) sts. remain. Keeping neck edge straight, continue to dec. at armhole edge as before until 2 sts. remain. Work 1 row. K.2 tog. and fasten off. Slip the centre 17 (19, 19, 21, 21, 23) sts. on to a stitch holder.

Join yarn to remaining sts. at neck edge, patt. to last 2 sts., k.2 tog. Complete to match first side of neck.

LONG SLEEVES (make 2 alike)
With No. 13 needles cast on 46 (48, 50, 52, 54, 56) sts. and work 2½ in. in k.1, p.1 rib, ending with a right-side row.

Next row: rib 5 (6, 2, 4, 5, 6), * work twice into next st., rib 3 (3, 4, 3, 3, 3); rep. from * to last 5 (6, 3, 4, 5, 6) sts., work twice into next st., rib 4 (5, 2, 3, 4, 5): 56 (58, 60, 64, 66, 68) sts.

Change to No. 11 needles and st.st.

Inc. 1 st. at each end of the 3rd and every foll. 5th (5th, 6th, 7th, 7th, 7th) row until there are 86 (90, 94, 98, 102, 106) sts. on the needle.

Cont. without further shaping until work measures 11 (12, 13½, 15, 16, 17) in. from beg. ending with a p. row.

Shape Raglan Top. Cast off 1 (1, 1, 2, 2, 2) sts. at the beg. of the next 2 rows.

For size 26 only. Next row: k.2 tog., k. to last 2 sts., k.2 tog.

Work 3 rows straight: 86 sts.

For sizes 28, 30, 32 and 34. Dec. 1 st. at each end of the next and every foll. 4th row until 86 (86, 86, 88) sts. remain, ending with a p. row.

For all sizes. Dec. 1 st. at each end of the next and every foll. alt. row until 10 (10, 10, 10, 12, 12) sts. remain, ending with a p. row. Leave these sts. on a safety pin or stitch holder.

SHORT SLEEVES (make 2 alike)
With No. 13 needles cast on 66 (70, 74, 78, 82, 86) sts. and work ¾ in. in k.1, p.1 rib, ending with a right-side row.

Next row: rib 6 (4, 6, 8, 5, 7), * work twice into next st., rib 5 (6, 6, 6, 7, 7); rep. from * to last 6 (3, 5, 7, 5, 7) sts., work twice into next st., rib 5 (2, 4, 6, 4, 6): 76 (80, 84, 88, 92, 96) sts.

Change to No. 11 needles and st.st.

Inc. at each end of every foll. 3rd (3rd, 3rd, 4th, 4th, 4th) row until there are 86 (90, 94, 98, 102, 106) sts. on the needle.

Cont. without further shaping until work measures 2½ (2½, 2½, 3, 3, 3) in. from beg. ending with a p. row.

Shape Raglan Top. Work as for Long Sleeves.

Jumper is worked in alternate panels of stocking stitch and lacy pattern

NECKBAND
Using a backstitch, join raglan seams, leaving left back raglan seam open. With right side of work facing and with No. 13 needles, k. across the 10 (10, 10, 10, 12, 12) sts. on top of Left Sleeve, pick up and k.23 (23, 23, 23, 24, 24) sts. down left side of front neck, k. across 17 (19, 19, 21, 21, 23) sts. at centre, pick up and k.23 (23, 23, 23, 24, 24) sts. up right side of neck, k. across the 10 (10, 10, 10, 12, 12) sts. on top of Right Sleeve and the 37 (39, 41, 43, 45, 47) sts. on back neck: 120 (124, 126, 130, 138, 142) sts.

Work 1 in. in k.1, p.1 rib. Cast off in rib.

TO COMPLETE
Join left back raglan seam and neckband seam. Join side and sleeve seams.

Version 2: in 4-Ply Yarn
BACK
With No. 12 needles cast on 90 (98, 104, 110, 118, 124) sts. and work 1½ in. in k.1, p.1 rib, ending with a right-side row.

Next row: rib 5 (7, 8, 5, 9, 7), *work twice into next st., rib 9 (13, 10, 9, 9, 10); rep. from * to last 5 (7, 8, 5, 9, 7) sts., work twice into next st., rib 4 (6, 7, 4, 8, 6): 99 (105, 113, 121, 129, 135) sts. ***

Change to No. 10 needles and st.st. (see page 23).

Cont. until work measures 9½ (10½, 11½, 12, 12½, 13) in. from beg., ending with a p. row.

Shape Raglan Armholes. Cast off 1 (1, 1, 2, 2, 2) sts. at the beg. of the next 2 rows.

Dec. 1 st. at each end of the next and every foll. alt. row until 33 (35, 37, 39, 41, 43) sts. remain, ending with a p. row. Leave these sts. on a stitch holder.

FRONT
Work as for Back to ***.

Change to No. 10 needles and patt. thus:

1st row: k.23 (26, 30, 34, 38, 41), *p.2, sl.1, k.1, p.s.s.o., y.fwd., k.3, y.fwd., k.2 tog., p.2, k.10; rep. from * twice, k.13 (16, 20, 24, 28, 31).

2nd row: p.23 (26, 30, 34, 38, 41), *k.2, p.7, k.2, p.10; rep. from * twice, p.13 (16, 20, 24, 28, 31).

3rd row: k.23 (26, 30, 34, 38, 41), *p.2, k.2, y.fwd., sl.1, k.2 tog., p.s.s.o., y.fwd., k.2, p.2, k.10; rep. from * twice, k.13 (16, 20, 24, 28, 31).

4th row: as 2nd row.

These 4 rows form patt. Cont. in patt. until work measures 9½ (10½, 11½, 12, 12½, 13) in. from the beg., ending with a wrong-side row.

Shape Raglan Armholes. Cast off 1 (1, 1, 2, 2, 2) sts. at the beg. of next 2 rows. Dec. 1 st. at each end of next and every foll. alt. row until 57 (59, 61, 63, 67, 69) sts. remain, ending with a wrong-side row.

Shape Neck. Next row: k.2 tog., patt. 19 (19,

20, 20, 22, 22) sts.; turn and leave remaining sts. on a stitch holder.

Dec. 1 st. at each end of every alt. row until 6 (6, 5, 5, 5, 5) sts. remain. Keeping neck edge straight, continue to dec. at armhole edge as before until 2 sts. remain.

Work 1 row.

K.2 tog. and fasten off.

Slip the centre 15 (17, 17, 19, 19, 21) sts. on to a stitch holder.

Join yarn at neck edge to remaining sts., patt. to last 2 sts., k.2 tog. Complete to match first side of neck.

LONG SLEEVES (make 2 alike)

With No. 12 needles cast on 42 (44, 46, 48, 50, 52) sts. and work 2½ in. in k.1, p.1 rib, ending with a right-side row.

Next row: rib 3 (4, 5, 3, 2, 3), *work twice into next st., rib 4 (4, 4, 5, 4, 4); rep. from * to last 4 (5, 6, 3, 3, 4) sts., work twice into next st., rib 3 (4, 5, 2, 2, 3): 50 (52, 54, 56, 60, 62) sts.

Change to No. 10 needles and st.st.

Inc. 1 st. at each end of the 7th and every foll. 5th (5th, 6th, 6th, 7th, 7th) row until there are 74 (78, 82, 86, 90, 94) sts. on the needle.

Cont. without further shaping until work measures 11 (12, 13½, 15, 16, 17) in. from beg. ending with a p. row.

Shape Raglan Top. Cast off 1 (1, 1, 2, 2, 2) sts. at the beg. of next 2 rows.

For size 28 only. Next row: k.2 tog., k. to last 2 sts., k.2 tog.

Work 3 rows straight: 76 sts.

For sizes 30, 32 and 34 only. Dec. 1 st. at each end of the next and every foll. 4th row until 76 (76, 80) sts. remain, ending with a p. row.

For all sizes. Dec. 1 st. at each end of the next and every foll. alt. row until 8 (8, 8, 8, 10, 10) sts. remain, ending with a p. row.

Leave these sts. on a safety pin or stitch holder.

SHORT SLEEVES (make 2 alike)

With No. 12 needles, cast on 58 (62, 66, 70, 74, 78) sts. and work ¾ in. in k.1 p.1 rib, ending with a right-side row.

Next row: rib 7 (4, 6, 4, 6, 8), *work twice into next st., rib 4 (5, 5, 6, 6, 6); rep. from * to last 6 (4, 6, 3, 5, 7) sts., work twice into next st., rib 5 (3, 5, 2, 4, 6): 68 (72, 76, 80, 84, 88) sts.

Change to No. 10 needles and st.st.

Inc. 1 st. at each end of every foll. 4th (4th, 4th, 5th, 5th, 5th) row until there are 74 (78, 82, 86, 90, 94) sts. on the needle.

Cont. without further shaping until work measures 2½ (2½, 2½, 3, 3, 3) in. from beg., ending with a p. row.

Shape Raglan Top. Work as for Long Sleeves.

NECKBAND

Using backstitch, join raglan seams, leaving left back raglan seam open. With right side of work facing and No. 12 needles, k. across the 8 (8, 8, 8, 10, 10) sts. on top of Left Sleeve, pick up and k.21 (21, 21, 21, 22, 22) sts. down left side of front neck, k. across the 15 (17, 17, 19, 19, 21) sts. at centre, pick up and k.21 (21, 21, 21, 22, 22) sts. up right side of neck, k. across the 8 (8, 8, 8, 10, 10) sts. on top of Right Sleeve and the 33 (35, 37, 39, 41, 43) sts. on back neck: 106 (110, 112, 116, 124, 128) sts. Work 1 in. in k.1, p.1 rib. Cast off in rib.

TO COMPLETE

Join left back raglan seam and neckband seam. Join side and sleeve seams.

Version 3: in Double Knitting Yarn

BACK

With No. 10 needles, cast on 74 (76, 82, 88, 94, 98) sts. and work 1½ in. in k.1, p.1 rib, ending with a wrong-side row and inc. 1 st. at end of last row: 75 (77, 83, 89, 95, 99) sts.****

Change to No. 8 needles and st.st. (see page 23). Cont. until work measures 9½ (10½, 11½, 12, 12½, 13) in. from the beg., ending with a p. row. Mark each end of last row with a coloured thread.

Shape Raglan Armholes. Dec. 1 st. at each end of the next and every foll. 4th row until 69 (67, 73, 81, 87, 89) sts. remain, then 1 st. at each end of every alt. row until 23 (25, 27, 27, 29, 31) sts. remain, ending with a p. row. Leave these sts. on a stitch holder.

FRONT

Work as Back to ****.

Change to No. 8 needles and patt. thus:

1st row: k.11 (12, 15, 18, 21, 23), *p.2, sl.1, k.1, p.s.s.o., y.fwd., k.3, y.fwd., k.2 tog., p.2, k.10; rep. from * twice, k.1 (2, 5, 8, 11, 13).

2nd row: p.11 (12, 15, 18, 21, 23), *k.2, p.7, k.2, p.10; rep. from * twice, p.1 (2, 5, 8, 11, 13).

3rd row: k.11 (12, 15, 18, 21, 23), *p.2, k.2, y.fwd., sl.1, k.2 tog., p.s.s.o., y.fwd., k.2, p.2, k.10; rep. from * twice, k.1 (2, 5, 8, 11, 13).

4th row: as 2nd row.

These 4 rows form patt. Cont. in patt. until work measures 9½ (10½, 11½, 12, 12½, 13) in. from beg., ending with a wrong-side row. Mark each end of last row with a coloured thread.

Shape Raglan Armholes. Dec. 1 st. at each end of next and every foll. 4th row until 69 (67, 73, 81, 87, 89) sts. remain, then 1 st. at each end of every alt. row until 43 (45, 47, 47, 51, 63) sts. remain, ending with a wrong-side row.

Shape Neck. Next row: k.2 tog., patt. 15 (15, 16, 16, 17, 18) sts.; turn and leave remaining sts. on a stitch holder. Dec. 1 st. at each end of every alt. row until 6 (6, 5, 5, 6, 5) sts. remain. Keeping neck edge straight, cont. to dec. at armhole edge as before until 2 sts. remain. Work 1 row. K.2 tog. and fasten off. Slip the centre 9 (11, 11, 11, 13, 13) sts. on to a stitch holder. Join yarn at neck edge to remaining sts., patt. to last 2 sts., k.2 tog. Complete to match first side of neck.

LONG SLEEVES (make 2 alike)
With No. 10 needles, cast on 40 (42, 44, 46, 48, 50) sts. and work 2½ in. in k.1, p.1 rib, ending with a wrong-side row.
Change to No. 8 needles and st.st. Inc. 1 st. at each end of the 7th and every foll. 7th (8th, 8th, 9th, 10th, 10th) row until there are 56 (58, 62, 64, 66, 70) sts. on the needle. Cont. without further shaping until work measures 11 (12, 13½, 15, 16, 17) in. from beg. ending with a p. row. Mark each end of last row with a coloured thread.
Shape Raglan Top. Dec. 1 st. at each end of the next and every foll. 4th row until 48 (48, 52, 52, 50, 54) sts. remain, then 1 st. at each end of every alt. row until 6 (6, 6, 6, 8, 8) sts. remain, ending with a p. row. Leave these sts. on a safety pin or stitch holder.

SHORT SLEEVES (make 2 alike)
With No. 10 needles cast on 50 (52, 56, 58, 60, 64)

sts. and work ¾ in. in k.1, p.1 rib ending with a wrong-side row.
Change to No. 8 needles and st.st. Inc. 1 st. at each end of every foll. 3rd (3rd, 3rd, 4th, 4th, 4th) row until there are 56 (58, 62, 64, 66, 70) sts. on the needle.
Cont. without further shaping until work measures 2½ (2½, 2½, 3, 3, 3) in. from beg., ending with a p. row. Mark each end of last row with a coloured thread.
Shape Raglan Top. Work as for Long Sleeves.

NECKBAND
Using backstitch, join raglan seams, matching coloured threads. Leave left back raglan seam open. With right side of work facing and with No. 10 needles, k. across the 6 (6, 6, 6, 8, 8) sts. on top of Left Sleeve, pick up and k.18 (18, 18, 19, 19, 19) sts. down left side of front neck, k. across the 9 (11, 11, 11, 13, 13) sts. at centre, pick up and k.18 (18, 18, 19, 19, 19) sts. up right side of neck, k. across the 6 (6, 6, 6, 8, 8) sts. on top of Right Sleeve and the 23 (25, 27, 27, 29, 31) sts. on back neck: 80 (84, 86, 88, 96, 98) sts.
Work 1 in. in k.1, p.1 rib. Cast off in rib.

TO COMPLETE
Join left back raglan seam and neckband seam. Remove coloured threads. Using backstitch, join side and sleeve seams.

Boy's zip-up jacket
– in double knitting or tripleknit yarn, with or without hood
(photographed in black and white on page 120)

MATERIALS
For version 1: 10 (12, 14, 16, 18, 19) balls Emu Scotch Double Knitting *or*, Double Crêpe *or* Bri-Nylon Double Knitting (see note on wools and yarns, page 20). **For version 2:** 12 (14, 16, 18, 20, 21) balls. **For both versions:** one pair each Nos. 8 and 10 knitting needles (see page 26); a 14 (16, 18, 18, 20, 22)-in. open-ended zip fastener.
For version 3: 5 (6, 7, 8, 9, 10) balls Emu Tripleknit (see note on wools and yarns, page 20). **For version 4:** 6 (7, 8, 9, 10, 11) balls. **For both versions:** one pair each Nos. 6 and 8 knitting needles (see page 26); a 14 (16, 18, 18, 20, 22)-in. open-ended zip fastener.

MEASUREMENTS
To fit chest size 24 (27, 29, 31, 33, 34) in.; length at centre back 14½ (16½, 18½, 18½, 20¾, 22½) in.; sleeve seam 11 (12, 13½, 15, 16, 17) in.

TENSION
Double Knitting: 6½ sts. and 8 rows to 1 in. with No. 8 needles. **Tripleknit:** 4½ sts. and 6 rows to 1 in. with No. 6 needles (see note on tension, page 15).

ABBREVIATIONS
See page 26; k.1b., k. into back of st.

Version 1: in Double Knitting Yarn without Hood
BACK
With No. 10 needles cast on 80 (92, 98, 104, 110, 116) sts. and work 10 rows in k.1, p.1 rib inc. 1 st. at end of last row: 81 (93, 99, 105, 111, 117) sts. Change to No. 8 needles.
1st row (right side): k.3, *p.3, k.3; rep. from * to end.

2nd row: p.3, *k.1b., p.1, k.1b., p.3; rep. from * to end.

3rd row: k.3, *p.1, k.1b., p.1, k.3; rep from * to end.

4th row: k.1b., p.1, k.1b., *p.3, k.1b., p.1, k.1b.: rep. from * to end.

5th row: p.3, *k.3, p.3; rep. from * to end.

6th row: as 4th row.

7th row: p.1, k.1b., p.1, *k.3, p.1, k.1b., p.1; rep. from * to end.

8th row: as 2nd row.

These 8 rows form patt.

Cont. in patt. until work measures 8½ (9¾, 11, 10½, 11¾, 12¾) in. from the beg., ending with a wrong-side row.

Shape Raglan Armholes. Keeping continuity of patt. cast off 5 (8, 7, 8, 6, 6) sts. at the beg. of next 2 rows. Dec. 1 st. at each end of the next and every foll. alt. row until 25 (25, 27, 27, 29, 29) sts. remain, ending with a wrong-side row. Leave these sts. on a stitch holder.

LEFT FRONT

With No. 10 needles cast on 42 (48, 54, 54, 60, 60) sts.

1st row (right side): *k.1, p.1; rep. from * to last 4 sts., k.4.

2nd row: k.3, *p.1, k.1; rep. from * to last st., p.1. Rep. the last 2 rows 4 times.

Change to No. 8 needles.

1st row: (right side): k.3, *p.3, k.3; rep. from * to last 3 sts., k.3.

2nd row: k.3, p.3, *k.1b., p.1, k.1b., p.3; rep. from * to end.

3rd row: k.3, *p.1, k.1b., p.1, k.3; rep. from * to last 3 sts., k.3.

4th row: k.3, k.1b., p.1, k.1b., *p.3, k.1b., p.1, k.1b.; rep. from * to end.

5th row: p.3, *k.3, p.3; rep. from * to last 3 sts., k.3.

6th row: as 4th row.

7th row: p.1, k.1b., p.1, *k.3, p.1, k.1b., p.1; rep. from * to last 3 sts., k.3.

8th row: as 2nd row.

Cont. in patt. keeping garter st. border at front edge correct, until work measures same as Back to armhole shaping, ending at side edge.

Shape Raglan Armhole. Keeping continuity of patt. and garter-st. border, cast off 5 (8, 7, 8, 6, 6) sts. at beg. of next row. Work 1 row. Dec. 1 st. at beg. of next and every foll. alt. row until 20 (20, 24, 21, 26, 22) sts. remain, ending at neck edge.

Shape Neck. Next row: patt. 8 (8, 12, 9, 12, 10) sts., slip these sts. on to a stitch holder, patt. remaining sts.

Cont. in patt. dec. 1 st. at each end of next and every

Instructions for this casual style jacket give a range of six different sizes

foll. alt. row until 2 sts. remain, ending with a wrong-side row. Work 2 sts. tog., and fasten off.

RIGHT FRONT

With No. 10 needles, cast on 42 (48, 54, 54, 60, 60) sts.

1st row (right side): k.4, *p.1, k.1; rep. from * to end.

2nd row: p.1, *k.1, p.1; rep. from * to last 3 sts., k.3. Rep. last 2 rows 4 times. Change to No. 8 needles.

1st row (right side): k.3, *k.3, p.3; rep. from * to last 3 sts., k.3.

2nd row: p.3, *k.1b., p.1, k.1b., p.3; rep. from * to last 3 sts., k.3.

These 2 rows set patt.

Complete to match Left Front; cont. to reverse patt. and shapings.

SLEEVES (make 2 alike)

With No. 10 needles, cast on 44 (44, 44, 50, 50, 50) sts. and work 14 rows in k.1, p.1 rib, inc. 1 st. at end of last row: 45 (45, 45, 51, 51, 51) sts.

Change to No. 8 needles and work in patt. as given for Back, inc. and working into patt. 1 st. at each end of the 13th (5th, 5th, 5th, 17th, 5th) and every foll. 12th (8th, 7th, 8th, 6th, 6th) row until there are 55 (61, 69, 75, 81, 87) sts. on the needle.

Cont. without further shaping until Sleeve measures 11 (12, 13½, 15, 16, 17) in. from the beg., ending with a wrong-side row.

Shape Raglan Top. Keeping continuity of patt., cast off 5 (7, 7, 8, 6, 6) sts. at the beg. of the next 2 rows. Dec. 1 st. at each end of the next 2 rows. Dec. 1 st. at each end of the next and every foll. 4th row until 35 (33, 41, 45, 57, 63) sts. remain, ending with a wrong-side row.

Now dec. 1 st. at each end of the next and every foll. alt. row until 7 (7, 9, 9, 9, 9) sts. remain, ending with a wrong-side row. Leave these sts. on a stitch holder.

NECKBAND

Using backstitch, join raglan seams. With right side of work facing, and No. 10 needles, rejoin yarn to inner edge of 8 (8, 12, 9, 12, 10) sts. left on stitch holder on Right Front, pick up and k. 12 sts. up right side of neck, k. across 7 (7, 9, 9, 9, 9) sts. on Right Sleeve, 25 (25, 27, 27, 29, 29) sts. on back neck, 7 (7, 9, 9, 9, 9) sts. on Left Sleeve, pick up and k. 12 sts. down left side of neck, k. across the 8 (8, 12, 9, 12, 10) sts. on stitch holder: 71 (71, 81, 78, 83, 81) sts.

Next row: k.3, *p.1, k.1; rep. from * and work across sts. left on stitch holder on Right Front to last 4 sts., p.1, k.3: 79 (79, 93, 87, 95, 91) sts.

Next row (right side): k.3, *k.1, p.1; rep. from * to last 4 sts., k.4.

Next row: k.3, *p.1, k.1; rep. from * to last 4 sts., p.1, k.3.

Rep. the last 2 rows twice more. Cast off.

TO COMPLETE

Join side and sleeve seams. Sew zip fastener to centre fronts.

Version 2: in Double Knitting Yarn with Hood

Work as for Version 1 but do not cast off sts. of Neckband.

HOOD

Next row: cast off 5 (5, 9, 6, 10, 8) sts., rib to last 4 sts., k. 4.

Next row: cast off 5 (5, 9, 6, 10, 8) sts., rib 5 (5, 8, 8, 8, 8) including st. used in casting off, * inc. 1 st. in next st., rib 1; rep. from * to last 4 (4, 7, 7, 7, 7) sts., rib to end: 99 (99, 105, 105, 105, 105) sts.

Change to No. 8 needles and work 2½ (2½, 2½, 3, 3, 3) in. in patt. as given for Back, ending with a wrong-side row.

Keeping continuity of patt. dec. 1 st. at each end of the next and every foll. alt. row until 93 (93, 99, 99, 99, 99) sts. remain.

Work straight in patt. for 5 (5½, 5½, 6, 6, 6) in. measured from last dec. row.

Shape Top. Next row: patt. 45 (45, 48, 48, 48, 48) sts., work 2 tog.; turn, leaving remaining sts. on a stitch holder.

** Keeping patt. correct, cast off 4 sts. at the beg. of the next and every foll. alt. row until 22 (22, 25, 25, 25, 25) sts. remain. Cast off.** Rejoin yarn to inner edge of remaining sts., patt. to end.

Next row: patt. to end.

Work as for other side from ** to **.

Using backstitch, join top seam. With right side of work facing and with No. 10 needles, pick up and k. 97 (101, 101, 109, 111, 115) sts. round face edge, starting and finishing at inner edge of garter-st. border.

1st row: p.1, *k.1, p.1; rep. from * to end.

2nd row: k.1, *p.1, k.1; rep. from * to end.

Rep. the last 2 rows once.

Next row: p.1, *k.1, p.1; rep. from * to end. Cast off.

TO COMPLETE

Join side and sleeve seams. Sew down Hood ribbing at neck. Sew zip fastener down centre fronts.

Version 3: in Tripleknit Yarn without Hood

BACK

With No. 8 needles, cast on 56 (62, 68, 74, 74, 80) sts. and work 8 rows in k.1, p.1 rib, inc. 1 st. at end of last row: 57 (63, 69, 75, 75, 81) sts.

Change to No. 6 needles.

1st row (right side): k.3, *p.3, k.3; rep. from * to end.

2nd row: p.3, *k.1b., p.1, k.1b., p.3; rep. from * to end.

3rd row: k.3, *p.1, k.1b., p.1, k.3; rep. from * to end.

4th row: k.1b., p.1, k.1b., *p.3, k.1b., p.1, k.1b.; rep. from * to end.

5th row: p.3, *k.3, p.3; rep. from * to end.

6th row: as 4th row.

7th row: p.1, k.1b., p.1, *k.3, p.1, k.1b., p.1; rep. from * to end.

8th row: as 2nd row.

These 8 rows form patt.

Cont. in patt. until work measures 8½ (9¾, 11, 10½, 11¾, 12¾) in. from the beg. ending with a wrong-side row.

Shape Raglan Armholes. Keeping continuity of patt. cast off 3 (4, 4, 5, 1, 2) sts. at the beg. of the next 2 rows. Dec. 1 st. at each end of the next and every foll. alt. row until 17 (17, 19, 19, 21, 21) sts. remain, ending with a wrong-side row. Leave these sts. on a stitch holder.

LEFT FRONT

With No. 8 needles cast on 30 (36, 36, 42, 42, 42) sts.

1st row (right side): *k.1, p.1; rep. from * to last 4 sts., k.4.

2nd row: k.3, *p.1, k.1; rep. from * to last st., p.1. Rep. the last 2 rows 3 times.

Change to No. 6 needles.

1st row (right side): k.3, *p.3, k.3; rep. from * to last 3 sts., k.3.

2nd row: k.3, p.3, *k.1b., p.1, k.1b., p.3; rep. from * to end.

3rd row: k.3, *p.1, k.1b., p.1, k.3; rep. from * to last 3 sts., k.3.

4th row: k.3, k.1b., p.1, k.1b., *p.3, k.1b., p.1, k.1b.; rep. from * to end.

5th row: p.3, *k.3, p.3; rep. from * to last 3 sts., k.3.

6th row: as 4th row.

7th row: p.1, k.1b., p.1, *k.3, p.1, k.1b., p.1; rep. from * to last 3 sts., k.3.

8th row: as 2nd row.

Cont. in patt., keeping garter-st. border correct, until work measures same as Back to armhole shaping, ending at side edge.

Shape Raglan Armhole. Keeping continuity of patt. and garter-st. border, cast off 3 (4, 4, 5, 1, 2) sts. at the beg. of next row. Work 1 row. Dec. 1 st. at beg. of next and every foll. alt. row until 15 (18, 16, 19, 20, 17) sts. remain, ending at neck edge.

Shape Neck. Next row: patt. 5 (8, 6, 9, 10, 7) sts., slip these sts. on to a stitch holder, patt. remaining sts. Cont. in patt. dec. 1 st. at each end of the next and every foll. alt. row until 2 sts. remain, ending with a wrong-side row. Work 2 sts. tog. and fasten off.

RIGHT FRONT

With No. 8 needles cast on 30 (36, 36, 42, 42, 42) sts.

1st row (right side): k.4, *p.1, k.1; rep. from * to end.
2nd row: p.1, *k.1, p.1; rep. from * to last 3 sts., k.3.
Rep. the last 2 rows 3 times.
Change to No. 6 needles.
1st row (right side): k.3, *k.3, p.3; rep. from * to last 3 sts., k.3.
2nd row: p.3, *k.1b., p.1, k.1b., p.3; rep. from * to last 3 sts., k.3.
These 2 rows set patt.
Complete to match Left Front; cont. to reverse patt. and shapings.

SLEEVES (make 2 alike)
With No. 8 needles, cast on 32 (32, 32, 38, 38, 38) sts. and work 12 rows in k.1, p.1 rib, inc. 1 st. at end of last row: 33 (33, 33, 39, 39, 39) sts.
Change to No. 6 needles and work in patt. as given for Back, inc. and working into patt. 1 st. at each end of the 13th (11th, 9th, 11th, 5th, 11th) row and every foll. 15th (9th, 8th, 11th, 8th, 7th) row until there are 39 (43, 47, 51, 57, 61) sts. on the needle.
Cont. without further shaping until sleeve measures 11 (12, 13½, 15, 16, 17) in. from the beg., ending with a wrong-side row.
Shape Raglan Top. Keeping continuity of patt., cast off 3 (4, 4, 5, 1, 2) sts. at the beg. of the next 2 rows. Work 2 rows in patt.
Next row: work 2 sts. tog., patt. to last 2 sts., work 2 sts. tog.
Work 3 rows in patt.
For sizes 24, 27, 29, 31 and 34 only: rep. the last 4 rows until 27 (27, 31, 31, 53) sts. remain.
For all sizes: dec. 1 st. at each end of the next and every foll. alt. row until 7 sts. remain, ending with a wrong-side row.
Leave these sts. on a stitch holder.

NECKBAND
Using backstitch, join raglan seams. With right side of work facing and with No. 8 needles, rejoin yarn to inner edge of sts. left on stitch holder on Right Front, pick up and k. 10 sts. up right side of neck, k. across the 7 sts. on Right Sleeve, 17 (17, 19, 19, 21, 21) sts. on back neck, 7 sts. on Left Sleeve, pick up and k. 10 sts. down left side of neck, k. across the 5 (8, 6, 9, 10, 7) sts. on stitch holder: 56 (59, 59, 62, 65, 62) sts.
Next row: k.3, *p.1, k.1; rep. from * and work across sts. left on stitch holder on Right front to last 4 sts., p.1, k.3: 61 (67, 65, 71, 75, 69) sts.
Next row (right side): k.3, *k.1, p.1; rep. from * to last 4 sts., k.4.

Next row: k.3, *p.1, k.1; rep. from * to last 4 sts., p.1, k.3.
Rep. the last 2 rows once more. Cast off.

TO COMPLETE
Using a backstitch, join side and sleeve seams. Sew in zip fastener to centre fronts.

Version 4: in Tripleknit Yarn with Hood
Work as for Version 3 but do not cast off sts. of Neckband.

HOOD
Next row: cast off 5 (8, 7, 7, 9, 6) sts., rib to last 4 sts., k.4.
Next row: cast off 5 (8, 7, 7, 9, 6) sts., rib 2 (2, 2, 5, 5, 5) including st. used in casting off, * inc. 1 st. in next st., rib 1; rep. from * to last 1 (1, 1, 4, 4, 4) sts., rib to end: 75 (75, 75, 81, 81, 81) sts.
Change to No. 6 needles and work 2½ (2½, 2½, 3, 3, 3) in. in patt. as given for Back, ending with a wrong-side row.
Keeping continuity of patt. dec. 1 st. at each end of the next and every foll. alt. row until 69 (69, 69, 75, 75, 75) sts. remain.
Work straight in patt. for 5 (5½, 5½, 6, 6, 6) in. measured from last dec. row.
Shape Top. Next row: patt. 33 (33, 33, 36, 36, 36) sts., work 2 tog., turn, leaving remaining sts. on a stitch holder.
***Keeping patt. correct, cast off 4 sts. at the beg. of the next and every foll. alt. row until 14 (14, 14, 17, 17, 17) sts. remain.
Cast off. ***
Rejoin yarn to inner edge of remaining sts., patt. to end.
Next row: patt. to end.
Work as for other side from *** to ***.
Using backstitch, join top seam. With right side of work facing and with No. 8 needles, pick up and k.69 (73, 79, 81, 83, 85) sts. round face edge, starting and finishing at inner edge of garter-st. border.
1st row: p.1, *k.1, p.1; rep. from * to end.
2nd row: k.1, *p.1, k.1; rep. from * to end.
Rep. the last 2 rows once more.
Cast off.

TO COMPLETE
Join side and sleeve seams and sew rib edges of hood down at neck. Sew zip fastener to centre fronts.

Chapter 5

Picked for Playtime

Pastel-striped dress

(photographed in colour on page 113)

MATERIALS

7 (8, 8, 9) oz. Lister Lavenda Double Knitting in blue, 1 oz. in purple and 1 oz. in pink (see note on wools and yarns, page 20); one pair each Nos. 9 and 11 knitting needles (see page 26); 3 buttons $\frac{1}{2}$ in. in diameter.

MEASUREMENTS

To fit chest size 22 (24, 26, 28) in.; length 16 (18, 20, 22) in.

TENSION

6 sts. and 8 rows to 1 in. with No. 9 needles (see note on tension, page 15).

ABBREVIATIONS

See page 26; B., blue; Pu., purple; Pk., pink.

FRONT

With No. 9 needles and B., cast on 85 (92, 99, 106) sts.

1st row: k.3, *p.2, k.5; rep. from * to last 5 sts., p.2, k.3.

2nd row: p.3, *k.2, p.5; rep. from * to last 5 sts., k.2, p.3.

These 2 rows form rib patt. Rep. patt. until work measures 7 (8$\frac{1}{2}$, 10, 11$\frac{1}{2}$) in. from beg. ending with a 2nd row.

Still working in rib patt., work stripes thus:

Join Pu., and work 4 rows.

Rejoin B., and work 4 rows.

Join Pk., and work 4 rows.

Rejoin B., and work 4 rows.

Rejoin Pu., and work 4 rows.

Rep. last 16 rows once.

Rejoin B., and work a further 4 rows.

Shape Armholes. Cast off 4 sts. at beg. of next 2 rows, then work 2 sts. tog. at each end of next 8 rows: 61 (68, 75, 82) sts.

Keeping rib patt. correct, cont. straight until work measures 14$\frac{1}{2}$ (16$\frac{1}{2}$, 18$\frac{1}{2}$, 20$\frac{1}{2}$) in. from beg. ending with a 2nd row.

Shape Neck. Next row: patt. 21 (24, 27, 30) sts., k.2 tog.; turn.

Cont. on these sts. working 2 sts. tog. at neck edge on next 7 rows. Work 4 rows straight.

Shape Shoulders. Cast off 5 (6, 7, 8) sts. at beg. of next and foll. 2 alt. rows.

Slip centre 15 (16, 17, 18) sts. on to stitch holder.

Rejoin yarn to remaining 23 (26, 29, 32) sts. and work to match first side, reversing shapings.

BACK

Work as Front until Back measures 13$\frac{1}{2}$ (15$\frac{1}{2}$, 17$\frac{1}{2}$, 19$\frac{1}{2}$) in. from beg., having completed armhole shaping, and ending with a 2nd row.

Divide for Back Opening. Next row: patt. 28 (31, 35, 38) sts., k.4; turn. Work on these sts. only.

Next row: k.4, patt. to end.

Work 4 more rows, keeping border of 4 sts. in garter st. at centre edge.

Next (buttonhole) row: patt. to last 4 sts., k.2 tog., y.r.n., k.2.

Work 13 more rows, keeping garter st. border, making another buttonhole on the 12th row.

Shape Shoulders. Cast off 5 (6, 7, 8) sts. at beg. of next and foll. 2 alt. rows. Work 1 row straight.

Leave remaining 17 (17, 18, 18) sts. on stitch holder.

Rejoin yarn to 29 (33, 36, 40) sts. on left side of back opening, cast on 4 sts., k. these 4 sts., then patt. to end.

Complete to match first side, omitting buttonholes, and reversing shapings.

SLEEVES (make 2 alike)

With No. 11 needles and B., cast on 43 (50, 57, 64) sts. and work 4 rows in k.1, p.1 rib.

Change to No. 9 needles and work in rib patt. as for

Front until work measures 3 in.

Shape Top. Cast off 4 sts. at beg. of next 2 rows then work 2 sts. tog. at beg. of every row until 19 (20, 21, 22) sts. remain. Work 2 sts. tog. at each end of next 6 rows.

Cast off.

NECKBAND

Join shoulder seams. With right side of work facing and with No. 11 needles and B., k. across 17 (17, 18, 18) sts. of left back neck, pick up and k. 13 (14, 13, 14) sts. round left side of front neck, k. across centre 15 (16, 17, 18) sts. of front neck, pick up and k. 14 (14, 14, 14) sts. round right side of front neck and k. across 17 (17, 18, 18) sts. of right back neck: 76 (78, 80, 82) sts.

Work 7 rows in k.1, p.1 rib, keeping two borders of 4 sts. in garter st. at centre back, and making a buttonhole at end of 4th row.

Cast off.

TO COMPLETE

Sew in sleeves, sew side and sleeve seams. Catch down 4 cast-on sts. at bottom of centre back opening. Sew buttons to left side of back opening to match buttonholes.

Pink dress

(photographed in colour on the back cover and in black and white below)

MATERIALS

10 (11, 13) oz. Lee Target Motoravia Double Knitting (see note on wools and yarns, page 20); one pair each Nos. 7, 8 and 10 knitting needles (see page 26); a 4-in. zip fastener.

MEASUREMENTS

To fit chest size 24 (26, 28) in.; length 19 (21, 23) in.

TENSION

$5\frac{1}{2}$ sts. and $7\frac{1}{2}$ rows to 1 in. with No. 8 needles (see note on tension, page 15).

ABBREVIATIONS

See page 26.

BACK

With No. 7 needles cast on 92 (100, 108) sts. and work 3 rows in garter st. (see page 23).

1st row (right side): k.2, *k.6, k.2 tog., y.fwd.; rep. from * to last 2 sts., k.2.

2nd row: k.2, *k.1, y.r.n., p.2 tog., k.5; rep. from * to last 2 sts., k.2.

3rd row: k.2, *k.4, k.2 tog., y.fwd., k.2; rep. from * to last 2 sts., k.2.

4th row: k.2, *k.3, y.r.n., p.2 tog., k.3; rep. from * to last 2 sts., k.2.

5th row: k.2, *k.2, k.2 tog., y.fwd., k.4; rep. from * to last 2 sts., k.2.

6th row: k.2, *k.5, y.r.n., p.2 tog., k.1; rep. from * to last 2 sts., k.2.

7th row: k.2, *k.2 tog., y.fwd., k.6; rep. from * to last 2 sts., k.2.

8th row: k.2, *k.6, p.2 tog. t.b.l., y.o.n.; rep. from * to

Main part of dress is in stocking stitch, sleeves and hemband are patterned

last 2 sts., k.2.

9th row: k.2, *k.1, y.fwd., k.2 tog. t.b.l., k.5; rep. from * to last 2 sts., k.2.

10th row: k.2, *k.4, p.2 tog. t.b.l., y.o.n., k.2; rep. from * to last 2 sts., k.2.

11th row: k.2, *k.3, y.fwd., k.2 tog. t.b.l., k.3; rep. from * to last 2 sts., k.2.

12th row: k.2, *k.2, p.2 tog. t.b.l., y.o.n., k.4; rep. from * to last 2 sts., k.2.

13th row: k.2, *k.5, y.fwd., k.2 tog. t.b.l., k.1; rep. from * to last 2 sts., k.2.

14th row: k.2, *p.2 tog. t.b.l., y.o.n., k.6; rep. from * to last 2 sts., k.2.

The last 14 rows form 1 patt.

Change to No. 8 needles and work 1 patt.

Work 1 more patt., working 2 sts. tog. at each end of first row.

Work 2 rows in garter st., working 2 sts. tog. at each end of first row. Cont. in st.st. working 2 sts. tog. at each end of 5th and every foll. 7th row until 72 (78, 84) sts. remain.

Cont. straight until work measures 12¾ (14½, 16¼) in. ending with a p. row.

Shape Armholes. Cast off 3 (4, 5) sts. at beg. of next 2 rows. Work 2 sts. tog. at each end of next and every alt. row until 56 (60, 64) sts. remain. ** Cont. straight until armholes measure 3½ (3¾, 4) in., ending with a p. row.

Divide for Centre Back Opening. Next row: k.28 (30, 32); turn.

Next row: k.1, p. to end.

Rep. these 2 rows until armhole measures 6¼ (6½, 6¾) in., ending at armhole edge.

Shape Shoulders. Next row: cast off 5 (6, 6) sts., work to end.

Work 1 row straight. Rep. these 2 rows once.

Cast off 6 (5, 6) sts. at beg. of next row.

Work 1 row straight. Cast off remaining 12 (13, 14) sts.

Rejoin yarn to remaining 28 (30, 32) sts. and complete second side to match first.

FRONT

Work as Back to **. Cont. straight until armholes measure 5 (5, 5¼) in. ending with a p. row.

Shape Neck and Shoulders. Next row: k.20 (22, 23); turn.

Work on these sts. only. Work 2 sts. tog. at neck edge on every k. row until 16 (17, 18) sts. remain. Cont. straight until armhole measures same as Back to shoulder shaping, ending at armhole edge.

Cast off 5 (6, 6) sts. at beg. of next and foll. alt. row.

Cast off remaining sts.

Rejoin yarn to remaining 36 (38, 41) sts., cast off 16 (16, 18) sts., then work on remaining stitches and complete to match first side.

SLEEVES (make 2 alike)

With No. 10 needles cast on 52 (52, 54) sts. and work 3 rows in garter st. Change to No. 8 needles and, with right side facing, work in patt. as for Back.

For size 28 only: work an extra k. st. at each end of every row.

For all sizes: inc. 1 st. at each end of 5th and every foll. 6th row (working extra sts. in garter st.) until there are 58 (60, 62) sts. Cont. straight until Sleeve measures 3 in., ending with a wrong-side row.

Shape Top. Keeping patt. correct, cast off 3 (4, 5) sts. at beg. of next 2 rows, then work 2 sts. tog. at each end of every 3rd row until 44 (40, 36) sts. remain, and then at each end of every alt. row until 26 sts. remain. Work 2 sts. tog. at each end of each of next 4 rows. Cast off 3 sts. at beg. of next 2 rows. Cast off.

NECKBAND

Join shoulder seams. With right side of work facing, and with No. 10 needles, pick up and k. 72 (76, 80) sts. evenly round neck and work 5 rows in garter st.

6th row: k.0 (2, 0), *k.2 tog., k.7 (7,8); rep. from * to last 0 (2, 0) sts., k.0 (2, 0).

Work 5 more rows in garter st.

Cast off.

TO COMPLETE

Using backstitch, sew in sleeves, join side and sleeve seams. Sew zip in centre back opening.

Green and yellow dress and jacket

(photographed in colour on page 114)

MATERIALS

14 (16, 17, 19) balls Wendy Courtelle Crêpe 4-ply in green and 4 (5, 5, 6) balls in yellow (see note on wools and yarns, page 20); one pair each Nos. 10, 11 and 12 knitting needles (see page 26); 6 buttons ⅝ in. in diameter; an 8 (8, 10, 10)-in. zip fastener to match yellow yarn.

MEASUREMENTS

To fit chest size 22 (24, 26, 28) in.; length of dress 16 (18, 21, 24) in.; length of jacket 10½ (12½, 15, 16½) in.; jacket sleeve seam 8 (9½, 11, 12) in.

TENSION

7½ sts. and 9½ rows to 1 in over st.st. with No. 11

needles (see note on tension, page 15).

ABBREVIATIONS
See page 26; G., green; Y., yellow.

DRESS
FRONT
With No. 12 needles and G., cast on 109 (109, 121, 121) sts.

Work 7 rows in st.st.

Next row (hem ridge): k.

Change to No. 10 needles and patt.

1st row (right side): p.1, *p.1, k.9, p.2; rep. from * to end.

2nd row: k.1, *k.1, p.9, k.2; rep. from * to end.

3rd row: k.1, *p.2, k.7, p.2, k.1; rep. from * to end.

4th row: p.1, *p.1, k.2, p.5, k.2, p.2; rep. from * to end.

5th row: k.1, *k.2, p.2, k.3, p.2, k.3; rep. from * to end.

6th row: p.1, *p.3, k.2, p.1, k.2, p.4; rep. from * to end.

7th row: k.1, *k.4, p.3, k.5; rep. from * to end.

8th row: p.1, *p.4, k.3, p.5; rep. from * to end.

9th row: k.1, *k.3, p.2, k.1, p.2, k.4; rep. from * to end.

10th row: p.1, *p.2, k.2, p.3, k.2, p.3; rep. from * to end.

11th row: k.1, *k.1, p.2, k.5, p.2, k.2; rep. from * to end.

12th row: p.1, *k.2, p.7, k.2, p.1; rep. from * to end.

These 12 rows form patt. Rep. patt. rows, working 2 sts. tog. at each end of 25th row from hem ridge and every foll. 8th (12th, 12th, 20th) row, until work measures 4 (4, 5, 6) in. from hem ridge.

Change to No. 11 needles and cont. in patt. still dec. until 66 (72, 78, 96) rows from hem ridge have been worked: 97 (101, 111, 113) sts.

Join Y., and work in st.st., dec. as before until 89 (95, 103, 109) sts. remain. **

Work straight until Front measures 11½ (13, 15½, 18) in. from hem ridge, ending with a p. row.

Shape Armholes. Cast off 4 sts. at beg. of next 2 rows then work 2 sts. tog. at each end of next 5 (6, 7, 8) rows and of foll. 2 alt. rows. Work on remaining 67 (71, 77, 81) sts. until armhole measures 3½ (4, 4½, 5) in., ending after a p. row.

Shape Front Neck. K.22 (23, 25, 26); turn.

Work 3 rows on these sts., working 2 sts. tog. at neck edge on each p. row.

Shape Shoulders. Next row: cast off 6 (6, 7, 7) sts., k. to end.

Next row: p.2 tog., p. to end.

Rep. last 2 rows once.

Cast off.

Slip centre 23 (25, 27, 29) sts. on to a stitch holder. Join yarn to remaining 22 (23, 25, 26) sts. and work to match first side, reversing shapings.

BACK
Work as Front to ** then cont. straight until Back measures 8½ (10½, 11½, 14½) in. from hem ridge, ending with a p. row.

Divide for Back Opening. Where necessary cont. to dec. as before at side edge after dividing for back opening until 10 (7, 9, 6) sts. in all have been taken off each side edge.

1st row: patt. until there is 1 st. fewer on right-hand needle than on left; turn.

Next row: k. twice into first st., p. to end.

Cont. in st.st., keeping border of 2 sts. in garter st. at centre edge, until Back measures same as Front to beg. of armhole shaping, ending at side edge: 45 (48, 52, 55) sts.

Shape Armhole. Cast off 4 sts. at beg. of next row then work 2 sts. tog. at side edge on next 5 (6, 7, 8) rows and on foll. 2 alt. rows.

Work remaining 34 (36, 39, 41) sts. until Back measures same as Front to shoulder shaping, ending at side edge.

Shape Shoulders. Cast off 6 (6, 7, 7) sts. at beg. of next and foll. alt. row and 6 (7, 7, 8) sts. at beg. of next alt. row. Leave remaining 16 (17, 18, 19) sts. on stitch holder.

Rejoin yarn to other group of sts. and k. 1 row.

Next row: p. to last 2 sts., k.2.

Now complete to match first side, reversing shapings.

SLEEVES (make 2 alike)
With No. 12 needles and Y., cast on 56 (62, 68, 74) sts. and work 6 rows in k.1, p.1 rib.

Change to No. 11 needles and starting with a k. row work 2 in. in st.st., ending with a p. row.

Shape Top. Cast off 4 sts. at beg. of next 2 rows, then work 2 sts. tog. at beg. of next 6 rows.

Cast off 2 sts. at beg. of foll. 12 (14, 16, 20) rows. Cast off.

NECKBAND
Sew shoulder seams. With right side of work facing, No. 12 needles and Y., start at centre edge of left side of back neck and k. across 16 (17, 18, 19) sts., pick up and k. 11 sts. round left side of front neck, k. across 23 (25, 27, 29) sts. of centre front neck, pick up and k. 11 sts. from right side of front neck and k. across 16 (17, 18, 19) sts. of right back neck: 77 (81, 85, 89) sts.

Work 5 rows in k.1, p.1 rib. Cast off in rib.

TO COMPLETE
Sew zip fastener down centre back opening. Turn up hem at lower edge of skirt and slipstitch in place. Sew in sleeves and join side and sleeve seams.

JACKET
LEFT FRONT (worked from side edge)
With No. 10 needles and G., cast on 21 (21, 33, 33)

sts.

1st row: p.1, (p.1, k.9, p.2) 1 (1, 2, 2) times, k.8.

2nd row: p.7, leave yarn at front and sl.1 purlwise, y.b., k.1, *k.1, p.9, k.2; rep. from * to end; cast on 12 sts.

3rd row: k.1, *p.2, k.7, p.2, k.1; rep. from * to last 8 sts, k.8.

4th row: p.7, leave yarn at front and sl.1 purlwise, p.1, *p.1, k.2, p.5, k.2, p.2; rep. from * to end; cast on 12 sts.

5th row: k.1, *k.2, p.2, k.3, p.2, k.3; rep. from * to last 8 sts, k.8: 45 (45, 57, 57) sts.

6th row: p.7, leave yarn at front and sl.1 purlwise, p.1, *p.3, k.2, p.1, k.2, p.4; rep. from * to end; cast on 0 (12, 12, 18) sts.: 45 (57, 69, 75) sts.

Keeping st.st. border (for hem) as set correct, cont. in patt. as Dress Front skirt until 17 (19, 21, 23) rows from beg. have been worked, ending at hem edge.

Complete Armhole. Next row: patt. to end, cast on 36 (36, 42, 48) sts.: 81 (93, 111, 123) sts. Now work 24 (26, 28, 30) rows in patt., inc. 1 st. at shoulder edge on 8th and 16th (18th, 20th, 20th) rows: 83 (95, 113, 125) sts. ***

Shape Front Neck. Next row: cast off 5 sts., patt. to end.

Patt. 6 rows working 2 sts. tog. at neck edge on every alt. row. Work 10 (12, 14, 16) rows in patt. on remaining 75 (87, 105, 117) sts., ending at hem edge.****

Next row: cast off 8 sts., patt. to end: 67 (79, 97, 109) sts.

Front Band. Change to No. 12 needles and k. 13 rows. Cast off.

RIGHT FRONT (worked from side edge)

Cast on as for Left Front.

1st row: k.8, p.1, (p.1, k.9, p.2) 1 (1, 2, 2) times; cast on 12 sts.

2nd row: k.1, *k.1, p.9, k.2; rep. from * to last 8 sts., y.fwd., sl.1 purlwise, p.7.

Now cont. as for Left Front on these sts. as set, casting on on 3rd and 5th rows, and then reversing shapings, until Right front measures same as Left front to ****.

Front Band. Change to No. 12 needles. **1st row:** cast off 8 sts., k. to end: 67 (79, 97, 109) sts.

2nd-6th rows: k.

Make Buttonholes. Next row: k.7 (9, 17, 19), *k.1, cast off 2, k.9 (11, 13, 15); rep. from * 4 times.

Next row: *k.9 (11, 13, 15), cast on 2, k.1; rep. from * 4 times; k. to end.

K. another 5 rows. Cast off.

BACK (worked from right edge)

Work as Left Front to beg. of neck shaping ***, ending at shoulder edge: 83 (95, 113, 125) sts. Mark this point with a piece of contrasting yarn.

Back of Neck. Work 46 (50, 54, 58) rows in patt.

Mark this point.

Shape Shoulders. Work 24 (26, 28, 30) rows in patt., working 2 sts. tog. at shoulder edge on the 8th (8th, 8th, 10th) row and on the 16th (18th, 20th, 22nd) row: 81 (93, 111, 123) sts.

Shape Armhole. Next row: cast off 36 (36, 42, 48) sts. at beg. of next row: 45 (57, 69, 75) sts.

Patt. 13 (13, 15, 17) rows.

Cast off 12 (12, 12, 18) sts. at beg. of next row and then 12 sts. at beg. of every right-side row until 21 (21, 33, 33) sts. remain. Cast off on next right-side row.

SLEEVES (make 2 alike)

With No. 12 needles and G., cast on 49 sts. and k. 14 rows.

Change to No. 10 needles and patt. as for Dress Front skirt, inc. 1 st. at each end of every 4th (5th, 6th, 7th) row until there are 73 sts.

Cont. straight until 66 (84, 84, 96) patt. rows in all have been worked.

For size 26 only: patt. another 12 rows, inc. 1 st. at each end of every right-side row.

For size 28 only: patt. another 12 rows, inc. 1 st. at each end of every row.

For all sizes. Shape Top. Patt 12 (14, 16, 18) rows. Cast off.

NECKBAND

Sew shoulder seams (contrasting yarn on Back marks end of shoulder seams — remove yarn). With right side facing and with No. 12 needles and G., start at centre edge of Right Front and pick up and k. 19 (20, 21, 22) sts. around neck to shoulder seam, 40 (42, 44, 46) sts. across back of neck and 19 (20, 21, 22) sts. around other side of neck to centre edge of Left Front: 78 (82, 86, 90) sts.

1st row: k.6 (8, 6, 8), *k.2 tog., k.6; rep. from * to last 8 (10, 8, 10) sts., k.2 tog., k. to end: 69 (73, 76, 80) sts.

Make Buttonhole. Next row: k.4; turn.

Work another 4 rows on these 4 sts. Join a separate ball of yarn to the 65 (69, 72, 76) sts. on left-hand needle and k.4 rows on these sts. Break off new yarn and use original yarn to k. these sts. on to the right-hand needle holding 4 sts. K. 2 more rows. Cast off.

TO COMPLETE

Sew side seams. Turn up hem and slipstitch in place. Sew each sleeve seam to within 12 (14, 16, 18) rows of cast-off edge. Place these rows against the horizontal lower edges of armholes on Jacket and sew Sleeves into armholes squarely. Sew buttons on Left Front to correspond with buttonholes on Right Front.

Aran-patterned sweater dress — instructions start on page 130

Polo-necked sweater dress

(photographed in black and white on page 129)

MATERIALS

22 (24, 26, 28) oz. Maggie wool (see note on wools and yarns, page 20); one pair each Nos. 10 and 8 knitting needles (see page 26); one cable needle.

MEASUREMENTS

To fit chest size 26 (28, 30, 32) in.; length 25 (26, 27, 28) in.; sleeve seam 13 (14, 15, 16) in.

TENSION

12 sts. to 2 in. over garter st. with No. 8 needles (see note on tension, page 15).

ABBREVIATIONS

See page 26; k.1b., knit into back of st.; sl.1f., slip next st. on to cable needle and keep at front of work; sl.1b., slip next st. on to cable needle and keep at back of work; tw.2, k. into front of 2nd st. on left-hand needle, then k. into back of first st., slip both off needle tog.; c.4b., slip next 2 sts. on to cable needle and leave at back of work, k. next 2 sts., k. sts. from cable needle; c.4f., slip next 2 sts. on to cable needle and leave at front of work, k. next 2 sts., k. sts. from cable needle; I.M.S., Irish moss stitch; S.H., small honeycomb; C., cable; D., diamond.

IRISH MOSS STITCH PATTERN

1st row: (k.1, p.1) 2 (3, 4, 5) times.
2nd row: (k.1, p.1) 2 (3, 4, 5) times.
3rd row: (p.1, k.1) 2 (3, 4, 5) times.
4th row: (p.1, k.1) 2 (3, 4, 5) times.

SMALL HONEYCOMB PATTERN

1st row: p.12.
2nd row: (sl.1b., k.1, k.1 from cable needle, sl.1f., k.1, k.1 from cable needle) 3 times.
3rd row: p.12.
4th row: (sl.1f., k.1, k.1 from cable needle, sl.1b., k.1, k.1 from cable needle) 3 times.

CABLE PATTERN

1st row: p.8.
2nd row: c.4b., c.4f.
3rd row: p.8.
4th row: k.8.

DIAMOND PATTERN

1st row: k.7, p.4, k.6.
2nd row: p.6, k.2b., sl.2f., p.1, k.2b. from cable needle, p.6.
3rd row: k.6, p.2, k.1, p.2, k.6.
4th row: p.5, sl.1b., k.2b., p.1 from cable needle, k.1, sl.2f., p.1, k.2b. from cable needle, p.5.

5th row: k.5, p.2, k.1, p.1, k.1, p.2, k.5.
6th row: p.4, sl.1b., k.2b., p.1 from cable needle, k.1, p.1, k.1, sl.2f., p.1, k.2b. from cable needle, p.4.
7th row: k.4, p.2, (k.1, p.1) twice, k.1, p.2, k.4.
8th row: p.3, sl.1b., k.2b., p.1 from cable needle, (k.1, p.1) twice, k.1, sl.2f., p.1, k.2b. from cable needle, p.3.
9th row: k.3, p.2, (k.1, p.1) 3 times, k.1, p.2, k.3.
10th row: p.2, sl.1b., k.2b., p.1 from cable needle, (k.1, p.1) 3 times, k.1, sl.2f., p.1, k.2b. from cable needle, p.2.
11th row: k.2, p.2, (k.1, p.1) 4 times, k.1, p.2, k.2.
12th row: p.2, sl.2f., p.1, k.2b. from cable needle, (p.1, k.1) 3 times, p.1, sl.1b., k.2b., p.1 from cable needle, p.2.
13th row: as 9th row.
14th row: p.3, sl.2f., p.1, k.2b. from cable needle, (p.1, k.1) twice, p.1, sl.1b., k.2b., p.1 from cable needle, p.3.
15th row: as 7th row.
16th row: p.4, sl.2f., p.1, k.2b. from cable needle, p.1, k.1, p.1, sl.1b., k.2b., p.1 from cable needle, p.4.
17th row: as 5th row.
18th row: p.5, sl.2f., p.1, k.2b. from cable needle, p.1, sl.1b., k.2b., p.1 from cable needle, p.5.
19th row: as 3rd row.
20th row: p.6, sl.3f., k.2b., k.2b. from cable needle, p.1 from cable needle, p.6.

BACK

With No. 10 needles cast on 86 (90, 94, 98) sts. and work 6 rows in k.1b., p.1 rib.
Next row: k., inc. 11 sts. evenly across row: 97 (101, 105, 109) sts. Change to No. 8 needles.
1st row: work first row of I.M.S. patt., *k.2, p.2, k.2, work first row of S.H. patt., k.2, p.2, k.2*, work first row of C. patt., k.2, p.2, work first row of D. patt., p.2, k.2, C. patt. 8 (first row); rep. from * to *, I.M.S. patt. 4 (6, 8, 10) (first row).
2nd row: I.M.S. patt. 4 (6, 8, 10) (2nd row), *p.2, tw.2, p.2, S.H. patt. 12 (2nd row), p.2, tw.2, p.2*, C. patt. 8 (2nd row), p.2, tw.2, D. patt. 17 (2nd row), tw.2, p.2, C. patt. 8; rep. from * to *, I.M.S. patt. 4 (6, 8, 10). Cont. in patts. as set until work measures 18 (19, 20, 21) in., or desired length, to armholes allowing for a 1-in. drop, ending with right side facing.
Shape Armholes. Cast off 6 sts. at beg. of next 2 rows.
Shape Raglan. 1st row: k.1, sl.1, k.1, p.s.s.o., patt.

Matching sweater and jacket, Aran style — instructions start on page 133

to last 3 sts., k.2 tog., k.1.
2nd row: k.1, p.1, patt. to last 2 sts., p.1, k.1.
Rep. last 2 rows until 31 (33, 33, 35) sts. remain.
Leave sts. on stitch holder.

FRONT
Work as Back until armholes measure 5 (5¼, 5½, 5¾) in., ending with right side facing.
Shape Neck. Next Row: patt. to centre 13 sts.; place centre sts. on stitch holder; turn and work left side of neck.
Dec. 1 st. at neck edge on every row 9 (10, 10, 11) times, and at the same time cont. to dec. at armhole edge, until all sts. are worked off.
Work right side of neck to match left.

SLEEVES (make 2 alike)
With No. 10 needles cast on 40 (40, 42, 42) sts. Work 2½ in. in k.1b., p.1 rib.
Next row: k., inc. 6 sts. evenly across row: 46 (46, 48, 48) sts.
Change to No. 8 needles.
1st row: k.1 (1, 2, 2), S.H. patt. 12 (first row), k.2, p.2, k.2, C. patt. 8, k.2, p.2, k.2, S.H. patt. 12, k.1 (1, 2, 2).
2nd row: p.1 (1, 2, 2), S.H. patt. 12 (2nd row), p.2, tw.2, p.2, C. patt. 8, p.2, tw.2, p.2, S.H. patt. 12, p.1 (1, 2, 2).

Now cont. in patts. as set, inc. 1 st. at beg. and end of next and every foll. 4th row until there are 64 (68, 72, 76) sts. and sleeve measures 13 (14, 15, 16) in. or desired length to armholes. Work inc. sts. in I.M.S. patt. as sides of Back.
Shape Top. Cast off 6 sts. at beg. of next 2 rows. Now work first and 2nd rows of Back raglan shaping until 2 sts. remain. Leave on safety pin.

POLO COLLAR
With right side facing and No. 10 needles, k. 31 (33, 33, 35) sts. from back of neck, k.2 sts. from top of left sleeve, pick up and k.18 (19, 20, 21) sts. from left side of front neck, k.13 centre sts. from stitch holder, pick up and k.18 (19, 20, 21) sts. from right side of front neck, k.2 sts. from top of right sleeve. Work 1 in. in k.1b., p.1 rib. Change to No. 8 needles and cont. in rib for a further 4 in. Cast off in rib.

BELT
With No. 10 needles cast on 10 sts. and work 56 (58, 60, 62) in. or required length in k.1b., p.1 rib. Cast off.

TO COMPLETE
Set in sleeves and sew side of polo collar. Fold collar in half on to right side.
Join side and sleeve seams.

Matching Aran sweater and jacket
(photographed in colour on page 131 and in black and white on page 134)

MATERIALS
For sweater: 16 (18, 20, 22) oz. Maggie wool (see note on wools and yarns, page 20). **For jacket:** 18 (20, 22, 24) oz. of Maggie wool; 6 buttons ¾ in. in diameter. **For both:** one pair each Nos. 8 and 10 knitting needles (see page 26); one cable needle.

MEASUREMENTS
To fit chest size 26 (28, 30, 32) in.; length 16½ (18, 19½, 21) in.; sleeve seam 14 (15, 16, 17) in.

TENSION
12 sts. to 2 in. over garter st. with No. 8 needles (see note on tension, page 15).

ABBREVIATIONS
See page 26; I.M.S., Irish moss stitch; C., cable; D., diamond; H., honeycomb; k.1b., knit into back of st., p.1b., purl into back of st.; c.4b., slip next 2 sts. on to cable needle and put to back of work, k. next 2

Opposite: pinafore, jumper and socks in red, white and navy (see page 141)

sts., then k. 2 sts. from cable needle; sl.1f., slip 1 st. on to cable needle and keep to front of work; sl.1b., slip 1 st. on to cable needle and keep to back of work.

IRISH MOSS STITCH PATTERN
1st row: (k.1, p.1) 1 (2, 3, 4) times.
2nd row: (k.1, p.1) 1 (2, 3, 4) times.
3rd row: (p.1, k.1) 1 (2, 3, 4) times.
4th row: (p.1, k.1) 1 (2, 3, 4) times.

CABLE PATTERN
1st row: p.4.
2nd row: k.4.
3rd row: p.4.
4th row: c.4b.

DIAMOND PATTERN
1st row: k.6, p.2, k.5.
2nd row: p.5, k.1b., sl.1f., p.1, k.1b. from cable needle, p.5.
3rd row: k.5, p.1, k.1, p.1, k.5.
4th row: p.4, sl.1b., k.1b., p.1 from cable needle,

k.1, sl.1f., p.1, k.1b. from cable needle, p.4.
5th row: k.4, (p.1, k.1) twice, p.1, k.4.
6th row: p.3, sl.1b., k.1b., p.1 from cable needle, k.1, p.1, k.1, sl.1f., p.1, k.1b. from cable needle, p.3.
7th row: k.3, (p.1, k.1) 3 times, p.1, k.3.
8th row: p.2, sl.1b., k.1b., p.1 from cable needle, (k.1, p.1) twice, k.1, sl.1f., p.1, k.1b. from cable needle, p.2.
9th row: k.2, (p.1, k.1) 4 times, p.1, k.2.
10th row: p.1, sl.1b., k.1b., p.1 from cable needle, (k.1, p.1) 3 times, k.1, sl.1f., p.1, k.1b. from cable needle, p.1.
11th row: k.1, (p.1, k.1) 5 times, p.1, k.1.
12th row: p.1, sl.1f., p.1, k.1b. from cable needle, (p.1, k.1) 3 times, p.1, sl.1b., k.1b., p.1 from cable needle, p.1.
13th row: as 9th row.
14th row: p.2, sl.1f., p.1, k.1b. from cable needle, (p.1, k.1) twice, p.1, sl.1b., k.1b., p.1 from cable needle, p.2.
15th row: as 7th row.
16th row: p.3, sl.1f., p.1, k.1b. from cable needle, p.1, k.1, p.1, sl.1b., k.1b., p.1 from cable needle, p.3.
17th row: as 5th row.
18th row: p.4, sl.1f., p.1, k.1b. from cable needle, p.1, sl.1b., k.1b., p.1 from cable needle, p.4.
19th row: as 3rd row.
20th row: p.5, sl.2b., k.1b., k.1b. from cable needle, p.1 from cable needle, p.5.

HONEYCOMB PATTERN (24 sts., except sleeves and jacket fronts, 16 sts.)
1st row: p.24.
2nd row: (sl.2b., k.2, k.2 sts. from cable needle, sl.2f., k.2, k.2 sts. from cable needle) 3 times.
3rd row: p.24.
4th row: k.24.
5th row: p.24.
6th row: (sl.2f., k.2, k.2 sts. from cable needle, sl.2b., k.2, k.2 sts. from cable needle) 3 times.
7th row: p.24.
8th row: k.24.

SWEATER
BACK
With No. 10 needles cast on 76 (80, 84, 88) sts. and work 12 rows in k.1b., p.1 rib.
Next row: k.10 (12, 10, 12), *k. twice into next st., k.7 (7, 8, 8); rep. from * 6 times, k. twice into next st., k.9 (11, 10, 12): 84 (88, 92, 96) sts.
Change to No. 8 needles.
1st row: work first row of I.M.S. patt., k.2, p.1b., *k.2, work first row of C. patt., work first row of D. patt., work first row of C. patt., k.2*, work first row of H. patt.; rep. from * to *, p.1b., k.2, I.M.S. patt. 2 (4, 6, 8) (first row).
2nd row: I.M.S. patt. 2 (4, 6, 8) (2nd row), p.2, k.1b., *p.2, C. patt. 4 (2nd row), D. patt. 13 (2nd

row), C. patt. 4, p.2*, H. patt. 24; rep. from * to *, k.1b., p.2, I.M.S. patt. 2 (4, 6, 8).
Cont. working in patts. as set until work measures 10 (11, 12, 13) in. ending with right side of work facing.
Shape Armholes. Cast off 2 (3, 3, 4) sts. at beg. of next 2 rows.
Shape Raglan. 1st row: k.1, sl.1, k.1, p.s.s.o., patt. to last 3 sts., k.2 tog., k.1.
2nd row: k.1, p.1, patt. to last 2 sts., p.1, k.1.
Rep. last 2 rows 19 times.
Next row: k.1, sl.1, k.2 tog., p.s.s.o., patt. to last 4 sts., k.3 tog., k.1.
Next row: as 2nd row of raglan shaping.
Rep. last 2 rows until 26 (26, 28, 28) sts. remain.
Leave sts. on stitch holder.

FRONT
Work as Back until armholes measure 3¾ (4, 4¼, 4½) in., ending with right side facing.
Next row: patt. to centre 12 sts.; turn and work left side of neck. Dec. 1 st. at neck edge on every row 7 (7, 8, 8) times, and at the same time cont. to dec. at armhole edge until all sts. are worked off.
Slip centre 12 sts. on to a stitch holder or safety pin. Work right side of neck to match left.

SLEEVES (make 2 alike)
With No. 10 needles, cast on 36 (38, 40, 42) sts. and work 14 rows in k.1b., p.1 rib.
Next row: k.4 (5, 6, 7), *k. twice into next st., k.2; rep. from * 8 times, k. twice into next st., k.4 (5, 6, 7): 46 (48, 50, 52) sts. Change to No. 8

needles.
First row: p.1 (2, 3, 4), k.2, H. patt. 16, k.2, C. patt. 4, k.2, H. patt. 16, k.2, p.1 (2, 3, 4). Cont. in patts. as set, inc. 1 st. at beg. and end of next and every foll. 6th row until there are 68 (72, 76, 80 sts. and sleeve measures 14 (15, 16, 17) in. Use p. sts. at sides for C. patt. as soon as inc. permits then work inc. in I.M.S. patt. as on sides of Back.
Shape Top. Work as for Back until 6 sts. remain. Leave on a safety pin.

NECKBAND
With right side facing and No. 10 needles, k.26 (26, 28, 28) sts. from back of neck, k. 6 sts. from top of left sleeve, pick up and k.9 (10, 11, 12) sts. down left side of neck, k. 12 sts. from stitch holder or safety pin, pick up and k.9 (10, 11, 12) sts. from right side of neck and k. 6 sts. from top of right sleeve.
Work 16 rows in k.1b., p.1 rib. Cast off loosely in rib.

TO COMPLETE
Set in sleeves and sew side of neckband. Join side and sleeve seams. Fold neckband in half on to wrong side and slipstitch down.

JACKET
BACK AND SLEEVES
Work as for Back and Sleeves of Sweater.

POCKET LININGS (make 2 alike)
With No. 10 needles cast on 21 sts. and work 20 rows in k.1b., p.1 rib.
Leave sts. on a stitch holder.

RIGHT FRONT
With No. 10 needles cast on 38 (40, 42, 44) sts. and work 12 rows in k.1b., p.1 rib.
Next row: k.7 (8, 5, 6), *k. twice into next st., k.2 (2, 3, 3); rep. from * 7 times, k. twice into next st., k.7 (8, 5, 6): 47 (49, 51, 53) sts.
Change to No. 8 needles.**
1st row: I.M.S. patt. 2 (4, 6, 8), k.2, p.1b., k.2, C. patt. 4, D. patt. 13, C. patt. 4, k.2, H. patt. 16, k.1.
Now work in patts. as set. and k. 1 st. at front edge on every row. Cont. until 20 rows have been com-
pleted.
Next row: patt. 7 (9, 11, 13) sts., slip next 21 sts. on to stitch holder, patt. 21 sts. of one pocket lining, patt. to end.
Cont. until work measures same as Back to armholes.
Shape Armhole. Work armhole as given for left side of Sweater Back. Cont. until armhole measures 4 (4¼, 4½, 4¾) in.
Shape Neck. Dec. 1 st. at neck edge on every row 18 (18, 19, 19) times, and at the same time cont. dec. at armhole edge until all sts. are worked off.

LEFT FRONT
Work as Right Front to **.
Next row: k.1, H. patt. 16, k.2, C. patt. 4, D. patt. 13, C. patt. 4, k.2, p.1b., k.2, I.M.S. patt. 2 (4, 6, 8). Cont. as Right Front, reversing shapings.

FRONT BANDS
Right Band. With No. 10 needles cast on 8 sts. and work 4 rows in k.1b., p.1 rib.
1st buttonhole row: rib 3, cast off 2 sts., rib 3.
2nd buttonhole row: rib 3, cast on 2 sts., rib 3.
Work 5 more buttonholes in this way at 2¼ (2½, 2¾, 3) in. intervals. Work 2 rows in rib after last buttonhole and leave sts. on safety pin.
Left Band. Work as right band, omitting buttonholes.

COLLAR
With right side facing and with No. 10 needles, rib across 8 sts. of right band, pick up and k.17 (18, 19, 20) sts. from right front neck, k. 6 sts. from top of right sleeve, k.26 (26, 28, 28) from back of neck, k. 6 sts. from top of left sleeve, pick up and k.17 (18, 19, 20) sts. from left front neck and rib 8 sts. of left band. Now work 4 (4¼, 4½, 4¾) in. in k.1b., p.1 rib. Cast off in rib.

TO COMPLETE
Set in sleeves. Sew side and sleeve seams.
Pockets. With No. 10 needles work 6 rows in k.1b., p.1 rib on pocket tops. Sew around pocket linings and sides of pocket tops.
Bands. Join right and left bands to Fronts. Sew buttons on to left band to match buttonholes.

Cowboy sweater
(photographed in black and white on page 136)

MATERIALS
8 (8, 9) hanks (2-oz.) Hayfield Brig (see note on wools and yarns, page 20); one pair each Nos. 9 and 11 knitting needles (see page 26); one crochet hook approx. International Standard Size 4·00.

MEASUREMENTS
To fit chest size 26 (28, 30) in.

TENSION
5 sts. and 7 rows to 1 in. with No. 9 needles (see

note on tension, page 15).

ABBREVIATIONS
See page 26.

BACK
With No. 11 needles cast on 70 (76, 82) sts. and work 2 (2½, 3) in. in k.1, p.1 rib.
Change to No. 9 needles and work in st.st. (see page 00) until Back measures 10½ (11½, 12½) in., ending with a p. row.
Shape Armholes. Next row: cast off 5 sts., k. to end.
Yoke Ridge. Next row: Cast off 5 sts., k. to end.**
Now cont. in st.st. beg. with a k. row, and working 2 sts. tog. at each end of every k. row until 52 (56, 60) sts. remain.
Cont. straight until work measures 6 (6½, 7) in. from beg. of armhole shaping, ending with a p. row.
Shape Shoulders. Cast off 8 sts. at beg. of next 2 rows and 7 (8, 9) sts. at beg. of next 2 rows.
Leave remaining 22 (24, 26) sts. on a stitch holder.

FRONT
Work as Back to **.
Next row: k.2 tog., k.28 (31, 34); turn.
Next row: k.2, p. to end.
Make Holes for Lacing. Next row: k.2 tog., k. to last 6 sts., y.fwd., k.2 tog., k. to end.
Cont. on these sts. keeping border of 2 sts. in garter st. at centre edge, and working 2 sts. tog. at armhole edge on alt. rows until 26 (28, 30) sts. remain, and at the same time making a lacing hole on every 7th (8th, 8th) row until 4 in all are made. Cont. until work measures 5 (5½, 5¾) in. from yoke ridge, ending with a k. row.
Next row: k.2, p.3, slip these 5 sts. on to a safety pin or stitch holder, p. to end. Now work 2 sts. tog. at neck edge on every row until 15 (16, 17) sts. remain. Cont. until armhole measures 6 (6½, 7) in., ending with a p. row.
Shape Shoulder. Cast off 8 sts. at beg. of next row. Work 1 row straight. Cast off.
Rejoin yarn to remaining 30 (33, 36) sts. and com-

plete to match first side, reversing shapings.

SLEEVES (make 2 alike)
With No. 11 needles cast on 34 (36, 40) sts. and work 2 (2½, 3) in. in k.1, p.1 rib.
Change to No. 9 needles.
Next row: k.16 (17, 19), p.2, k. to end.
Next row: p.16 (17, 19), k.2, p. to end.
Rep. these 2 rows, keeping centre panel of 2 sts. in garter st., and at the same time inc. 1 st. at each end of every 7th row until there are 52 (56, 60) sts., ending with a p. row.
Shape Top. Cast off 5 sts. at beg. of next 2 rows and then work 2 sts. tog. at beg. of every row until 28 sts. remain, then work 2 sts. tog. at each end of every row until 18 sts. remain.
Work 4 rows without shaping. Cast off.

COLLAR
Join shoulder seams. With right side of work facing and No. 11 needles, k. 5 sts. at right side of front neck, pick up and k. 15 (15, 17) sts. round right side of neck, k. across 22 (24, 26) sts. of back neck, pick up and k. 15 (15, 17) sts. round left side of neck and k. across 5 sts. at left side of neck: 62 (64, 70) sts.
1st row: k.2, k. twice into next st., k. to last 3 sts., k. twice into next st., k.2.
2nd row: k. 2, p. to last 2 sts., k.2.
Now rep. these 2 rows until there are 72 (82, 88) sts., ending with a first row, k. 2 rows. Cast off.

TO COMPLETE
Sew in sleeves and join side and sleeve seams.
Fringe. Make fringe down centre panel of sleeves and across back and front yoke ridges. Cut yarn into 6-in. lengths. Use 2 lengths of yarn together and double in half. Slip crochet hook through 1 st. of ridge, put looped end of yarn over hook and draw through loop. Slip ends of yarn through loop and draw up tightly. Work 1 loop into each st. of ridges.
Lacing. Make lacing either by working a length of crochet chain (see page 24) or by plaiting 3 strands of yarn. It should be about 3½ ft. long. Thread through lacing holes.

Cowboy sweater is worked mainly in simple stocking stitch, with fringing and lace-up front fastening added afterwards

Check dress
(photographed in black and white on page 138)

MATERIALS
7 (8, 9) oz. Paton's Totem Double Knitting in 1st colour and 4 (5, 6) oz. in 2nd colour (see note on wools and yarns, page 20); one pair each Nos. 8 and 10 knitting needles (see page 26); 2 small and 4 medium-sized ball buttons; a 4-in zip fastener.

MEASUREMENTS

To fit chest size 22 (24, 26) in.; length 17½ (19½, 21) in.; sleeve seam 9½ (10½, 11½) in.

TENSION

6 sts. to 1 in. with No. 8 needles (see note on tension, page 15).

ABBREVIATIONS

See page 26.

BACK

With No. 8 needles and 1st colour cast on 92 (96, 100) sts.

Work 1 in. in garter st. (every row k.).

Join 2nd colour and start patt.

1st row: * with 2nd colour k.4, with 1st colour k.4; rep. from * to last 4 (0, 4) sts., with 2nd colour k.4 (0, 4).

For sizes 22 and 26 only. 2nd row: * with 2nd colour p.4, with 1st colour p.4; rep. from * to last 4 sts., with 2nd colour p.4.

For size 24 only. 2nd row: *with 1st colour p.4, with 2nd colour p.4; rep. from * to end.

For all sizes. Rep. last 2 rows once.

5th row: *with 1st colour k.4, with 2nd colour k.4; rep. from * to last 4 (0, 4) sts., with 1st colour k.4 (0, 4).

For sizes 22 and 26 only. 6th row: *with 1st colour p.4, with 2nd colour p.4; rep. from * to last 4 sts., with 1st colour p.4.

For size 24 only. 6th row: *with 2nd colour p.4, with 1st colour p.4; rep. from * to end.

For all sizes. Rep. last 2 rows once.

These 8 rows form patt.

Rep. patt. until work measures 3 in., ending with a p. row.

Work 2 sts. tog. at each end of next row and at 1-in. intervals until 74 (74, 80) sts. remain.

Cont. straight until work measures 11¾ (13½, 14¾) in., ending with a p. row.

Shape Armholes. Keeping patt. correct, cast off 3 sts. at beg. of next 2 rows, then work 2 sts. tog. at each end of every k. row until 60 (64, 66) sts. remain **. Cont. straight until armholes measure 1¼ (1½, 1¾) in. ending with a p. row.

Next row: patt. 28 (30, 31) sts., with 1st colour k.2; turn and work on these sts. only.

Next row: with 1st colour k.2, patt. to end.

Rep. these 2 rows until armhole measures 5¼ (5½, 5¾) in., ending with a p. row.

Cast off 7 sts. at beg. of next row. Work 1 row straight. Cast off 7 (8, 9) sts. at beg. of next row.

Buttoned side tabs and collar tips add a pretty finishing touch to this long-sleeved check dress

Leave remaining 16 (17, 17) sts. on stitch holder. Rejoin yarn to remaining 30 (32, 33) sts., and complete to match first side reversing shapings.

FRONT

Work as Back to **. Cont. straight until armholes measure 4 (4, 4¼) in., ending with a p. row.

Next row: patt. 20 (21, 22) sts., k.2 tog.; turn. Work on these sts. only in patt., working 2 sts. tog. at neck edge on every row until 14 (15, 16) sts. remain. Cont. straight until armhole measures 5¼ (5½, 5¾) in., ending with a p. row.

Cast off 7 sts. at beg. of next row, work 1 row straight; cast off.

Slip centre 16 (18, 18) sts. on to stitch holder.

Rejoin yarn to remaining 22 (23, 24) sts. and complete to match first side, reversing shapings.

SLEEVES (make 2 alike)

With No. 10 needles and 1st colour, cast on 36 (40, 44) sts. and work ¾ (¾, 1) in. in garter st.

Change to No. 8 needles and work patt. as for Back, inc. 1 st. at each end of every 5th row until there are 54 (58, 60) sts. Cont. straight until work measures 9½ (10½, 11½) in., ending with a p. row.

Shape Armholes. Cast off 3 sts. at beg. of next 2 rows. Work 2 sts. tog. at beg. of every row until 36 (38, 40) sts. remain, then at each end of every row until 16 (18, 16) sts. remain. Cast off.

COLLAR

Join Front and Back at shoulders. With No. 10 needles and 1st colour and with right side of work facing, k. across 16 (17, 17) sts. of left back neck, pick up and k. 13 (14, 15) sts. down left side of front neck, k. across 8 (9, 9) of centre sts.: 37 (40, 41 sts.

Work in garter st., inc. 1 st. at each end of next and every alt. row until there are 55 (60, 65) sts. Cast off. Work other side of Collar to match.

SIDE TABS (make 2 alike)

With No. 10 needles and 1st colour, cast on 40 (42, 46) sts. Work 1 k. row.

Now work in garter st., inc. 1 st. at each end of next and every alt. row until there are 52 (54, 60) sts.

Work 1 row straight. Now work 2 sts. tog. at each end of next and every alt. row until there are 40 (42, 46) sts. Cast off.

TO COMPLETE

Sew in sleeves and join side and sleeve seams. Place tabs round sides at hip level (see photograph opposite) and stitch points to dress. Stitch a medium-sized button to each point of each tab. Turn collar down and stitch front points to dress. Sew one small button to each front point. Sew zip down centre back opening.

Zipped sweater dress

(photographed in black and white on page 165)

MATERIALS

14 (15, 16, 18) oz. of Wendy Nylonised Double Knitting (see note on wools and yarns, page 20); one pair each Nos. 8, 9, 10 and 11 knitting needles (see page 26); a 12 (12, 14, 16)-in. zip fastener.

MEASUREMENTS

To fit chest size 24 (26, 28, 30) in.; length 18 (20, 23, 26) in.; length of sleeve seam 9 (10½, 12, 13½) in.

TENSION

6 sts. to 1 in. over bodice patt. with No. 8 needles (see note on tension, page 15).

ABBREVIATIONS

See page 26.

FRONT

With No. 11 needles cast on 88 (96, 100, 108) sts. and k. 5 rows.

6th row (hem ridge): k.

Change to No. 9 needles and k. 2 rows.

Skirt Patt. 1st row (right side): k.

2nd row: p.

3rd-6th rows: k.

These 6 rows form skirt patt. Rep. 6 skirt patt. rows 6 (9, 11, 13) times.

Change to No. 10 needles and cont. in patt. until work measures 6 (8, 9, 10) in. from hem ridge, ending after a 6th patt. row.

Change to No. 8 needles.

Divide for Front Opening. Next row: k.44 (48, 50, 54); turn.

Bodice Patt. 1st row (wrong side): k.2, *p.3, k.2; rep. from * to last 2 (1, 3, 2) sts., p. to end.

2nd row: k.

These last 2 rows form bodice patt. Rep. 2 bodice patt. rows working 2 sts. tog. at side edge on 5th and every foll. 9th (7th, 11th, 11th) row until 39 (42, 45, 48) sts. remain. Work straight until Front measures 13 (14½, 17, 19½) in. from hem ridge, ending at side edge.

Shape Armhole. Keeping patt. correct, cast off 3 sts. at beg. of next row, then work 2 sts. tog. at side edge on next 4 (5, 6, 7) rows and then on foll. 2 alt. rows. Work straight in patt. on remaining 30 (32, 34, 36) sts. until armhole measures 4 (4½, 5, 5½) in., ending at side edge.

Shape Neck and Shoulders. Next row: patt. 21 (22, 23, 24) sts.; turn and leave remaining 9 (10, 11, 12) sts. on stitch holder.

Patt. 3 rows, working 2 sts. tog. at neck edge on every row.

Next row: cast off 5 (5, 6, 6) sts., patt. to end.

Next row: work 2 sts. tog., patt. to end.

Rep. last 2 rows once. Cast off.

Rejoin yarn to remaining 44 (48, 50, 54) sts. for other side of bodice.

Next row: k.

Bodice Patt. 1st row (wrong side): p.2 (1,3,2) sts., *k.2, p.3; rep. from * to last 2 sts., k.2.

2nd row: k.

Work to match first side, reversing shapings.

BACK

Work as Front to beg. of front opening.

For size 28 only: inc. 1 st. at end of last row.

For all sizes: change to No. 8 needles.

Next row: k.

Bodice Patt. 1st row (wrong side): p.3 (2, 2, 3); *k.2, p.3; rep. from * to last 5 (4, 4, 5) sts., k.2, p. to end.

2nd row: k.

Keeping bodice patt. correct as set, cont. in patt. working 2 sts. tog. at each end of 5th and every foll. 9th (7th, 11th, 11th) row until 78 (84, 91, 96) sts. remain. Work straight until Back matches Front to beg. of armholes.

Shape Armholes. Keeping patt. correct, cast off 3 sts. at beg. of next 2 rows, then work 2 sts. tog. at each end of next 4 (5, 6, 7) rows and then on foll. 2 alt. rows. Work straight on remaining 60 (64, 69, 72) sts. until Back matches Front to beg. of shoulders.

Shape Shoulders. Cast off 5 (5, 6, 6) sts. at beg. of next 4 rows and 6 (7, 6, 7) sts. at beg. of next 2 rows. Leave remaining 28 (30, 33, 34) sts. on stitch holder.

SLEEVES (make 2 alike)

With No. 11 needles cast on 31 (34, 37, 40) sts. and k. 2 rows. Work 6-row skirt patt. 3 times.

For sizes 26 and 30 only: inc. 1 st. at end of last row.

For all sizes: change to No. 8 needles.

Inc. row: k.1 (2, 1, 2), *k. twice into next st., k.2; rep. from * to end: 41 (46, 49, 54) sts.

1st patt. row (wrong side): p.2 (2, 1, 1), *k.2, p.3; rep. from * to last 4 (4, 3, 3) sts., k.2, p. to end.

2nd patt. row: k.

Cont. in patt. and, keeping patt. correct, inc. 1 st. at each end of every 5th row until there are 51 (58, 63, 64) sts. Cont. straight until work measures 9 (10½, 12, 13½) in., ending after first patt. row.

Shape Top. Cast off 3 sts. at beg. of next 2 rows, then work 2 sts. tog. at each end of next 6 (8, 8, 8) rows and 2 sts. at beg. of foll. 10 (12, 14, 14) rows.

Cast off.

NECKBAND

Sew shoulder seams. With right side of work facing and with No. 10 needles, k. across 9 (10, 11, 12) sts. of right side of Front, pick up and k. 9 sts. from right side of front neck, k. across 28 (30, 33, 34) sts. of back neck, pick up and k.9 (9, 8, 9) sts. from left side of front neck and k. across 9 (10, 11, 12) sts. of left side of Front: 64 (68, 72, 76) sts.

1st row: k.3, *k.2 tog., k.2; rep. from * to last st., k.1.
2nd-4th rows: k.
5th row: k.2, p. to last 2 sts., k.2.
6th-8th rows: k. Cast off.

TO COMPLETE

Sew in sleeves and join side and sleeve seams. Turn up hem of skirt and slipstitch in position. Sew zip fastener down centre front.

Tassel. Cut a piece of card about 2 in. by 1 in. and wind yarn lengthwise round card about 25 times. Thread a short length of yarn beneath loops at top of card, draw up loops and tie length of yarn to secure. Cut through bottom loops and remove card. Now tie another short length of yarn round tassel about ½ in. from top.
Use ends of yarn drawing up top loops to attach tassel to zip slider.

Pinafore, jumper and socks

(photographed in colour on page 132)

MATERIALS

8 (9, 10, 12, 13) balls Wendy Tricel/Nylon Double Knitting in navy, 15 (16, 19, 20, 21) balls in white and 2 balls in red (see note on wools and yarns, page 20); one pair each Nos. 8, 9, 10 and 11 knitting needles (see page 26); a 10 (12, 14, 16, 18)-in. open-ended zip fastener.

MEASUREMENTS

To fit chest size 24 (26, 28, 30, 32) in.; length of pinafore 18 (20, 23, 26, 28) in.; length of jumper 13 (15, 17, 19, 21) in.; jumper sleeve seam (including 2-in. cuff) 10 (11½, 13, 14½, 16) in.; socks seam (including 2-in. turnover at top) 8 (10, 11½, 12, 12½) in.

TENSION

7½ sts. and 8 rows to 1 in. over ribbed patt. with No. 8 needles (see note on tension, page 15).

ABBREVIATIONS

See page 26; N., navy; W., white; R., red.

PINAFORE
LEFT FRONT

With No. 8 needles and N. cast on 55 (59, 63, 67, 71) sts.

1st row: p.1, *k.3, p.1; rep. from * to last 2 sts., k.2.
2nd row: k.2, *k.1, p.3; rep. from * to last st., k.1.
Rep. these 2 rows 7 times. Keeping the garter st. border of 2 sts. on front edge, cont. in rib working 2 sts. tog. at side edge on next and every foll. 10th (12th, 14th, 18th, 20th) row until 49 (53, 57, 61, 65) sts. remain. Work straight until Front measures 11 (13, 15, 17, 19) in., ending with right side facing.
Shape Front Slope and Armhole Edging. 1st row: k.2, patt. to last 4 sts., p.2 tog., k.2.

2nd row: k.3, p.2, patt. to last 3 sts., k.3.
3rd row: k.4, patt. to last 4 sts., p.2 tog., k.2.
4th row: k.3, p.1, patt. to last 5 sts., k.5.
5th row: k.6, patt. to last 4 sts., p.2 tog., k.2.
6th row: k.3, patt. to last 7 sts., k.7.
Shape Armhole. 7th row: cast off 4 sts., k.3, patt. to last 4 sts., p.2 tog., k.2.
8th row: k.2, patt. to last 4 sts., k.4.
9th row: k.3, k.2 tog., patt. to last 4 sts., p.2 tog., k.2.
10th row: k.2, patt. to last 5 sts., k.2 tog., k.3. Cont. to dec. for front slope at neck edge on every right-side row and at the same time dec. for armhole at side edge by k. tog. 4th and 5th sts. from edge on next 5 (6, 7, 8, 9) rows and on foll. 2 alt. rows. Then, keeping the garter st. border of 4 sts. on side edge correct, work side edge straight but dec. at neck edge on every 4th row until 22 (23, 24, 26, 28) sts. remain. Work straight until Front measures 17½ (19½, 22½, 25½, 27½) in., ending at side edge.
Shape Shoulder. Cast off 6 (7, 7, 8, 8) sts. at beg. of next and foll. alt. row and 8 (7, 8, 8, 10) sts. at beg. of next alt. row. Leave remaining 2 sts. on a safety pin.

RIGHT FRONT

With No. 8 needles and N. cast on 55 (59, 63, 67, 71) sts.

1st row: k.2, *p.1, k.3; rep. from * to last st., p.1.
2nd row: k.1, *p.3, k.1; rep. from * to last 2 sts., k.2.
Now work as Left Front reading rows from end of row to beg. to reverse shapings.

BACK

With No. 8 needles and N., cast on 109 (117, 125, 133, 141) sts.

1st row: p.1, *k.3, p.1; rep. from * to end.
2nd row: k.1, *p.3, k.1; rep. from * to end.

Rep. these 2 rows 7 times. Cont. in patt., working 2 sts. tog. at each end of next and every foll. 10th (12th, 14th, 18th, 20th) row until there are 97 (105, 113, 121, 129) sts. Cont. straight until Back measures same as fronts to beg. of armhole edgings, ending with right side facing.

Armhole Edgings. 1st row: k.2, patt. to last 2 sts., k.2.

2nd row: k.3, patt. to last 3 sts., k.3.

Work 4 more rows, working 1 more st. in garter st. at each end of every row.

Shape Armholes. 7th row: cast off 4 sts., k.3, patt. to last 8 sts., k.8.

8th row: cast off 4 sts., k.3, patt. to last 4 sts., k.4.

9th row: k.3, k.2 tog., patt. to last 5 sts., k.2 tog., k.3.

10th row: k.3, k.2 tog., patt. to last 5 sts., k.2 tog., k.3.

Dec. in same way at each end of next 5 (6, 7, 8, 9) rows and foll. 2 alt. rows. Cont. in patt. on remaining 71 (77, 83, 89, 95) sts., keeping garter st. edgings correct, until Back measures same as Fronts to shoulder shaping.

Shape Shoulders. Cast off 6 (7, 7, 8, 8) sts. at beg. of next 4 rows and 8 (7, 8, 8, 10) sts. at beg. of next 2 rows. Cast off remaining 31 (35, 39, 41, 43) sts.

TO COMPLETE

With No. 8 needles, work on each set of 2 sts. on fronts in garter st., until each is long enough to go halfway round back of neck. Cast off. Join shoulder and side seams. Join ends of neckbands and sew in position round back neck. Sew zip fastener to centre front edges, setting lower ends 1 in. above cast-on edges.

JUMPER
FRONT

With No. 11 needles and W., cast on 70 (76, 82, 88, 94) sts. and work 2 in. in k.1, p.1 rib.

Inc. row: k.1, *p.2, p. into front and k. into back of next st.; rep. from * to last 3 sts., p.2, p. into front and back of last st.: 93 (101, 109, 117, 125) sts.

Change to No. 9 needles.

1st row: p.1, *k.3, p.1; rep. from * to end.

2nd row: k.1, *p.3, k.1; rep. from * to end. Rep. last 2 rows until work measures 8½ (10, 11, 13, 14½) in., ending with right side facing.

Shape Armholes. Cast off 4 (4, 5, 5, 5) sts. at beg. of next 2 rows then work 2 sts. tog. at each end of next 5 (6, 6, 7, 8) rows and foll. 3 alt. rows.**

Cont. straight on remaining 69 (75, 81, 87, 93) sts. until armholes measure 3 (3½, 4, 4½, 5) in. ending with right side facing.

Shape Neck. Next row: patt. 25 (26, 27, 29, 31) sts.; turn.

Work 9 rows in patt. on these sts., working 2 sts. tog. at neck edge on next and every foll. alt. row: 20 (21, 22, 24, 26) sts.

Shape Shoulders. Cast off 6 (7, 7, 8, 8) sts. at beg. of next and foll. alt. row. Work 1 row straight. Cast off.

Slip centre 19 (23, 27, 29, 31) sts. on to a stitch holder, then work on remaining 25 (26, 27, 29, 31) sts. on other side to match first, reversing shapings.

BACK

Work as Front to **. Cont. straight on remaining 69 (75, 81, 87, 93) sts. until Back measures same as Front to shoulder shapings.

Shape Shoulders. Cast off 6 (7, 7, 8, 8) sts. at beg. of next 4 rows and 8 (7, 8, 8, 10) sts. at beg. of next 2 rows. Leave remaining 29 (33, 37, 39, 41) sts. on a stitch holder.

SLEEVES (make 2 alike)

With No. 11 needles and W., cast on 34 (36, 42, 42, 48) sts. and work 4 rows in k.1, p.1 rib.

Join R., and k. 1 row then rib 7 rows.

Join W., k. 1 row then rib until work measures 4 in. ending with right side facing (remembering that cuff folds back).

For sizes 26 (28, 30, 32): inc. 1 st. at end of last row: 34 (37, 43, 43, 49) sts.

For all sizes. Inc. row: k.1, *p.2, p. into front and k. into back of next st.; rep. from * to end: 45 (49, 57, 57, 65) sts.

Change to No. 9 needles.

1st row: p.1, *k.3, p.1; rep. from * to end.

2nd row: k.1, *p.3, k.1; rep. from * to end.

Cont. in patt. inc. 1 st. at each end of 7th and every foll. 8th row until there are 53 (57, 65, 73, 81) sts. Work straight until Sleeve measures 10 (11½, 13, 14½, 16) in. ending with right side facing.

Shape Top. Cast off 4 (4, 5, 5, 5) sts. at beg. of next 2 rows, then cast off 2 sts. at beg. of next 10 (12, 12, 16, 18) rows and 3 sts. at beg. of next 2 (2, 4, 4, 4) rows.

Cast off.

POLO COLLAR

Join right shoulder seam. With No. 11 needles and W., and with right side of work facing, pick up and k. 15 sts. from left side of front neck, k. across centre 19 (23, 27, 29, 31) sts., pick up and k. 15 sts. along right side of front neck and k. across 29 (33, 37, 39, 41) sts. of back neck: 78 (86, 94, 98, 102) sts.

Work 8 rows in k.1, p.1 rib.

Change to No. 9 needles and work a further 8 rows.

Join R., and k. 1 row, then rib 7 rows.

Join W., and k. 1 row then rib 3 rows. Cast off in rib.

TO COMPLETE

Join left shoulder and collar seams. Sew in sleeves and join side and sleeve seams.

SOCKS

TO MAKE (2 alike)

With No. 11 needles and W., cast on 46 (48, 52, 54, 58) sts. Work 4 rows in k.1, p.1 rib.

Join R., and k. 1 row, then rib 7 rows.

Join W., and k. 1 row, then rib 2 rows.

Now k. 1 row (which forms ridge for turnover at top of sock) and then rib a further 15 rows.

For sizes 26 and 30: inc. 1 st. at end of last row: 46 (49, 52, 55, 58) sts.

For all sizes: change to No. 9 needles and patt.:

1st row (right side): p.1, *k.2, p.1; rep. from * to end.

2nd row: k.1, *p.2, k.1; rep. from * to end.

Work 1½ (3, 4, 4, 4) in. in patt., then cont. in patt. working 2 sts. tog. at each end of next and every foll. 4th (4th, 5th, 6th, 7th) row until 34 (37, 40, 43, 46) sts. remain.

Change to No. 11 needles and cont. straight until work measures 6 (8, 9½, 10, 10½) in. from ridge row, ending with right side facing.

Shape Heel. Next 2 rows: k.7 (8, 8, 9, 9); turn, sl.1, p. back.

Rep. these 2 rows 5 (6, 7, 8, 9) times.

Next row: k. to last 3 sts., k.2 tog. t.b.l., k.1.

Next row: sl.1, p. to end.

Rep. these 2 rows until 5 (5, 5, 6, 6) sts. remain ending with right side facing.

Next row: k.3 (3, 3, 4, 4), k.2 tog. t.b.l., pick up and k.7 (9, 10, 11, 12) loop sts. along side of heel, and keeping ribbing from leg correct, rib 20 (21, 24, 25, 28) sts., k. to end.

Next 2 rows: p.7 (8, 8, 9, 9) sts.; turn, sl.1, k. back. Complete this side of heel to match first side: 42 (47, 52, 57, 62) sts.

Next row: k.9 (11, 12, 14, 15), k.2 tog., rib 20 (21, 24, 25, 28), k.2 tog., k.9 (11, 12, 14, 15).

Next row: p.10 (12, 13, 15, 16), rib 20 (21, 24, 25, 28), p.10 (12, 13, 15, 16).

Next row: k.8 (10, 11, 13, 14), k.2 tog., rib 20 (21, 24, 25, 28), k.2 tog., k.8 (10, 11, 13, 14).

Cont. thus, dec. 2 sts. every right-side row until 34 (37, 40, 43, 46) sts. remain. Keeping centre rib panel correct, cont. side panels straight in st.st., until work measures 5 (5½, 6, 6½, 7) in. from back of heel, ending after a wrong-side row.

Shape Toe. 1st row: k.7 (8, 9, 10, 11), k.2 tog., k.2 tog. t.b.l., k.12 (13, 14, 15, 16), k.2 tog., k.2 tog. t.b.l., k.7 (8, 9, 10, 11).

2nd row: p.

3rd row: k.6 (7, 8, 9, 10), k.2 tog., k.2 tog. t.b.l., k.10 (11, 12, 13, 14), k.2 tog., k.2 tog. t.b.l., k.6 (7, 8, 9, 10).

Cont. thus dec. 4 sts. every right-side row until 18 (21, 20, 23, 26) sts. remain.

Cast off.

TO COMPLETE

Sew seam under sole and up back of leg; fold foot flat and sew seam at toe.

Red, blue and white suit and beret

(photographed in colour on page 149)

MATERIALS

15 (15, 17) oz. Wendy Fashionflake Double Knitting in red, 2 oz. in blue and 2 oz. in white (see note on wools and yarns, page 20); one pair each Nos. 9 and 11 knitting needles (see page 26); one crochet hook International Standard Size 4·00 (optional); 5 buttons each ⅝ in. in diameter; a waist length of narrow elastic.

MEASUREMENTS

Suit: to fit chest size 24 (26, 28) in.; length of jacket 16¼ (17¼, 18¼) in.; jacket sleeve seam 11 (12½, 14) in.; length of skirt 11 (12½, 14) in. **Beret:** to fit an average-sized head.

TENSION

6 sts. and 8 rows to 1 in. over st.st. with No. 9 needles (see note on tension, page 15).

ABBREVIATIONS

See page 26; R., red; B., blue; W., white.

JACKET

BACK

With No. 11 needles and R., cast on 76 (82, 88) sts. and work 8 rows in k.1, p.1 rib.

Change to No. 9 needles and patt. thus:

For sizes 24 and 26. 1st row: k.10 (13), *p.1, k.3, p.1, k.12; rep. from * to last 15 (18) sts., p.1, k.3, p.1, k.10 (13).

For size 28. 1st row: k.3, p.1, k.12, *p.1, k.3, p.1, k.12; rep. from * to last 21 sts., p.1, k.3, p.1, k.12, p.1, k.3.

For all sizes. 2nd row: p.

Rep. these 2 rows 3 times.

Join B.

9th and 10th rows: with B., k.

Join R. and work first and 2nd rows twice.

Join W.

15th and 16th rows: with W., k.

Join R. and work first and 2nd rows 4 times.

These 24 rows form patt. Rep. patt. rows until work measures 8½ (9½, 10½) in., ending with right side facing.

Shape Armholes. Keeping patt. correct, cast off 2 (3, 4) sts. at beg. of next 2 rows, then work 2 sts. tog. at each end of next 3 rows, then at each end of next 3 (4, 5) alt. rows: 60 (62, 64) sts.

Cont. straight until armhole measures 3½ (3¾, 4) in. then inc. 1 st. at each end of next and foll. 8th (10th, 10th) row: 64 (66, 68) sts.

Cont. straight until work measures 15½ (16½, 17½) in., ending with right side facing.

Shape Shoulders. Keeping patt. correct, cast off 7 sts. at beg. of next 6 (4, 4) rows and 0 (8, 8) sts. at beg. of next 2 rows. Cast off 22 (22, 24) remaining sts.

POCKET LININGS (make 2 alike)

With No. 9 needles and R., cast on 24 (25, 26) sts. and work 22 rows in st.st. Leave sts. on a stitch holder.

LEFT FRONT

With No. 11 needles and R., cast on 46 (50, 54) sts. and work 8 rows in k.1, p.1 rib.

Change to No. 9 needles and patt. thus:

For sizes 24 and 26. 1st row: k.10 (13), p.1, k.3, p.1, k.12, p.1, k.3, p.1, k.6, slip last 8 (9) sts. on to a safety pin or stitch holder.

For size 28. 1st row: k.3, p.1, k.12, p.1, k.3, p.1, k.12, p.1, k.3, p.1, k.6, slip last 10 sts. on to a stitch holder.

For all sizes. 2nd row: p.

Work in patt. as for Back on these sts. until 22 patt. rows in all have been completed.

Next row: patt. 4 (5, 6) sts., slip next 24 (25, 26) sts. on to spare length of yarn, patt. across 24 (25, 26) pocket lining sts. on stitch holder, then patt. last 10 (11, 12) sts.

Cont. in patt. until Front measures same as Back to armhole shaping, ending with right side facing.

Shape Armhole and Front Slope. Cast off 2 (3, 4) sts., patt. to last 2 sts., k.2 tog.

Now work 2 sts. tog. at armhole edge on next 3 rows and on foll. 3 (4, 5) alt. rows, and at the same time work 2 sts. tog. at front edge on every 4th row from previous dec. When armhole measures 3½ (3¾, 4) in. inc. 1 st. at armhole edge on next and foll. 8th (10th, 10th) row. Cont. to dec. at front edge on every 4th row until 21 (22, 22) sts. remain. Cont. straight until work measures same as Back to start of shoulder shaping.

Shape Shoulder. Cast off 7 sts. at beg. of next and foll. alt. row. Work 1 row straight. Cast off.

RIGHT FRONT

With No. 11 needles and R., cast on 46 (50, 54) sts. and work 4 rows in k.1, p.1 rib.

5th row: rib 3 (3, 4), cast off 2 (3, 2) sts. (for buttonhole), rib to end.

6th row: rib 41 (44, 48), cast on 2 (3, 2) sts., rib 3 (3, 4).

Work 2 more rows in rib.

Change to No. 9 needles and patt. thus:

For sizes 24 and 26. 1st row: slip first 8 (9) sts. on to a stitch holder or safety pin, k.6, p.1, k.3, p.1, k.12, p.1, k.3, p.1, k.10 (13).

For size 28. 1st row: slip first 10 sts. on to a stitch holder, k.6, p.1, k.3, p.1, k.12, p.1, k.3, p.1, k.12, p.1, k.3.

For all sizes. 2nd row: p.

Work in patt. as for Back on these sts. until 22 patt. rows in all have been completed.

Next row: patt. 10 (11, 12) sts., slip next 24 (25, 26) sts. on to spare length of yarn, patt. across pocket lining sts. on stitch holder, patt. 4 (5, 6) sts. Now work as Left Front reversing shapings.

SLEEVES (make 2 alike)

With No. 11 needles and R., cast on 34 (36, 38) sts. and work 11 (15, 19) rows in k.1, p.1 rib.

Inc. row: *rib 4 (5, 5), work twice into next st.; rep. from * to last 4 (0, 2) sts., rib to end: 40 (42, 44) sts.

Change to No. 9 needles and patt. thus:

1st row: k.9 (10,11), p.1, k.3, p.1, k.12, p.1, k.3, p.1, k.9 (10, 11).

2nd row: p.

Cont. in patt. as for Back on these sts., inc. 1 st. at each end of 7th and every foll. 6th row, taking sts. into patt., until there are 60 (64, 68) sts. Cont. straight until work measures 11 (12½, 14) in., ending with right side facing.

Shape Top. Cast off 2 (3, 4) sts. at beg. of next 2 rows. Work 2 sts. tog. at each end of next 3 rows, then at each end of next 3 alt. rows.

Work 2 sts. tog. at each end of every 3rd row 2 (4, 6) times, then on every alt. row 3 times, then on next and every row until 26 sts. remain. Cast off.

TO COMPLETE

Join shoulder seams and sew in sleeves; join side and sleeve seams.

Pocket Tops (work both alike). With right side of work facing, and with No. 11 needles and R., transfer 24 (25, 26) sts. for pocket top from spare yarn to needle and work 6 rows in k.1, p.1 rib. Cast off in rib. Sew sides of pocket tops to jacket, and sew down pocket linings.

Bands. Join R. to inner side of 8 (9, 10) sts. of Left Front border and with No. 11 needles cont. in rib as set until strip reaches up front and halfway along back of neck. Cast off.

Join R. to inner edge of Right Front border and with No. 11 needles cont. in rib, making a further button- hole in the same way as first every 14 (16, 18) rows until there are 5 in all, then cont. straight until band is the same length as the first. Cast off.

Join two ends of bands neatly and sew whole band in place up Fronts and round back of neck. Sew buttons to left band to match buttonholes.

Vertical Stripes (these can be crocheted or sewn). The positions of the vertical stripes are indicated by lines of p. sts. above ribbing on right side of work, and stripes are worked alternately in B. and W. as follows (see also photograph on page 149). On the Fronts the left-hand of the double stripes are worked in B. and the right-hand in W. On the Back the left-hand are worked in W. and the right-hand in B., so Front and Back stripes match at the shoulders. The Right Sleeve is worked as Back and the Left as Fronts.

To crochet stripes: with right side of work facing, hold yarn for stripe beneath work, and, starting above ribbing, use crochet hook to draw a loop of yarn through knitting. Insert crochet hook 2 sts. higher up and pull through a second loop, drawing it through both knitting and first loop.
Cont. thus, working ch. up stripe.
To sew stripes: using correct yarn, work chain stitch up p. guide lines.

SKIRT

TO MAKE (worked in 1 piece from waist downwards)
With No. 11 needles and R., cast on 147 (161, 175) sts. and work 1 in. in k.1, p.1 rib.
Change to No. 9 needles and work in st.st. Cont. for 2½ in. ending with a p. row.
Next row: *k.6, k. into front and back of next st.; rep. from * to end: 168 (184, 200) sts.
Cont. straight until work measures 4½ in., ending with a p. row.
Next row: *k.7, k. into front and back of next st.; rep. from * to end: 189 (207, 225) sts.
Cont. until work measures 7½ in. ending with a p. row.
Next row: *k.8, k. into front and back of next st.; rep. from * to end: 210 (230, 250) sts.
Work straight until skirt measures 10¾ (11¼, 11¾) in. ending with a p. row.
Next row: *k.9, k. into front and back of next st.;

rep. from * to end: 231 (253, 275) sts.
Cont. straight until work measures 11 (12½, 14) in. ending with a k. row.
Next row (hem ridge): k.
Beg. with a k. row, work 6 (8, 10) rows in st.st. Cast off.

TO COMPLETE
Join centre back seam, turn up hem and slipstitch in place. Join elastic in a circle to desired size, and attach to inside of waist ribbing with herring-bone stitch.

BERET
TO MAKE
With No. 11 needles and R., cast on 120 sts. and work 7 rows in k.1, p.1 rib.
Inc. row: *k.1, p. into front and back of next st.; rep. from * to end: 180 sts.
Change to No. 9 needles and st.st.
Work 16 rows.
17th row: *k.7, k.2 tog.; rep. from * to end.
Work 5 rows straight.
23rd row: *k.6, k.2 tog.; rep. from * to end.
Work 5 rows straight.
29th row: *k.5, k.2 tog.; rep. from * to end.
Work 3 rows straight.
33rd row: *k.4, k.2 tog.; rep. from * to end.
Work 3 rows straight.
37th row: *k.3, k.2 tog.; rep. from * to end.
Work 3 rows straight.
41st row: *k.2, k.2 tog.; rep. from * to end.
Work 1 row straight.
43rd row: *k.1, k.2 tog.; rep. from * to end.
Work 1 row straight.
45th row: *k.2 tog.; rep. from * to end.
Thread yarn through sts. and draw up; fasten off securely.

TO COMPLETE
Sew centre back seam. Using R., B. and W. yarn, make a pompon (see page 82) with card circles 1½ in. in diameter, centre hole ⅜ in.; sew this to centre of beret.

Patterned jumper and socks
(photographed in black and white on page 146)

MATERIALS
For sweater: 11 (12, 13, 15, 16, 17) balls of Emu Scotch Double Knitting **or** Double Crêpe **or** Bri-Nylon Double Knitting (see note on wools and yarns, page 20); one pair each Nos. 8 and 10 knitting needles (see page 26); one cable needle. **For socks:** 4 (4, 5, 5) balls Scotch 4-ply **or** Super Crêpe **or** Bri-Nylon 4-ply (see note on wools and yarns, page 20); one set of four No. 12 needles, pointed at both ends (see page 26); one cable needle.

MEASUREMENTS
Sweater: to fit chest size 24 (26, 28, 30, 32, 34) in.; length 16¾ (17¾, 19¼, 20¾, 21¾, 22½) in.; sleeve

seam 12½ (14, 15, 16, 16½, 17) in. **Socks:** length of foot 7 (8, 9, 10) in.; length of leg 12½ (13½, 14½, 15½) in.

TENSION
Sweater: 7 sts. and 8 rows to 1 in. over patt. with No. 8 needles. **Socks:** 8½ sts. to 1 in. over st.st. (see note on tension, page 15).

ABBREVIATIONS
See page 26.

JUMPER
BACK
With No. 10 needles cast on 84 (90, 96, 100, 106, 112) sts. and work 2½ in. in k.1, p.1 rib, ending with wrong side facing.

Next row: rib 7 (6, 7, 6, 7, 4), * work twice into next st., rib 9 (10, 8, 7, 6, 7); rep. from * to last 7 (7, 8, 6, 8, 4) sts., work twice into next st., rib 6 (6, 7, 5, 7, 3): 92 (98, 106, 112, 120, 126) sts.
Change to No. 8 needles and patt.

1st row: p.9 (12, 16, 19, 23, 26), *(k.2 tog. and leave sts. on left-hand needle, k. first st. again, then slip sts. off needle: tw.2), p.1, k.4, p.1, tw.2, p.8, (slip next st. on to cable needle and leave at back of work: sl.1b.), k.2, k.1 t.b.l. from cable needle, (slip next 2 sts. on to cable needle and leave at front of work: sl.2f.), p.1, k.2 from cable needle, p.8; rep. from * once, tw.2, p.1, k.4, p.1, tw.2, p.9 (12, 16, 19, 23, 26).

2nd row: k.9 (12, 16, 19, 23, 26), *p.2, k.1, p.4, k.1, p.2, k.8, p.2, k.1, p.1 t.b.l., p.2, k.8; rep. from * once, p.2, k.1, p.4, k.1, p.2, k.9 (12, 16, 19, 23, 26).

3rd row: p.9 (12, 16, 19, 23, 26), *tw.2, p.1, (slip next 2 sts. on to cable needle and leave at front of work, k. next 2 sts., then k. 2 sts. from cable needle: c.4f), p.1, tw.2, p.7, sl.1b., k.2, p.1 from cable needle, k.1 t.b.l., p.1, sl.2f., k.1 t.b.l., k.2 from cable needle, p.7; rep. from * once, tw.2, p.1, c.4f., p.1, tw.2, p.9 (12, 16, 19, 23, 26).

4th row: k.9 (12, 16, 19, 23, 26), *p.2, k.1, p.4, k.1, p.2, k.7, p.2, (p.1 t.b.l., k.1) twice, p.2, k.7; rep. from * once, p.2, k.1, p.4, k.1, p.2, k.9 (12, 16, 19, 23, 26).

5th row: p.9 (12, 16, 19, 23, 26), * tw.2, p.1, k.4, p.1, tw.2, p.6, sl.1b., k.2, k.1 t.b.l. from cable needle, (p.1, k.1 t.b.l) twice, sl. 2f., p.1, k.2 from cable needle, p.6; rep. from * once, tw.2, p.1, k.4, p.1, tw.2, p.9 (12, 16, 19, 23, 26).

6th row: k.9 (12, 16, 19, 23, 26), *p.2, k.1, p.4, k.1, p.2, k.6, p.2, (k.1, p.1 t.b.l) 3 times, p.2, k.6; rep. from * once, p.2, k.1, p.4, k.1, p.2, k.9 (12, 16, 19, 23, 26).

7th row: p.9 (12, 16, 19, 23, 26), * tw.2, p.1, c.4f., p.1, tw.2, p.5, sl.1b., k.2, p.1 from cable needle,

The jumper cable pattern is repeated down the side of each knee-high sock

(k.1 t.b.l., p.1) 3 times, sl.2f., k.1 t.b.l., k.2 from cable needle, p.5; rep. from * once, tw.2, p.1, c.4f., p.1, tw.2, p.9 (12, 16, 19, 23, 26).

8th row: k.9 (12, 16, 19, 23, 26), *p.2, k.1, p.4, k.1, p.2, k.5, p.2, (p.1 t.b.l., k.1) 4 times, p.2, k.5; rep. from * once, p.2, k.1, p.4, k.1, p.2, k.9 (12, 16, 19, 23, 26).

9th row: p.9 (12, 16, 19, 23, 26), * tw.2, p.1, k.4, p.1, tw.2, p.4, sl.1b., k.2, k.1 t.b.l. from cable needle, (p.1, k.1 t.b.l.) 4 times, sl.2f., p.1, k.2 from cable needle, p.4; rep. from * once, tw.2, p.1, k.4, p.1, tw.2, p.9 (12, 16, 19, 23, 26).

10th row: k.9 (12, 16, 19, 23, 26), *p.2, k.1, p.4, k.1, p.2, k.4, p.2, (k.1, p.1 t.b.l) 5 times, p.2, k.4; rep. from * once, p.2, k.1, p.4, k.1, p.2, k.9 (12, 16, 19, 23, 26).

11th row: p.9 (12, 16, 19, 23, 26), *tw.2, p.1, c.4f., p.1, tw.2, p.3, sl.1b., k.2, p.1 from cable needle, (k.1 t.b.l., p.1) 5 times, sl.2f., k.1 t.b.l., k.2 from cable needle, p.3; rep. from * once, tw.2, p.1, c.4f., p.1, tw.2, p.9 (12, 16, 19, 23, 26).

12th row: k.9 (12, 16, 19, 23, 26), *p.2, k.1, p.4, k.1, p.2, k.3, p.2, (p.1 t.b.l., k.1) 6 times, p.2, k.3; rep. from * once, p.2, k.1, p.4, k.1, p.2, k.9 (12, 16, 19, 23, 26).

13th row: p.9 (12, 16, 19, 23, 26), *tw.2, p.1, k.4, p.1, tw.2, p.3, sl.2f., p.1, k.2 from cable needle, (k.1 t.b.l., p.1) 5 times, sl.1b., k.2, p.1 from cable needle, p.3; rep. from * once, tw.2, p.1, k.4, p.1, tw.2, p.9 (12, 16, 19, 23, 26).

14th row: k.9 (12, 16, 19, 23, 26), *p.2, k.1, p.4, k.1, p.2, k.4, p.2, (k.1, p.1 t.b.l.) 5 times, p.2, k.4; rep. from * once, p.2, k.1, p.4, k.1, p.2, k.9 (12, 16, 19, 23, 26).

15th row: p.9 (12, 16, 19, 23, 26), * tw.2, p.1, c.4f., p.1, tw.2, p.4, sl.2f., p.1, k.2 from cable needle, (p.1, k.1 t.b.l.) 4 times, sl.1b., k.2, p.1 from cable needle, p.4; rep. from * once, tw.2, p.1, c.4f., p.1, tw.2, p.9 (12, 16, 19, 23, 26).

16th row: k.9 (12, 16, 19, 23, 26), *p.2, k.1, p.4, k.1, p.2, k.5, p.2, (p.1 t.b.l., k.1) 4 times, p.2, k.5; rep. from * once, p.2, k.1, p.4, k.1, p.2, k.9 (12, 16, 19, 23, 26).

17th row: p.9 (12, 16, 19, 23, 26), *tw.2, p.1, k.4, p.1, tw.2, p.5, sl.2f., p.1, k.2 from cable needle, (k.1 t.b.l., p.1) 3 times, sl.1b., k.2, p.1 from cable needle, p.5; rep. from * once, tw.2, p.1, k.4, p.1, tw.2, p.9 (12, 16, 19, 23, 26).

18th row: k.9 (12, 16, 19, 23, 26), *p.2, k.1, p.4, k.1, p.2, k.6, p.2, (k.1, p.1 t.b.l.) 3 times, p.2, k.6; rep. from * once, p.2, k.1, p.4, k.1, p.2, k.9 (12, 16, 19, 23, 26).

19th row: p.9 (12, 16, 19, 23, 26), *tw.2, p.1, c.4f., p.1, tw.2, p.6, sl.2f., p.1, k.2 from cable needle, (p.1, k.1 t.b.l.) twice, sl.1b., k.2, p.1 from cable needle, p.6; rep. from * once, tw.2, p.1, c.4f., p.1, tw.2, p.9 (12, 16, 19, 23, 26).

20th row: k.9 (12, 16, 19, 23, 26), *p.2, k.1, p.4,

k.1, p.2, k.7, p.2, (p.1 t.b.l, k.1) twice, p.2, k.7; rep. from * once, p.2, k.1, p.4, k.1, p.2, k.9 (12, 16, 19, 23, 26).

21st row: p.9 (12, 16, 19, 23, 26), *tw.2, p.1, k.4, p.1, tw.2, p.7, sl.2f., p.1, k.2 from cable needle, k.1 t.b.l., p.1, sl.1b., k.2, p.1 from cable needle, p.7; rep. from * once, tw.2, p.1, k.4, p.1, tw.2, p.9 (12, 16, 19, 23, 26).

22nd row: k.9 (12, 16, 19, 23, 26), *p.2, k.1, p.4, k.1, p.2, k.8, p.2, k.1, p.1 t.b.l., p.2, k.8; rep. from * once, p.2, k.1, p.4, k.1, p.2, k.9 (12, 16, 19, 23, 26).

23rd row: p.9 (12, 16, 19, 23, 26), *tw.2, p.1, c.4f., p.1, tw.2, p.8, sl.2f., p.1, k.2 from cable needle, sl.1b., k.2, p.1 from cable needle, p.8; rep. from * once, tw.2, p.1, c.4f., p.1, tw.2, p.9 (12, 16, 19, 23, 26).

24th row: k.9 (12, 16, 19, 23, 26), *p.2, k.1, p.4, k.1, p.2, k.9, sl.2f., p.2, p.2 from cable needle, k.9; rep. from * once, p.2, k.1, p.4, k.1, p.2, k.9 (12, 16, 19, 23, 26).

25th row: p.9 (12, 16, 19, 23, 26), *tw.2, p.1, k.4, p.1, tw.2, p.9, k.4, p.9; rep. from * once, tw.2, p.1, k.4, p.1, tw.2, p.9 (12, 16, 19, 23, 26).

26th row: k.9 (12, 16, 19, 23, 26), *p.2, k.1, p.4, k.1, p.2, k.9, p.4, k.9; rep. from * once, p.2, k.1, p.4, k.1, p.2, k.9 (12, 16, 19, 23, 26).

27th row: p.9 (12, 16, 19, 23, 26), *tw.2, p.1, c.4f., p.1, tw.2, p.9, c.4f., p.9; rep. from * once, tw.2, p.1, c.4f., p.1, tw.2, p.9 (12, 16, 19, 23, 26).

28th row: as 26th row.

Rep. last 4 rows once.

These 32 rows form patt. Cont. in patt. until work measures 10 (10½, 11½, 12½, 13, 13½) in., ending with a wrong-side row.

Shape Armholes. Cast off 5 (6, 7, 7, 8, 8) sts. at beg. of next 2 rows. Dec. 1 st. at each end of next and every foll. alt. row until 76 (78, 82, 84, 88, 92) sts. remain.**

Cont. without further shaping until armholes measure 6 (6½, 7, 7½, 8, 8¼) in. ending with a wrong-side row.

Shape Shoulders. Cast off 5 (5, 6, 6, 6, 7) sts. at beg. of the next 6 rows and 7 (7, 5, 6, 7, 5) sts. at the beg. of the foll. 2 rows. Leave remaining 32 (34, 36, 36, 38, 40) sts. on a stitch holder.

FRONT

Work as Back to **.

Continue without further shaping until armholes measure 3¾ (4¼, 4½, 5, 5½, 5¾) in. ending with a wrong-side row.

Shape Neck. Next row: patt. 30 (31, 32, 33, 34, 36) sts.; turn. Leave remaining sts. on a stitch holder. Dec. 1 st. at neck edge on next 8 (9, 9, 9, 9, 10) rows. Cont. without further shaping until work measures same as Back to shoulder, ending at armhole edge.

Shape Shoulder. Cast off 5 (5, 6, 6, 6, 7) sts. at beg. of the next and 2 foll. alt. rows. Work 1 row.

Cast off remaining 7 (7, 5, 6, 7, 5) sts. Slip centre 16 (16, 18, 18, 20, 20) sts. on to a stitch holder. Join yarn to neck edge of remaining sts., patt. to end. Complete to match first side of neck.

SLEEVES (make 2 alike)

With No. 10 needles cast on 48 (50, 52, 54, 56, 58) sts. and work 3 in. in k.1, p.1 rib, ending with a wrong-side row.

Change to No. 8 needles and st.st. Inc. 1 st. at each end of the 11th and every foll. 12th (12th, 12th, 14th, 13th, 13th) row until there are 58 (62, 64, 66, 70, 72) sts. on needle. Cont. without further shaping until work measures 12½ (14, 15, 16, 16½, 17) in., ending with a p. row.

Shape Top. Cast off 5 (6, 7, 7, 8, 8) sts. at the beg. of next 2 rows. Dec. 1 st. at each end of the next and every foll. 4th row until 42 (44, 42, 44, 46, 48) sts. remain, then 1 st. at each end of every alt. row until 30 (30, 28, 30, 30, 32) sts. remain. Now dec. 1 st. at each end of every row until 16 (16, 18, 20, 20, 22) sts. remain. Cast off.

NECKBAND

Using a backstitch, join right shoulder seam. With right side of work facing and with No. 10 needles, pick up and k.23 (24, 24, 24, 24, 25) sts. down left side of neck, k. across the 16 (16, 18, 18, 20, 20) sts. at centre, pick up and k.23 (24, 24, 24, 24, 25) sts. up right side of neck, then k. across the 32 (34, 36, 36, 38, 40) sts. on back neck: 94 (98, 102, 102, 106, 110) sts.

Work 2 in. in k.1, p.1 rib. Cast off loosely in rib.

TO COMPLETE

Join side and sleeve seams. Join left shoulder seam and neckband. Set in sleeves. Fold neckband in half on to wrong side and slipstitch down.

SOCKS

TO MAKE (2 alike)

Using the set of four No. 12 needles, cast on 54 (60, 66, 72) sts.: 16 (18, 20, 22) sts. on first and third needles and 22 (24, 26, 28) sts. on second needle.

Work 3 in. in k.1, p.1 rib.

Change to st.st. (every round k.) and cont. until work measures 6½ (7, 7½, 8) in.

1st round. First needle: k.8 (10, 12, 14), p.1, tw.2, p.1, k.4; **second needle:** p.1, tw.2, p.1, k.14 (16, 18, 20), p.1, tw.2, p.1; **third needle:** k.4, p.1, tw.2, p.1, k. to end.

Rep. first round once.

3rd round. First needle: k.8 (10, 12, 14), p.1, tw.2, p.1, c.4f.; **second needle:** p.1, tw.2, p.1, k.14

Opposite: red, blue and white suit with matching beret (instructions on page 143)

(16, 18, 20), p.1, tw.2, p.1; **third needle:** c.4f., p.1, tw.2, p.1, k. to end.
Rep. the first round once.
These 4 rounds form patt. Cont. in patt. until work measures 7½ (8, 8½, 9) in. Keeping patt. correct. dec. 1 st. at each end of the next round (i.e. at beg. of first needle and at end of last needle) and at each end of every following 6th round until 44 (50, 56, 62) sts. remain. Cont. straight until work measures 12½ (13½, 14½, 15½) in.
Next row: k.11 (13, 15, 17) sts. then slip last 11 (13, 15, 17) sts. of round on to same needle for heel, leaving remaining sts. on 2 needles for instep. Work on heel sts. in st.st. (1 row k., 1 row p.), commencing with a p. row, until 19 (21, 23, 25) rows in all have been worked.
Next row: k.13 (16, 19, 22) sts., sl.1, k.1, p.s.s.o.; turn.
Next row: p.5 (7, 9, 11) sts., p.2 tog.; turn.
Next row: k.5 (9, 11) sts., sl.1, k.1, p.s.s.o.; turn.
Rep. the last 2 rows until all sts. are again on the needle.

Next row: k.3 (4, 5, 6) sts. (This will halve heel sts. again.) Place all instep sts. on to one needle.
Next round. First needle: using a spare needle, k. across remaining 3 (4, 5, 6) heel sts., pick up and k.13 (15, 17, 19) sts. along side of heel; **second needle:** k.; **third needle:** pick up and k.13 (15, 17, 19) sts. along second side of heel, then k. across 3 (4, 5, 6) sts. to centre of heel.
Next round: k.
Next round. First needle: k. to last 2 sts., k.2 tog.; **second needle:** k.; **third needle:** k.2 tog., k. to end.
Rep last 2 rounds 5 (6, 7, 8) times. Cont. straight for 2¾ (3¼, 3¾, 4¼) in.
Next round. First needle: k. to last 2 sts., k.2 tog.; **second needle:** k.2 tog., k. to last 2 sts., k.2 tog.; **third needle:** k.2 tog., k. to end.
Work 2 rounds without shaping.
Rep. the last 3 rounds until 18 (20, 22, 24) sts. remain on round. Place remaining sts. on two needles right side of work to right side, then cast off both group of sts. together.

Windcheater

– in double knitting or tripleknit yarn.
(photographed in black and white on page 152)

MATERIALS
11 (12, 13, 14, 15, 16) balls of Emu Scotch Double Knitting **or** Double Crêpe **or** Bri-Nylon Double Knitting **or** 6 (7, 8, 9, 10, 11) balls Emu Tripleknit (see note on wools and yarns, page 20); one pair each Nos. 8 and 10 knitting needles for double knitting yarn **or** one pair each Nos. 6 and 8 knitting needles for tripleknit yarn (see page 26); one cable needle; a 14 (16, 16, 18, 18, 18)-in. open-ended zip fastener.

MEASUREMENTS
To fit chest size 24 (26, 28, 30, 32, 34) in.; length 16½ (18, 18½, 20, 20¾, 21½) in.; sleeve seam 11½ (12½, 14, 15½, 16½, 17) in.

TENSION
5½ sts. and 8 rows to 1 in. over st.st. with No. 8 needles and double knitting yarn; 4½ sts. and 5½ rows to 1 in. over st.st. with No. 6 needles and tripleknit yarn (see note on tension, page 15).

ABBREVIATIONS
See page 26.

Opposite: sleeveless pullover and toggle-fastening waistcoat (see page 159)

Version 1: in Double Knitting Yarn
BACK
With No. 10 needles, cast on 72 (78, 84, 88, 94, 100) sts., and work 2 in. in k.1, p.1 rib.
Change to No. 8 needles and st.st. (see page 23). Cont. until work measures 9½ (10¾, 10¾, 11¾, 12¼, 12½) in., ending with a p. row. Mark each end of last row with a coloured thread.
Shape Raglan Armholes.
For sizes 24 and 30 only. Next row: k.2, sl.1, k.1, p.s.s.o., k. to last 4 sts., k.2 tog., k.2.
Work 3 rows straight.
For all sizes. Next row: k.2, sl.1, k.1, p.s.s.o., k. to last 4 sts., k.2 tog., k.2.
Next row: p.
Rep. last 2 rows until 18 (20, 22, 24, 26, 28) sts. remain, ending with a p. row. Leave these sts. on a stitch holder.

LEFT FRONT
With No. 10 needles, cast on 40 (44, 46, 48, 52, 54) sts. and work 2 in. in k.1, p.1 rib.
Change to No. 8 needles and patt.
1st row: k.12 (14, 15, 16, 18, 19), p.2, k.12, p.2, k. to end.
2nd row: p.12 (14, 15, 16, 18, 19), k.2, p.12, k.2, p. to end.
Rep. these 2 rows 3 times.
9th row: k.12 (14, 15, 16, 18, 19), p.2, (slip next

3 sts. on to cable needle and leave at back of work, k. next 3 sts. then k. sts. from cable needle: c.6b.), (slip next 3 sts. on to cable needle and leave at front of work, k. next 3 sts., then k. sts. from cable needle: c.6f.), p.2, k. to end.

10th row: as 2nd row.

These 10 rows form patt.

Cont. in patt. until work measures same as Back to armhole, ending with a wrong-side row. Mark end of last row with a coloured thread.

Shape Raglan Armhole. Next row: k.2, sl.1, k.1, p.s.s.o., patt. to end.

Next row: patt. to end.

Rep. these 2 rows until 22 (25, 25, 26, 29, 30) sts. remain, ending at front edge.

Shape Neck. Next row: cast off 5 (6, 7, 7, 8, 8) sts., patt. to end. Still dec. at armhole edge as before, dec. 1 st. at neck edge on the next and every foll. alt. row until 7 (5, 6, 7, 5, 6) sts. remain.

Keeping neck edge straight, dec. at armhole edge as before until 2 sts. remain, working dec. at outer armhole edge when they can no longer be worked inside a border of 2 sts.

Work 1 row. K.2 tog. and fasten off.

RIGHT FRONT

Work as Left Front, reversing all shapings and working armhole shapings k.2 tog., k.2.

SLEEVES (make 2 alike)

With No. 10 needles cast on 40 (42, 44, 46, 48, 48) sts. and work 2½ in. in k.1, p.1 rib.

Change to No. 8 needles and st.st. Inc. 1 st. at each end of the 7th and every foll. 6th (7th, 7th, 8th, 8th, 8th) row until there are 58 (60, 66, 68, 72, 74) sts. on the needle.

Cont. without further shaping until work measures 11½ (12½, 14, 15½, 16½, 17) in., ending with a p. row. Mark each end of last row with a coloured thread.

Shape Raglan Top. Next row: k.2, sl.1, k.1, p.s.s.o., k. to last 4 sts., k.2 tog., k.2.

Work 3 rows straight.

For sizes 24, 30 and 34 only: rep. the last 4 rows once.

For all sizes. Next row: k.2, sl.1, k.1, p.s.s.o., k. to last 4 sts., k.2 tog., k.2.

Next row: p.

Rep. the last 2 rows until 6 sts. remain, ending with a p. row. Leave these sts. on a stitch holder.

NECKBAND

Using a back stitch, and matching up coloured threads, join raglan seams. With right side of work facing and with No. 10 needles, pick up and k.20 (20, 22, 22, 24, 24) sts. up right side of front neck,

Windcheater is cable-patterned with a zip-up centre front fastening

k. across 6 sts. at top of Right Sleeve, 18 (20, 22, 24, 26, 28) sts. across back neck, 6 sts. at top of Left Sleeve, pick up and k. 20 (20, 22, 22, 24, 24) sts. down left side of neck: 70 (72, 78, 80, 86, 88) sts. Work 2 in. in k.1, p.1 rib. Cast off loosely in rib.

FRONT EDGINGS

With right side of work facing, and with No. 10 needles, pick up and k.82 (92, 96, 106, 110, 116) sts. evenly along front edge of Right Front from bottom to neck.

K.3 rows. Cast off.

Rep. for Left Front but pick up sts. from neck edge to bottom.

TO COMPLETE

Using backstitch, join side and sleeve seams. Sew in zip, placing top of zip to base of neckband. Fold neckband in half on to wrong side and slipstitch down. Neaten short edges of neckband.

Version 2: in Tripleknit Yarn

BACK

With No. 8 needles, cast on 60 (64, 68, 72, 78, 82) sts. and work 2 in. in k.1, p.1 rib.

Change to No. 6 needles and st.st. (see page 23). Cont. until work measures 9½ (10¾, 10¾, 11¾, 12¼, 12½) in. ending with a p. row.

Shape Raglan Armholes. Cast off 3 (3, 4, 3, 4, 5) sts. at beg. of the next 2 rows.

Next row: k.2, sl.1, k.1, p.s.s.o., k. to last 4 sts., k.2 tog., k.2.

Next row: p.

Rep. last 2 rows until 18 (20, 20, 22, 24, 24) sts. remain, ending with a p. row. Leave these sts. on a stitch holder.

LEFT FRONT

With No. 8 needles, cast on 34 (36, 38, 40, 44, 46) sts. and work 2 in. in k.1, p.1 rib.

Change to No. 6 needles and patt.

1st row: k.9 (10, 11, 12, 14, 15), p.2, k.12, p.2, k. to end.

2nd row: p.9 (10, 11, 12, 14, 15), k.2, p.12, k.2, p. to end.

Rep. these 2 rows 3 times.

9th row: k.9 (10, 11, 12, 14, 15), p.2, c.6b., c.6f., p.2, k. to end. (NOTE. For c.6b. and c.6f., see Version 1, Left Front, 9th row.)

10th row: as 2nd row.

These 10 rows form patt.

Cont. in patt. until work measures same as Back to armhole, ending with a wrong-side row.

Shape Raglan Armhole. Next row: cast off 3 (3, 4, 3, 4, 5) sts., patt. to end.

Next row: patt. to end.

Next row: k.2, sl.1, k.1, p.s.s.o., patt. to end.

Rep. last 2 rows until 20 (22, 22, 24, 27, 28) sts. remain, ending at front edge.
Shape Neck. Next row: cast off 6 (6, 7, 7, 8, 8) sts., patt. to end.
Still dec. at armhole edge as before, dec. 1 st. at neck edge on the next and every foll. alt. row until 4 (4, 5, 5, 5, 6) sts. remain.
Keeping neck edge straight, dec. at armhole edge as before until 2 sts. remain, working dec. at outer armhole edge when they can no longer be worked inside a border of 2 sts.
Work 1 row. K.2 tog. and fasten off.

RIGHT FRONT
Work as for Left Front, reversing all shapings and working armhole shapings, k.2 tog., k.2.

SLEEVES (make 2 alike)
With No. 8 needles, cast on 36 (36, 38, 38, 40, 42) sts. and work 2½ in., in k.1, p.1 rib.
Change to No. 6 needles and st.st. Inc. 1 st. at each end of the 5th and every foll. 6th row until there are 48 (50, 54, 56, 60, 62) sts. on the needle.
Cont. without further shaping until work measures 11½ (12½, 14, 15½, 16½, 17) in., ending with a p. row.
Shape Raglan Top. Cast off 3 (3, 4, 3, 4, 4) sts. at beg. of the next 2 rows.
Next row: k.2, sl.1, k.1, p.s.s.o., k. to last 4 sts., k.2 tog., k.2.

Next row: p.
Rep. the last 2 rows until 6 sts. remain, ending with a p. row. Leave these sts. on a stitch holder.

NECKBAND
Using backstitch, join raglan seams. With right side of work facing and with No. 8 needles, pick up and k.16 (18, 18, 20, 22, 22) sts. up right side of front neck, k. across 6 sts. at top of Right Sleeve, 18 (20, 20, 22, 24, 24) sts. across back neck, 6 sts. at top of Left Sleeve, pick up and k.16 (18, 18, 20, 22, 22) sts. down left side of neck: 62 (68, 68, 74, 80, 80) sts. Work 2 in. in k.1, p.1 rib. Cast off loosely in rib.

FRONT EDGINGS
With right side of work facing, and with No. 8 needles, pick up and k.66 (72, 74, 82, 84, 86) sts. evenly along front edge of Right Front from bottom to neck.
K.3 rows. Cast off.
Rep. for Right Front but pick up sts. from neck edge to bottom.

TO COMPLETE
Using backstitch, join side and sleeve seams. Sew in zip, placing top of zip to base of neckband. Fold neckband in half on to wrong side and slipstitch down.
Neaten short edges of neckband.

Cable-patterned pinafore dress

MATERIALS
8 (9) hanks (2-oz.) Robin Aran (see note on wools and yarns, page 20); one pair each Nos. 7 and 10 knitting needles (see page 26); one cable needle; one buckle 1 in. wide.

MEASUREMENTS
To fit chest size 30 (32) in.; length 28 (30) in.

TENSION
5 sts. and 6 rows to 1 in. with No. 7 needles (see note on tension, page 15).

ABBREVIATIONS
See page 26.

BACK
With No. 7 needles cast on 98 (104) sts. and work 7 rows in st.st.
Next row (hem ridge): k.
1st row: k.38 (41), p.2, k.1, p.2, k.12, p.2, k.1, p.2, k. to end.

2nd row: p.38 (41), k.2, p.1, k.2, p.12, k.2, p.1, k.2, p. to end.
3rd row: k.38 (41), p.2, (make bobble: into next st. work k.1, p.1, k.1, p.1, turn, p. these 4 sts., turn, k. these 4 sts., slip 4th, 3rd and 2nd sts. over first: m.b.), p.2, (slip next 3 sts. on to cable needle and put to back of work, k. next 3 sts., then k.3 sts. from cable needle: c.3b.), (slip next 3 sts. on to cable needle and put to front of work, k. next 3 sts., then k. 3 sts. from cable needle: c.3f.), p.2, m.b., p.2, k. to end.
4th row: as 2nd row.
5th row: as first row.
6th row: as 2nd row.
7th row: k.38 (41), p.2, m.b., p.2, k.12, p.2, m.b., p.2, k. to end.
8th row: as 2nd row.
These 8 rows form patt. Cont. in patt. until work measures 3 in. from hem ridge and then work 2 sts.

With a jumper or blouse, the pinafore is ideal for holiday or school wear

tog. at each end of the next row. Cont. in patt. dec. as above at 2-in. intervals until 80 (86) sts. remain. Cont. straight until work measures 20 (21½) in. from hem ridge, ending with a wrong-side row.

Shape Armholes. Cast off 7 sts. at beg. of next 2 rows.**

Now work 2 sts. tog. at each end of the next and every alt. row until 56 (60) sts. remain. Cont straight until armholes measure 8 (8½) in. ending with a wrong-side row.

Shape Shoulders. Cast off 7 (7) sts. at beg. of next 2 rows and 6 (7) sts. at beg. of next 2 rows. Leave remaining 30 (32) sts. on stitch holder.

FRONT

Work as Back to **.

Shape Neck. Next row: k.2 tog., patt. 31 (34); turn.

Next row: p. 2 tog., patt. to end.

Now work 2 sts. tog. at neck edge on every 3rd row, but cont. to work patt. at neck edge until all patt. sts. have been worked off, and at the same time work 2 sts. tog. at armhole edge on every right-side row until 4 (5) more decs. have been worked. Cont. to dec. at neck edge until 13 (14) sts. remain. Cont. straight until armhole measures 8 (8½) in., ending with a wrong-side row.

Shape Shoulder. Cast off 7 sts. at beg. of next row. Work 1 row straight. Cast off.

Rejoin yarn to remaining 33 (36) sts. and complete to match first side, reversing shapings.

NECK EDGING

Join right shoulder seam. With right side of work facing, and with No. 10 needles, pick up and k. 39 (42) sts. down left side of V-neck, 1 st. in centre of V and 39 (42) sts. up right side of V-neck, and k. across 30 (32) sts. of back neck: 109 (117) sts. Work in k.1, p.1 rib on these sts., but work centre st. at base of V in garter st., and work 2 sts. tog. at each side of this centre st. on every row. Cont. until edging measures 1 in. Cast off in rib.

ARMHOLE EDGINGS (both alike)

Join left shoulder seam. With right side of work

facing and with No. 10 needles, pick up and k. 94 (100) sts. around armhole and work 1 in. in k.1, p.1 rib. Cast off in rib.

BELT

With No. 10 needles cast on 13 sts.

1st row: k.1, *k.1, p.1; rep. from * to end.

2nd row: *k.1, p.1; rep. from * to last st., k.1.

Rep. these 2 rows until work measures 34 in. Now work 2 sts. tog. at each end of every alt. row until 3 sts. remain. Work 3 sts. tog. Fasten off.

TO COMPLETE

Join side seams. Turn up hem and slipstitch in place. Stitch straight end of belt to buckle bar.

Lattice-bordered suit

MATERIALS

18 (19, 20) oz. Wendy Nylonised Double Knitting (see note on wools and yarns, page 20); one pair each Nos. 7 and 8 knitting needles (see page 26); 6 buttons ⅝ in. in diameter; a waist length of elastic ¾ in. wide.

MEASUREMENTS

To fit chest size 26½ (28¾, 31) in.; length of jacket

Jacket buttons neatly to the neck, and the skirt is gently flared

$15\frac{3}{4}$ ($16\frac{3}{4}$, 18) in.; jacket sleeve seam $11\frac{1}{2}$ ($12\frac{1}{2}$, $13\frac{1}{2}$) in.; length of skirt 14 ($15\frac{1}{2}$, $17\frac{1}{2}$) in.

TENSION
11 sts. to 2 in. over main patt. with No. 8 needles (see note on tension, page 15).

ABBREVIATIONS
See page 26.

JACKET
BACK
With No. 8 needles cast on 74 (78, 82) sts.
Main patt. 1st row: k.sts. t.b.l.
2nd row: k.
3rd row: as first row.
4th row: p.
These 4 rows form main patt.
Rep. these 4 rows once, then rep. first, 2nd and 3rd rows once.
Next row: p.5 (3, 5), *p. into front and back of next st., p.8 (9, 9); rep. from * 6 times, p. into front and back of next st., p.5 (4, 6): 82 (86, 90) sts.
Change to No. 7 needles.
Border Patt. 1st row: k.1, *k.2 tog., y.r.n. twice, sl.1, k.1, p.s.s.o.; rep. from * to last st., k.1.
2nd row: *p.2, k.1, k.1 t.b.l.; rep. from * to last 2 sts., p.2.
3rd row: (k. into back of 2nd st., then k. into front of first st., slip both off needle tog.: tw. 2b.), *p.2, tw.2b.; rep. from * to end.
4th row: *p.2, k.2; rep. from * to last 2 sts., p.2.
5th row: k.1, y.fwd., *sl.1, k.1, p.s.s.o., k.2 tog., y.r.n. twice; rep. from * to last 5 sts., sl.1, k.1, p.s.s.o., k.2 tog., y.fwd., k.1.
6th row: k.2, *p.2, k.1, k.1 t.b.l.; rep. from * to end.
7th row: p.2, *tw.2b., p.2; rep. from * to end.
8th row: *k.2, p.2; rep. from * to last 2 sts., k.2.
Rep. first to 8th border-patt. rows once, then work first to 4th border-patt. rows again.
Change to No. 8 needles.
Next row: k.5 (3, 5) t.b.l., *k.2 tog. t.b.l., k.8 (9, 9) t.b.l.; rep. from * 6 times, k.2 tog. t.b.l., k.5 (4, 6) t.b.l.: 74 (78, 82) sts.
Work 2nd, 3rd and 4th main-patt. rows, then rep. 4 main-patt. rows until work measures $9\frac{3}{4}$ ($10\frac{1}{4}$, 11) in., ending with right side facing.
Shape Armholes. Still working main patt., cast off 3 sts. at beg. of next 2 rows then 2 sts. at beg. of foll. 2 rows.
Now work 2 sts. tog. at each end of every alt. row until 54 (58, 62) sts. remain.
Cont. straight until armholes measure $5\frac{1}{2}$ (6, $6\frac{1}{2}$) in., ending with right side facing.
Shape Shoulders. Cast off loosely 4 (5, 5) sts. at beg. of next 2 (2, 4) rows, then 4 sts. at beg. of foll. 6 (6, 4) rows.
Leave remaining 22 (24, 26) sts. on stitch holder.

RIGHT FRONT
With No. 8 needles cast on 34 (38, 42) sts. Work 4 main-patt. rows as given for Back twice, then first, 2nd and 3rd main-patt. rows once.
12th row: p., inc. 1 st. purlwise in every 8th (8th, 9th) st.: 38 (42, 46) sts.
Change to No. 7 needles and work 8 border-patt. rows as given for Back twice, then work first to 4th border-patt. rows again.**
Next row: slip first 9 (13, 17) sts. on a stitch holder, rejoin yarn to remaining sts. and with No. 8 needles k. sts. t.b.l., working 2 sts. tog. at every 9th (10th, 15th) st.: 26 (27, 28) sts.
Cont. working main patt. until work measures same as Back to beg. of armhole shaping, ending at side edge.
Shape Armhole. Still working in main patt., cast off 3 sts. at beg. of next row and 2 sts. at beg. of foll. alt. row. Now work 2 sts. tog. at side edge on next 5 alt. rows: 16 (17, 18) sts.
Cont. straight until armhole measures same as Back armholes ending at side edge.
Shape Shoulder. Cast off loosely 4 (5, 5) sts. at beg. of next row, 4 (4, 5) sts. at beg. of next alt. row and 4 sts. at beg. of next alt. row.
Work 1 row straight. Cast off.

LEFT FRONT
Work as Right Front to **.
Next row: with No. 8 needles, k. sts. t.b.l., working 2 sts. tog. at every 9th (10th, 15th) st., to last 9 (13, 17) sts., slip these sts. on to stitch holder: 26 (27, 28) sts. Cont. as right front, reversing shapings.

LEFT FRONT BORDER
With right side of work facing, and No. 7 needles, rejoin yarn to inner edge of 9 (13, 17) sts. of Left Front border, cast on 1 st. and put on left-hand needle. Work 5th row of border patt. across all sts.
Work 6th to 8th rows of border patt., then rep. 8 border-patt. rows until work measures $13\frac{1}{4}$ ($14\frac{1}{4}$, $15\frac{1}{2}$) in., ending at front edge.
Shape Neck. Keeping patt. correct, cast off 2 (4, 4) sts. at beg. of next row and 2 (3, 4) sts. at beg. of next alt. row. Now work 2 sts. tog. at this edge on every 3rd (3rd, 2nd) row until 2 sts. remain. Fasten off.

RIGHT FRONT BORDER
With right side of work facing, and with No. 7 needles, rejoin yarn to front edge of 9 (13, 17) sts. of Right Front border, then work 5th row of border patt., casting on 1 st. at end of row.
Now complete to match Left Front border and sew to Right Front.

SLEEVES (make 2 alike)
With No. 8 needles cast on 37 (38, 41) sts. and rep. 4

main-patt. rows, inc. 1 st. at each end of 10th (8th, 14th) and every foll. 13th row until there are 53 (56, 59) sts.

Cont. straight in main patt. until work measures 11½ (12½, 13½) in.

Shape Top. Still working in main patt., cast off 3 sts. at beg. of next 2 rows then 2 sts. at beg. of foll. 4 rows. Now work 2 sts. tog. at each end of every foll. 3rd row until 23 (26, 29) sts. remain. Work 2 sts. tog. at each end of next 3 alt. rows. Cast off 2 sts. at beg. of next 4 rows. Cast off remaining 9 (12, 15) sts.

NECKBAND

Join shoulder seams. With right side facing and No. 8 needles, pick up and k. 15 (17, 19) sts. from neck edge of Right Front, k. across 22 (24, 26) sts. of back neck, pick up and k. 15 (17, 19) sts. from neck edge of Left Front: 52 (58, 64) sts. Work 2nd, 3rd and 4th main-patt. rows once, then first to 4th main-patt. rows once. Work first row again. Cast off knitwise.

RIGHT FRONT BAND

With right side of work facing and with No. 8 needles, pick up evenly and k. 78 (84, 90) sts. from bottom of front edge of Right Front to neck and 6 sts. from edge of neckband: 84 (90, 96) sts.

Work 2nd to 4th main-patt. rows once.

Next 2 rows: k.4 (5, 6) t.b.l., *cast off 2 sts., k. 13 (14, 15) t.b.l.; rep. from * 4 times, cast off 2 sts., work to end; turn; k. back, casting on 2 sts. over cast-off sts. Work 3rd and 4th main-patt. rows once, then first row once. Cast off knitwise.

LEFT FRONT BAND

Work as Right Front band, omitting buttonholes.

Matching waistcoat and sleeveless pullover

(photographed in colour on page 150)

MATERIALS

For waistcoat: 5 (5, 6) balls Sirdar Pullman; 4 toggles.

For pullover: 6 (7, 7) balls Sirdar Pullman (see note on wools and yarns, page 20).

For both: one pair each Nos. 4 and 6 knitting needles (see page 26).

MEASUREMENTS

To fit chest size 30 (32, 34) in.

TENSION

7½ sts. and 10 rows to 2 in. over st.st. with No. 4 needles (see note on tension, page 15).

TO COMPLETE

Sew in sleeves and join side and sleeve seams.
Sew buttons on left front band to correspond with buttonholes.

SKIRT

MAIN PIECE (make 2 alike)

With No. 8 needles cast on 94 (102, 114) sts. and work first to 4th main-patt. rows twice, then first to 3rd main-patt. rows once.

Next row: p.8 (8, 7), *inc. 1 st. in next st. purlwise, p.10 (11, 8); rep. from * 6 (6, 10) times, inc. 1 st. in next st. purlwise, p. 8 (9, 7): 102 (110, 126) sts. Change to No. 7 needles and work first to 8th border-patt. rows twice, then first to 4th border-patt. rows once.

Change to No. 8 needles.

Next row: k.8 (8,7) t.b.l., *k.2 tog. t.b.l., k.10 (11, 8) t.b.l.; rep. from * 6 (6, 10) times, k.2 tog. t.b.l., k.8 (9, 7) t.b.l.: 94 (102, 114) sts. Work 2nd to 4th main-patt. rows once then first to 3rd rows once.

Next row: p.22 (24, 28), p.2 tog., p.46 (50, 54), p.2 tog., p. to end. Work first to 3rd main-patt. rows once.

Next row: p.21 (23, 27), p.2 tog., p.46 (50, 54), p.2 tog., p. to end: 90 (98, 110) sts.

Cont. in this way, dec. twice on every 4th main-patt. row, each time working 1 st. fewer before making first dec., until 62 (66, 70) sts. remain.

Cont. straight until work measures 13 (14½, 16½) in. Work 1 in. in k.1, p.1 rib. Cast off in rib.

TO COMPLETE

Join side seams. Join elastic in a circle of required size. Place inside waist ribbing and herringbone-stitch over it to hold it in place.

ABBREVIATIONS

See page 26.

WAISTCOAT

RIGHT FRONT

With No. 4 needles cast on 34 (37, 38) sts.

1st row (wrong side): k.1 (1, 2), *p.2, k.1; rep. from * to end.

2nd row: k.1, *(k. into front of 2nd st. then into back of first st., slip both off needle tog.: tw. 2f.), p.1; rep. from * to last 3 (3, 4) sts., tw. 2f., p. to end.

Rep. these 2 rows twice. **For size 32 only:** work 2 sts. tog. at end of last row.

For all sizes. 7th row: p. to last 7 sts., patt. 7.

8th row: patt. 7, k. to end.

Cont. thus, keeping edging correct, until 48 (54, 60) rows have been completed, ending with wrong side facing.

Armhole Edging and Front Slope. 1st row: k.1, p.1, (pick up loop between sts. on previous row and p. t.b.l.: make 1 p.), k.1, p. to last 7 sts., patt. 7.

2nd row: patt 6, p. 2 tog., k. to last 4 sts., p.1, tw.2f., k.1.

3rd row: k.1, p.2, k.1, p.1, make 1 p., k.1, p. to last 7 sts., patt. 7.

4th row: patt. 7, k. to last 7 sts., (p.1, tw.2f.) twice, k.1.

5th row: (k.1, p.2) twice, k.1, p.1, make 1 p., k.1, p. to last 7 sts., patt. 7.

6th row: patt. 6, p.2 tog., k. to last 10 sts., (p.1, tw.2f.) 3 times, k.1: 35 (37, 39) sts.

Shape Armholes. Next row: cast off 3 sts., (p.2, k.1) twice, p. to last 7 sts., patt. 7.

Next row: patt. 7, k. to last 8 sts., p. 2 tog., tw.2f., p.1, tw.2f., k.1.

Next row: patt. 6, k.2 tog., p. to last 7 sts., patt. 7.

Next row: patt. 6, p. 2 tog., k. to last 8 sts., p.2 tog., patt. 6. Cont. to dec. on every 4th row for the neck shaping and at the same time complete armhole shaping by dec. 1 st. on next and foll. 1 (1, 2) alt. rows. Then keeping edgings correct, cont. to dec. for neck shaping until 22 (23, 24) sts. remain. Cont. straight until work measures 16 (18, 20) in., ending at side edge.

Shape Shoulders. Cast off 7 sts. at beg. of next row, 4 sts. at beg. of next alt. row and 4 (5, 6) sts. at beg. of foll. alt. row. Work in patt. on remaining 7 sts. for 5 in., then cast off.

LEFT FRONT

Cast on as for Right Front.

1st row (wrong side); *k.1, p.2; rep. from * to last 1 (1, 2) sts., k. to end.

2nd row: p.1 (1, 2), tw.2f., *p.1, tw.2f.; rep. from * to last st., k.1.

3rd (buttonhole) row: k.1, p.2 tog., y.r.n. twice, *k.1, p.2; rep. from * to last 1 (1, 2) sts., k. to end.

4th row: as 2nd row, but drop extra loop at buttonhole.

Rep. first and 2nd rows once. **For size 32 only:** work 2 sts. tog. at beg. of last row.

For all sizes. 7th row: patt. 7, p. to end.

8th row: k. to last 7 sts., patt. 7.

Now cont. as Right Front, reversing shapings and making a buttonhole every 14 (16, 18) rows until 4 in all are made.

BACK

With No. 4 needles cast on 61 (64, 70) sts.

1st row (wrong side): k.1, *p.2, k.1; rep. from * to end.

2nd row: k.1, *tw.2f., p.1; rep. from * to end.

Rep. these 2 rows twice.

Starting with a p. row cont. in st.st.

For size 30 only: work 2 sts. tog. at beg. of first row.

For size 34 only: k.2 sts. tog. each end of first row.

For all sizes: work in st.st. until Back measures same as Fronts to beg. of armhole edging, ending with a k. row.

Armhole Edgings. 1st row: k.1, p.1, make 1 p., k.1, p. to last 3 sts., k.1, make 1 p., p.1, k.1.

2nd row: k.1, tw.2f., p.1, k. to last 4 sts., p.1, tw.2f., k.1.

3rd row: k.1, p.2, k.1, p.1, make 1 p., k.1, p. to last 6 sts., k.1, make 1 p., p.1, k.1, p.2, k.1.

4th row: k.1, (tw.2f., p.1) twice, k. to last 7 sts., (p.1, tw.2f.) twice, k.1.

5th row: (k.1, p.2) twice, k.1, p.1, make 1 p., k.1, p. to last 9 sts., k.1, make 1 p., p.1, k.1, (p.2, k.1) twice.

6th row: k.1, (tw.2f., p.1) 3 times, k. to last 10 sts., (p.1, tw.2f.) 3 times, k.1: 66 (70, 74) sts.

Shape Armholes. Next row: cast off 3 sts., patt. 6, p. to last 10 sts., patt. 10.

Next row: cast off 3 sts., patt. 6, k. to last 7 sts., patt. 7.

Next row: patt. 6, p. 2 tog., k. to last 8 sts., p.2 tog., patt. 6.

Next row: patt. 6, p. 2 tog., k. to last 8 sts., k.2 tog., patt. 6.

Cont. to dec. 1 st. at each end of next 2 rows and at each end of foll. 1 (1, 2) alt. rows. Keeping edgings correct, work on remaining 50 (54, 56) sts. until Back measures same as Fronts to beg. of shoulder shaping.

Shape Shoulders. Cast off 7 sts., at beg. of next 2 rows, 4 sts. at beg. of next 2 rows and 4 (5, 6) sts. at beg. of next 2 rows. Cast off remaining sts.

TO COMPLETE

Sew shoulder seams and side seams. Join ends of neckbands tog. and sew bands in position round neck. Sew toggles to Right Front to match button-holes.

SLEEVELESS PULLOVER
FRONT

Work as Waistcoat Back to beg. of armhole edgings. Work another 2 in. in st.st., ending after a k. row.

Armhole and V-Neck Edgings. 1st row: k.1, p.1, make 1 p., k.1, p. 24 (26, 28), k.1, make 1 p., p.1, k.2, p.1, make 1 p., k.1, p. 24 (26, 28), k.1, make 1 p., p.1, k.1.

2nd row: k.1, tw.2f., p.1, k.24 (26, 28), (p.1, tw.2f., p.1) twice, k.24 (26, 28), p.1, tw. 2f., k.1.

3rd row: k.1, p.2, k.1, p.1, make 1 p., k.1, p.20 (22, 24), k.1, make 1 p., p.1, (k.1, p.2, k.1) twice, p.1, make 1 p., k.1, p.20 (22, 24), k.1, make 1 p., p.1, k.1, p.2, k.1: 68 (72, 76) sts.

4th row: k.1, (tw.2f., p.1) twice, k.20 (22, 24), (p.1, tw.2f.) twice, p.2, (tw.2f., p.1) twice, k.20

(22, 24), (p.1, tw.2f.) twice, k.1

5th row: (k.1, p.2) twice, k.1, p.1, make 1 p., k.1, p.18 (20, 22), (k.1, p.2) twice, k.2, (p.2, k.1) twice, p.18 (20, 22), k.1, make 1 p., p.1, k.1, (p.2, k.1) twice.

6th row: patt. 10, k.18 (20, 22), patt. 6, p.2, patt. 6, k.18 (20, 22), patt. 10

Shape Armhole and V-Neck. Next row: cast off 3 sts., patt. 6, p.18 (20, 22), patt. 7; turn.

Next row: k.1, patt. 5, p.2 tog., k. to last 8 sts., p.2 tog., patt. 6.

Next row: patt. 6, k.2 tog., p. to last 7 sts., patt. 7. Cont. to dec. at neck edge on every 4th row, and at the same time dec. 1 st. at armhole edge on next 2 rows and on foll. 1 (1, 2) alt. rows. Then, keeping edgings correct, cont. to dec. at neck edge as before until 22 (23, 24) sts. remain.

Work straight until Front measures 18 (20, 22) in., ending at side edge, and then shape shoulder as for Right Front of Waistcoat. Rejoin yarn to rem. sts. Complete to match first side, reversing shapings.

BACK

Work as Sleeveless Pullover Front to beg. of armhole edging. Now work edgings, armholes and shoulder shapings at 18 (20, 22) in. from beg. as Waistcoat Back.

TO COMPLETE

Sew shoulder and side seams. Join ends of neck-bands tog. and sew band round neck.

Chapter 6

Time for Teenagers

Girl's two-way jumper

MATERIALS
For Mini Top: 5 (5) oz. Sirdar Courtelle Crêpe Double Knitting.
For Jumper: 9 (10) oz. Sirdar Courtelle Crêpe Double Knitting (see note on wools and yarn, page 20). **For both:** one pair No. 9 knitting needles (see page 26).

MEASUREMENTS
To fit chest or bust size 30 (32) in.; length of mini top 12 (12½) in.; length of jumper 20½ (21) in.

TENSION
6 sts. to 1 in. (see note on tension, page 15).

ABBREVIATIONS
See page 26.

MINI TOP
BACK (worked from shoulders downwards).
Cast on 28 (30) sts.
Foundation row: k. into back of sts.
1st row (front of work): cast on 6 sts., *k.1, p.1; rep. from * to end.
2nd row: cast on 6 (7) sts., k. to end.
3rd row: cast on 6 (7) sts., *p.1, k.1; rep. from * to end.
4th row: as 2nd row.
5th row: cast on 6 sts., *k.1, p.1; rep. from * to end.
6th row: cast on 6 sts., k. to end.
7th row: cast on 6 sts., * p.1, k.1; rep. from * to end.
8th row: as 6th row: 76 (82) sts.
Cont. on these sts. in patt. as set in 5th-8th rows omitting cast-on sts. until armhole measures 4½ in., ending after a first patt. row.
Shape Armholes. 1st row: inc. 1 st. into first st., k. to last st., inc. 1 st. in this st.
Next row: * k.1, p.1; rep. from * to end. Rep. last 2 rows 5 times: 88 (94) sts.

Cast on 6 sts. at beg. of next 2 rows: 100 (106) sts. **
Cont. on these sts. for a further 30 (34) rows, then work in k.1, p.1 rib for 14 rows. Cast off in rib.

FRONT
Left Shoulder. Cast on 6 (7) sts. and k. into back of these.
1st row (front of work): * k.1, p.1; rep. from * to end.
2nd row: cast on 6 (7) sts., k. to end.
3rd row: * p.1, k.1; rep. from * to end.
4th row: cast on 6 sts., k. to end.
5th row: as first row.
6th row: cast on 6 sts., k. to end.
7th row: *p.1, k.1; rep. from * to end: 24 (26) sts.
8th row: k. to end.
Work 13 rows on these sts.
*** **Shape Neck. 1st row:** k. to last st., inc. 1 st. in this st.
2nd row: * k.1, p.1; rep. from * to end.
Rep. last 2 rows until 30 (32) sts. are on needle, ending with a k. row.
Next row: cast on 3 (4) sts., patt. to end: 33 (36) sts. Cont. on these sts. until work measures 4½ in., ending before a k. row.
Shape Armhole. 1st row: inc. 1 st. in first st., k. to end.
2nd row: patt. to end.
Rep. these 2 rows 5 times: 39 (42) sts.
Cast on 6 sts. at beg. of next row: 45 (48) sts. Work 4 more rows on these sts., *** casting on 10 sts. at end of last row (a k. row). Leave sts. on a stitch holder.
Right Shoulder. 1st row: cast on 6 (7) sts., * k.1, p.1; rep. from * to end.
2nd row: k. to end.

Maxi or mini length — either way this jumper is tops with trousers!

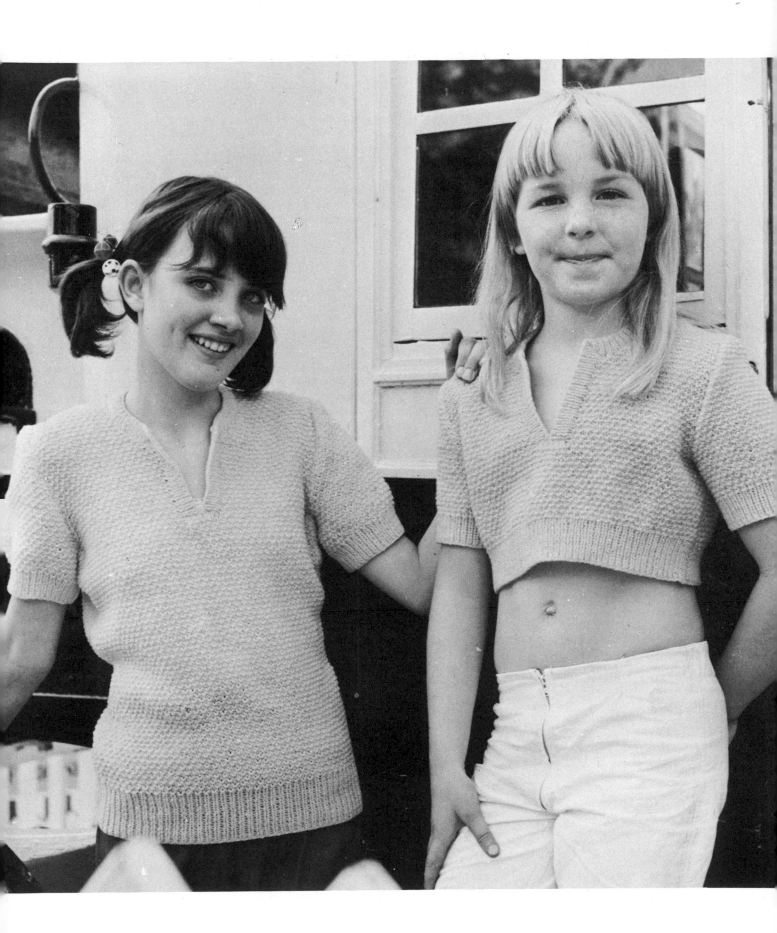

3rd row: cast on 6 (7) sts., * p.1, k.1; rep. from * to end.

4th row: k. to end.

Rep. these 4 rows once but for both sizes cast on 6 sts. on first and 3rd rows: 24 (26) sts. Work 14 rows on these sts. Now work from *** to *** of Left Shoulder, working patt. rows for k. rows and vice versa to reverse shaping.

Next row: patt. 45 (48) sts. then patt. over the 10 cast-on sts. of left shoulder, patt. to end: 100 (106) sts. ****

Cont. on these sts. till Front measures the same as Back to ribbing. Work 14 rows in k.1, p.1 rib and cast off in rib.

NECK RIBBING

With right side of work facing, pick up and k. 32 (34) sts. from right side of front opening working from lower edge to neck edge.

1st row: work p.1, k.1 into first st. p.1, * k.1, p.1; rep. from * to end.

2nd row: * k.1, p.1; rep. from * to last st., k.1, p.1 into last st.

Rep. these 2 rows once: 36 (38) sts.

5th row: * k.1, p.1; rep. from * to end. Cast off.

Now with right side of work facing, begin at neck edge of left side of front opening and pick up and k. 32 (34) sts. down left side to lower edge of opening. Work in rib on these as for other side, inc. at end of first row and beg. of 2nd, and complete to match first side.

With right side of work facing begin at right neck edge of Front and pick up and k. 31 (33) sts. round right side of neck, 26 (28) sts. round back neck and 31 (33) sts. round left side of neck: 88 (94) sts.

Now work in k.1, p.1 rib on these sts., working twice into first and last st. of every row for 4 rows: 96 (102) sts.

Rib 1 more row and cast off in rib.

SLEEVES (make 2 alike)

Cast on 16 (18) sts.

1st row: k. to end.

2nd row: cast on 2 sts., *k.1, p.1: rep. from * to end.

3rd row: cast on 2 sts., k. to end.

4th row: cast on 2 sts., * p.1, k.1; rep. from * to end.

5th row: as 3rd row.

6th row: work p.1, k.1 into first st., rib to last st., (p.1, k.1) into this st.

7th row: k. to end.

Rep. last 2 rows 17 (19) times: 60 (66) sts.

Next row: cast on 6 sts., * k.1, p.1; rep. from * to end.

Next row: cast on 6 sts., k. to end: 72 (78) sts.

Work on these sts. for 16 rows, then work in k.1, p.1 rib for 10 rows and cast off in rib.

TO COMPLETE

Sew sleeves in armholes and join side seams.

JUMPER

BACK

Work as Mini Top Back to ** when armhole shaping is complete.*****

Cont. straight on these sts. until 3 (3½) in. have been worked from armhole shaping, then work 2 sts. tog. at each end of next and every foll. 6th row until 88 (94) sts. remain. Cont. straight until work measures 13 (13½) in. from armhole shaping, then work in k.1, p.1 rib for 3 in. Cast off in rib.

FRONT

Work as Mini Top Front to ****, then work as Jumper Back from *****.

SLEEVES (make 2 alike)

Work as Mini Top Sleeves.

TO COMPLETE

Work as for Mini Top.

Ribbed sweater dress

(photographed in black and white opposite, right)

MATERIALS

21 (23) oz. Lee Target Motoravia Double Knitting (see note on wools and yarns, page 20); one pair each Nos. 8 and 10 knitting needles (see page 26); 2 buttons ⅝ in. in diameter; 1 buckle 1–1½ in. wide.

MEASUREMENTS

To fit bust size 32 (34) in.; length 31 (32) in.; sleeve seam 17 in.

TENSION

6 sts. and 6½ rows to 1 in. over rib patt. with No. 8 needles (see note on tension, page 15).

ABBREVIATIONS

See page 26.

BACK

With No. 8 needles cast on 102 (106) sts. and work 5 rows in garter st. (see page 23).

Next row: k.1, p. to last st., k.1.

Rep. last 6 rows until work measures 15½ (16) in., ending with right side facing.

Junior sweater dresses with a top-fashion look – instructions for zipped dress (left) are on page 140

Next row: k.2, * p.2, k.2; rep. from * to end.
Next row: k.1, p.1, * k.2, p.2; rep. from * to last 4 sts., k.2, p.1, k.1.
Rep. last 2 rows until work measures 24½ (25) in., ending with right side facing.
Shape Armholes. Cast off 4 sts. at beg. of next 2 rows then work 2 sts. tog. at each end of next 3 rows. Work 2 sts. tog. at each end of next 2 alt. rows. **
Cont. straight on these 84 (88) sts. until work measures 31 (32) in., then cast off 9 sts. at beg. of next 2 rows.
Next row: cast off 9 sts., patt. 11 (12) sts.; leave these sts. on a stitch holder, cast off 26 (28) sts., patt. to end.
Next row: working on last set of sts. only, cast off 9 sts., patt. to last 2 sts., k.2 tog.
Next row: k.2 tog., patt. to end. Cast off remaining 9 (10) sts.
Rejoin yarn to sts. on stitch holder and work to match first side, reversing shapings.

FRONT

Work as for Back to **, ending with right side facing.
Divide for Neck. Next row: k.1, patt. 37 (39) sts., cast on 8 sts. for underflap; turn, leaving other sts. on a stitch holder.
Work on first set of sts. only thus:
1st row: k.8, patt. to end.
2nd row: k.1, patt. to last 8 sts., k.8.
Rep. these 2 rows once.
5th row: k.1, p.7, patt. to end.
6th row: as 2nd row.
Rep. last 6 rows until work is 12 rows less than Back to shoulder shapings, ending with wrong side facing.
Shape Neck. Cast off 12 (13) sts., patt. to end. Work 2 sts. tog. at neck edge on each of next 3 rows then on every alt. row until 27 (28) sts. remain.
Shape Shoulders. Next row (armhole edge): cast off 9 sts., patt. to end.
Next row: k.1, patt. to end.
Rep. these 2 rows once. Cast off. Rejoin yarn to sts. on stitch holder.
1st row: k.8, patt. to end.

2nd row: k.1, patt. to last 8 sts., k.8.
Rep. these 2 rows once.
5th row: as first row.
6th row: k.1, patt. to last 8 sts., p.7, k.1.
7th row (buttonhole row): k.3, cast off 2 sts., k.3, patt. to end.
8th row: work in patt., casting on 2 sts. over 2 cast-off sts. Complete to match first side, reversing shapings and working another buttonhole on 5th and 6th rows down from neck shaping.

SLEEVES (make 2 alike)

The sleeves are worked entirely in garter st. patt.
With No. 10 needles cast on 43 (45) sts., and work 18 rows in garter st. patt.
Change to No. 8 needles and inc. 1 st. at each end of next and every foll. 8th row until there are 75 (77) sts. Cont. straight until work measures 17 in., ending with right side facing.
Shape Top. Cast off 4 sts. at beg. of next 2 rows then work 2 sts. tog. at each end of next 3 rows. Work 2 sts. tog. at each end of every alt. row until 39 sts. remain. Cast off 5 sts. at beg. of next 6 rows. Cast off.

TO COMPLETE

Sew shoulder seams.
Neckband. With right side of work facing, and with No. 10 needles, and beg. 8 sts. from right front edge, pick up and k. 22 (23) sts. round side of neck, 32 (34) sts. across back of neck and 22 (23) round other side of neck, ending 8 sts. in from left front edge: 76 (80) sts.
Work 4 rows in garter st.
5th row: k.1, p. to last st., k.1.
Work 5 rows in garter st., then rep. 5th row.
Work 3 rows in garter st. Cast off.
Belt. With No. 10 needles cast on 186 (190) sts. and work 5 rows in garter st.
Next row: k.1, p. to last st., k.1.
Rep. last 6 rows once. Work 5 rows in garter st. Cast off.
To Make Up. Sew in sleeves; sew up side and sleeve seams. Sew buttons to match buttonholes and attach buckle to one end of belt.

Green waistcoat and trousers

(photographed in colour opposite)

MATERIALS

26 (27) oz. Hayfield Gaylon Double Knitting (see note on wools and yarns, page 20); one pair each Nos. 8 and 10 knitting needles (see page 26); one cable needle; 8 buttons ¾ in. in diameter; waist length of elastic, 1 in. wide.

MEASUREMENTS

Waistcoat: to fit chest size 28 (30) in.; length 27 (28½) in.

Cable pattern on the long-line waistcoat is repeated down sides of trousers

Trousers: to fit hip size 30 (32) in.; inside leg measurement 25½ (26) in.

TENSION
5½ sts. to 1 in. with No. 8 needles (see note on tension, page 15).

ABBREVIATIONS
See page 26; c.6b., slip next 3 sts. on to cable needle and put to back of work, k. next 3 sts., then k. sts. from cable needle; c.6f., slip next 3 sts. on to cable needle and put to front of work, k. next 3 sts., then k. sts. from cable needle.

WAISTCOAT
BACK
With No. 8 needles cast on 104 (110) sts. and work 6 rows in k.1, p.1 rib.
1st patt. row: k.24 (26), p.3, k.6, p.3, k.32 (34), p.3, k.6, p.3, k.24 (26).
2nd patt. row: p.24 (26), k.3, p.6, k.3, p.32 (34), k.3, p.6, k.3, p.24 (26).
3rd patt. row: k.24 (26), p.3, c.6b., p.3, k.32 (34), p.3, c.6f., p.3, k.24 (26).
4th patt. row: as 2nd row.
Rep. first and 2nd patt. rows twice.
Now cont. in patt. as above, working a cable row every 8 rows. When work measures 4½ (5) in. work 2 sts. tog. at each end of the next row, and then at 1-in. intervals until 76 (82) sts. remain. Cont. straight until work measures 20 (21) in. ending with a p. row.
Shape Armholes. Cast off 6 sts. at beg. of next 2 rows and then work 2 sts. tog. at each end of every k. row until 56 (62) sts. remain. Cont. straight until armhole measures 7 (7½) in., then cast off 8 sts. at beg. of next 2 rows and 7 (8) sts. at beg of next 2 rows. Cast off.

LEFT FRONT
With No. 8 needles cast on 52 (55) sts. and work 6 rows in k.1, p.1 rib.
1st patt. row: k.24 (26), p.3, k.6, p.3, k. to end.
2nd patt. row: p.16 (17), k.3, p.6, k.3, p. to end.
3rd patt. row: k.24 (26), p.3, c.6b., p.3, k. to end.
Now work as for Back on these sts., working a cable row every 8 rows. When work measures 4½ (5) in., with right side facing, work 2 sts. tog. at beg. of next row and at the beg. of a right-side row at 1-in. intervals until 38 (41) sts. remain. Cont. straight until work measures 20 (21) in. ending with right side facing.
Shape Armholes and Front Slope. Next row: cast off 6 sts., patt. to last 2 sts., k.2 tog.

Pretty for the beach — a button-up shift with striped pockets (see page 170)

Cont. on these sts., working 2 sts. tog. at armhole edge on every right-side row until 4 (4) dec. in all have been worked, and at the same time work 2 sts. tog. at front edge at ½-in. intervals until 15 (16) sts. remain. Cont. straight until armhole measures 7 (7½) in., ending with right side facing. Cast off 8 sts. at beg. of next row. Patt. 1 row. Cast off.

RIGHT FRONT
With No. 8 needles cast on 52 (55) sts. and work first 6 rows in rib as for Left Front.
Next row: k.16 (17), p.3, k.6, p.3, k. to end.
Next row: p.24 (26), k.3, p.6, k.3, p. to end.
Next row: k.16 (17), p.3, c.6f., p.3, k. to end.
Cont. on these sts. to match Left Front, reversing all shapings.

ARMHOLE EDGINGS (make 2 alike)
With No. 10 needles cast on 9 sts. and work in k.1, p.1 rib until band is long enough to go all round one armhole. Cast off in rib.

FRONT BANDS
Left Band. With No. 10 needles cast on 9 sts. and work in k.1, p.1 rib until strip is long enough to go up Left Front and halfway round back of neck. Cast off. Mark 8 evenly spaced points for buttons on this strip, the top one level with the bottom of armhole.
Right Band. Work as Left Band, but work buttonholes to match marked points on left band.
1st buttonhole row: rib 3, cast off 3, rib to end.
2nd buttonhole row: rib 3, cast on 3, rib to end.

TROUSERS
LEFT LEG
With No. 8 needles cast on 104 (110) sts. and work 5 rows in st.st. (see page 23).
Next row: k. (this makes hem ridge).
Next row: k. 48 (51), p.3, k.6, p.3, k. to end.
Next row: p.44 (47), k.3, p.6, k.3, p. to end.
Next row: k.48 (51), p.3, c.6b., p.3, k. to end.
Work as for Back Waistcoat on these sts., working a cable row every 8 rows, and working 2 sts. tog. at each end of every 9th row until 82 (88) sts. remain. Cont. straight until work measures 15½ (16) in. from hem ridge, then inc. 1 st. at each end of the next and every foll. 5th row until there are 110 (116) sts. Cont. straight until work measures 25½ (26) in. from hem ridge ending with right side facing.
Shape Crutch. Cast off 3 sts. at beg. of next 4 rows then work 2 sts. tog. at each end of every 3rd row until 82 (88) sts. remain. Work 2 sts. tog. at each end of every foll. 4th row until 60 (64) sts. remain. Cont. straight until work measures 35¾ (36¼) in. from hem ridge, ending with a p. row.**
Next 2 rows: patt. 50 sts.; turn and work back.
Next 2 rows: patt. 40 sts.; turn and work back.
Cont. working thus with 10 sts. fewer each alt. row

until the foll. row has been completed: patt. 10; turn and work back.
Now work 6 rows in k.1, p.1 rib.
Cast off in rib.

RIGHT LEG
Cast on and work first 6 rows as for Left Leg.
Next row: k.44 (47), p.3, k.6, p.3, k. to end.
Next row: p.48 (51), k.3, p.6, k.3, p. to end.
Next row: k.44 (47), p.3, c.6f., p.3, k. to end.
Work as for Left Leg on these sts. to **, ending with a k. row.
Complete to match Left Leg.

TO COMPLETE
Waistcoat. Join shoulder and side seams. Sew bands to Fronts and join at back of neck; sew on buttons to match buttonholes. Sew bands round armholes.
Trousers. Join front and back and inside leg seams. Sew elastic into a circle of desired size and attach to inside waist ribbing with herringbone-st.

Cream boucle shift
(photographed in colour on page 168)

MATERIALS
18 (19) balls Robin Tricel-Nylon Boucle in cream, 1 ball in pink, 1 ball in brown and 1 ball in ginger (see note on wools and yarns, page 20); one pair each Nos. 8 and 10 knitting needles (see page 26); 8 cream buttons, $\frac{7}{8}$ in. in diameter.

MEASUREMENTS
To fit bust size 32 (34) in.; length 29 (31) in.

TENSION
6 sts. to 1 in. with No. 8 needles (see note on tension, page 15).

ABBREVIATIONS
See page 26; C., cream; Pk., pink; B., brown; G., ginger.

BACK
With No. 8 needles and C., cast on 116 (124) sts.
1st row: *k.2, p.2; rep. from * to end of row.
Rep. first row 5 times.
Work in st.st. (see page 23) until work measures 3 in. from beg. **Now dec. 1 st. (k.2 tog.) at each end of the next row and then work 2 in. straight.**
Rep. from ** to ** until 96 (104) sts. remain. Cont. straight until work measures 22 (23) in. from beg., ending with a p. row.
Shape Armholes. Cast off 7 sts. at beg. of next 2 rows, then k. 2 sts. tog. at each end of every k. row until 60 (64) sts. remain. Cont. straight until Back measures 29 (31) in., ending with a p. row.
Shape Neck. Cast off 5 sts. at beg. of next 2 rows, then 4 sts. at beg. of foll. 4 rows. Leave remaining 34 (38) sts. on a stitch holder.

LEFT FRONT
With No. 8 needles and C., cast on 58 (62) sts. and work 6 rows in k.2, p.2 rib as for Back. Work in st.st. until work measures 3 in. from beg., ending with a p. row. *** Dec. 1 st. at beg. of next row, then work 2 in., ending with a p. row. *** Rep. from *** to *** until 48 (52) sts. remain. Cont. straight until work measures 22 (23) in. from beg., ending with a p. row.
Shape Armholes. Cast off 7 sts. at beg. of next row and then k. 2 sts. tog. at armhole edge on every k. row until 30 (32) sts. remain. Cont. straight until work measures 25½ (27) in., ending with a k. row.
Shape Neck. Cast off 6 sts. at beg. of next row, then dec. 1 st. at neck edge of every row until 13 (13) sts. remain.
Cont. until work measures 29 (31) in. ending with a p. row. Cast off 5 sts. at beg. of next row.
Work 1 row. Cast off 4 sts. at beg. of next row.
Work 1 row. Cast off.

RIGHT FRONT
Work as Left Front, but reverse all shapings.

LEFT FRONT BAND
With No. 10 needles and C., cast on 13 sts. and work in k.1, p.1 rib until band is long enough to go up Left Front. Leave sts. on a stitch holder.

RIGHT FRONT BAND
With No. 10 needles and C., cast on 13 sts. and work in k.1, p.1 rib for ½ (1) in.
1st buttonhole row: rib 5, cast off 3, rib to end.
2nd buttonhole row: rib 5, cast on 3, rib to end.
Cont. in rib, working a buttonhole every 3½ (3¾) in. from previous buttonhole until 7 in all are made. Cont. in rib until strip is same length as Left Front Band. Leave sts. on a stitch holder.

TO COMPLETE
Join Back and Fronts at shoulder seams, and join

Bands to Fronts.

Neck Ribbing. With No. 10 needles and C., k. across sts. of Right Front Band, pick up and k. 36 (38) sts. round neck of Right Front, k. across 34 (38) sts. of Back, pick up and k. 36 (38) sts. round neck edge of Left Front, k. across 13 sts. of Left Front Band: 132 (140) sts.

Work in k.2, p.2 rib on these sts. for 1 in., making a buttonhole on Right Front Band on the 3rd and 4th rows. Cast off in rib.

Armhole Ribbing. With No. 10 needles and C., pick up and k. 102 (110) sts. round one armhole and work in k.2, p.2 rib for 1 in. Cast off in rib. Rep. for other armhole.

Pockets (make 2 alike). With No. 8 needles and Pk., cast on 30 sts. Working 6 rows st.st. **** Join B. and work 4 rows in st.st. Join C., and work 2 rows in st.st. Join G. and work 4 rows in st.st. Join Pk. and work 4 rows st.st. Rep. from **** once, then work 2 more rows in Pk. Cast off.

To make up. Join side seams. Sew on pockets, positioning them 6 in. up from lower edge, 3 in. in from centre front edges, with the stripes running vertically (see photograph on page 168). Sew buttons on Left Front to correspond with button-holes.

Blue Aran suit

(photographed in colour on page 185)

MATERIALS
13 balls (2-oz.) Regency Bainin wool (see note on wools and yarns, page 20); one pair each Nos. 8 and 10 knitting needles (see page 26); one cable needle; 18-in. open-ended zip fastener; waist length of elastic, 1 in. wide.

MEASUREMENTS
Top: to fit bust size 34 in.; length 22½ in.
Skirt: to fit hip size 36 in.; length 18½ in.

TENSION
5 sts. and 6½ rows to 1 in. over double moss st. with No. 8 needles (see note on tension, page 15).

ABBREVIATIONS
See page 26; tw.2f., k. into front of 2nd st. on left-hand needle, then k. into front of first st., slip both off needle tog.; tw.2b., k. into back of 2nd st., then into front of first st. and slip both off tog.; c.4b., put next 2 sts. on to cable needle and put to back of work, k. next 2 sts., then k. 2 sts. from cable needle; c.4f., put next 2 sts. on to cable needle and put to front of work, k. next 2 sts., then k. 2 sts. from cable needle; cr.2b., take needle behind first st. on left-hand needle and p. into back of 2nd st., k. first st. and slip both off needle tog.; cr.2f., take needle in front of first st. on left-hand needle and k. into front of 2nd st., p. first st. and slip both sts. off needle tog.

PATTERN A (36 sts.)
1st row: p.1, tw.2f., p.1, k.4, p.1, k.4, p.1, tw.2b., p.1., k.10, p.1, tw.2f., p.1, k.4, p.1.
2nd and every alt. row: k. all k. sts., p. all p. sts.
3rd row: p.1, tw.2f., p.1, c.4b., p.1, c.4f., p.1, tw.2b., p.1, cr.2b., k.6, cr.2f., p.1, tw.2f., p.1, c.4b., p.1.
5th row: p.1, tw.2f., p.1, k.4, p.1, k.4, p.1, tw.2b., p.2, cr.2b., k.4, cr.2f., p.2, tw.2f., p.1, k.4, p.1.
7th row: p.1, tw.2f., p.1, c.4b., p.1, c.4f., p.1, tw.2b., p.3, cr.2b., k.2, cr.2f., p.3, tw.2f., p.1, c.4b., p.1.
9th row: p.1, tw.2f., p.1, k.4, p.1, k.4, p.1, tw.2b., p.4, cr.2b., cr.2f., p.4, tw.2f., p.1, k.4, p.1.
11th row: p.1, tw.2f., p.1, c.4b., p.1, c.4f., p.1, tw.2b., p.5, tw.2f., p.5, tw.2f., p.1, c.4b., p.1.
13th row: p.1, tw.2f., p.1, k.4, p.1, k.4, p.1, tw.2b., p.5, tw.2f., p.5, tw.2f., p.1, k.4, p.1.
15th row: p.1, tw.2f., p.1, c.4b., p.1, c.4f., p.1, tw.2b., p.4, tw.2f., tw.2b., p.4, tw.2f., p.1, c.4b., p.1.
17th row: p.1, tw.2f., p.1, k.4, p.1, k.4, p.1, tw.2b., p.3, tw.2f., k.2, tw.2b., p.3, tw.2f., p.1, k.4, p.1.
19th row: p.1, tw.2f., p.1, c.4b., p.1, c.4f., p.1, tw.2b., p.2, tw.2f., k.4, tw.2b., p.2, tw.2f., p.1, c.4b., p.1.
21st row: p.1, tw.2f., p.1, k.4, p.1, k.4, p.1, tw.2b., p.1, tw.2f., k.6, tw.2b., p.1, tw.2f., p.1, k.4, p.1.
22nd row: as 2nd row.
The 3rd–22nd rows form patt.

PATTERN B (36 sts.)
1st row: p.1, k.4, p.1, tw.2b., p.1, k.10, p.1, tw.2f., p.1, k.4, p.1, k.4, p.1, tw.2b., p.1.
2nd and every alt. row: k. all k. sts., p. all p. sts.
3rd row: p.1, c.4f., p.1, tw.2b., p.1, cr.2b., k.6, cr.2f., p.1, tw.2f., p.1, c.4b., p.1, c.4f., p.1, tw.2b., p.1.
5th row: p.1, k.4, p.1, tw.2b., p.2, cr.2b., k.4, cr.2f., p.2, tw.2f., p.1, k.4, p.1, k.4, p.1, tw.2b., p.1.
7th row: p.1, c.4f., p.1, tw.2b., p.3, cr.2b., k.2, cr.2f., p.3, tw.2f., p.1, c.4b., p.1, c.4f., p.1, tw.2b., p.1.
9th row: p.1, k.4, p.1, tw.2b., p.4, cr.2b., cr.2f., p.4, tw.2f., p.1, k.4, p.1, k.4, p.1, tw.2b., p.1.
11th row: p.1, c.4f., p.1, tw.2b., p.5, tw.2f., p.5, tw.2f., p.1, c.4b., p.1, c.4f., p.1, tw.2b., p.1.
13th row: p.1, k.4, p.1, tw.2b., p.5, tw.2f., p.5,

tw.2f., p.1, k.4, p.1, k.4, p.1, tw.2b., p.1.

15th row: p.1, c.4f., p.1, tw.2b., p.4, tw.2f., tw.2b., p.4, tw.2f., p.1, c.4b., p.1, c.4f., p.1, tw.2b., p.1.

17th row: p.1, k.4, p.1, tw.2b., p.3, tw.2f., k.2, tw.2b., p.3, tw.2f., p.1, k.4, p.1, k.4, p.1, tw.2b., p.1.

19th row: p.1, c.4f., p.1, tw.2b., p.2, tw.2f., k.4, tw.2b., p.2, tw.2f., p.1, c.4b., p.1, c.4f., p.1, tw.2b., p.1.

21st row: p.1, k.4, p.1, tw.2b., p.1, tw.2f., k.6, tw.2b., p.1, tw.2f., p.1, k.4, p.1, k.4, p.1, tw.2b., p.1.

22nd row: as 2nd row.

The 3rd—22nd rows form patt.

SKIRT

MAIN PIECE (make 2 alike)

With No. 8 needles cast on 107 sts.

1st row: k.2, *p.1, k.1; rep. from * to last st., k.1.

2nd row: *k.1, p.1; rep. from * to last st., k.1.

Rep. first and 2nd rows once, then first row again.

Next row: rib 19, p. into front and back of next st., rib 11, (p. into front and back of next st., rib 5) 3 times, p. into front and back of next st., rib 7, (p. into front and back of next st., rib 5) 3 times, p. into front and back of next st., rib 11, p. into front and back of next st., rib to end: 117 sts.

1st patt. row: (p.1, k.1) 9 times, work first row of Patt. A, (k.1, p.1) 4 times, k.1, work first row of Patt. B, (k.1, p.1) 9 times.

2nd patt. row: k. all k. sts., p. all p. sts.

3rd patt. row: (k.1, p.1) 9 times, 3rd row of Patt. A, (p.1, k.1) 4 times, p.1, work 3rd row of Patt. B, (p.1, k.1) 9 times.

4th patt. row: as 2nd patt. row.

Now cont. in patt. working double moss st. and the 2 patt. panels as set.

Work 8 more rows straight, then work 2 sts. tog. at each end of the next and every foll. 12th row until 107 sts. remain.

Work straight until skirt measures $11\frac{1}{2}$ in. from beg. Now work 2 sts. tog. at each end of the next and every foll. 6th row until 97 sts. remain, then dec. 1 st. at each end of every 4th row until 89 sts. remain. Cont. until skirt measures $18\frac{1}{2}$ in. Cast off in patt.

JACKET

BACK

With No. 10 needles cast on 91 sts. and work 11 rows in rib as for beg. of Skirt.

Next row: rib 11, p. into front and back of next st., rib 11, (p. into front and back of next st., rib 5) 3 times, p. into front and back of next st., rib 7, (p. into front and back of next st., rib 5) 3 times, p. into front and back of next st., rib 11, p. into front and back of next st., rib to end: 101 sts.

Change to No. 8 needles.

1st patt. row: (p.1, k.1) 5 times, work first row of Patt. A, (k.1, p.1) 4 times, k.1, work first row of Patt. B, (k.1, p.1) 5 times.

2nd patt. row: k. all k. sts., p. all p. sts.

3rd patt. row: (k.1, p.1) 5 times, work 3rd row of Patt. A, (p.1, k.1) 4 times, p.1, work 3rd row of Patt. B, (p.1, k.1) 5 times.

4th patt. row: as 2nd patt. row.

Cont. thus working double moss st. and the 2 patt. panels.

Work 18 more rows. Then work 2 sts. tog. at each end of the next and every foll. 6th row until 93 sts. remain. Work until Back measures $9\frac{1}{2}$ in. from beg., ending with right side facing, then inc. 1 st. at each end of the next and every foll. 8th row until there are 101 sts.

Work until Back measures $14\frac{3}{4}$ in., ending with right side facing.

Shape Armholes. Cast off 4 sts. at beg. of next 2 rows, then work 2 sts. tog. at beg. of every row until 83 sts. remain. Cont. straight until armhole measures $7\frac{1}{2}$ in., ending with right side facing.

Shape Shoulder. Cast off 7 sts. very firmly, patt. 15 sts. (including st. already on needle), cast off 39 sts., patt. to end. Work on last set of sts. only.

1st row: cast off 7 sts., patt. to last 2 sts., work last 2 sts. tog.

2nd row: work 2 sts. tog., patt. to end.

3rd row: cast off 6 sts., patt. to last 2 sts., work last 2 sts. tog.

4th row: work in patt.

Cast off remaining sts.

Rejoin yarn to 15 sts. on other side at neck edge.

1st row: work 2 sts. tog., patt. to end.

2nd row: cast off 6 sts., patt. to last 2 sts., work last 2 sts. tog.

3rd row: as first row.

Cast off.

LEFT FRONT

With No. 10 needles cast on 47 sts. and work 11 rows rib as for Skirt.

Next row: (rib 5, p. into front and back of next st.) 4 times, rib 11, p. into front and back of next st., rib to end: 52 sts.

Change to No. 8 needles.

1st patt. row: (p.1, k.1) 5 times, work first row of Patt. A, (k.1, p.1) 3 times.

2nd patt. row: k. all k. sts., p. all p. sts.

3rd patt. row: (k.1, p.1) 5 times, work 3rd row of Patt. A, (p.1, k.1) 3 times.

4th patt. row: as 2nd patt. row.

Cont. thus, working double moss st. and panel of Patt. A.

Work 18 more rows, then work 2 sts. tog. at beg. of next and every foll. 6th row until 48 sts. remain. Cont. straight until work measures $9\frac{1}{2}$ in., ending with right side facing. Inc. 1 st. at beg. of next and every foll. 8th row until there are 52 sts. Cont. straight until Front measures $14\frac{3}{4}$ in., ending with right side facing.

Shape Armhole. Cast off 4 sts. at beg. of next row, then work 1 row. Work 2 sts. tog. at beg. of next and every alt. row until 43 sts. remain.
Work 4 rows, ending at front edge.
Shape Neck. 1st row: cast off 9 sts., patt. to end. Keeping armhole edge straight, work 2 sts. tog. at neck edge on every row 9 times, and then on every alt. row 6 times. Cont. on remaining 19 sts. until armhole measures 7½ in., ending at armhole edge.
Shape Shoulder. Cast off 7 sts. at beg. of next row and 6 sts. at beg. of next alt. row. Work 1 row. Cast off.

RIGHT FRONT

With No. 10 needles cast on 47 sts. and work 11 rows rib as for Left Front.
Next row: rib 11, p. into front and back of next st., rib 11, (p. into front and back of next st., rib 5) 4 times: 52 sts.
Change to No. 8 needles.
1st patt. row: (p.1, k.1) 3 times, work first row of Patt. B, (k.1, p.1) 5 times.
Now complete to match Left Front, working double moss st. and panel of Patt. B, and reversing shapings.

TO COMPLETE

Sew shoulder seams.
Neck Border. With No. 10 needles and with right side of work facing pick up and k. 40 sts. from neck edge of Right Front, 49 sts. from Back neck edge and k. 40 sts. from Left Front neck edge.
1st row: *k.1, p.1; rep. from * to last st., k.1.
2nd row: k.2, *p.1, k.1; rep. from * to last st., k.1.
Rep. these 2 rows twice then first row once. Cast off in rib.
Armhole Borders. With No. 10 needles and with right side of work facing, pick up and k. 86 sts. round one armhole. Work 7 rows in k.1, p.1 rib. Cast off in rib.
Rep. for other armhole.
To Make Up. Jacket: sew side seams and insert zip fastener down centre front.
Skirt: sew side seams. Join elastic in circle to desired size, and sew one edge to top of skirt on the inside. Work over the elastic with herringbone st. to hold it in position.

Short-sleeved coat dress

(photographed in black and white on page 174)

MATERIALS
16 balls Sirdar Pullman in main shade and 1 ball in contrast shade (see note on wools and yarns, page 20); one pair each Nos. 3 and 5 knitting needles (see page 26); one circular No. 5 needle or one set of four No. 5 needles; 6 buttons, ¾ in. in diameter. (Note. Our dress is made in white, with navy trim and gold buttons.)

MEASUREMENTS
To fit bust size 34 in.; length 30 in.

TENSION
4 sts. and 5 rows to 1 in. over patt. with No. 3 needles (see note on tension, page 15).

ABBREVIATIONS
See page 26; M., main shade; C., contrast shade.

BACK
With No. 5 needles and M., cast on 86 sts. and work 5 rows in garter st. (see page 23). Join C. and k. 2 rows, then rejoin M. and k. 1 row.
Change to No. 3 needles and patt.
1st patt. row (wrong side): working into backs of loops, p.3, *k.1, p.1, k.1, p.4; rep. from * to last 6 sts., k.1, p.1, k.1, p.3.
2nd patt. row: working into backs of loops, k.3, *p.1, k.1, p.1, k.4; rep. from * to last 6 sts., p.1, k.1, p.1, k.3.
These 2 rows form patt. Rep. patt., working 2 sts. tog. at each end of every 14th row until 72 sts. remain. Work straight until Back measures 22½ in., ending with right side facing.
Shape Armholes. Cast off 5 sts. at beg. of next 2 rows, then work 2 sts. tog. at each end of next 5 rows. Work until armholes measure 7½ in.
Shape Shoulders. Cast off 6 sts. at beg. of next 4 rows and 5 sts. at beg. of next 2 rows. Cast off remaining 18 sts.

POCKET LININGS (make 2 alike)
With No. 3 needles cast on 25 sts.
1st row: working into backs of loops, p.4, *k.1, p.1, k.1, p.4; rep. from * to end.
2nd row: working into backs of loops, k.4, *p.1, k.1, p.1, k.4; rep. from * to end.
Rep. these 2 rows until work measures 5 in. and leave sts. on a stitch holder.

LEFT FRONT
With No. 5 needles and M., cast on 44 sts. and work first 8 rows as for Back. Now change to No. 3 needles and patt. as for Back, beg. with a first patt. row. Working 2 sts. tog. at side edge only on every 14th row until 37 sts. remain, and at the same time

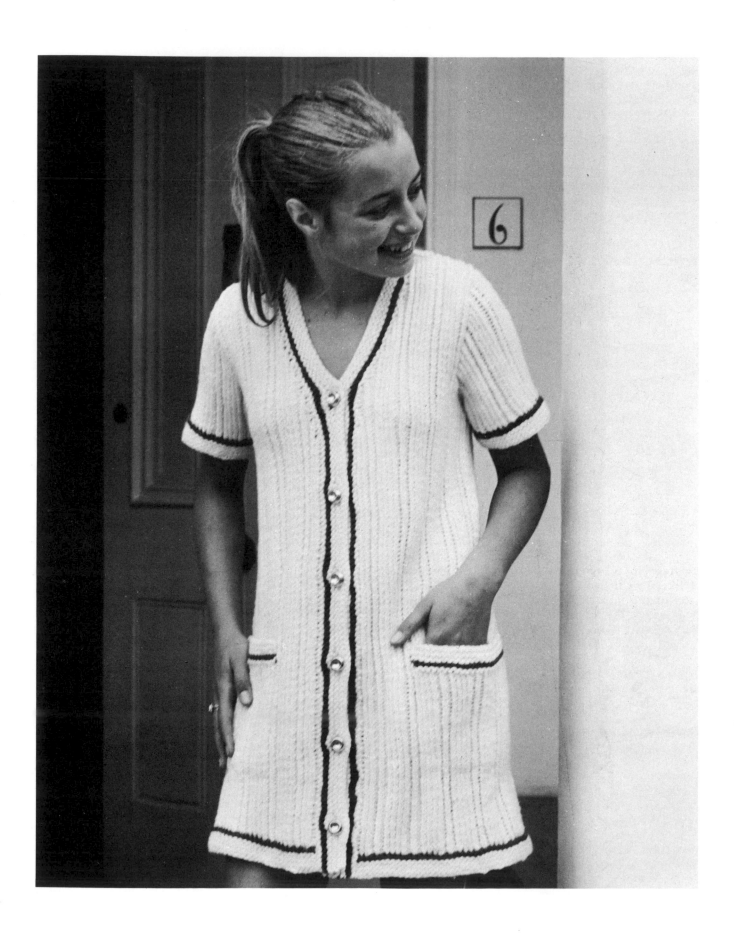

when work measures 10 in., ending at centre front edge, work thus:

Next row: patt. across 13 sts., slip next 25 sts. on to a length of yarn, patt. across 25 sts. of one pocket lining, patt. to end.

Now work on these sts., shaping at side edge as above, until work measures 21 in., ending at centre front edge.

Shape Slope. Work 2 sts. tog. at beg. of next and every foll. 4th row until 10 sts. in all have been dec., and *at the same time* when Front measures same as Back to armhole begin to shape armhole.

Shape Armhole (side edge). Cast off 5 sts. at beg. of row, then work 2 sts. tog. at this side on each of next 5 rows. Cont. straight, dec. as before on front slope only, until Front measures same as Back to shoulder, ending at armhole edge.

Shape Shoulder. Cast off 6 sts. at beg. of next row and next alt. row, patt. 1 row, then cast off.

RIGHT FRONT

Work as for Left Front, reversing all shapings.

POCKET TOPS (make 2 alike)

With right side of work facing, slip the 25 sts. off yarn on to No. 5 needle and, with M., k. 1 row. Join C. and k. 2 rows. Join M. and k. 5 rows. Cast off.

LEFT FRONT BAND

Join shoulder seams. With right side of work facing, using either a circular No. 5 needle or a set of four No. 5 needles and M., pick up and k. 125 sts. from centre of back of neck down Left Front to lower edge. Working backwards and forwards in rows, k. 1 row,

join C., k. 2 rows, join M., k. 6 rows. Cast off.

RIGHT FRONT BAND

Mark places for buttonholes with pins: set one level with beg. of armhole shaping, one 2 in. from hemline and the remaining four at regular intervals between these two. Now pick up 125 sts. as for Left Front Band down Right Front and with circular needle or set of 4, and M. k. 1 row. Join C and k. 2 rows.

Next row: with M., k., casting off 3 sts. at each buttonhole point.

Next row: k., casting on 3 sts. above every set of cast-off sts.

Work 2 more k. rows and cast off.

SLEEVES (make 2 alike)

With No. 5 needles and M., cast on 51 sts. and work first 8 rows as for Back.

Change to No. 3 needles and patt. as for Back, beg. with first patt. row and inc. 1 st. at each end of every 4th row, taking new sts. into patt., until there are 57 sts.

Work until sleeve measures $3\frac{1}{2}$ in., ending with right side facing.

Shape top. Cast off 5 sts. at beg. of next 2 rows, then work 2 sts. tog. at each end of next and every alt. row until 37 sts. remain, then at each end of every row until 21 sts. remain. Cast off 3 sts. at beg. of next 2 rows. Cast off.

TO COMPLETE

Sew in sleeves and join side and sleeve seams. Sew buttons on Left Front to match buttonholes. Catch down pocket linings.

Boy's cabled polo-neck sweater

(photographed in colour on page 186)

MATERIALS

12 (13, 14, 14) balls Sirdar Pullman (see note on wools and yarns, page 20); one pair each Nos. 4 and 6 knitting needles (see page 26); one cable needle.

MEASUREMENTS

To fit chest size 30 (32, 34, 36) in.; length 21 (22, 23, 24) in.; sleeve seam 15 (16, 17, 18) in.

TENSION

4 sts. and 5 rows to 1 in. over st.st. with No. 4 needles (see note on tension, page 15).

Sailor-style coat dress has deep pockets and a smart contrast trimming

ABBREVIATIONS

See page 26; c.6b., slip next 3 sts. on to a cable needle and put to back of work, k. next 3 sts., then k. sts. from cable needle; c.6f., slip next 3 sts. on to cable needle and put to front of work, k. next 3 sts., then k. sts. from cable needle.

FRONT

With No. 6 needles cast on 66 (70, 74, 78) sts. and work 3 in. in k.1, p.1 rib, inc. 1 st. at end of last row.

Next row: p.12 (13, 14, 15), k. twice into next st., p.6, k. twice into next st., p.6 (7, 8, 9), (k. twice into next st., p.6) twice, k. twice into next st., p.6 (7, 8, 9), k. twice into next st., p.6, k. twice into next st., p.12 (13, 14, 15): 74 (78, 82, 86) sts.

Change to No. 4 needles.

1st patt. row: k.12 (13, 14, 15), p.2, k.6, p.2, k.6

(7, 8, 9), p.2, k.6, p.2, k.6, p.2, k.6 (7, 8, 9), p.2, k.6, p.2, k. to end.

2nd patt. row: p.12 (13, 14, 15), k.2, p.6, k.2, p.6 (7, 8, 9), k.2, p.6, k.2, p.6, k.2, p.6 (7, 8, 9), k.2, p.6, k.2, p. to end.

Rep. these 2 rows twice.

7th patt. row: k.12 (13, 14, 15), p.2, c.6b., p.2, k.6 (7, 8, 9), p.2, c.6b., p.2, c.6f., p.2, k.6 (7, 8, 9), p.2, c.6f., p.2, k. to end.

8th patt. row: as 2nd row.

These last 8 rows form patt. Rep. patt. until work measures 14½ (15, 15½, 16) in., ending with right side facing.

Shape Armholes. Keeping patt. correct, cast off 3 sts. at beg. of next 2 rows, then work 2 sts. tog. at each end of next 2 (3, 3, 4) rows and foll 2 alt. rows. Work straight on remaining 60 (62, 66, 68) sts. until work measures 6 (6½, 7, 7½) in. from beg. of armholes, ending with right side facing.**

Shape Shoulders. Patt. 18 (19, 20, 21), k.2 tog.; turn.

Work another 3 rows in patt. working 2 sts. tog. at neck edge on every row: 16 (17, 18, 19) sts.

Cast off 5 (5, 6, 6) sts. at beg. of next row and 11 (12, 12, 13) sts. at beg. of next alt. row. Slip 20 (20, 22, 22) centre sts. on to a stitch holder and complete other side to match first, reversing shapings.

BACK

Work as for Front to **

Shape Shoulders. Cast off 5 (5, 6, 6) sts. at beg. of next 2 rows and 11 (12, 12, 13) sts. at beg. of next 2 rows. Leave remaining 28 (28, 30, 30) sts. on a stitch holder.

SLEEVES (make 2 alike)

With No. 6 needles cast on 28 (30, 32, 34) sts. and

work 3 in. in k.1, p.1 rib, inc. 1 st. at end of last row.

Next row: p.7 (8, 9, 10), (k. twice into next st., p.6) twice, k. twice into next st., p.7 (8, 9, 10): 32 (34, 36, 38) sts.

Change to No. 4 needles.

1st patt. row: k.7 (8, 9, 10), p.2, (k.6, p.2) twice, k.7 (8, 9, 10).

2nd patt. row: p.7 (8, 9, 10), k.2, (p.6, k.2) twice, p.7 (8, 9, 10).

Inc. 1 st. at each end of next row, rep. these last 2 rows twice.

7th patt. row: k.8 (9, 10, 11), p.2, c.6b., p.2, c.6f., p.2, k.8 (9, 10, 11).

8th patt. row: as 2nd patt. row.

These 8 rows form patt. Cont. in patt., inc. 1 st. at each end of next and every foll. 5th row until there are 50 (54, 58, 62) sts. Cont. straight until work measures 15 (16, 17, 18) in., ending with right side facing.

Shape Top. Cast off 3 sts. at beg. of next 2 rows, then cast off 2 sts. at beg. of next 14 (16, 18, 20) rows. Cast off.

TO COMPLETE

Join right shoulder seam.

Polo Neck. With right side of work facing and with No. 6 needles, pick up and k. 7 sts. from left side of front neck, k. across 20 (20, 22, 22) centre sts., pick up and k. 7 sts. from right side of front neck and k. across 28 (28, 30, 30) sts. of Back: 62 (62, 66, 66) sts.

Work in k.1, p.1 rib on these sts. for 1 in., then change to No. 4 needles.

Work another 3 in. and cast off loosely in rib.

To Make Up. Join second shoulder seam and polo collar seam. Sew in sleeves; join side and sleeve seams.

Two-colour waistcoat

MATERIALS

15 oz. Sirdar Sportswool in the main shade and 4 oz. in contrast shade (see note on wools and yarns, page 20); one pair No. 9 knitting needles (see page 26); 2 buttons, 1¼ in. in diameter.

MEASUREMENTS

To fit bust size 34 in.; length 23 in.

TENSION

9½ sts. to 2 in. before pressing (see note on tension, page 15).

ABBREVIATIONS

See page 26; M., main shade; C., contrast shade.

BACK

With M., cast on 89 sts. and k. into back of sts.

1st patt. row (right side): *k.1, p.1; rep. from * to last st., k.1.

2nd patt. row: k.

3rd patt. row: *p.1, k.1; rep. from * to last st., p.1.

4th patt. row: k.

These 4 rows form patt. Cont. in patt. until work measures 16 in., ending with right side facing.

Contrast trimming round front edge and armholes is added after rest of waistcoat has been worked. Pockets are in stripes of the main and contrast shades

Shape Armholes. Cast off 6 sts. at beg. of next 2 rows, then work 2 sts. tog. at beg. of next 6 rows: 71 sts.

Cont. until work measures 23 in. ending with right side facing.

Shape Shoulders. Cast off 6 sts. at beg. of next 4 rows, then cast off 5 sts. at beg. of next 4 rows. Cast off remaining 27 sts.

LEFT FRONT

With M., cast on 41 sts. and work as for Back until work measures 14 in. ending with wrong side facing.

Shape Front Slope. Work 2 sts. tog. at beg. of next and every foll. 6th row until work measures the same as Back to armhole shaping, ending with right side facing.

Shape Armhole. Still dec. at front edge on every 6th row, cast off 6 sts. at beg. of next row, then work 2 sts. tog. at beg. of next 3 alt. rows. Cont. to dec. on every 6th row at front edge until 22 sts. remain. Cont. straight until armhole measures the same as Back armhole, ending at armhole edge.

Shape Shoulder. Cast off 6 sts. at beg. of next and foll. alt. row, then cast off 5 sts. at beg. of next alt. row. Work 1 row. Cast off.

RIGHT FRONT

Work as for Left Front, reversing shaping.

POCKETS (make 2 alike)

With M., cast on 30 sts. and work 2 rows in st.st. (see page 23). Join C. and k. 1 row. Now work 3 rows in st.st., beg. with a k. row.

These 6 rows form the patt. Rep. 10 times, then cont. in C. and work 4 rows in st.st., beg. with a k.

row (this forms hem at top). Cast off.

TO COMPLETE

Join shoulder seams.

Armhole Edgings. With right side of work facing and with M., pick up and k. 86 sts. round one armhole.

1st row: p.

2nd row: join C., k.

Work 3 rows in st.st., beg. with a k. row. Again beg. with a k. row, work 4 rows in st.st. (this forms hem). Cast off.

Work other armhole edging in same way.

Front Band. With M. and with right side of work facing, pick up and k. 130 sts. along front edge of Right Front, starting at bottom and working to right shoulder, then pick up and k. 26 sts. across back neck, then 130 sts. down Left Front: 286 sts.

1st row: p.

2nd row: join C., k., then work 3 rows in st.st., beg. with a k. row.

6th row: join M., k. 54, cast off 4 sts., k. to last 58 sts., cast off 4 sts., k. to end.

7th row: p., casting on 4 sts. over 2 sets of cast-off sts. in 6th row.

Join C. and k. 1 row, then work 2 rows in st.st., beg. with a k. row.

Cast off knitwise.

To Make Up. Turn under 4 rows of st.st. on armhole borders and slipstitch down. Sew side seams. Turn under last rows of pockets and slipstitch down, then sew on pockets, placing the cast-on edge of each against the cast-on edge of Front and the outer sides against side seams. Join buttons with a 1½-in. chain of C. yarn and use as link through buttonholes.

Double-breasted coat

MATERIALS

29 oz. Sirdar Double Knitting (see note on wools and yarns, page 20); one pair each Nos. 8 and 11 knitting needles (see page 26); 6 buttons, 1 in. in diameter.

MEASUREMENTS

To fit bust size 34 in.; length 32 in.; sleeve seam 17 in.

TENSION

6½ sts. and 7½ rows to 1 in. over patt. with No. 8 needles (see note on tension, page 15).

ABBREVIATIONS

See page 26.

PATTERN

1st row (right side): k.

2nd row: p.

3rd row: as first row.

4th row: *p.2 tog. and leave on left-hand needle, p. again into first of these 2 sts., slip both off needle tog.; rep. from * to last st., p.1.

5th row: *sl.1 knitwise, k.1, p.s.s.o., leaving st. on left-hand needle, k. into back of this st.; rep. from *

For special occasions, this elegant coat is quick and easy to make in double knitting yarn

to last st., k.1.
6th row: p.

BACK
With No. 8 needles, cast on 125 sts. Work in patt., beg. with a 6th row (wrong side), until Back measures 24¾ in., ending with right side facing.
Shape Armholes. Cast off 4 sts. at beg. of next 2 rows then work 2 sts. tog. at each end of next 10 rows. Work on remaining 97 sts. until armhole measures 8¼ in.
Shape Shoulders. Cast off 8 sts. at beg. of next 6 rows and 7 sts. at beg. of next 2 rows. Cast off remaining 35 sts.

LEFT FRONT
With No. 8 needles cast on 81 sts. and patt. as for Back until work measures 20½ in.
Shape Front Slope. Work 2 sts. tog. at neck edge (at end of right-side row) on next and every foll. alt. row until 20 sts. have been dec. **At the same time** when Front measures same as Back to armhole begin to shape armhole.
Shape Armhole (side edge). Cast off 4 sts. at beg. of next row then work 2 sts. tog. at this side on each of next 10 rows.
Cont. shaping front slope only until 31 sts. remain and work until Front armhole measures the same as the Back armhole.
Shape Shoulder (side edge). Cast off 8 sts. at beg. of next and every alt. row until 7 sts. remain. Work 1 row. Cast off.

RIGHT FRONT
First place 3 pins in Left Front for button positions, which should be in centre of st.st., the top one just below front slope shaping, the next 4¼ in. below it, and the next 4¼ in. below this. Now work Right Front as for Left, reversing all shapings, and making 3 sets of buttonholes to correspond with pins, starting each on a first row.
1st buttonhole row (front edge): k.4, cast off 4 sts., k.18, cast off 4 sts., k. to end.
2nd buttonhole row: p. to first set of cast-off sts., cast on 4 sts. above them, p.18, cast on 4 sts., p.4.

SLEEVES (make 2 alike)
With No. 8 needles cast on 55 sts. and beg. patt. with a 6th row. Patt. 3 in. then inc. 1 st. at each end of next and every foll. 5th row, taking new sts. into patt., until there are 95 sts. Cont. straight until sleeve measures 17 in., ending with the same wrong-side row at this point as at bottom of Back armhole.
Shape Top. Cast off 4 sts. at beg. of next 2 rows, then work 2 sts. tog. at each end of next and every alt. row until 61 sts. remain. Cast off 5 sts. at beg. of next 4 rows, 4 sts. at beg. of next 4 rows and 3 sts. at beg. of next 2 rows.
Cast off remaining 19 sts.

BRAID
With No. 11 needles cast on 7 sts.
1st row (wrong side): k.1, p.2, k.1, p.2, k.1.
2nd row: p.1, k.2 tog. and leave on left-hand needle, k. again into first of these 2 sts. then slip both off needle tog., p.1, k.2 tog. and leave on left-hand needle, k. again into first of 2 sts., and slip both sts. off needle tog., p.1.
These 2 rows form patt. Rep. patt. until strip is long enough to fit round hem, up front, round neck and down front to meet at hem. Cast off. Make two shorter strips in the same way for the two sleeve edges.

TO COMPLETE
Join shoulder seams, sew in sleeves. Sew braid to sleeve edges and join sleeve seams. Join side seams and sew braid to hem and fronts. Sew buttons on to left front to match buttonholes.

Knickerbocker suit and beret

MATERIALS
For knickerbocker suit: 15 (18, 20, 22) balls (2-oz.) Mahony's Blarney Bainin (see note on wools and yarns, page 20); one pair each Nos. 7, 9 and 10 knitting needles (see page 26); one cable needle; one large and two small buckles; waist length of elastic ¾ in. wide.
For beret: 2 (3) balls Mahony's Blarney Bainin (see note on wools and yarns, page 20); one pair each Nos. 7 and 10 knitting needles (see page 26); one No. 7 circular needle or an extra pair No. 7 needles; one cable needle.

MEASUREMENTS
Sweater: to fit chest or bust size 28 (30, 32, 34) in.; length 23 (25, 27, 28) in.; sleeve seam 14 (15½, 16½, 17½) in.
Knickerbockers: to fit hip size 30 (32, 34, 36) in.; length (measured at side) 19 (20½, 22, 23½) in.

A trendsetting suit for all sizes, all seasons — long-line top is neatly belted

Beret: to fit head size 20/21 (22/23) in.; width across top 10½ (12) in.

TENSION
16 sts. to 3 in. and 6 rows to 1 in. over cross-st. patt. with No. 7 needles (see note on tension, page 15).

ABBREVIATIONS
See page 26; p.f.b., purl into front and back of next st.; s.k.p.k., slip 1 knitwise, k.1, p.s.s.o. but leave on left-hand needle and k. it through back; claw patt. 7, slip next 2 sts. on to cable needle and leave at back of work, k.1, then k.2 from cable needle, k.1, slip next st. on to cable needle and leave at front of work, k.2, then k.1 from cable needle; k. loop, pick up loop lying between needles and k. into back of it; p. loop, pick up loop lying between needles and p. into back of it.

SWEATER
BACK
With No. 9 needles cast on 71 (77, 81, 85) sts.

1st row (right side): k.2, *p.1, k.1; rep. from * to last st., k.1.

2nd row: k.1, *p.1, k.1; rep. from * to end. Rep. these 2 rows 5 times then rep. first row again.

14th row (wrong side): p.4, p.f.b., p.3, k.1, (p.1, p.f.b.) twice, p.1, k.1, p.5 (5, 6, 7), p.f.b., p.5 (5, 6, 7), *k.1, (p.1, p.f.b.) twice, p.1; rep. from * 2 (3, 3, 3) times, k.1, p.5 (5, 6, 7), p.f.b., p.5 (5, 6, 7), k.1, (p.1, p.f.b.) twice, p.1, k.1, p.3, p.f.b., p.4: 85 (93, 97, 101) sts.

Change to No. 7 needles.

1st patt. row: k.1, (s.k.p.k.) 4 times, p.1, k.7, p.1, (s.k.p.k.) 6 (6, 7, 8) times, (p.1, k.7) 3 (4, 4, 4) times, p.1, (s.k.p.k.) 6 (6, 7, 8) times, p.1, k.7, p.1, (s.k.p.k.) 4 times, k.1.

2nd patt. row: p.9, k.1, p.7, k.1, p.12 (12, 14, 16), (k.1, p.7) 3 (4, 4, 4) times, k.1, p.12 (12, 14, 16), k.1, p.7, k.1, p.9.

3rd patt. row: k.2, (s.k.p.k.) 3 times, k.1, p.1, claw patt. 7, p.1, k.1, (s.k.p.k.) 5 (5, 6, 7) times, k.1, (p.1, claw patt. 7) 3 (4, 4, 4) times, p.1, k.1, (s.k.p.k.) 5 (5, 6, 7) times, k.1, p.1, claw patt. 7, p.1, k.1, (s.k.p.k.) 3 times, k.2.

4th patt. row: as 2nd patt. row.

These 4 rows form one patt. Cont. in patt. until work measures 6 (7, 7, 8) in. from beg., then inc. 1 st. at each end of next row and every foll. 18th row until there are 91 (99, 105, 109) sts. Cont. straight until work measures 15¾ (17½, 19¼, 20) in. from beg.

Shape Armholes. Cast off 6 sts. at beg. of next 2 rows and 5 (6, 6, 7) sts. at beg. of next 2 rows: 69 (75, 81, 83) sts. Cont. straight until work measures 22 (24, 26, 27) in. from beg., ending with a wrong-side row.

Shape Shoulders. Cast off 8 sts. at beg. of next 2 rows and 6 (7, 8, 8) sts. at beg. of next 4 rows.

Cast off remaining 29 (31, 33, 35) sts. for back neck.

FRONT
Work as given for Back until you have worked 8 (8, 10, 10) rows fewer than on Back to start of shoulder shaping, ending with a wrong-side row.

Shape Neck and Shoulders. 1st row: patt. 29 (31, 35, 35) sts. and leave on a stitch holder. Cont. along row, cast off 11 (13, 11, 13) sts., patt. to end. Cont. on the 29 (31, 35, 35) sts. now remaining on needle at right side of Front. ** Dec. 1 st. at neck edge on next 8 (8, 10, 10) rows. Cast off 8 sts. for shoulder at beg. of next row and dec. 1 st. at neck edge on foll. row. Cast off 6 (7, 8, 8) sts. at beg. of next row, work 1 row, then cast off remaining 6 (7, 8, 8) sts.** With wrong side facing, rejoin yarn to inner edge of left side of Front sts., patt. to end. Complete to match other side from ** to **.

SLEEVES (make 2 alike)
With No. 9 needles cast on 37 (41, 45, 45) sts. and work 13 rows in rib as for Back.

14th row: p.6 (7, 8, 8), p.f.b., p.5 (6, 7, 7), *k.1, (p.1, p.f.b.) twice, p.1; rep. from * once, k.1, p.5 (6, 7, 7), p.f.b., p.6 (7, 8, 8): 43 (47, 51, 51) sts.

Change to No. 7 needles.

1st patt. row: k.1, (s.k.p.k.) 6 (7, 8, 8) times, p.1, k.7, p.1, k.7, p.1, (s.k.p.k.) 6 (7, 8, 8) times, k.1.

Cont. in patt. as now set having 2 claw patts. in centre and when first patt. is completed inc. 1 st. at each end of next row and every foll. 5th row until there are 73 (77, 79, 83) sts. keeping extra sts. at sides in the cross-st. patt. Cont. straight until work measures 14 (15½, 16½, 17½) in. from beg. Place marker loops of contrast yarn at each end of last row, then work 12 (13, 13, 15) rows straight. Cast off 5 sts. at beg. of next 6 rows, 6 (7, 7, 6) sts. at beg. of next 2 (2, 2, 4) rows and 6 (7, 8, 5) sts. at beg. of next 2 rows.

Cont. on remaining 19 sts. working 2 claw patt. with 2 sts. on either side until this strip is long enough to fit across front shoulder edge.

Cast off tightly.

NECKBANDS
For Short Neckband (as on teenager's sweater). With No. 9 needles, cast on 102 (106, 110, 114) sts.

1st row: k.2, *p.1, k.1; rep. from * to end.

Rep. this row 3 times, change to No. 10 needles and work 8 rows in same rib, change back to No. 9 needles and work 4 more rows.

Cast off ribwise.

For Deep Neckband. Work as for short neckband but continue on No. 9 needles for 7 rows then change to No. 10 needles and work 12 rows, then change back to No. 9 needles and work 7 rows. Cast off ribwise.

BELT

With No. 9 needles cast on 11 (11, 11, 13) sts. and work in rib as on Back welt (first 8 rows) for 22 (24, 26, 28) in. Dec. 1 st. at each end of every row until 3 sts. remain. Cast off.

TO COMPLETE

Press work lightly on wrong side with warm iron and damp cloth avoiding ribbing. Pin sleeves in place matching markers to beg. of casting-off at armholes, pinning these cast-off edges to sides of sleeves above markers, cast-off edges of sleeves to sides of armholes and sides of extension strip to shoulder shaping. Cast-off edge of extension strips forms part of neck edge. Sew sleeves in place as pinned, backstitching these and all seams. Remove markers. Press seams. Join side and sleeve seams and press. Join ends of neckband. With right sides tog. and seam level with left back shoulder, sew cast-on edge to neck edge. Press seam with point of iron. Fold band in half to wrong side and slip-stitch cast-off edge to previous seam. Oversew cast-on edge of belt to centre bar of large buckle.

KNICKERBOCKERS
RIGHT LEG

With No. 9 needles cast on 63 (67, 75, 83) sts.
Foundation row: p.5 (6, 7, 8), p.f.b., p.4 (5, 6, 7), *k.1, (p.1, p.f.b.) twice, p.1, k.1, p.5 (5, 6, 7), p.f.b., p.5 (5, 6, 7); rep. from * once, k.1, (p.1, p.f.b.) twice, p.1, k.1, p.4 (5, 6, 7), p.f.b., p.5 (6, 7, 8): 73 (77, 85, 93) sts.
Change to No. 7 needles.
1st row: k.1, (s.k.p.k.) 5 (6, 7, 8) times, *p.1, k.7, p.1, (s.k.p.k.) 6 (6, 6, 8) times; rep. from * once, p.1, k.7, p.1, (s.k.p.k.) 5 (6, 7, 8) times, k.1.
Cont. in patt. as now set working 3 claw patts. with cross-st. patt. between and at ends, but inc. 1 st. at each end of 4th row of every patt. until there are 99 (107, 119, 129) sts. keeping extra sts. at sides in cross-st. patt. Cont. straight until work measures $9\frac{1}{4}$ ($10\frac{1}{4}$, $11\frac{1}{4}$, $12\frac{1}{2}$) in. from beg., ending with a wrong-side row.***
****Shape Crutch. 1st row:** cast off 2 (2, 2, 3) sts., patt. to end.
2nd row: cast off 5 (5, 5, 6) sts., patt. to end.
3rd row: cast off 1 (1, 1, 2) sts., patt. to end.
4th row: cast off 2 (2, 3, 4) sts., patt. to end.
Work 1 row straight, then dec. 1 st. at each end of next row.
For sizes 30 and 32: rep. last 2 rows once.
For size 34: rep. last 2 rows twice.
For all sizes: work 1 row straight, dec. 1 st. at beg. of foll. row, work 1 row then dec. 1 st. at each end of next row. Rep. last 4 rows again.
For sizes 32 and 34: rep. last 4 rows once more: 95 (99) sts.
For all sizes: now dec. 1 st. at each end of every

foll. 6th (5th, 4th, 4th) row until 69 (73, 77, 81) sts. remain. Cont. straight until work measures $18\frac{1}{2}$ (20, $21\frac{1}{2}$, 23) in. from beg., ending with a wrong-side row.****
Shape Waist. Cast off 14 (15, 16, 17) sts. at beg. of next row and next 3 alt. rows. Cast off remaining 13 sts.

LEFT LEG

Work as for Right Leg as far as *** but ending with a right-side row. Cont. as for Right Leg from **** to **** but again ending with a right-side row. Work waist shaping as for Right Leg.

LEGBANDS (make 2 alike)

With No. 9 needles cast on 9 sts. and work in rib as for welt of Sweater (first 8 rows of Back), for $11\frac{1}{2}$ (12, 13, 14) in. Dec. 1 st. at each end of next 3 rows. Cast off.

TO COMPLETE

Press main parts lightly on wrong side with warm iron and damp cloth. Join inner leg seams to beg. of crutch shaping, backstitching these and all seams. Press seams. Join front and back seams from beg. of crutch shaping to waist. Press seams. Cut elastic to fit waist size required, overlap ends $\frac{1}{2}$ in. to form a ring and sew securely. Pin inside waist edge and hold in place with a row of herringbone-st. working from side to side across elastic but not into it.
With right sides tog. pin each Legband to lower edge of each leg having cast-on edge at centre of the claw which is at outside of leg and easing in fullness so that pointed end overlaps about 1 in. Backstitch in place but leave about 1 in. of leg free at pointed end of band so that it can be pleated when band is fastened.
Oversew cast-on edge of each band to centre bar of each small buckle.

BERET
TO MAKE

With No. 10 needles cast on 98 (106) sts.
1st row: k.2, *p.1, k.1; rep. from * to end. Rep. this row 6 times.
Inc. row (wrong side): k.2, *p.1, (p.f.b., p.1) twice, k.1, p.2 (4), (p.f.b., p.2) 5 times, k.1; rep. from * 3 times: 126 (134) sts.
Change to No. 7 needles.
1st row: k.1, *k.1, (s.k.p.k.) 10 (11) times, k.1, p.1, k.7, p.1; rep. from * 3 times, k.1.
2nd row: k.1, *k.1, p.7, k.1, p.22 (24); rep. from * 3 times, k.1.
Now start to inc. noting that when you have too many sts. to fit on to one needle you should take the circular needle or the extra pair of No. 7 needles, still working backwards and forwards in rows.
Next row: k.1, *k. loop, (s.k.p.k.) 11 (12) times,

k. loop, p.1, claw patt. 7, p.1; rep. from * 3 times, k.1.

Next row: k.1, *k.1, p.7, k.1, p. loop, p.24 (26), p. loop; rep. from * 3 times, k.1.

Cont. to inc. at each side of the 4 cross-st. panels on every row taking extra sts. into this patt. until you have worked 11 (12) rows in patt. from beg. and you have 198 (214) sts. on needle.

Work 3 (2) rows straight, then start to dec. changing back to 1 pair of needles when possible.

15th row: k.1, *k.2 tog. t.b.l., patt. to the last 2 sts. of the cross-st. panel, k.2 tog., p. 1, claw patt. 7, p.1; rep. from * to last st., k.1.

16th row: k.1, *k.1, p.7, k.1, p.2 tog., p. to last 2 sts. of panel, p.2 tog. t.b.l.; rep. from * 3 times, k.1.

17th row: k.1, *k.2 tog. t.b.l., patt. to last 2 sts. of panel, k.2 tog., p.1, k.7, p.1; rep. from * to last st., k.1.

18th row: patt. without shaping.

Rep. last 4 rows 5 times more: 54 (70) sts.

For small size only. 39th row: k.1, *k.2 tog. t.b.l., k.2 tog., p.1, claw patt. 7, p.1; rep. from * 3 times, k.1.

40th row: *k.2 tog., p.7, k.2 tog. t.b.l.; rep. from * 3 times, k.2 tog.

41st row: k.1, *p.1, k.2 tog., k.1, k.2 tog. t.b.l., k.1, p.1; rep. from * 3 times, but ending last rep. k.2 instead of k.1, p.1.

42nd row: k.1, *p.1, p.3 tog., p.1, k.2 tog.; rep. from * 3 times.

Break yarn and thread end through remaining sts., pull up tightly and fasten off.**

For large size only: after 38th row, rep. 15th and 16th rows again: 54 sts.

41st row: k.1, *k.2 tog. t.b.l., k.2 tog., p.1, k.7, p.1; rep. from * 3 times, k.1. Complete as for small size from ** to **

TO COMPLETE

Join seam of beret, pull over sleeve board and press seam. Working from right side press beret gently into a flat rounded shape. Make pompon (see page 82) with card circles 1½ in. in diameter, and sew to top of beret.

Round or polo-neck sweater
(photographed in black and white on page 188)

MATERIALS

For round-neck sweater: 12 (13, 14, 15, 16, 17) balls Emu Scotch Double Knitting **or** Double Crêpe **or** Bri-Nylon Double Knitting (see note on wools and yarns, page 20). **For polo-neck sweater:** 14 (15, 16, 17, 18, 19) balls Emu Scotch Double Knitting **or** Double Crêpe **or** Bri-Nylon Double Knitting (see note on wools and yarns, page 20). **For both sweaters:** one pair each Nos. 8 and 10 knitting needles (see page 26); one cable needle.

MEASUREMENTS

To fit chest size 24 (26, 28, 30, 32, 34) in.; length 16¼ (16¾, 17¾, 20½, 21¼, 22¼) in.; sleeve seam 10½ (12, 13½, 15, 16, 17) in.

TENSION

5½ sts. and 8 rows to 1 in. over st.st. with No. 8 needles (see note on tension, page 15).

ABBREVIATIONS

See page 26.

ROUND-NECK SWEATER
BACK

With No. 10 needles, cast on 72 (78, 84, 88, 94, 100) sts. and work in k.1, p.1 rib for 1½ (1½, 2, 2, 2½, 2½) in., ending with wrong side facing.

Next row: rib 3 (6, 3, 5, 8, 4), * work twice into next st., rib 4 (4, 5, 5, 5, 6); rep. from * to last 4 (7, 3, 5, 8, 5) sts., work twice into next st., rib 3 (6, 2, 4, 7, 4): 86 (92, 98, 102, 108, 114) sts.

Change to No. 8 needles.

1st row: k.6 (8, 11, 12, 15, 17), *p.4, k.3, p.4, k.6, p.4, k.3, p.4, *k.18 (20, 20, 22, 22, 24); rep. from * to * once, k.6 (8, 11, 12, 15, 17).

2nd row: p.6 (8, 11, 12, 15, 17), *k.4, p.3, k.4, p.6, k.4, p.3, k.4, *p.18 (20, 20, 22, 22, 24); rep. from * to * once, p.6 (8, 11, 12, 15, 17).

3rd row: as first row.

4th row: as 2nd row.

5th row: k.6 (8, 11, 12, 15, 17), *p.4, k.3, p.4, (slip next 3 sts. on to cable needle and put to back of work, k. next 3 sts., k. sts. from cable needle: c.6b.), p.4, k.3, p.4, *k.18 (20, 20, 22, 22, 24); rep. from * to * once, k.6 (8, 11, 12, 15, 17).

6th row: as 2nd row.

7th row: k.6 (8, 11, 12, 15, 17), *p.4, ** (slip next 3 sts. on to cable needle and leave at front of work: sl.3f.), p.1, k.3 from cable needle, p.2, (slip next st. on to cable needle and leave at back of work: sl.1b.), k.3, p.1 from cable needle; rep. from ** once, p.4, *k.18 (20, 20, 22, 22, 24); rep. from * to * once, k.6 (8, 11, 12, 15, 17).

8th row: p.6 (8, 11, 12, 15, 17), *k.5, (p.3, k.2) 4 times, k.3, *p.18 (20, 20, 22, 22, 24); rep. from * to *

Opposite: matching Aran-patterned skirt and zip-up waistcoat (see page 171)

once, p.6 (8, 11, 12, 15, 17).

9th row: k.6 (8, 11, 12, 15, 17), *p.5, (sl.3f., p.1, k.3 from cable needle, sl.1b., k.3, p.1 from cable needle, p.2) twice, p.3, *k.18 (20, 20, 22, 22, 24); rep. from * to * once, k.6 (8, 11, 12, 15, 17).

10th row: p.6 (8, 11, 12, 15, 17), *k.6, p.6, k.4, p.6, k.6, *p.18 (20, 20, 22, 22, 24); rep. from * to * once, p.6 (8, 11, 12, 15, 17).

11th row: k.6 (8, 11, 12, 15, 17), *p.6, (slip next 3 sts. on to cable needle and put to front of work, k. next 3 sts., k. sts. from cable needle: c.6f.), p.4, c.6f., p.6, *k.18 (20, 20, 22, 22, 24); rep. from * to * once, k.6 (8, 11, 12, 15, 17).

12th row: as 10th row.

13th row: k.6 (8, 11, 12, 15, 17), *p.5, (sl.1b., k.3, p.1 from cable needle, sl.3f., p.1, k.3 from cable needle, p.2) twice, p.3, *k.18 (20, 20, 22, 22, 24); rep. from * to * once, k.6 (8, 11, 12, 15, 17).

14th row: as 8th row.

15th row: k.6 (8, 11, 12, 15, 17), *p.4, (sl.1b., k.3, p.1 from cable needle, p.2, sl.3f., p.1, k.3 from cable needle) twice, p.4, *k.18 (20, 20, 22, 22, 24); rep. from * to * once, k.6 (8, 11, 12, 15, 17).

16th row: as 2nd row.

17th row: as 5th row.

Rows 2 to 17 inclusive form patt. Rep. patt. 2 (2, 2, 3, 3, 3) times, then 2nd to 16th rows inclusive once.

Next row: k.10 (12, 15, 16, 19, 21), *k.3 tog., k.4, (k.2 tog.) 3 times, k.4, k.3 tog., *k.26 (28, 28, 30, 30, 32); rep. from * to * once, k.10 (12, 15, 16, 19, 21): 72 (78, 84, 88, 94, 100) sts.

Next row: p.

Mark each end of last row with a coloured thread to help when joining raglan seams.

Shape Raglan Armholes. Next row: k.2, sl.1, k.1, p.s.s.o., k. to last 4 sts., k.2 tog., k.2.

Next row: p.

Next row: k.

Next row: p.

Rep. the last 4 rows 2 (1, 1, 2, 3, 3) times.

Next row: k.2, sl.1, k.1, p.s.s.o., k. to last 4 sts., k.2 tog., k.2.

Next row: p.

Rep. the last 2 rows *** until 32 (32, 34, 34, 36, 38) sts. remain, ending with right side facing.

Shape Neck. Next row: k.2, sl.1, k.1, p.s.s.o., k.7 sts.; turn, leaving remaining sts. on a stitch holder.

Next row: cast off 3 sts., p. to end.

Next row: k.2, sl.1, k.1, p.s.s.o., k. to end.

Next row: cast off 3 sts., p. to end.

Next row: k.2 tog., k.1. Cast off remaining 2 sts. Slip the centre 10 (10, 12, 12, 14, 16) sts. on to a stitch holder. Join yarn at neck edge to remaining

Sporting choice for a teenage boy — cabled polo-neck sweater (see page 175)

sts., k. to last 4 sts., k.2 tog., k.2.

Next row: p.

Next row: cast off 3 sts., k. to last 4 sts., k.2 tog., k.2.

Next row: p.

Next row: cast off 3 sts. (the 4th st. is used in casting off), k.2 tog. Cast off remaining 2 sts.

FRONT

Work as Back to *** until 46 (46, 48, 48, 50, 52) sts. remain, ending with right side facing.

Shape Neck. Next row: k.2, sl.1, k.1, p.s.s.o., k.14 sts.; turn, leaving remaining sts. on a stitch holder.

Still dec. at armhole edge as before, dec. 1 st. at neck edge on every row until 8 sts. remain. Keeping neck edge straight, continue to dec. at armhole edge until 2 sts. remain, working dec. at outer armhole edge when they can no longer be worked inside a border of 2 sts. Cast off remaining 2 sts. Slip the centre 10 (10, 12, 12, 14, 16) sts. on to a stitch holder. Join in yarn at neck edge to remaining sts., k. to last 4 sts., k.2 tog., k.2.

Complete to match first side of neck.

SLEEVES (make 2 alike)

With No. 10 needles, cast on 40 (42, 44, 46, 48, 50) sts. and work in k.1, p.1 rib for 3 in., ending with right side facing. Change to No. 8 needles and st.st. (see page 23). Inc. 1 st. at each end of the 3rd and every following 6th (8th, 8th, 9th, 10th, 10th) row until there are 56 (58, 62, 64, 66, 70) sts. on the needle. Continue without further shaping until work measures 10½ (12, 13½, 15, 16, 17) in. from beg., ending with a p. row. Mark each end of last row with a coloured thread.

Shape Raglan Top. Next row: k.2, sl.1, k.1, p.s.s.o., k. to last 4 sts., k.2 tog., k.2.

Next row: p.

Next row: k.

Next row: p.

Rep. the last 4 rows 2 (3, 3, 5, 7, 7) times.

Next row: k.2, sl.1, k.1, p.s.s.o., k. to last 4 sts., k.2 tog., k.2.

Next row: p.

Rep. the last 2 rows until 10 sts. remain, ending with a p. row. Leave these sts. on a safety pin or stitch holder.

NECKBAND

Using a flat stitch, join raglan seams, leaving left back raglan seam open. With right side of work facing and No. 8 needles, k. across the 10 sts. on top of Left Sleeve, pick up and k. 17 sts. down left side of front neck, k. across the 10 (10, 12, 12, 14, 16) sts. at centre front, pick up and k. 17 sts. up right side of front neck, k. across the 10 sts. on top of Right Sleeve, pick up and k. 6 sts. down right

side of back neck, k. across the 10 (10, 12, 12, 14, 16) sts. at centre back, pick up and k. 6 sts. up left side of back neck: 86 (86, 90, 90, 94, 98) sts. ****
Work in k.1, p.1 rib for 1 in. Change to No. 10 needles and work ½ in. Change to No. 8 needles and work 1 in.
Cast off loosely in rib.

TO COMPLETE
Join left back raglan seam and neckband with a flat stitch. Using backstitch, join side and sleeve seams.
Fold neckband in half on to wrong side of work and slipstitch down.

Aran trouser suit
(photographed in black and white on page 190)

MATERIALS
25 (27) balls (2-oz.) Paton's Capstan (see note on wools and yarns, page 20); one pair each Nos. 10 and 8 knitting needles (see page 26); a waist length of elastic 1 in. wide.

MEASUREMENTS
Sweater: to fit bust size 33/34 (35/36) in.; length 22½ (23) in.; length of sleeve seam 16½ in.
Trousers: to fit hip size 35/36 (37/38) in.; inside leg measurement 27 (28) in.

TENSION
10 sts. and 13 rows to 2 in. over st.st. with No. 8 needles (see note on tension, page 15).

ABBREVIATIONS
See page 26; cr.2f., take needle in front of first st. on left-hand needle, k. into front of 2nd st., p. first st. and slip both sts. off needle tog.; cr.2b., take needle behind first st. on left-hand needle, p. into back of 2nd st., k. first st. and slip both off needle tog.; m.b. (make bobble): into next st. work (k.1, p.1) twice, turn, k.4, turn, p.4, slip 2nd, 3rd and 4th sts. over first; tw.2b., k. into back of 2nd st., then into front of first st. and slip both off tog.; tw.2f., k. into front of 2nd st. on left-hand needle, then k. into front of first st., slip both off needle tog.; b.3 (bramble 3): work k.1, p.1, k.1 into next st.

PANEL PATTERN (21 sts.)
1st row: k.3, cr.2f., cr.2b., (p.1, k.1) 3 times, p.1, cr.2f., cr.2b., k.3.
2nd row: p.4, k.2, p.1, (p.1, k.1) 3 times, p.2, k.2, p.4.

Sweater with a choice of necklines – instructions start on page 184

POLO-NECK SWEATER
BACK, FRONT AND SLEEVES
Work as for Round-Neck Sweater.

POLO NECKBAND
Follow instructions for Round-Neck Sweater to ****.
Work in k.1, p.1 rib for 2½ in. Change to No. 10 needles and work 1 in. Change to No. 8 needles and work a further 3 in. Cast off loosely in rib.

TO COMPLETE
Join left back raglan seam and neckband with a flat stitch. Using backstitch, join side and sleeve seams. Fold neckband in half on to right side.

3rd row: k.2, cr.2f., p.2, cr.2b., (k.1, p.1) twice, k.1, or.2f., p. 2, cr.2b., k.2.
4th row: p.3, k.4, p.1, (k.1, p.1) 3 times, k.4, p.3.
5th row: k.1, cr.2f., p.4, cr.2b., p.1, k.1, p.1, cr.2f., p.4, cr.2b., k.1.
6th row: p.2, k.6, p.2, k.1, p.2, k.6, p.2.
7th row: cr.2f., p.6, cr.2b., m.b., cr.2f., p.6, cr.2b.
8th row: p.1, k.8, p.1, k.1, p.1, k.8, p.1.
9th row: tw.2b., p.6, tw.2f., k.1, tw.2b., p.6, tw.2f.
10th row: as 6th row.
11th row: k.1, tw.2b., p.4, tw.2f., p.1, k.1, p.1, tw.2b., p.4, tw.2f., k.1.
12th row: as 4th row.
13th row: k.2, tw.2b., p.2, tw.2f., (k.1, p.1) twice, k.1, tw.2b., p.2, tw.2f., k.2.
14th row: as 2nd row.
15th row: k.3, tw.2b., tw.2f., (p.1, k.1) 3 times, p.1, tw.2b., tw.2f., k.3.
16th row: p.6, (k.1, p.1) 4 times, k.1, p.6. These 16 rows form panel patt.

SWEATER
BACK
With No. 10 needles, cast on 84 (92) sts.
1st row: k.1, *p.2, k.2; rep. from * to last 3 sts., p.2, k.1.
2nd row: p.1, *k.2, p.2; rep. from * to last 3 sts., k.2, p.1.
Rep. first and 2nd rows for 3 in., ending with a first row.
Next row: rib 2 (6), (inc. 1 st. in next st., rib 5) 13 times, inc. 1 st. in next st., rib to end: 98 (106) sts.
Change to No. 8 needles and work in patt.
1st row: p.1, cr.2b., k.7, cr.2f., cr.2b., k.4, work first row of panel patt. (21 sts.), p.20 (28), panel patt. 21 (first row), k.4, cr.2f., cr.2b., k.7, cr.2f., p.1.
2nd row: k.2, p.9, k.2, p.5, panel patt. 21 (2nd row), (b.3, p.3 tog.) 5 (7) times, panel patt. 21 (2nd row),

p.5, k.2, p.9, k.2.

3rd row: p.2, cr.2b., k.5, cr.2f., p.2, cr.2b., k.3, panel patt. 21, p.20 (28), panel patt. 21, k.3, cr.2f., p.2, cr.2b., k.5, cr.2f., p.2.

4th row: k.3, p.7, k.4, p.4, panel patt. 21, (p.3 tog., b.3) 5 (7) times, panel patt. 21, p.4, k.4, p.7, k.3.

5th row: p.3, cr.2b., k.3, cr.2f., p.4, cr.2b., k.2, panel patt. 21, p.20 (28), panel patt. 21, k.2, cr.2f., p.4., cr.2b., k.3, cr.2f., p.3.

6th row: k.4, p.5, k.6, p.3, panel patt. 21, (b.3, p.3 tog.) 5 (7) times, panel patt. 21, p.3, k.6, p.5, k.4.

7th row: p.4, cr.2b., m.b., cr.2f., p.6, cr.2b., m.b., panel patt. 21, p.20 (28), panel patt. 21, m.b., cr.2f., p.6, cr.2b., m.b., cr.2f., p.4.

8th row: k.5, p.3, k.8, p.2, panel patt. 21, (p.3 tog., b.3) 5 (7) times, panel patt. 21, p.2, k.8, p.3, k.5.

9th row: p.4, tw.2f., k.1, tw.2b., p.6, tw.2f., k.1, panel patt. 21, p.20 (28), panel patt. 21, k.1, tw.2b., p.6, tw.2f., k.1, tw.2b., p.4.

10th row: as 6th row.

11th row: p.3, tw.2f., k.3, tw.2b., p.4, tw.2f., k.2, panel patt. 21, p.20 (28), panel patt. 21, k.2, tw.2b., p.4, tw.2f., k.3, tw.2b., p.3.

12th row: as 4th row.

13th row: p.2, tw.2f., k.5, tw.2b., p.2, tw.2f., k.3, panel patt. 21, p.20 (28), panel patt. 21, k.3, tw.2b., p.2, tw.2f., k.5, tw.2b., p.2.

14th row: as 2nd row.

15th row: p.1, tw.2f., k.7, tw.2b., tw.2f., k.4, panel patt. 21, p.20 (28), panel patt. 21, k.4, tw.2b., tw.2f., k.7, tw.2b., p.1.

16th row: p.18, panel patt. 21, (p.3 tog., b.3) 5 (7) times, panel patt. 21, p.18.

Now work in st.st. (see page 23) with centre panel patt. as follows:

1st row: k.18, panel patt. 21, p.20 (28), panel patt. 21, k. 18.

2nd row: p.18, panel patt. 21, (b.3, p.3 tog.), 5 (7) times, panel patt. 21, p.18.

3rd row: k.18, panel patt. 21, p.20 (28), panel patt. 21, k.18.

4th row: p.18, panel patt. 21, (p.3 tog., b.3) 5 (7) times, panel patt. 21, p. 18.

Cont. in this way until Back measures 15½ in., ending with right side facing.

Shape Armholes. Cast off 4 (5) sts. at beg. of next 2 rows, then dec. 1 st. at each end of next and every alt. row until 70 (74) sts. remain. **Work straight until Back measures 22½ (23) in., ending with right side facing.

Shape Shoulders. Cast off 6 (7) sts. at beg. of next 4 rows, 7 (6) sts. at beg. of next 2 rows. Leave remaining 32 (34) sts. on a length of yarn.

The Aran pattern is continued down sides of trousers and round lower hem

FRONT

Work as Back to **: 70 (74) sts. Work straight until Front measures 20 (20½) in., ending with right side facing.

Shape Neck. Next row: patt. 25 (26) sts.; turn and leave remaining sts. on a length of yarn.

Dec. 1 st. at neck edge on next and every alt. row until 19 (20) sts. remain.

Work a few rows straight until Front measures same as Back at armhole edge, ending with right side facing.

Shape Shoulder. Cast off 6 (7) sts. at beg. of next and following alt. row. Work 1 row. Cast off.

With right side facing, leave centre 20 (22) sts. on a length of yarn, rejoin yarn to remaining sts. and complete to match first side, reversing shapings.

SLEEVES (make 2 alike)

With No. 10 needles, cast on 40 sts. and work 3 in. in rib as on Back, inc. 5 sts. evenly across on last row: 45 sts.

Change to No. 8 needles and work in patt.

1st row: k.4, cr.2f., cr.2b., k.4, panel patt. 21 (first row), k.4, cr.2f., cr.2b., k.4.

2nd row: p.5, k.2, p.5, panel patt. 21 (2nd row), p.5, k.2, p.5.

3rd row: k.3, cr.2f., p.2, cr.2b., k.3, panel patt. 21, k.3, cr.2f., p.2, cr.2b., k.3.

4th row: p.4, k.4, p.4, panel patt. 21, p.4, k.4, p.4.

5th row: inc. 1 st. in first st., k.1, cr.2f., p.4, cr.2b., k.2, panel patt. 21, k.2, cr.2f., p.4, cr.2b., k.1, inc. in last st.: 47 sts.

6th row: p.4, k.6, p.3, panel patt. 21, p.3, k.6, p.4.

7th row: k.1, m.b., cr.2f., p.6, cr.2b., m.b., panel patt. 21, m.b., cr.2f., p.6, cr.2b., m.b., k.1.

8th row: p.3, k.8, p.2, panel patt. 21, p.2, k.8, p.3.

9th row: k.2, tw.2b., p.6, tw.2f., k.1, panel patt. 21, k.1, tw.2b., p.6, tw.2f., k.2.

10th row: p.4, k.6, p.3, panel patt. 21, p.3, k.6, p.4.

11th row: inc. 1 st. in first st., k.2, tw.2b., p.4, tw.2f., k.2, panel patt. 21, k.2, tw.2b., p.4, tw.2f., k.2, inc. in last st.: 49 sts.

12th row: p.6, k.4, p.4, panel patt. 21, p.4, k.4, p.6.

13th row: k.5, tw.2b., p.2, tw.2f., k.3, panel patt. 21, k.3, tw.2b., p.2, tw.2f., k.5.

14th row: p.7, k.2, p.5, panel patt. 21, p.5, k.2, p.7.

15th row: k.6, tw.2b., tw.2f., k.4, panel patt. 21, k.4, tw.2b., tw.2f., k.6.

16th row: p.14, panel patt. 21, p.14.

Now work in st.st. (see page 23), working panel patt. over centre 21 sts. (next row first row of panel patt.), inc. 1 st. at each end of next and every foll. 7th (6th) row until there are 67 (71) sts.

Work a few rows straight until sleeve seam measures 16½ in., ending with right side facing.

Shape Top. Cast off 4 (5) sts. at beg. of next 2 rows, then dec. 1 st. at each end of next and every alt. row until 39 sts. remain. Work 1 row. Cast off 3 sts. at beg. of next 8 rows. Cast off.

POLO NECK
Using a fine backstitch, join right shoulder seam. With right side facing and No. 10 needles, pick up and k. 19 sts. down left side of front neck, k. across 20 (22) sts. on length of yarn, pick up and k. 19 sts. up right side of neck, k. across 32 (34) sts. on length of yarn on back neck, dec. 2 sts. evenly: 88 (92) sts.
Starting with a first row, work in rib as on Back for 6 in.
Cast off evenly in rib.

TO COMPLETE
With wrong side of work facing, block each piece by pinning out round edges and, omitting ribbing, press each piece using a warm iron and damp cloth (see page 16). Using a flat seam for ribbing and a fine backstitch for remainder, join remaining shoulder, polo neck, side and sleeve seams. Insert sleeves. Press seams.

TROUSERS
RIGHT LEG
With No. 10 needles, cast on 101 sts. and work in st.st. for 2½ in., ending with a k. row.
Next row: k., thus forming ridge for hemline.
Change to No. 8 needles and work in patt.:
1st row: p.1, cr.2b., k.4, (k.3, cr.2f., cr.2b., k.4) 3 times, panel patt. 21 (first row), (k.4, cr.2f., cr.2b., k.3) 3 times, k.4, cr.2f., p.1.
2nd row: k.2, p.5, (p.4, k.2, p.5) 3 times, panel patt. 21 (2nd row), (p.5, k.2, p.4) 3 times, p.5, k.2.
3rd row: p.2, cr.2b., k.3, (k.2, cr.2f., p.2, cr.2b., k.3) 3 times, panel patt. 21, (k.3, cr.2f., p.2, cr.2b., k.2) 3 times, k.3, cr.2f., p.2.
4th row: k.3, p.4, (p.3, k.4, p.4) 3 times, panel patt. 21, (p.4, k.4, p.3) 3 times, p.4, k.3.
5th row: p.3., cr.2b., k.2, (k.1, cr.2f., p.4, cr.2b., k.2) 3 times, panel patt. 21, (k.2, cr.2f., p.4, cr.2b., k.1) 3 times, k.2, cr.2f., p.3.
6th row: k.4, p.3, (p.2, k.6, p.3) 3 times, panel patt. 21, (p.3, k.6, p.2) 3 times, p.3, k.4.
7th row: p.4, cr.2b., m.b., (cr.2f., p.6, cr.2b., m.b.) 3 times, panel patt. 21, (m.b., cr.2f., p.6, cr.2b.) 3 times, m.b., cr.2f., p.4.
8th row: k.5, p.2, (p.1, k.8, p.2) 3 times, panel patt. 21, (p.2, k.8, p.1) 3 times, p.2, k.5.
9th row: p.4, tw.2f., k.1, (tw.2b., p.6, tw.2f., k.1) 3 times, panel patt. 21, (k.1, tw.2b., p.6, tw.2f.) 3 times, k.1, tw.2b., p.4.
10th row: as 6th row.
11th row: p.3, tw.2f., k.2, (k.1, tw.2b., p.4, tw.2f., k.2) 3 times, panel patt. 21, (k.2, tw.2b., p.4, tw.2f., k.1) 3 times, k.2, tw.2b., p.3.
12th row: as 4th row.

13th row: p.2, tw.2f., k.3, (k.2, tw.2b., p.2, tw.2f., k.3) 3 times, panel patt. 21, (k.3, tw.2b., p.2, tw.2f., k.2) 3 times, k.3, tw.2b., p.2.
14th row: as 2nd row.
15th row: p.1, tw.2f., k.4, (k.3, tw.2b., tw.2f., k.4) 3 times, panel patt. 21, (k.4, tw.2b., tw.2f., k.3) 3 times, k.4, tw.2b., p.1.
16th row: p.40, panel patt. 21, p. 40.
Now work in st.st., working panel patt. over centre 21 sts. (next row first row of panel patt.), until work measures 24 (23) in. from ridge for hemline, ending with right side facing.
Shape Leg. Inc. 1 st. at each end of next and every foll. 4th row until there are 111 (117) sts.
Work 3 rows straight, thus ending with right side facing.
Place a marker at centre of last row. Cast off 2 sts. at beg. of next 2 rows, then dec. 1 st. at each end of next and every alt. row until 95 (99) sts. remain. Cont. dec. at back edge on every alt. row, but at front edge on every foll. 4th row until 83 (90) sts. remain. Keeping front edge straight, continue dec. at back edge only on every foll. 4th row until 77 (83) sts. remain. Work a few rows straight until work measures 9 (9½) in. from marked point (measured at centre of work), ending at back edge (wrong side facing).
Now work in st.st., shaping back as follows:
1st row: p.45 (48); turn.
2nd and every alt. row: sl.1, k. to end.
3rd row: p.37 (40); turn.
5th row: p.29 (32); turn.
7th row: p.21 (24); turn.
9th row: p.13 (16); turn.
11th row: p. all across.
Change to No. 10 needles and work 1 in. in k.1, p.1 rib, with right-side rows having a k.1 at each end. Cast off loosely in rib.

LEFT LEG
Work to match Right Leg reversing all shapings, noting that when shaping back, first row will be right side of work facing and reading k. for p. and p. for k.

TO COMPLETE
With wrong side of work facing, block each piece by pinning out round edges and, omitting ribbing, press each piece using a warm iron and damp cloth. Using a flat seam for ribbing and a fine backstitch seam for remainder, join leg seams to marked points, then join front and back seams.
Fold lower edge at ridge to wrong side and slip-stitch hem loosely in position.
Join elastic in circle to desired size and sew one edge to top of trousers on the inside. Work over elastic with herringbone-st.

Chapter 7
Classics

Toddler's zip-up jacket

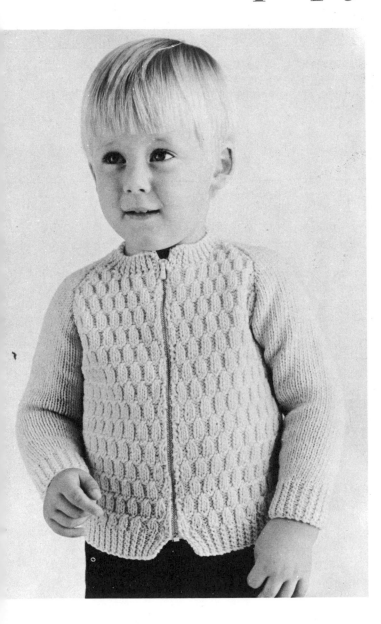

MATERIALS
6 (6, 7) oz. Sirdar Double Crêpe (see note on wools and yarns, page 20); 1 pair each Nos. 8 and 10 knitting needles (see page 26); 10 (12, 12)-in. open-ended zip.

MEASUREMENTS
To fit chest size 20 (22, 24) in.; sleeve seam 7 (8, 9) in.

TENSION
6 sts. and 8 rows to 1 in. on No. 8 needles (see note on tension, page 15).

ABBREVIATIONS
See page 26; tw.2f. (twist 2 front), k. into front of 2nd st. on needle, then into first st. and sl. both off needle tog.

BACK
With No. 10 needles cast on 60 (66, 72) sts.
Work in k.1, p.1 rib for 12 rows. Change to No. 8 needles and st.st. until work is 7 (8, 9) in., ending with a p. row.
Shape Raglan. K.2 tog., k. to last 2 sts., k.2 tog.
Work 3 rows without shaping. Cont. to take 2 tog. at each end of next and every alt. row until there are 20 (22, 24) sts. Leave these on a stitch holder.

LEFT FRONT
With No. 10 needles cast on 34 (36, 40) sts. and work in k.1, p.1, rib for 11 rows.
Next row: *rib 3, inc. in next st.; rep. from * 3 (5, 5) more times, rib to end: 38 (42, 46) sts. Change to No. 8 needles and work in patt.:
1st row: *k.2, p.2; rep. from * to last 2 sts., k.2.

Patterned front contrasts with stocking stitch back and sleeves

needles and work in st.st., inc. at each end of 7th and every 9th (10th, 11th) row until there are 44 (48, 54) sts., ending with a p. row.

Shape Raglan. K.2 tog., k. to last 2 sts., k.2 tog. Work 3 rows in st.st.

Rep. these 4 rows until there are 38 (42, 50) sts., ending with a p. row, then take 2 tog. at each end of next and every alt. row until 6 sts. rem. Leave on a stitch holder.

NECKBAND

Join raglan seams and, with No. 10 needles and right side of work facing, k. across 12 sts. on right Front, pick up and k. 7 (8, 9) sts. up right side of front, k. across 6 sts. of right sleeve, 20 (22, 24) sts. at top of Back, 6 sts. of second sleeve, pick up and k. 7 (8, 9) down left side of front and k. 12 sts. of left front: 70 (74, 78) sts. Work 6 rows of k.1, p.1 rib on these sts.
Cast off in rib.

TO COMPLETE

Sew side and sleeve seams. Sew in zip fastener at centre front.

Two-colour sweaters

– with round, button-up neck for a girl, V-neck for a boy
(photographed in colour on page 203)

MATERIALS

4 oz. Sirdar Fontein Crêpe 4-ply in main colour and 3 oz. in contrasting shade (see note on wools and yarns, page 20); one pair each Nos. 10 and 11 knitting needles (see page 26); 3 small buttons for the round-necked (girl's) sweater.

MEASUREMENTS

To fit chest size 18 (20, 22) in.; sleeve seam 7½ (8½, 9) in.

TENSION

17 sts. and 18 rows to 2 in. on No. 10 needles (see note on tension, page 15).

ABBREVIATIONS

See page 26; M., main shade; C., contrasting shade.

BACK (for both versions)

With No. 11 needles and M., cast on 96 (104, 112) sts. Work 12 rows in k.1, p.1 rib.
Change to No. 10 needles.

1st row: join in C., *k.2 M., k.2 C.; rep. from * to end of row.

2nd row: p.1 M., *p.2 C., p.2 M.; rep. from * to last 3 sts., p.2 C., p.1 M.

3rd row: k.1 C., *k.2 M., k.2 C.; rep. from * to last

2nd row: *p.2, k.2; rep. from * to last 2 sts., p.2.

3rd and 4th rows: as first and 2nd rows.

5th row: *tw.2f., p.2; rep. from * to last 2 sts., tw.2f. Rep. first and 2nd rows twice more and then first row again.

11th row: *p.2, tw.2f.; rep. from * to last 2 sts., p.2.

12th row: as 2nd row.

Cont. in patt. until work is 7 (8, 9) in., ending with a wrong-side row.

Shape Armhole. Take 2 tog. at beg. of next and every alt. row until 24 (26, 27) sts. rem., finishing at armhole edge.

Shape Neck. K.2 tog., patt. 10 (12, 13) sts.; turn. Now work on these sts., taking 2 tog. each end of 2nd and every alt. row until 3 (3, 2) sts. rem. Work these sts. tog. and fasten off. Leave rem. sts. on a stitch holder.

RIGHT FRONT

Work as for Left Front but reverse all shapings.

SLEEVES (make 2 alike)

With No. 10 needles cast on 36 (38, 42) sts.
Work in k.1, p.1 rib for 1½ (2, 2) in. Change to No. 8

3 sts., k.2 M., k.1 C.

4th row: *p.2 C., p.2 M.; rep. from * to end of row. Rep. these 4 rows until work is 7 (7½, 8) in., ending with a wrong-side row.**

Shape Armholes. Keeping patt. correct cast off 4 sts. at beg. of next 2 rows, then take 2 tog. at each end of every right-side row until there are 80 (88, 94) sts. Cont. till armhole is 3½ (3¾, 4) in., ending with a wrong-side row.

Shape Shoulder. Cast off 7 (8, 9) sts. at beg. of next 6 rows.
Leave rem. 38 (40, 40) sts. on a stitch holder.

FRONT (girl's jersey)

Work as for Back until **.

Shape Armhole and Neck. Keeping patt. correct cast off 4 sts. at beg. of next row, patt. 41 (45, 49), sl. next 6 sts. on to a safety pin, and working on left side of front only cont. in patt., taking 2 tog. at armhole edge on every k. row until there are 37 (41, 44) sts. Cont. until armhole is 2¾ (3, 3¼) in., ending with a p. row.

Next row: patt. 26 (29, 32), sl. next 11 (12, 12) sts. on to a stitch holder and cont. in patt. taking 2 tog. at neck edge on every row until there are 21 (24, 27) sts. Cont. until armhole is 3½ (3¾, 4) in., ending with a p. row.

Shape Shoulder. Cast off 7 (8, 9) sts. at beg. of next and foll. 2 alt. rows. Cast off.

Rejoin yarn to rem. 45 (49, 53) sts. and k. to end. Cast off 4 sts. at beg. of next row. Now complete to match first side, reversing all shapings.

FRONT (boy's jersey)

Work as for Back until work is 6½ (7, 7½) in., ending with a p. row.

Shape Neck and Armholes. Keeping patt. correct, k.46 (50, 54), k.2 tog.; turn, p. to end.

Working on this side of the neck:

Next row: k. to last 2 sts., k. 2 tog. **Next row:** p.

Next row: cast off 4 sts., k. to last 2 sts., k. 2 tog.

Next and alt. rows: p.

Take 2 tog. at each end of next and every k. row until there are 33 (37, 39) sts. then take 2 tog. at end of every k. row until 24 (27, 30) sts. then take 2 tog. at end of every row until 21 (24, 27) sts., ending with a p. row.

Shape Shoulder. Cast off 7 (8, 9) sts. at beg. of next 3 k. rows. Cast off. Rejoin yarn to rem. sts. and work other side to match, reversing all shapings.

SLEEVES (both versions – make 2 alike)

With No. 11 needles and M., cast on 52 (56, 60) sts. Work 14 rows in k.1, p.1 rib.

Change to No. 10 needles and work in patt. as for Back inc. at each end of 5th and every foll. 6th row until there are 70 (74, 76) sts. Cont. until work is 7½ (8½, 9) in., ending with a p. row.

Shape Top. Cast off 4 sts. at beg. of next 2 rows, then take 2 tog. at each end of every k. row, until there are 54 (58, 58) sts. Cast off 4 sts. at beg. of next 8 rows. Cast off.

FRONT EDGING AND NECKBAND (girl's jersey)

With No. 11 needles and M., sl. 6 sts. from safety pin on to needle and work 10 rows k.1, p.1 rib.

Next row (buttonhole row): k.1, p.1, y.fwd., k.2 tog., k.1, p.1.

Cont. in rib, making another buttonhole on 21st row, until strip measures the same as front opening. Leave sts. on safety pin or stitch holder.

Make Other Front Edging. With No. 11 needles and M., cast on 6 sts. and work in rib until strip measures same as front opening. Leave on a safety pin or stitch holder.

Make Neckband. Sew buttonhole edging strip to right side of front opening and plain edging strip to left side. Sew shoulder seams. With right side of work facing, No. 11 needles and M., rib 6 sts. from front buttonhole edging, k.11 (12, 12) sts. from stitch holder at right front, pick up and k. 9 (10, 12) sts. up right side of neck, k.38 (40, 40) sts. of back, pick up and k.9 (10, 12) sts. down left side of neck, k.11 (12, 12) sts. from stitch holder at left front and rib 6 sts. from left front edging: 90 (96, 100) sts. Work in k.1, p.1 rib for 3 rows.

4th row: k.1, p.1, k.2 tog., y.fwd., rib to end. Work 3 more rows in rib. Cast off in rib.

NECKBAND (boy's jersey)

Join right shoulder seam. With right side of work facing, No. 11 needles and M., pick up and k. 36 (38, 40) down left side of neck, pick up yarn between sts. at centre of neck to make 1 st., pick up and k.36 (38, 40) up right side of neck, and k.38 (40, 40) from back: 111 (117, 121) sts. Work on these sts. in k.1, p.1 rib, beg. first row with a p. st. so that centre st. is a k. st. Work 5 rows in rib, working k. 2 tog. on each side of the centre st. on 2nd and 4th rows. Cast off in rib.

TO COMPLETE

Girl's jersey. Sew in sleeves and join side and sleeve seams. Catch down bottom of left front edging at inside of work, and sew on buttons opposite buttonholes.

Boy's jersey. Join left shoulder seam. Sew in sleeves and join side and sleeve seams.

Fair Isle sweater

(photographed in colour on page 204)

MATERIALS

4 (6) oz. Emu Scotch Double Knitting in white, 4 (6) oz. in red, 2 (4) oz. in green (see note on wools and yarns, page 20); one pair each Nos. 8 and 10 knitting needles, and a set of four No. 10 knitting needles (see page 26).

MEASUREMENTS

To fit chest size 24/26 (28/30) in.; sleeve seam 12½ (15½) in.

TENSION

13 sts. to 2 in. on No. 8 needles over patt. (see note on tension, page 15).

ABBREVIATIONS

See page 26; G., green; R., red; W., white.

Note. *Each square on chart overleaf equals 1 st., and each complete line of squares, reading across the chart, equals 1 row. One complete pattern*

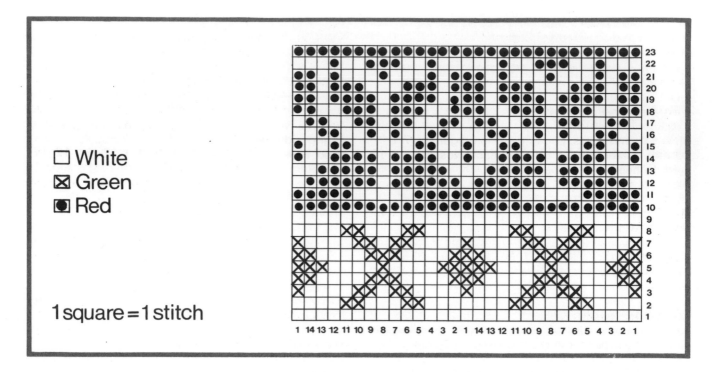

□ White
☒ Green
◉ Red

1 square = 1 stitch

Chart row numbers (right side): 23, 22, 21, 20, 19, 18, 17, 16, 15, 14, 13, 12, 11, 10, 9, 8, 7, 6, 5, 4, 3, 2, 1

Chart stitch numbers (bottom): 1 14 13 12 11 10 9 8 7 6 5 4 3 2 1 14 13 12 11 10 9 8 7 6 5 4 3 2 1

equals 14 sts. and 23 rows; numbers down right-hand side of chart refer to rows; numbers along bottom refer to sts. Read k. rows from right to left, and p. rows from left to right, working odd st. at end of k. rows and beg. of p. rows (see also note on Colour Knitting, page 23).

BACK

With No. 10 needles and G., cast on 84 (98) sts. Work in k. 1, p.1 rib for 1¼ in., inc. at end of last row. Change to No. 8 needles and work in st.st., following the colour patt. chart above.

Cont. until work is 11½ (12¾) in., ending with a wrong-side row.

Shape Armholes. Cast off 5 (7) sts. at beg. of next 2 rows then, keeping patt. correct, take 2 tog. at each end of next and alt. rows until there are 63 (71) sts. **.

Cont. until armhole is 5 (6) in., ending with a wrong-side row.

Shape Shoulders. Cast off 7 (8) sts. at beg. of next 4 rows and 6 (7) sts. at beg. of next 2 rows. Slip rem. 23 (25) sts. on a stitch holder.

FRONT

Work as for Back until **.

Cont. till armhole is 3¼ (3¾) in., ending with a p. row.

Shape Neck. K.24 (28); turn, work on these sts. taking 2 tog. at neck edge on next and alt. rows until there are 20 (23) sts. Cont. until work measures same as Back to shoulder, ending at armhole edge.

Shape Shoulder. Cast off 7 (8) sts. at beg. of next and alt. rows. Work 1 row. Cast off.

Slip centre 15 sts. on to a stitch holder and complete second side to match, reversing shapings.

SLEEVES (make 2 alike)

With No. 10 needles and G., cast on 36 (42) sts. Work in k.1, p.1 rib for 2 in., inc. 1 st. at end of last row. Change to No. 8 needles and cont. in st.st. working from colour chart thus:

1st size. 1st row: work from 11th-14th sts., then work 1st-14th sts. twice, then 1st-5th.

Cont. in patt. as set.

2nd size: work from chart.

Both sizes. Keeping patt. correct inc. each end of 5th and every foll. 6th (7th) row until 59 (67) sts. Cont. till work is 12½ (15½) in. from beg. ending with a wrong-side row.

Shape Top. Cast off 5 (6) sts. at beg. of next 2 rows then take 2 tog. at each end of next and alt. rows until 37 (41) sts. rem. ending with a p. row. Cast off 4 sts. at beg. of next 6 rows. Cast off.

NECKBAND

Join shoulders. With the set of No. 10 needles and G., k. across 23 (25) sts. of back neck, pick up and k.19 (24) sts. down left front, k. across 15 sts. at centre, pick up and k. 19 (24) sts. up right front: 76 (88) sts. Work in k.1, p.1 rib on these sts. for 1¾ (2) in. Cast off loosely in rib.

TO COMPLETE

Sew in sleeves, then join side and sleeve seams. Fold neckband in half to wrong side and slipstitch in position.

Girl's twin set

– in 4-ply or double knitting yarn

(photographed in black and white on page 198)

MATERIALS

For version 1: 8 (9, 10, 11, 12, 13) oz. Emu Super Crêpe *or* Scotch 4-ply *or* Bri-Nylon 4-ply (see note on wools and yarns, page 20) for cardigan, 6 (7, 8, 9, 10, 11) oz. for jumper; one pair each Nos. 10 and 12 knitting needles (see page 26).

For version 2: 13 (14, 15, 16, 17, 18) oz. Emu Scotch Double Knitting *or* Double Crêpe *or* Bri-Nylon Double Knitting (see note on wools and yarns, page 20) for cardigan, 9 (10, 11, 12, 13, 14) oz. for jumper; one pair each Nos. 8 and 10 knitting needles (see page 26).

For both versions: a 4-in. zip fastener; 5 medium buttons.

MEASUREMENTS

To fit chest size 26 (28, 30, 32, 34, 36) in.; length at centre back 17$\frac{1}{4}$ (18$\frac{3}{4}$, 19$\frac{3}{4}$, 21, 22$\frac{1}{4}$, 23$\frac{1}{4}$) in. (cardigan), 16$\frac{3}{4}$ (18$\frac{1}{4}$, 19$\frac{1}{4}$, 20$\frac{1}{2}$, 21$\frac{3}{4}$, 22$\frac{3}{4}$) in. (jumper); sleeve seam 12$\frac{1}{2}$ (14, 15$\frac{1}{2}$, 16$\frac{1}{2}$, 17$\frac{1}{2}$, 18) in. (cardigan), 2$\frac{1}{2}$ (2$\frac{1}{2}$, 2$\frac{1}{2}$, 3, 3, 3) in. (jumper).

TENSION

Version 1: 7$\frac{1}{2}$ sts. and 9$\frac{1}{2}$ rows to 1 in. over st.st.
Version 2: 5$\frac{1}{2}$ sts. and 8 rows to 1 in. over st.st. (see note on tension, page 15).

ABBREVIATIONS

See page 26.

Version 1: in 4-Ply Yarn
CARDIGAN
BACK

With No. 12 needles, cast on 98 (106, 112, 118, 126, 132) sts. and work in k.1, p.1 rib for 2$\frac{1}{2}$ in. ending with a wrong-side row.
Next row: k.7 (7, 7, 9, 9, 7), *m.1, k.12 (13, 14, 11, 12, 13); rep. from * to last 7 (8, 7, 10, 9, 8) sts., m.1, k.7 (8, 7, 10, 9, 8) sts.: 106 (114, 120, 128, 136, 142) sts.
Next row: p.
Change to No. 10 needles and st. st. Cont. until work measures 10 (11, 11$\frac{1}{2}$, 12, 12$\frac{1}{2}$, 13) in. from the beg., ending with a p. row.
Shape Raglan Armholes. ** Cast off 3 (3, 3, 3, 2, 2) sts. at the beg. of the next 2 rows.
Next row: k.2, p.2 tog., k. to last 4 sts., p.2 tog., k.2.
Next row: p.
Rep. the last 2 rows ** until 34 (36, 38, 40, 42, 44) sts. rem. ending with a wrong-side row.
Cast off.

LEFT FRONT

With No. 12 needles cast on 46 (50, 52, 56, 60, 62) sts. and work in k.1, p.1 rib for 2$\frac{1}{2}$ in., ending with a wrong-side row.
Next row: k.5 (4, 2, 4, 2, 1), *m.1, k.12 (14, 12, 12, 14, 12); rep. from * to last 5 (4, 2, 4, 2, 1) sts., m.1, k.5 (4, 2, 4, 2, 1): 50 (54, 57, 61, 65, 68) sts.
Next row: p.
Change to No. 10 needles and st.st.
Cont. until work measures the same as Back to the armholes, ending with a p. row.
Shape Raglan Armhole and Neck. Next row: cast off 3 (3, 3, 3, 2, 2) sts., k. to end.
Next row: p.
Next row: k.2, p.2 tog., k. to end.
Next row: p.
Rep. these 2 rows until 39 (42, 45, 48, 51, 54) sts. rem.
1st row: k.2, p.2 tog., k. to last 2 sts., k.2 tog.
2nd row: p.
3rd row: k.2, p.2 tog., k. to end.
4th row: p.
Rep. these 4 rows until 3 sts. rem. working dec. at outer armhole edge when they can no longer be worked inside a border of 2 sts. Work 1 row. K.3 tog. Fasten off.

RIGHT FRONT

Work to match Left Front, reversing all shapings.

SLEEVES (make 2 alike)

With No. 12 needles, cast on 42 (44, 46, 48, 50, 52) sts. and work in k.1, p.1 rib for 2$\frac{1}{2}$ (2$\frac{1}{2}$, 2$\frac{1}{2}$, 3, 3, 3) in., ending with a wrong-side row.
Next row: k.3 (4, 5, 3, 2, 3), *m.1, k.5 (5, 5, 6, 5, 5); rep. from * to last 4 (5, 6, 3, 3, 4) sts., m.1, k.4 (5, 6, 3, 3, 4): 50 (52, 54, 56, 60, 62) sts.
Next row: p.
Change to No. 10 needles and st.st., inc. 1 st. at each end of every foll. 5th (6th, 6th, 6th, 6th, 6th) row until there are 78 (84, 88, 94, 100, 104) sts. on the needle. Cont. without further shaping until work measures 12$\frac{1}{2}$ (14, 15$\frac{1}{2}$, 16$\frac{1}{2}$, 17$\frac{1}{2}$, 18) in. from the beg. ending with a p. row.
Shape Raglan Top. Follow instructions for Back from ** to ** until 6 sts. rem., ending with a wrong-side row.

FRONT BAND

With No. 12 needles cast on 11 sts.
1st row: k.1, *p.1, k.1, rep. from * to end.
2nd row: p.1, *k.1, p.1, rep. from * to end. Rep. these 2 rows until work measures $\frac{3}{4}$ ($\frac{1}{2}$, $\frac{3}{4}$, $\frac{1}{2}$, $\frac{3}{4}$, $\frac{1}{2}$) in. from the beg.

1st buttonhole row: rib 4, cast off 3 sts., rib to end.
2nd buttonhole row: rib casting on over sts. cast off in previous row.

Cont. in rib working 4 more buttonholes at intervals of 2 (2¼, 2¼, 2½, 2½, 2¾) in. measured from base of previous buttonhole. Cont. until band is long enough slightly stretched, to fit up right front, across sleeve tops, back neck, and down left front. Cast off in rib.

JUMPER
BACK
***With No. 12 needles, cast on 94 (102, 108, 114, 122, 128) sts. and work in k.1, p.1 rib for 2½ in., ending with a wrong-side row.
Next row: k.5 (5, 5, 7, 7, 5), *m.1, k.12 (13, 14, 11, 12, 13); rep. from * to last 5 (6, 5, 8, 7, 6) sts., m.1, k.5 (6, 5, 8, 7, 6): 102 (110, 116, 124, 132, 138) sts.
Next row: p.
Change to No. 10 needles and st.st. Cont. until work measures 9½ (10½, 11, 11½, 12, 12½) in. from the beg., ending with a p. row. ***
Shape Raglan Armholes. Follow instructions for Back of Cardigan from ** to ** until 30 (32, 34, 36, 38, 40) sts. rem., ending with a wrong-side row. Leave these sts. on a stitch holder.

FRONT
Follow instructions for Back of Jumper from *** to ***.
Shape Raglan Armholes. Follow instructions for Back of Cardigan from ** to ** until 50 (54, 56, 60, 64, 66) sts. rem., ending with a wrong-side row.
Shape Neck. Next row: k.2, p.2 tog., k.11 (12, 13, 14, 16, 16), k.2 tog., turn, leaving rem. sts. on a stitch holder.
Next row: p.2 tog., p. to end.
Cont. dec. at armhole edge as before, **at the same time** dec. 1 st. at neck edge on the foll. 4 (4, 5, 5, 6, 6) rows. Keeping neck edge straight, dec. at armhole edge as before until 1 st. rem., working dec. at outer armhole edge when they can no longer be worked inside a border of 2 sts. Fasten off. Slip centre 16 (18, 18, 20, 20, 22) sts. on to a stitch holder. Join in yarn at neck edge to remaining sts. and work to match first side of neck, reversing shapings.

SLEEVES (make 2 alike)
With No. 12 needles, cast on 58 (64, 66, 70, 74, 78) sts. and work in k.1, p.1 rib for ¾ in., ending with a wrong-side row.
Next row: k.1 (4, 7, 2, 7, 1), *m.1, k.5 (5, 4, 5, 4, 5); rep. from * to last 2 (5, 7, 3, 7, 2) sts., m.1, k.2 (5, 7, 3, 7, 2): 70 (76, 80, 84, 90, 94) sts.
Next row: p.
Change to No. 10 needles and st.st., inc. 1 st. at

The jumper has neat short sleeves, the cardigan buttons up to a high V-neck

each end of the next and every foll. 4th row until there are 78 (84, 88, 94, 100, 104) sts. on the needle. Cont. without further shaping until work measures 2½ (2½, 2½, 3, 3, 3) in. from beg., ending with a p. row.
Shape Raglan Top. Follow instructions for Back of Cardigan from ** to ** until 6 sts. rem., ending with a wrong-side row. Leave these sts. on a stitch holder.

NECKBAND
Join raglan seams, leaving left back raglan seam open. With No. 12 needles and right side of work facing k. across the 6 sts. on top of left sleeve, pick up and k. 20 (22, 23, 24, 25, 26) sts. down left side of neck, k. across the 16 (18, 18, 20, 20, 22) sts. from centre front, pick up and k. 20 (22, 23, 24, 25, 26) sts. up right side of neck, k. across the 6 sts. on top of right sleeve and 30 (32, 34, 36, 38, 40) sts. from back neck: 98 (106, 110, 116, 120, 126) sts. Work in k.1, p.1 rib for 1 in. Cast off in rib.

TO COMPLETE
CARDIGAN
Join raglan, side and sleeve seams. Sew on front band, slightly stretching it as you work. Neaten buttonholes and sew on buttons opposite.

JUMPER
Join side and sleeve seams. Join left back raglan, leaving 4 in. open at neck. Sew in zip to this opening.

Version 2: in Double Knitting Yarn
CARDIGAN
BACK
With No. 10 needles, cast on 78 (84, 90, 96, 102, 108) sts. and work in k.1, p.1 rib for 2½ in., ending with a wrong-side row. Change to No. 8 needles and st.st. Cont. until work measures 10 (11, 11½, 12, 12½, 13) in., from the beg., ending with a p. row.
Shape Raglan Armholes. ** **Next row:** k.2, p.2 tog., k. to last 4 sts., p.2 tog., k.2.
Next row: p.
Next row: k.
Next row: p.
Rep. the last 4 rows 1 (1, 1, 2, 2, 2) times more.
Next row: k.2, p.2 tog., k. to last 4 sts., p. 2 tog., k.2.
Next row: p.
Rep. the last 2 rows ** until 24 (26, 28, 30, 30, 32) sts. rem., ending with a wrong-side row. Cast off.

LEFT FRONT
With No. 10 needles, cast on 38 (42, 44, 48, 50, 54) sts. and work in k.1, p.1 rib for 2½ in., ending with a wrong-side row and inc. at end of last row on **1st, 3rd and 5th sizes only:** 39 (42, 45, 48, 51, 54) sts. Change to No. 8 needles and st.st. Cont. until work measures 10 (11, 11½, 12, 12½, 13) in. from the beg., ending with a p. row.

Shape Raglan Armhole and Neck. 1st row: k.2, p.2 tog., k. to end.
2nd row: p.
3rd row: k.
4th row: p.
Rep. these 4 rows until 37 (40, 43, 45, 48, 51) sts. rem. Then rep. the first and 2nd rows until 33 (36, 39, 42, 42, 45) sts. rem.
Next row: k.2, p.2 tog., k. to last 2 sts., k.2 tog.
Next row: p.
Next row: k.2, p.2 tog., k. to end.
Next row: p.
Rep. these 4 rows until 3 sts. rem., working dec. at outer armhole edge when they can no longer be worked inside a border on 2 sts. Work 1 row. K.3 tog. Fasten off.

RIGHT FRONT
Work to match Left Front, reversing all shapings.

SLEEVES (make 2 alike)
With No. 10 needles, cast on 38 (40, 42, 44, 46, 48) sts. and work in k.1, p.1 rib for 2½ (2½, 2½, 3, 3, 3) in., ending with a wrong-side row.
Change to No. 8 needles and st.st. Inc. 1 st. at each end of the 7th and every foll. 6th (7th, 7th, 7th, 6th, 7th) row until there are 58 (62, 66, 70, 76, 80) sts. on the needle.
Cont. without further shaping until work measures 12½ (14, 15½, 16½, 17½, 18) in., from the beg., ending with a p. row.
Shape Raglan Top. Follow instructions for Back from ** to ** until 4 sts. rem., ending with a wrong-side row. Cast off.

FRONT BAND
With No. 10 needles, cast on 8 sts. and work ¾ (½, ¾, ½, ¾, ½) in. in k.1, p.1 rib.
1st buttonhole row: rib 3, cast off 2 sts., rib to end.
2nd buttonhole row: rib, casting on over sts. cast off in previous row.
Cont. in rib, working 4 more buttonholes at intervals of 2 (2¼, 2¼, 2½, 2½, 2¾) in., measured from base of previous buttonhole. Cont. until band is long enough slightly stretched to fit up right front, across sleeve tops, back neck, and down left front.
Cast off in rib.

JUMPER
BACK
*** With No. 10 needles cast on 74 (80, 86, 92, 98, 104) sts. and work in k.1, p.1 rib for 2½ in., ending with a wrong-side row and inc. 1 st. at end of last row: 75 (81, 87, 93, 99, 105) sts.
Change to No. 8 needles and st.st. Cont. until work measures 9½ (10½, 11, 11½, 12, 12½) in., from the beg., ending with a p. row.***
Shape Raglan Armholes. Follow instructions for Back of Cardigan from ** to ** until 21 (23, 25, 27, 27, 29) sts. rem. ending with a wrong-side row. Leave these sts. on a stitch holder.

FRONT
Follow instructions for Back of Jumper from *** to ***.
Shape Raglan Armholes. Follow instructions for Back of Cardigan from ** to ** until 37 (41, 45, 49, 51, 53) sts. rem., ending with a wrong-side row.
Shape Neck. Next row: k.2, p.2 tog., k.7 (9, 10, 12, 13, 13), k.2 tog., turn, leaving rem. sts. on a stitch holder.
Next row: p.2 tog., p. to end.
Cont. dec. at armhole edge as before, **at the same time** dec. 1 st. at neck edge of the foll. 2 (3, 3, 4, 4, 4) rows. Keeping neck edge straight, dec. at armhole edge as before until 1 st. rem., working dec. at outer armhole edge when they can no longer be worked inside a border of 2 sts. Fasten off. Slip centre 11 (11, 13, 13, 13, 15) sts. on to a stitch holder. Join in yarn at neck edge to rem. sts. and work to match first side of neck, reversing shapings.

SLEEVES (make 2 alike)
With No. 10 needles, cast on 42 (46, 52, 54, 58, 62) sts. and work in k.1, p.1 rib for ¾ in., ending with a wrong-side row.
Next row: k.3 (2, 5, 2, 2, 4), *m.1, k.5 (6, 6, 7, 6, 6) sts.; rep. from * to last 4 (2, 5, 3, 2, 4) sts., m.1, k.4 (2, 5, 3, 2, 4): 50 (54, 60, 62, 68, 72) sts.
Next row: p.
Change to No. 8 needles and st.st. inc. 1 st. at each end of the next and every foll. 4th row until there are 58 (62, 66, 70, 76, 80) sts. on the needle. Cont. without further shaping until work measures 2½ (2½, 2½, 3, 3, 3) in. from the beg., ending with a p. row.
Shape Raglan Top. Follow instructions for Back of Cardigan from ** to ** until 4 sts. rem., ending with a wrong-side row. Leave these sts. on a stitch holder.

NECKBAND
Join raglan seams, leaving left back raglan seam open. With No. 10 needles and right side of work facing, k. across the 4 sts. on top of left sleeve, pick up and k.15 (17, 18, 20, 22, 24) sts. down left side of neck, k. across the 11 (11, 13, 13, 13, 15) sts. from centre front, pick up and k. 15 (17, 18, 20, 22, 24) sts. up right side of neck, k. across the 4 sts. on top of right sleeve and 21 (23, 25, 27, 27, 29) sts. from back neck: 70 (76, 82, 88, 92, 100) sts.
Work in k.1, p.1 rib for 1 in. Cast off in rib.

TO COMPLETE
Follow instructions for 4-ply twin set.

Sturdy for schoolwear — a useful pullover to make in 4-ply or double knitting yarn (instructions start on page 202)

Schoolboy's pullover

— in 4-ply or double knitting yarn

(photographed in black and white on page 201)

MATERIALS

For version 1: 5 (6, 7, 7, 8, 9) balls of Emu Scotch 4-ply **or** Super Crêpe **or** Bri-Nylon 4-ply (see note on wools and yarns, page 20); one pair each Nos. 10 and 12 knitting needles (see page 26).

For version 2: 6 (8, 9, 9, 10,11) balls Emu Scotch Double Knitting **or** Double Crêpe **or** Bri-Nylon Double Knitting (see note on wools and yarns, page 20); one pair each Nos. 8 and 10 knitting needles (see page 26).

MEASUREMENTS

To fit chest size 24 (26, 28, 30, 32, 34) in.; length at centre back $16\frac{1}{2}$ (18, $19\frac{1}{2}$, $20\frac{1}{2}$, $21\frac{1}{2}$, $22\frac{1}{4}$) in.

TENSION

Version 1: $7\frac{1}{2}$ sts. and 8 rows to 1 in. over st. st.
Version 2: $5\frac{1}{2}$ sts. and 8 rows to 1 in. over st.st. (see note on tension, page 15).

ABBREVIATIONS

See page 26.

Version 1: in 4-Ply Yarn

BACK

** With No. 12 needles, cast on 99 (105, 113, 121, 129, 135) sts.

1st row: k.1, *p.1, k.1; rep. from * to end.
2nd row: p.1, *k.1, p.1; rep. from * to end.
Rep. these 2 rows for 2 in., ending with a wrong-side row. Change to No. 10 needles and st.st.
Cont. until work measures 10 (11, 12, $12\frac{1}{2}$, 13, $13\frac{1}{2}$) in. from the beg., ending with a p. row. **
Shape Armholes. Cast off 5 (5, 6, 6, 7, 7) sts. at beg. of the next 2 rows. Dec. 1 st. at each end of the next and every foll. alt. row until 77 (83, 87, 93, 99, 105) sts. rem. Cont. without further shaping until work measures 6 ($6\frac{1}{2}$, 7, $7\frac{1}{2}$, 8, $8\frac{1}{4}$) in. from beg. of armhole shaping, ending with a p. row.
Shape Shoulders. Cast off 6 (7, 7, 8, 8, 8) sts. at the beg. of the next 6 rows and 7 (6, 7, 6, 8, 10) sts. at the beg. of the foll. 2 rows. Leave the rem. 27 (29, 31, 33, 35, 37) sts. on a stitch holder.

FRONT

Follow instructions for Back from ** to **.
Shape Armhole and Neck. Next row: cast off 5 (5, 6, 6, 7, 7) sts., k.44 (47, 50, 54, 57, 60), inc. st. used in casting off, turn, leaving rem. sts. on a stitch holder, p. to end.
*** **Next row:** k.2 tog., k. to last 2 sts., k.2 tog.
Dec. 1 st. at neck edge on every foll. 4th row, **at the**

same time dec. 1 st. at armhole edge on every alt. row until 35 (38, 39, 42, 45, 48) sts. rem. Keeping armhole edge straight, cont. to dec. at neck edge as before until 25 (27, 28, 30, 32, 34) sts. rem. Cont. without further shaping until work measures the same as Back to shoulder, ending at armhole edge.
Shape Shoulder. Cast off 6 (7, 7, 8, 8, 8) sts. at beg. of the next and 2 foll. alt. rows. Work 1 row. Cast off the rem. 6 (6, 7, 6, 8, 10) sts. *** Slip the centre st. on to a safety pin. Join in yarn at neck edge to rem. sts., k. to end.
Next row: cast off 5 (5, 6, 6, 7, 7) sts., p. to end. Complete to match first side of neck, working from *** to ***

NECKBAND

Join right shoulder seam. With No. 12 needles and right side of work facing, pick up and k.56 (60, 64, 68, 74, 76) sts. down left side of neck, k. centre st. (mark this st. with a coloured thread), pick up and k.56 (60, 64, 68, 74, 76) sts. up right side of neck and k. across the 27 (29, 31, 33, 35, 37) sts. on back neck, inc. into last st.: 141 (151, 161, 171, 185, 191) sts.
1st row (wrong side): rib to within 2 sts. of centre st., sl.1, k.1, p.s.s.o., p.1, k.2 tog., rib to end.
2nd row: rib to within 2 sts. of centre st., sl.1, k.1, p.s.s.o., k.1, k.2 tog., rib to end. Rep. these 2 rows for 1 in. Cast off in rib, dec. on this row as before.

ARMBANDS (make 2 alike)

Join left shoulder seam. With No. 12 needles and right side of work facing pick up and k. 106 (114, 122, 128, 138, 142) sts. evenly around armhole edge. Work 6 rows in k.1, p.1 rib. Cast off in rib.

TO COMPLETE

Join side seams.

Version 2: in Double Knitting Yarn

BACK

** With No. 10 needles, cast on 73 (77, 83, 89, 95, 99) sts.

1st row: k.1, *p.1, k.1; rep. from * to end.
2nd row: p.1, *k.1, p.1; rep. from * to end.
Rep. these 2 rows for 2 in., ending with a wrong-side row. Change to No. 8 needles and st.st.

Continued on page 207

Opposite: two-colour sweaters with a choice of necklines for a boy or girl — instructions on page 194. Overleaf: traditional Fair Isle sweater (page 195)

Cont. until work measures 10 (11, 12, 12½, 13, 13½) in. from the beg. ending with a p. row. **

Shape Armholes. Cast off 4 (4, 5, 6, 6, 6) sts. at the beg. of the next 2 rows. Dec. 1 st. at each end of the next and every foll. alt. row until 57 (61, 65, 69, 73, 77) sts. rem. Cont. without further shaping until work measures 6 (6½, 7, 7½, 8, 8¼) in. from beg. of armhole shaping, ending with a p. row.

Shape shoulders. Cast off 6 (6, 6, 7, 7, 8) sts. at the beg. of the next 4 rows and 5 (6, 7, 6, 7, 7) sts. at the beg. of the next 2 rows. Leave the rem. 23 (25, 27, 29, 31, 31) sts. on a stitch holder.

FRONT

Follow instructions for Back from ** to **.

Shape Armhole and Neck. Next row: cast off 4 (4, 5, 6, 6, 6) sts., k.32 (34, 36, 38, 41, 43) including st. used in casting off; turn, leaving rem. sts. on a stitch holder, p. to end.

***Next row:** k.2 tog., k. to last 2 sts., k.2 tog. Dec. 1 st. at neck edge on every following 4th row, *at the same time* dec. 1 st. at armhole edge on every alt. row until 26 (28, 30, 32, 33, 35) sts. rem. Keeping armhole edge straight, cont. to dec. at neck edge as before until 17 (18, 19, 20, 21, 23) sts. rem. Cont. without further shaping until work measures the same as Back to shoulder, ending at armhole edge.

Shape Shoulder. Cast off 6 (6, 6, 7, 7, 8) sts. at the beg. of the next and following alt. row. Work 1 row.

Cast off the rem. 5 (6, 7, 6, 7, 7) sts.*** Slip the centre st. on to a safety pin. Join in yarn at neck edge to remaining sts., k. to end.

Next row: cast off 4 (4, 5, 6, 6, 6) sts., p. to end. Complete to match first side of neck, working from *** to ***.

NECKBAND

Join right shoulder seam. With No. 10 needles and right side of work facing, pick up and k.48 (50, 54, 58, 62, 66) sts. down left side of neck, k. centre st. (mark this st. with a coloured thread), pick up and k.48 (50, 54, 58, 62, 66) sts. up right side of neck and k. across the 23 (25, 27, 29, 31, 31) sts. on back neck, inc. into last st.: 121 (127, 137, 147, 157, 165) sts.

1st row (wrong side): rib to within 2 sts. of centre st., sl.1, k.1, p.s.s.o., p.1, k.2 tog., rib to end.

2nd row: rib to within 2 sts. of centre st., sl.1, k.1, p.s.s.o., k.1, k.2 tog., rib to end. Rep. these 2 rows for 1 in. Cast off in rib, dec. on this row as before.

ARMBANDS (make 2 alike)

Join left shoulder seam. With No. 10 needles and right side of work facing, pick up and k. 92 (98, 104, 110, 114, 118) sts. evenly around armhole edge. Work 6 rows in k.1, p.1 rib.
Cast off in rib.

TO COMPLETE

Join side seams.

Three-way cardigan

— with a high V-neck, low V-neck or button-up style
(photographed in black and white on page 208)

MATERIALS

7 (7, 8, 9, 10, 11) oz. Emu Scotch 4-ply *or* Super Crêpe *or* Bri-Nylon 4-ply for high V-neck cardigan, 6 (7, 8, 9, 10, 11) oz. for low V-neck cardigan, 7 (7, 8, 9, 10, 12) oz. for button-up cardigan (see note on wools and yarns, page 20); one pair each Nos. 10 and 12 knitting needles (see page 26); 5 medium buttons for high V-neck cardigan, 3 for low V-neck cardigan, 6 for button-up cardigan.

MEASUREMENTS

To fit chest size 22 (24, 26, 28, 30, 32) in.; length at centre back 14½ (15¼, 16, 17, 18½, 20) in.; sleeve seam 10½ (11½, 13½, 15, 16, 17) in.

TENSION

7½ sts. and 9½ rows to 1 in. over st. st. (see note on

Matching sweater and hat (page 212).
Previous page: school jersey (p. 210)

tension, page 15).

ABBREVIATIONS

See page 26.

HIGH V-NECK CARDIGAN
BACK

With No. 12 needles, cast on 90 (98, 106, 114, 120, 128) sts. and work in k.1, p.1 rib for 2 in. Change to No. 10 needles and st.st. (see page 23).
Cont. until work measures 9¼ (9½, 10, 10½, 11½, 12¼) in. from beg. ending with a p. row.

Shape Raglan Armholes. Cast off 4 (4, 5, 5, 5, 5) sts. at the beg. of the next 2 rows and 3 (4, 4, 5, 4, 4) sts. at the beg. of the foll. 2 rows: 76 (82, 88, 94, 102, 110) sts.

Next row: k.3, p.2 tog., k. to last 5 sts., p.2 tog., k.3.
Next row: p. to end.
Rep. the last 2 rows until 30 (32, 34, 36, 38, 40) sts. rem. ending with a p. row. Cast off.

LEFT FRONT

With No. 12 needles, cast on 44 (48, 52, 56, 60, 64) sts. and work in k.1, p.1 rib for 2 in., inc. 1 st. at the end of the last row on the **1st, 2nd, 3rd and 4th sizes: 45 (49, 53, 57, 60, 64) sts. Change to No. 10 needles and st.st. Cont. until work measures the same as Back to armhole shaping, ending with a p. row.

Shape Raglan Armhole. Cast off 4 (4, 5, 5, 5, 5) sts., k. to end.

Next row: p. to end.

Next row: cast off 3 (4, 4, 5, 4, 4) sts., k. to end.

Next row: p. to end. **

Shape Neck. Next row: k.3, p.2 tog., k. to last 2 sts., k.2 tog.

Next row: p.

Dec. in this way at armhole edge on next and every foll. alt. row and **at the same time,** dec., at neck edge on every foll. 3rd row until 4 (4, 5, 5, 7, 8) sts. rem. Keeping neck edge straight, cont. dec. at armhole edge as before until 1 st. rem. working dec. at outer armhole edge when they can no longer be worked within a border of 3 sts. Fasten off.

RIGHT FRONT

Work to match Left Front reversing all shapings.

SLEEVES (make 2 alike)

With No. 12 needles, cast on 34 (36, 38, 40, 42, 42) sts. and work in k.1, p.1 rib for 2½ in. ending with a right-side row.

Next row: rib 3 (3, 1, 2, 3, 3), *work twice into next st., rib 3 (3, 4, 4, 4, 4); rep. from * to last 3 (5, 2, 3, 4, 4) sts., work twice into next st., rib 2 (4, 1, 2, 3, 3): 42 (44, 46, 48, 50, 50) sts.

Change to No. 10 needles and st.st., inc. 1 st. at each end of 5th and every foll. 4th (4th, 5th, 5th, 5th, 5th) row until there are 74 (78, 80, 86, 90, 94) sts. on the needle. Cont. without further shaping until work measures 10½ (11½, 13½, 15, 16, 17) in. from beg., ending with a p. row.

Shape Raglan Top. Cast off 5 (5, 4, 5, 4, 4) sts. at the beg. of the next 2 rows, and 4 (4, 4, 4, 4, 3) sts. at the beg. of the foll. 2 rows: 56 (60, 64, 68, 74, 80) sts.

Next row: k.3, p.2 tog., k. to last 5 sts., p.2 tog., k.3.

Next row: p.

Rep. the last 2 rows until 10 sts. rem. Cast off.

FRONT BAND

** With No. 12 needles, cast on 11 sts.

Next row: *k.1, p.1; rep. from * to last st., k.1.

Next row: *p.1, k.1; rep. from * to last st., p.1.

Rep. these 2 rows for ½ (½, ¾, ½, ½, ½) in.

1st buttonhole row: rib 4, cast off 3, rib to end.

Six sizes, three classic styles — and all from the same pattern

2nd buttonhole row: rib, casting on over cast off sts. in previous row.**

Work 4 more buttonholes at intervals of 2 (2, 2, 2¼, 2½, 2¾) in. measured from base of previous buttonhole. Continue in rib until band is long enough slightly stretched, to fit up right front, across sleeve tops, across back neck and down left front. Cast off in rib.

TO COMPLETE

Join side and sleeve seams. Sew on front band. Neaten buttonholes and sew on buttons opposite.

LOW V-NECK CARDIGAN

BACK

Follow instructions for High V-Neck Cardigan.

LEFT FRONT

With No. 12 needles, cast on 44 (48, 52, 56, 60, 64) sts. and work in k.1, p.1 rib for 2 in. inc. 1 st. at the end of last row on **1st, 2nd, 3rd and 4th sizes only:** 45 (49, 53, 57, 60, 64) sts.

Change to No. 10 needles and st.st. Cont. until work measures 5 (5, 5, 5, 5½, 5½) in. from beg. ending with a p. row.

Next row: k. to last 2 sts., k. 2 tog. Dec. 1 st. at this edge on every foll. 6th (6th, 6th, 6th, 6th, 7th) row, 14 (15, 16, 17, 18, 19) times in all, **at the same time** when work measures 9¼ (9½, 10, 10½, 11½, 12¼) in. from the beg., commence raglan shaping by following instructions for Left Front of High V-Neck Cardigan. When front dec. are complete, cont. to dec. at armhole edge as before until 1 st. rem., working dec. at outer armhole edge when they can no longer be worked inside a border of 3 sts. Fasten off.

RIGHT FRONT

Work to match Left Front reversing all shapings.

SLEEVES (make 2 alike)

Follow instructions for High V-Neck Cardigan.

FRONT BAND

With No. 12 needles, cast on 11 sts.

Next row: *k.1, p.1; rep. from * to last st., k.1.

Next row: *p.1, k.1; rep. from * to last st., p.1.

Rep. these 2 rows for ½ in.

1st buttonhole row: rib 4, cast off 3, rib to end.

2nd buttonhole row: rib, casting on over cast-off sts. in previous row. Work 2 more buttonholes at intervals of 1¾ (1¾, 1¾, 1¾, 2, 2) in., measured from base of previous buttonhole.

Cont. in rib until band is long enough slightly stretched to fit up right front, across sleeve tops, across back neck and down left front. Cast off in rib.

TO COMPLETE

Follow instructions for High V-Neck Cardigan.

BUTTON-UP CARDIGAN

BACK
Follow instructions for High V-Neck Cardigan, but leave sts. on a stitch holder, instead of casting off.

LEFT FRONT
Follow instructions for left front of High V-Neck Cardigan from ** to **.

Next row: k.3, p.2 tog., k. to end.

Next row: p. to end.

Rep. the last 2 rows until 22 (23, 25, 27, 29, 30) sts. rem. ending with a p. row.

Shape Neck. K.3, p.2 tog., k.7 (7, 9, 11, 13, 13), k.2 tog. and turn, leaving rem. sts. on a stitch holder, p. to end.

Dec. as before at armhole edge and *at the same time* dec. at neck edge on the next and every foll. alt. row until 2 sts. rem. working dec. at outer armhole edge when they can no longer be worked within a border of 3 sts., k.2 tog. Fasten off.

RIGHT FRONT
Work to match Left Front reversing all shapings.

SLEEVES (make 2 alike)
Follow instructions for High V-Neck Cardigan, but leave sts. on a stitch holder, instead of casting off.

NECKBAND
Join raglan seams. With No. 12 needles and right side facing, k. across 8 (9, 9, 9, 9, 10) sts. at front neck, pick up and k.14 (15, 16, 17, 18, 18) sts. evenly up right side of neck, k. across 10 sts. from top of right sleeve, 30 (32, 34, 36, 38, 40) sts. from back neck and 10 sts. from top of left sleeve, pick up and k.14 (15, 16, 17, 18, 18) sts. down left side of neck, k. across 8 (9, 9, 9, 9, 10) sts. at front neck: 94 (100, 104, 108, 112, 116) sts.

Work in k.1, p.1 rib for 1 in.

Cast off in rib.

FRONT BANDS
Buttonhole Band. Follow instructions for front band of High V-Neck Cardigan from ** to **. Work 5 more buttonholes at intervals of 2 (2, 2¼, 2¼, 2½, 3) in. measured from base of previous buttonhole. Work a further ½ in. in rib. Cast off.

Button Band. Work to match Buttonhole Band omitting buttonholes.

TO COMPLETE
Follow instructions for High V-Neck Cardigan.

School jersey

– in 4-ply or double knitting yarn, with round or V-neck

(photographed in colour on page 205)

MATERIALS
For version 1: 6 (7, 8, 10, 11, 12) oz. Sirdar Fontein Crêpe 4-ply for round-neck jersey, 6 (7, 8, 9, 10, 11) oz. for V-neck jersey (see note on wools and yarns, page 20); one pair each Nos. 10 and 12 knitting needles, and a set of four No. 12 knitting needles (see page 26).

For version 2: 8 (9, 11, 12, 13, 15) oz. Sirdar Double Crêpe for round-neck jersey, 8 (9, 10, 11, 12, 14) oz. for V-neck jersey (see note on wools and yarns, page 20); one pair each Nos. 8 and 10 knitting needles, and a set of four No. 10 knitting needles (see page 26).

MEASUREMENTS
To fit chest size 24 (26, 28, 30, 32, 34) in.; length at centre back 15 (16½, 18, 19½, 21, 22½) in.; sleeve seam 12 (13, 14, 15, 16, 17) in.

TENSION
Version 1: 7 sts. to 1 in. on No. 10 needles.

Version 2: 5½ sts. to 1 in. on No. 8 needles (see note on tension, page 15).

ABBREVIATIONS
See page 26.

Version 1: in 4-Ply Yarn
BACK (round neck or V-neck)
With No. 12 needles cast on 91 (97, 105, 111, 119, 125) sts. Work in k.1, p.1 rib for 1 (1, 1, 1½, 1½, 1½) in. Change to No. 10 needles and cont. in st.st. (see page 23) until work is 10 (11, 12, 13, 14, 15) in. from beg., ending with a p. row.

Shape Armholes. Cast off 8 sts. at beg. of next 2 rows. ***

Next row: **k.1, sl.1, p.s.s.o., k. to last 3 sts., k.2 tog., k.1.

Next row: p. **

Rep. these last 2 rows until there are 27 (29, 31, 33, 35, 37) sts. Leave these sts. on a stitch holder.

FRONT (round neck)
Work as for Back until there are 45 (47, 49, 51, 53, 59) sts., ending with a p. row.

Shape Neck. K.1, sl.1, k.1, p.s.s.o., k.14 (14, 16, 16,

18, 18); turn.
Next row: p.
Next row: k.1, sl.1, k.1, p.s.s.o., k. to last 3 sts., k.2 tog., k.1.
Rep. these last 2 rows 5 (5, 6, 6, 7, 7) times more, then dec. at armhole edge only on alt. rows until 2 sts. rem.
Fasten off.
Slip centre 11 (13, 13, 15, 15, 17) sts. on to a stitch holder, k. to last 3 sts., k.2 tog., k.1.
Next row: p. to end.
Next row: k.1, sl.1, k.1, p.s.s.o., k. to last 3 sts., k.2 tog., k.1.
Complete to match first side.

FRONT (V-neck)
Work as for Back to ***.
Shape Neck. Next row: k.1, sl.1, k.1, p.s.s.o., k.34 (37, 41, 44, 48, 51); turn.
Next row: p.
Next row: k.1, sl.1, k.1, p.s.s.o., k. to last 3 sts., k.2 tog., k.1.
Cont. to dec. at neck edge on every 4th row 10 (11, 12, 13, 14, 15) times more, at the same time dec. at armhole edge on every alt. row until 2 sts. rem.
Fasten off.
Rejoin yarn to sts. on needle, leave first st. on a safety pin, k. to last 3 sts., k.2 tog., k.1.
Next row: p.
Next row: k.1, sl.1, k.1, p.s.s.o., k. to last 3 sts., k.2 tog., k.1.
Complete to match first side.

SLEEVES (make 2 alike)
With No. 12 needles cast on 43 (45, 47, 49, 51, 53) sts.
Work in k.1, p.1 rib for 2 (2, 2, 3, 3, 3) in. Change to No. 10 needles and work in st.st., inc. at each end of 5th and every foll. 6th row until there are 67 (71, 77, 81, 87, 91) sts. then work until sleeve is 13 (14, 15, 16½, 17½, 18½) in. (this length allows for 1 (1, 1, 1½, 1½, 1½) in. turn-up), ending with a p. row.
Work 10 rows.
Shape Top. Work as for Back from ** to ** until 41 sts. rem., ending with a p. row.
Next row: k. 1, sl.1, k.1, p.s.s.o., k.15, sl.1, k.1, p.s.s.o., k.1, k.2 tog., k.15, k.2 tog., k.1.
Cont. to dec. in centre of every 6th row 3 times more, at the same time dec. at each end of every alt. row as before until 11 sts. rem., ending with a p. row. Leave sts. on a stitch holder.

NECKBAND (round neck)
Join raglan seams, sewing the last 10 rows of sleeve seams to the cast-off sts. at armholes. With set of No. 12 needles and right side facing, k. sts. from stitch holder of back neck and left sleeve, knitting 2 tog. at seam,* pick up and k. 16 (16, 18, 18, 20, 20) sts.

down side of front neck, k.11 (13, 13, 15, 15, 17) sts. at centre front neck, pick up and k. 16 (16, 18, 18, 20, 20) sts. up other side of front neck, then the sts. on stitch holder of second sleeve, knitting last st. of sleeve tog. with first st. of back neck: 90 (94, 100, 104, 110, 114) sts.
Work in rounds of k.1, p.1 rib for 1½ (1½, 1½, 2, 2, 2) in. Cast off loosely in rib.

NECKBAND (V-neck)
Work as for round neck Neckband to *, pick up and k. 36 (40, 44, 48, 52, 56) sts. down side of front neck, k. centre front st., pick up and k. 36 (40, 44, 48, 52, 56) sts. up other side of front neck, then k. sts. of second sleeve, knitting last st. of sleeve tog. with first st. of back neck: 120 (130, 140, 150, 160, 170) sts.
Work in rounds of rib as follows:
Next round: rib to 2 sts. before centre st., p.2 tog., k.1, p.2 tog., rib to end.
Rep. this round for ¾ (¾, ¾, 1, 1, 1) in.
Cast off in rib with dec. at centre front.

TO COMPLETE
Join side and sleeve seams.
Round neck version. Fold neckband in half to inside and slipstitch in place.

Version 2: in Double Knitting Yarn
BACK (round neck or V-neck)
With No. 10 needles cast on 71 (77, 83, 89, 95, 101) sts. Work in k.1, p.1 rib for 1 (1, 1, 1½, 1½, 1½) in. Change to No. 8 needles and work in st.st. until work is 10 (11, 12, 13, 14, 15) in., ending with a p. row.
Shape Armholes. Cast off 6 sts. at beg. of next 2 rows. ***
Next row: **k.1, sl.1, k.1, p.s.s.o., k. to last 3 sts., k.2 tog., k.1.
Next row: p.**
Rep. the last 2 rows until there are 21 (23, 25, 27, 29, 31) sts., ending with a p. row. Leave these sts. on a stitch holder.

FRONT (round neck)
Work as for Back until there are 35 (37, 39, 43, 45, 47) sts. ending with a p. row.
Shape Neck. K.1, sl.1, k.1, p.s.s.o., k.11 (11, 11, 13, 13, 13); turn and p. to end.
Next row: k.1, sl.1, k.1, p.s.s.o., k. to last 3 sts., k.2 tog., k.1.
Rep the last 2 rows 3 (3, 3, 4, 4, 4) times more, then the first one again.
Next row: k.1, sl.1, k.2 tog., p.s.s.o., k.1.
Next row: p.
Next row: p.3 tog.
Fasten off.
Leave centre 7 (9, 11, 11, 13, 15) sts. on a stitch holder and work other side thus:

1st row: k. to last 3 sts., k.2 tog., k.1. Complete to match first side.

FRONT (V-neck)
Work as for Back to ***.

Shape Neck. K.1, sl.1, k.1, p.s.s.o., k.26 (29, 32, 35, 38, 41); turn.

Next row: p.

Next row: k.1, sl.1, k.1, p.s.s.o., k. to last 3 sts., k.2 tog., k.1.

Cont. to dec. at armhole edge as before on every alt. row at the same time dec. at neck edge on every 4th row 7 (8, 9, 10, 11, 12) times more until there are 2 sts. Work these 2 tog. and fasten off.

Rejoin yarn to sts. on needle, leave first st. on a safety pin, k. to last 3 sts., k.2 tog., k.1.

Complete to match first side.

SLEEVES (make 2 alike)
With No. 10 needles cast on 33 (35, 37, 39, 41, 43) sts.

Work in k.1, p.1 rib for 2 (2, 2, 3, 3, 3) in. Change to No. 8 needles and work in st.st., inc. at each end of 5th and every foll. 6th row until there are 53 (57, 61, 65, 69, 73) sts. then work until sleeve is 13 (14, 15, 16½, 17½, 18½) in. (this allows for 1 (1, 1, 1½, 1½, 1½) in. turn up), ending with a p. row. Work 8 rows.

Shape Top. Work as for Back from ** to ** until 31 sts. rem., ending with a p. row.

Next row: k.1, sl.1, k.1, p.s.s.o., k.10, sl.1, k.1, p.s.s.o., k.1, k.2 tog., k.10, k.2 tog., k.1.

Cont. to dec. in centre of every 4th row 3 times more, at the same time dec. at each end of every alt. row until 7 sts. rem., ending with a p. row. Leave sts. on a stitch holder.

NECKBAND (round neck)
Join raglan seams, sewing the last 8 rows of sleeve seams to the cast-off sts. at armholes. With set of No.10 needles and right side facing, k. sts. from stitch holder of back neck and left sleeve, knitting 2 tog. at seam,* pick up and k. 13 (13, 13, 15, 15, 15) sts. down side of front neck, k. 7 (9, 11, 11, 13, 15) sts. at centre front, pick up and k. 13 (13, 13, 15, 15, 15) sts. up other side of front neck, then the sts. on stitch holder of second sleeve, knitting last st. of sleeve tog. with first st. of back neck: 66 (70, 74, 80, 84, 88) sts. Work in rounds of k.1, p.1 rib for 1½ (1½, 1½, 2, 2, 2) in.

Cast off loosely in rib.

NECKBAND (V-neck)
Work as for round neck Neckband to *, pick up and k.29 (32, 35, 38, 41, 44) sts. down side of front neck, k. centre front st., pick up and k. 29 (32, 35, 38, 41, 44) sts. up other side of front neck, then k. sts. of second sleeve, knitting last st. of sleeve tog. with first st. of back neck: 92 (100, 108, 116, 124, 132) sts.

Work in rounds of rib as follows:

Next round: rib to 2 sts. before centre st., p.2 tog., k.1, p.2 tog., rib to end.

Rep. this round for ¾ (¾, ¾, 1, 1, 1) in.

Cast off in rib, still dec. at centre front.

TO COMPLETE
Join side and sleeve seams.

Round neck version. Fold neckband in half to inside and slipstitch in place.

Matching sweater and hat
(photographed in colour on page 206)

MATERIALS
12 (14, 16, 18, 20, 22) balls Emu Scotch Double Knitting **or** Double Crêpe **or** Bri-Nylon Double Knitting for sweater, 2 balls for hat (see note on wools and yarns, page 20); one pair each Nos. 8, 10 and 12 knitting needles (see page 26).

MEASUREMENTS
To fit chest size 24 (26, 28, 30, 32, 34) in.; length of sweater at centre back 17¼ (18¼, 19¼, 20¼, 21¾, 23¼) in.; sleeve seam 10½ (12, 13½, 15, 16, 17) in.

TENSION
5½ sts. and 10 rows to 1 in. over sweater patt. on No. 8 needles; 6½ sts. and 9 rows to 1 in. over st.st. on No. 10 needles (see note on tension, page 15).

ABBREVIATIONS
See page 26.

SWEATER
BACK
**With No. 10 needles, cast on 73 (77, 83, 89, 95, 99) sts.

1st row: *k.1, p.1; rep. from * to last st., k.1.

2nd row: *p.1, k.1; rep. from * to last st., p.1. Rep. these 2 rows for 2 in., ending with the 2nd row. Change to No. 8 needles and work in patt. thus:

1st row (right side): k.

2nd row: k.1, *k. into the st. below the next st. on left-hand needle, p.1; rep. from * to last 2 sts., k. into the st. below the next st. on left-hand needle, k.1.

These two rows form the patt. Cont. in patt. until work measures 9½ (10, 10½, 11, 12, 13) in. from the beg., ending with a wrong-side row. Mark each end of last row with a coloured thread.

Shape Raglan Armholes. Dec. 1 st. at each end of the next and every foll. 4th row until 49 (53, 57, 65, 69, 73) sts. remain, then 1 st. at each end of every alt. row ** until 25 (25, 27, 27, 29, 29) sts. remain, ending with a wrong-side row. Leave these sts. on a stitch holder.

FRONT

Follow instructions for Back from ** to ** until 47 (49, 53, 53, 57, 57) sts. remain, ending with a wrong-side row.

Shape Neck. Next row: k.2 tog., patt. 15 (16, 18, 17, 19, 19) sts. and turn, leaving remaining sts. on a stitch holder.

Still dec. at armhole edge as before, dec. 1 st. at neck edge on every foll. 4th row until 4 (5, 4, 6, 5, 5) sts. remain. Keeping neck edge straight, cont. to dec. at armhole edge until 2 sts. remain. Work 1 row. K.2 tog. and fasten off. Slip the centre 13 (13, 13, 15, 15, 15) sts. on to a stitch holder. Join in yarn at neck edge to remaining sts., patt. to last 2 sts., k.2 tog. Complete to match first side of neck.

SLEEVES (make 2 alike)

With No. 10 needles, cast on 45 (47, 49, 51, 53, 55) sts.

1st row: *k.1, p.1; rep. from * to last st., k.1.

2nd row: *p.1, k.1; rep. from * to last st., p.1.
Rep. these 2 rows for 2½ in., ending with the 2nd row. Change to No. 8 needles and patt. as given for Back. Inc. and work into patt. 1 st. at each end of the 13th and every foll. 12th (12th, 15th, 17th, 16th, 15th) row until there are 55 (59, 61, 63, 67, 71) sts. on the needle. Cont. without further shaping until work measures 10½ (12, 13½, 15, 16, 17) in. from the beg., ending with a wrong-side row. Mark each end of last row with a coloured thread.

Shape Raglan Top. Dec. 1 st. at each end of the next and every foll. 4th row until 27 (31, 29, 29, 31, 35) sts. remain, then 1 st. at each end of every alt. row until 11 sts. remain, ending with a wrong-side row. Leave these sts. on a safety pin or stitch holder.

NECKBAND

Join raglan seams, leaving left back raglan seam open. With No. 8 needles and right side of work facing, k. across the 11 sts. on top of left sleeve, pick up and k.17 (18, 19, 19, 20, 20) sts. down left side of neck, k. across the 13 (13, 13, 15, 15, 15) sts. at centre, pick up and k. 17 (18, 19, 19, 20, 20) sts. up right side of neck, k. across the 11 sts. on top of right sleeve and the 25 (25, 27, 27, 29, 29) sts. on back neck: 94 (96, 100, 102, 106, 106) sts.

Work in k.1, p.1 rib for 1 in. Change to No. 10 needles and work ½ in. in rib. Change to No. 8 needles and work a further 1 in. in rib. Cast off loosely in rib.

HAT
TO MAKE

With No. 12 needles, cast on 120 (128, 136) sts. and work in k.2, p.2 rib for 5 (5½, 6) in. Change to No. 10 needles.

1st row: k.

2nd and every alt. row: p.

3rd row: *k.13 (14, 15), k.2 tog.; rep. from * to end.

5th row: *k.12 (13, 14), k.2 tog.; rep. from * to end.
Cont. in this manner, making 8 decs. on every k. row until 8 sts. remain. Work 1 row. Break off yarn, thread through remaining sts., draw up and fasten off securely.

TO COMPLETE
SWEATER

Join left back raglan seam and neckband. Join side and sleeve seams. Fold neckband in half on to wrong side and slipstitch down.

HAT

Join back seam with a flat stitch. Make a pompon following instructions on page 82, but with card circles each 3 in., and centre hole ¾ in. Sew pompon to top of hat.

Chapter 8
Accessories and Toys

Baby's lacy shawl

MATERIALS
13 oz. Hayfield Crêpe or Gold Medal 4-ply (see note on wools and yarns, page 20); one pair No. 9 knitting needles (see page 26).

MEASUREMENTS
39 in. square, approx.

TENSION
11 sts. and 17 rows to 2 in. (see note on tension, page 15).

ABBREVIATIONS
See page 26.

CENTRE
Cast on 157 sts.
1st row: *k.1, y.fwd., sl.1, k.1, p.s.s.o., k.1, k.2 tog., y.fwd.; rep. from * to last st., k.1.
2nd and alt. rows: p.
3rd row: *k.2, y.fwd., k.3, y.fwd., k.1; rep. from * to last st., k.1.
5th row: k.2 tog., *y.fwd., sl.1, k.1, p.s.s.o., k.1, k.2 tog., y.fwd., sl.1, k.2 tog., p.s.s.o.; rep. from * ending last rep. sl.1, k.1, p.s.s.o.
7th row: *k.1, k.2 tog., y.fwd., k.1, y.fwd., sl.1, k.1, p.s.s.o.; rep. from * to last st., k.1.
9th row: as 3rd row.
11th row: *k.1, k.2 tog., y.fwd., sl.1, k.2 tog., p.s.s.o., y.fwd., sl.1, k.1, p.s.s.o.; rep. from * to last st., k.1.
12th row: p.
These 12 rows form centre patt. Rep. patt. until work measures 30 in. (approx. 21 patts.). Cast off.

Centre of shawl is worked first, then the stitches picked up along each side and the patterned border added

BORDERS (make 4 alike)

With right side of work facing pick up and k. 155 sts. along one side of centre. K.1 row.

1st row: k.1, y.fwd., k.2, *y.fwd., sl.1, k.1, p.s.s.o., k.5, k.2 tog., y.fwd., k.1; rep. from * to last 2 sts., k.1, y.fwd., k.1.

2nd and alt. rows: p.

3rd row: k.1, y.fwd., k.4, *y.fwd., sl.1, k.1, p.s.s.o., k.3, k.2 tog., y.fwd., k.3; rep. from * to last 2 sts., k.1, y.fwd., k.1.

5th row: k.1, y.fwd., k.6, *y.fwd., sl.1, k.1, p.s.s.o., k.1, k.2 tog., y.fwd., k.5; rep. from * to last 2 sts., k.1, y.fwd., k.1.

7th row: k.1, y.fwd., k.8, *y.fwd., sl.1, k.2 tog., p.s.s.o., y.fwd., k.7; rep. from * to last 2 sts., k.1, y.fwd., k.1.

9th row: k.1, y.fwd., *k.1, y.fwd., sl.1, k.1, p.s.s.o., k.2 tog., y.fwd.; rep. from * to the last 2 sts., k.1, y.fwd., k.1.

11th row: k.1, y.fwd., k.1, *k.1, y.fwd., sl.1, k.1, p.s.s.o., k.2 tog., y.fwd.; rep. from * to last 3 sts., k.2, y.fwd., k.1.

13th row: k.1, y.fwd., k.2 tog., y.fwd., *k.1, y.fwd., sl.1, k.1, p.s.s.o., k.2 tog., y.fwd.; rep. from * to last 4 sts., k.1, y.fwd., sl.1, k.1, p.s.s.o., y.fwd., k.1.

15th row: k.1, y.fwd., k.1, *k.2 tog., y.fwd., k.1, y.fwd., sl.1, k.1, p.s.s.o.; rep. from * to last 2 sts., k.1, y.fwd., k.1.

17th row: k.1, y.fwd., k.2, *k.2 tog., y.fwd., k.1, y.fwd., sl. 1, k.1, p.s.s.o.; rep. from * to last 3 sts., k.2, y.fwd., k.1.

19th row: k.1, y.fwd., k.2, *y.fwd., sl.1, k.1, p.s.s.o., k.3, k.2 tog., y.fwd., k.3; rep. from * ending last rep. k.2, y.fwd., k.1.

21st row: k.1, y.fwd., k.4, y.fwd., sl.1, k.1, p.s.s.o., k.1, *k.2 tog., y.fwd., k.5, y.fwd., sl.1, k.1, p.s.s.o., k.1; rep. from * to last 7 sts., k.2 tog., y.fwd., k.4, y.fwd., k.1.

23rd row: k.1, y.fwd., k.6, *y.fwd., sl.1, k.2 tog., p.s.s.o., y.fwd., k.7; rep. from * ending last rep. k.6, y.fwd., k.1.

25th row: as 15th row.

27th row: as 17th row.

29th row: as 9th row.

31st row: as 11th row.

33rd row: as 13th row.

35th row: k.1, y.fwd., k.5, *k.2 tog., y.fwd., k.3, y.fwd., sl.1, k.1, p.s.s.o., k.3; rep. from * to last 3 sts., k.2, y.fwd., k.1.

37th row: k.1, y.fwd., k.2, y.fwd., sl.1, k.1, p.s.s.o., *k.1, k.2 tog., y.fwd., k.5, y.fwd., sl.1, k.1, p.s.s.o.; rep. from * to last 6 sts., k.1, k.2 tog., y.fwd., k.2, y.fwd., k.1.

39th row: k.1, y.fwd., k.4, *y.fwd., sl.1, k.2 tog., p.s.s.o., y.fwd., k.7; rep. from * ending last rep. k.4, y.fwd., k.1.

40th row: k.

K. 2 rows.

Cast off.

TO COMPLETE

Join mitred edges at four corners of shawl.

Plain-edged bonnet, bootees and mitts

(photographed in black and white on page 216, left)

MATERIALS

3 oz. Emu Bri-Nylon Double Knitting **or** Scotch Double Knitting **or** Double Crêpe (see note on wools and yarns, page 20); one pair each Nos. 8 and 10 knitting needles (see page 26); one crochet hook approx. International Standard Size 4·00; 1 yard ribbon 1 in. wide; 1½ yards of baby ribbon.

MEASUREMENTS

To fit baby 1 to 3 months.

TENSION

6½ sts. and 9 rows to 1 in. with No. 8 needles (see note on tension, page 15).

ABBREVIATIONS

See page 26.

BONNET

TO MAKE

With No. 10 needles, cast on 68 sts. K.5 rows. Change to No. 8 needles.

1st row (right side): k.

2nd row: k.3, *p.2, k.3; rep. from * to end.

3rd row: p.3, *k.2 tog., but leave sts. on left-hand needle, k. into first st. again, then slip sts. off needle, p.3; rep. from * to end.

4th row: p.

These 4 rows form patt. Cont. in patt. until work measures 4½ in. from beg., ending with a wrong-side row.

Shape Back. 1st row: k.2, *sl.1, k.1, p.s.s.o., k.12, k.2 tog.; rep. from * 3 times, k.2: 60 sts.

2nd and alt. rows: p.

3rd row: k.2, *sl.1, k.1, p.s.s.o., k.10, k.2 tog.; rep.

Plain-edged bonnet, bootees and mitts | *Scalloped-edged bonnet, bootees, mitts*

from * 3 times, k.2: 52 sts.

5th row: k.2, *sl.1, k.1, p.s.s.o., k.8, k.2 tog.; rep. from * 3 times, k.2: 44 sts.

7th row: k.2, *sl.1, k.1, p.s.s.o., k.6, k.2 tog.; rep. from * 3 times, k.2: 36 sts.

9th row: k.2, *sl.1, k.1, p.s.s.o., k.4, k.2 tog.; rep. from * 3 times, k.2: 28 sts.

11th row: k.2, *sl.1, k.1, p.s.s.o., k.2, k.2 tog.; rep. from * 3 times, k.2: 20 sts.

13th row: *k.2 tog.; rep. from * to end: 10 sts. Break off yarn, thread through remaining sts., draw up and fasten off.

TO COMPLETE

Join back seam, starting at crown and working down side edges for 2½ in. Work a row of d.c. (see page 26) round neck edge (remaining side edges). Cut 1-in. ribbon in two and sew one piece to each side.

BOOTEES

TO MAKE (2 alike)

With No. 8 needles, cast on 33 sts.

Now work patt. as given for Bonnet and then rep. 4 patt. rows twice.

Make Eyelet Holes. Next row: k.1, *y.fwd., k.2 tog., k.2; rep. from * to end.**

Next row: *p.4, p.2 tog.; rep. from * to last 3 sts., p.3: 28 sts. **Next row:** k.18 sts., turn; p. 8 sts., turn. Work 14 rows in st.st. (see page 23) on these centre 8 sts. Break off yarn.

Join in yarn after the first 10 sts., pick up and k. 8 sts. along first side of instep, k.8 instep sts., pick up and k. 8 sts. along second side of instep, k. to end: 44 sts.

Next row: p.

Work 6 rows in st.st.

Next row: k.2 tog., k.16, sl.1, k.1, p.s.s.o., k.4, k.2 tog., k.16, k.2 tog.: 40 sts.

Next row: p.2 tog., p.14, p.2 tog., p.4, p.2 tog. t.b.l., p.14, p.2 tog.: 36 sts.

Next row: k.2 tog., k.12, sl.1, k.1, p.s.s.o., k.4, k.2 tog., k.12, k.2 tog.: 32 sts.

Next row: p.2 tog., p.10, p.2 tog., p.4, p.2 tog. t.b.l., p.10, p.2 tog.: 28 sts. Cast off.

TO COMPLETE

Join foot and leg seams. Cut baby ribbon into 4. Thread one length through eyelet holes on each bootee and tie in bow. (Keep rem. 2 lengths for Mitts.)

MITTS

TO MAKE (2 alike)

Work as Bootees to **.

Next row: p.2, *p.2, p.2 tog.; rep. from * to last 3 sts., p.3: 26 sts.

Work 2 in. in st.st. ending with a p. row.

Shape Top. 1st row: k.2, *k.2 tog., k.2; rep from * to end: 20 sts.

2nd row: p.

3rd row: k.2, *k.2 tog., k.1; rep. from * to end: 14 sts.

4th row: *p.2 tog.; rep. from * to end: 7 sts. Break off yarn, thread through remaining sts., draw up and fasten off.

TO COMPLETE

Join side seam. Thread rem. baby ribbon through eyelet holes, one piece to each mitt, and tie in bow.

Scalloped-edged bonnet, bootees and mitts

(photographed in black and white opposite, right,

MATERIALS

3 oz. Emu Bri-Nylon Double Knitting **or** Scotch Double Knitting **or** Double Crêpe (see note on wools and yarns, page 20); one pair each Nos. 8 and 10 knitting needles (see page 26); one crochet hook approx. International Standard Size 4·00; 1 yard ribbon 1 in. wide; 1½ yards baby ribbon.

MEASUREMENTS

To fit baby aged 1 to 3 months.

TENSION

7 sts. and 8 rows to 1 in. with No. 8 needles (see note on tension, page 15).

ABBREVIATIONS

See page 26.

BONNET
TO MAKE

With No. 10 needles, cast on 74 sts. K.1 row.
1st row: k.2, *y.fwd., k.2, sl.1, k.2 tog., p.s.s.o., k.2, y.fwd., k.1; rep. from * to end.
2nd row: p.
3rd row: k.1, *y.fwd., k.2, sl.1, k.2 tog., p.s.s.o., k.2, y.fwd., k.1; rep. from * to last st. k.1.
4th row: p.
These 4 rows form patt.
Change to No. 8 needles. Cont. in patt. until work measures 4½ in. from beg., ending with a p. row.
Shape Back. 1st row: k.1, *sl.1, k.1, p.s.s.o., k.14, k.2 tog.; rep. from * 3 times, k.1: 66 sts.
2nd and alt. rows: p.
3rd row: k.1, *sl.1, k.1, p.s.s.o., k.12, k.2 tog.: rep. from * 3 times, k.1: 58 sts.
5th row: k.1, *sl.1, k.1, p.s.s.o., k.10, k.2 tog.; rep. from * 3 times, k.1: 50 sts.
7th row: k.1, *sl.1, k.1, p.s.s.o., k.8, k.2 tog., rep. from * 3 times, k.1: 42 sts.
9th row: k.1, *sl.1, k.1, p.s.s.o., k.6, k.2 tog.; rep. from * 3 times, k.1: 34 sts.
11th row: k.1, *sl.1, k.1, p.s.s.o., k.4, k.2 tog.; rep. from * 3 times, k.1: 26 sts.
13th row: k.1, *sl.1, k.1, p.s.s.o., k.2, k.2 tog.; rep. from * 3 times, k.1: 18 sts.
15th row: *k.2 tog.; rep. from * to end: 9 sts.
Break off yarn, thread through remaining sts., draw up and fasten off.

TO COMPLETE

Join back seam, starting at crown and working down side edges for 2½ in. Work a row of d.c. (see page 26) round neck edge (remaining side edges). Cut 1-in. ribbon in two and sew one length to each side to form ties.

BOOTEES
TO MAKE (2 alike)

With No. 8 needles, cast on 34 sts. K.1 row.
Now work patt. as given for Bonnet and then rep. 4 patt. rows twice.
Make Eyelet Holes. Next row: k.2, *y.fwd., k.2 tog., k.2; rep. from * to end.**
Next row: *p.3, p.2 tog.; rep. from * to last 4 sts., p.4: 28 sts.
Next row: k.18 sts., turn; p. 8 sts., turn.
Work 14 rows in st.st. (see page 23) on these centre 8 sts. Break off yarn.
Join yarn after the first 10 sts., pick up and k. 8 sts. along first side of instep, k.8 instep sts., pick up and k. 8 sts. along second side of instep, k. to end: 44 sts.
Next row: p.
Work 6 rows in st.st., beg. with a k. row.
Next row: k.2 tog., k.16, sl.1, k.1, p.s.s.o., k.4, k.2 tog., k.16, k.2 tog.: 40 sts.
Next row: p.2 tog., p. 14, p.2 tog., p.4, p.2 tog. t.b.l., p.14, p.2 tog.: 36 sts.
Next row: k.2 tog., k.12, sl.1, k.1, p.s.s.o., k.4, k.2 tog., k.12, k.2 tog.: 32 sts.
Next row: p.2 tog., p.10, p.2 tog., p.4, p.2 tog. t.b.l., p. 10, p.2 tog.: 28 sts. Cast off.

TO COMPLETE

Join foot and leg seams. Cut baby ribbon into 4. Thread one length through eyelet holes on each bootee and tie in bow. (Keep rem. 2 lengths for Mitts.)

MITTS
TO MAKE (2 alike)

Work as Bootees to **.
Next row: *p.2, p.2 tog.; rep. from * to last 2 sts., p.2: 26 sts.
Work 2 in. in st.st., ending with a p. row.
Shape Top. 1st row: k.2, *k.2 tog., k.2; rep. from * to end: 20 sts.
2nd row: p.
3rd row: k.2, *k.2 tog., k.1; rep. from * to end: 14 sts.
4th row: *p.2 tog.; rep. from * to end: 7 sts.
Break off yarn, thread through remaining sts., draw up and fasten off.

TO COMPLETE

Join side seam. Thread rem. baby ribbon through eyelet holes, one piece to each mitt, and tie in bow.

Boy's socks

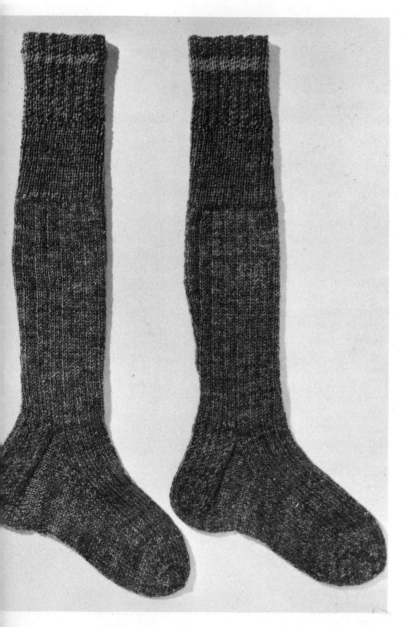

ABBREVIATIONS
See page 26; M., main shade; C., contrast.

TO MAKE (2 alike)
With M., cast on 64 sts.: 20 sts. on each of first two needles; 24 sts. on third needle.

Work 8 rounds in k.2, p.2 rib. Join C. and work 6 rounds in rib. Return to M. and work a further 18 rounds.

Note. *If 2 series of stripes or special arrangements of stripes are desired, they should be worked within this section.*

Work a further 26 rounds in rib.

Next round: *k.3, p.1; rep. from * to end of round. Cont. in this rib for 3 in., then work 2 sts. tog. at beg. and end of next round, then at beg. and end of every 7th round until 56 sts. remain. Cont. straight until work measures 13 in.

Divide for Heel.

Next row: rib 13, slip last 14 sts. of round on to beg. of same needle: 27 heel sts.

Put remaining 29 sts. for instep on stitch holder and leave. Now, beg. with a p. row, work 37 rows in st.st.

Turn Heel.

1st row: k.18, k.2 tog.; turn.

2nd row: p.10, p.2 tog.; turn.

3rd row: k.10, k.2 tog.; turn.

Rep. 2nd and 3rd rows 6 times then 2nd row once.

Next round: k.6, with another needle k. 5 remaining heel sts., pick up and k. 16 sts. along side of heel, with another needle rib. across 29 instep sts. from stitch holder, with needle with first heel sts. on it, pick up and k. 16 sts. from other side of heel then k. again across 6 heel sts.: 72 sts.

1st round. First needle: k.; **second needle:** rib; **third needle:** k.

2nd round. First needle: k. to last 2 sts., k.2 tog.; **second needle:** rib; **third needle:** k.2 tog., k. to end.

Cont. dec. on alt. rounds until 54 sts. remain then cont. straight until work measures 4½ in. from knitted-up sts. at heel.

Shape Toe. Next round. First needle: k. to last 2 sts., k.2 tog.; **second needle:** k.2 tog., k. to last 2 sts., k.2 tog.; **third needle:** k.2 tog., k. to end.

Next round: k.

Rep. last 2 rounds until 24 sts. remain. K. sts. from first needle on to third needle, place second and third needles next to each other and cast off both sets of sts. tog.

MATERIALS
3 oz. Paton's School Knitting 4-ply (see note on wools and yarns, page 20) in main shade, plus 1 oz. in contrast if desired; one set of four No. 12 knitting needles with points at both ends (see page 26).

MEASUREMENTS
To fit foot size 7½ in. approx.; length of leg 13 in.

TENSION
8 sts. to 1 in. over st.st. (see note on tension, page 15).

Striped beret

(photographed in black and white on right)

MATERIALS

2 balls Emu Scotch Double Knitting **or** Double Crêpe **or** Bri-Nylon Double Knitting (see note on wools and yarns, page 20) in main shade, 1 ball in 1st contrast shade and 1 ball in 2nd contrast shade; one pair each Nos. 8 and 11 knitting needles (see page 26).

MEASUREMENTS

To fit child aged 3 to 6 years.

TENSION

$5\frac{1}{2}$ sts. and 8 rows to 1 in. with No. 8 needles (see note on tension, page 15).

ABBREVIATIONS

See page 26; M., main shade; A., 1st contrast shade; B., 2nd contrast shade.

TO MAKE

With No. 11 needles and M., cast on 120 sts. and work 9 rows in k.1, p.1 rib.

Next row: rib 13, *work twice into next st., rib 2; rep. from * to last 14 sts., work twice into next st., rib 13: 152 sts.

Change to No. 8 needles and st.st. (see page 23). Work 10 rows. Join A and k. 2 rows. Join B. and, beg. with a k. row, work 6 rows in st.st. Change to A. and k. 2 rows.

Shape Crown. Change to M. and work in st.st. Work 2 rows straight.

Next row: *k.12, k.3 tog.; rep. from * to last 2 sts., k.2: 132 sts. Beg. with a p. row, work 5 rows straight.

Next row: *k.10, k.3 tog.; rep. from * to last 2 sts., k.2: 112 sts.

Next row: p. Change to A and k. 2 rows.

Change to B. and, beg. with a k. row, work 2 rows in st.st.

Next row: *k.8, k.3 tog.; rep. from * to last 2 sts., k.2: 92 sts.

Next row: p.

Change to A. and k. 2 rows.

Change to M. and, beg. with a k. row, work 2 rows in st.st.

Next row: *k.6, k.3 tog.; rep. from * to last 2 sts., k.2: 72 sts. Beg. with a p. row, work 3 rows straight in st.st.

Next row: *k.4, k.3 tog.; rep. from * to last 2 sts., k.2: 52 sts.

Top to bottom: striped beret, loopy hat (page 219), ridged beret (page 219)

Next row: p.
Next row: *k.2, k.3 tog.; rep. from * to last 2 sts.,
k.2: 32 sts.
Next row: *p.2 tog.; rep. from * to end: 16 sts.
Next row: *k.2 tog.; rep. from * to end: 8 sts.

Break off yarn, thread through remaining sts., draw
up and fasten off.

TO COMPLETE
Join seam.

Ridged beret

(photographed in black and white on page 219)

MATERIALS
3 balls Emu Scotch Double Knitting **or** Double
Crêpe **or** Bri-Nylon Double Knitting (see note on
wools and yarns, page 20); one pair each Nos. 8 and
11 knitting needles (see page 26).

MEASUREMENTS
To fit child aged 3 to 6 years.

TENSION
5½ sts. and 8 rows to 1 in. with No. 8 needles (see
note on tension, page 15).

ABBREVIATIONS
See page 26.

TO MAKE
With No. 11 needles, cast on 120 sts. and work 9
rows in k.1, p.1 rib.
Next row: rib 13, *work twice into next st., rib. 2;
rep. from * to last 14 sts., work twice into next st.,
rib 13: 152 sts.
Change to No. 8 needles.
1st row (right side): k.
2nd row: p.

3rd row: k.
4th row: k.
These 4 rows form patt. Rep. patt. 5 times.
Shape Crown. 1st row: *k.1, sl.1, k.1, p.s.s.o.,
k.19, k.2 tog., k.14; rep. from * to end: 144 sts.
2nd row: p.
3rd row: *k.1, sl.1, k.1, p.s.s.o., k.17, k.2 tog., k.14;
rep. from * to end: 136 sts.
4th row: k.
5th row: *k.1, sl.1, k.1, p.s.s.o., k.15, k.2 tog., k.14;
rep. from * to end: 128 sts.
Keeping continuity of patt., cont. to dec. in this way
on every alt. row until 72 sts. remain, ending with
a wrong-side row.
Next row: *k.1, sl.1, k.2 tog., p.s.s.o., k.14; rep.
from * to end: 64 sts.
Next row: work to end.
Next row: *k.3 tog., k.13; rep. from * to end: 56 sts.
Next row: *p.2 tog.; rep. from * to end: 28 sts.
Next row: *k.2 tog.; rep from * to end: 14 sts.
Break off yarn, thread through remaining sts., draw
up and fasten off securely.

TO COMPLETE
Join seam.

Loopy hat

(photographed in black and white on page 219)

MATERIALS
3 balls Emu Scotch Double Knitting **or** Double
Crêpe **or** Bri-Nylon Double Knitting (see note on
wools and yarns, page 20); one pair each Nos. 8 and
9 knitting needles (see page 26).

MEASUREMENTS
To fit child aged 3 to 6 years.

TENSION
5½ sts. and 8 rows to 1 in. with No. 8 needles (see
note on tension, page 15).

ABBREVIATIONS
See page 26.

TO MAKE
With No. 8 needles, cast on 6 sts.
1st row: *k. twice into next st.; rep. from * to last st.,
k.1: 11 sts.
2nd row: k.
3rd row: *k.1, k. twice into next st.; rep from * to
last st., k.1: 16 sts.
4th, 5th and 6th rows: k.
7th row: *k.1, k. twice into next st.; rep. from * to

end: 24 sts.

8th, 9th and 10th rows: k.

11th row: *k.1, k. twice into next st., rep. from * to end: 36 sts.

12th, 13th and 14th rows: k.

15th row: *k.3, k. twice into next st.; rep. from * to end: 45 sts.

16th, 17th and 18th rows: k.

19th row: *k.4, k. twice into next st.; rep. from * to end: 54 sts.

20th, 21st and 22nd rows: k.

23rd row: *k.5, k. twice into next st.; rep. from * to end: 63 sts.

24th, 25th and 26th rows: k.

27th row: *k.6, k. twice into next st.; rep. from * to end: 72 sts.

28th, 29th and 30th rows: k.

31st row: *k.7, k. twice into next st.; rep. from * to end: 81 sts.

32nd row: k.1, *insert right-hand needle knitwise into next st. on left-hand needle and wind yarn loosely twice, clockwise, round first and 2nd fingers of left hand, k. the st. into which right-hand needle is inserted, then k. loops round fingers, slip 2nd st. on right-hand needle over first st., k. next st. on left-hand needle; rep. from * to end.

33rd row: *k.8, k. twice into next st.; rep. from * to end: 90 sts.

34th row: k.

35th row: *k.9, k. twice into next st.; rep. from * to end: 99 sts.

36th row: as 32nd row.

37th row: *k.10, k. twice into next st.; rep. from * to end: 108 sts.

38th row: k.

39th row: k. to last st., inc. 1 st. in last st.: 109 sts.

40th row: as 32nd row.

41st, 42nd and 43rd rows: k.

44th row: as 32nd row.

Rep. last 4 rows twice.

53rd row: k.6, *k.2 tog., k.4; rep. from * to last 7 sts., k.2 tog., k.5: 92 sts.

Change to No. 9 needles.

K. 9 rows.

Cast off fairly loosely.

TO COMPLETE

Join seam.

Scarf hat

(photographed in colour on page 223)

MATERIALS

3 (4) oz. Twilley's Cortina Super Crochet Wool (see note on wools and yarns, page 20) in white and 1 (2) oz. in green or pink; one pair No. 12 knitting needles (see page 26).

MEASUREMENTS

To fit average sized head for small child (older child).

TENSION

8 sts. and 12 rows to 1 in. over slightly stretched rib (see note on tension, page 15).

ABBREVIATIONS

See page 26; W., white; C., contrast (green or pink).

TO MAKE

With W., cast on 132 (148) sts.

With W., k. 1 row. Work 31 (35) rows in k.1, p.1 rib.

Join C., and k. 1 row. Work 9 (11) rows in k.1, p.1 rib.

These 42 (48) rows form striped rib patt. Rep. patt. once.

Next row: join W., *k.2 tog.; rep. from * to end: 66 (74) sts.

Cont. in striped patt., beg. with 31 (35) rows in W. rib, until 7th contrast stripe from beg. has been worked.

Next row: with C., *k.2 tog.; rep. from * to end: 33 (37) sts.

Next row: with C., p.1, *p.2 tog.; rep. from * to end. Break off yarn, thread through remaining 17 (19) sts., draw up and secure firmly.

TO COMPLETE

Join seam, matching stripes. Make a tassel (see page 141) in C., using card 3 (4) in. long.

Panda

(photographed in black and white on page 222)

MATERIALS

4 oz. of Twilley's Bubbly (see note on wools and yarns, page 20) in white and 4 oz. in black; one pair No. 9 knitting needles (see page 26); foam filling (washable) or kapok for stuffing; ribbon 1½ in. wide for neck.

MEASUREMENTS
18 in. long and 7 in. wide approx.

TENSION
5 sts. and 8 rows to 1 in. (see note on tension, page 15).

ABBREVIATIONS
See page 26; W., white; B., black.

Note. *Yarn should be used double throughout.*

LEGS AND BACK BODY
First Leg. With 2 strands B., cast on 40 sts. Work 4 in. in st.st., ending with a p. row. Leave sts. on stitch holder.
Work another leg in the same way.
Back Body. Next row: cast off 20 sts., k.20, cast on 14 sts., k. 20 sts. from stitch holder, cast off remaining 20 sts.
Rejoin yarn to 54 sts. and p. 1 row.
Next row: k.18, k.2 tog., k.14, k.2 tog., k.18.
Next row: p.
Next row: k.18, k.2 tog., k.12. k.2 tog., k.18.
Next row: p.

Next row: k.18, k.2 tog., k.10, k.2 tog., k.18. Dec. in this way on every k. row until 38 sts. remain. P.1 row.
Next row: k.18, k.2 tog., k.18: 37 sts.
Cont. straight in st.st. until work measures 6 in. from leg joining row **.
Cast off 2 sts. at beg. of next 2 rows then dec. 1 st. at each end of every 4th row until 19 sts. remain. Cast off.

FRONT BODY
With 2 strands of W., cast on 13 sts. Work in st.st., inc. 1 st. at each end of 2nd and every foll. 3rd row until there are 37 sts. Cont. straight until work measures 6 in. from beg. Complete as back from **.

RIGHT ARM
With 2 strands of B., cast on 8 sts. Work in st.st., inc. 1 st. at each end of 2nd and foll. 3 rows: 16 sts. Cont. straight until work measures 2 in. ending with a p. row ***.
Next row: cast on 16 sts., k. to end: 32 sts.
Cont. straight until work measures 4½ in. from beg. Now dec. 1 st. at each end of next and every alt. row until 4 sts. remain. Cast off.

LEFT ARM
Work as Right Arm to *** but end with a k. row.
Next row: cast on 16 sts., p. to end.
Complete as Right Arm.

HEAD
Right Side. With 2 strands of W., cast on 26 sts. Work in st.st., beg. with a k. row, inc. 1 st. at end of 2nd row and every p. row until there are 36 sts. Work 4 rows straight. Now dec. 1 st. at shaped edge on next 4 rows, then dec. 1 st. at shaped edge every p. row until 22 sts. remain. Dec. 1 st. at shaped edge on next 4 rows. Cast off remaining 18 sts.
Left Side. Work as right side, but work p. for k. and k. for p., thus reversing shaped edge.
Gusset. With 2 strands of W., cast on 2 sts. Work in st.st., inc. 1 st. at each end of 2nd and every foll. 4th row until there are 20 sts. Work 4 in. straight. Now dec. 1 st. at each end of next and every foll. 4th row until 2 sts. remain. Cast off.

EARS (make 2 alike)
With 2 strands of B., cast on 16 sts. Work 6 rows in st.st. Now dec. 1 st. at each end of next and foll. 2 alt. rows. Work 1 row. Dec. 1 st. at each end of next 2 rows: 6 sts. Work 1 row. Inc. 1 st. at each end of sts. Work 4 rows straight. Dec. 1 st. at each end of next and every alt. row until 5 sts. remain. Cast off.

Opposite: warm scarf hats with tassel trimming for big and little sisters (see page 221)

FOOT PADS (make 2 alike)

With 2 strands of W., cast on 5 sts. Work in st.st. inc. 1 st. at each end of every alt. row until there are 13 sts. Work 4 rows straight. Dec. 1 st. at each end of next and every alt. row until 5 sts. remain. Cast off.

ARM PADS (make 2 alike)

With 2 strands of W., cast on 8 sts. Work in st.st., inc. 1 st. at each end of 2nd and foll. 3 rows: 16 sts. Cont. straight until work measures 2 in. from beg. Cast off.

EYE PATCHES (make 2 alike)

With 2 strands of B. cast on 4 sts. Working in st.st., inc. 1 st at each end of next 3 alt. rows: 10 sts. Work 4 rows straight. Dec. 1 st. each end of next and foll. 2 alt. rows. Cast off.

TO COMPLETE

Fold legs in half, with right sides facing, and oversew side seams of legs. Place front to back, with right sides facing, and sew front to legs and to back as far as 2 cast-off sts. Fold arms in half, with right sides facing, and sew side seams. Sew pads to front of arms. Turn arms right side out. Then, with right sides tog., join shaped sides of arms to shaped sides of back and front. Sew foot pads to bottom of legs. Turn whole body right side out and stuff legs, arms and body firmly with foam filling or kapok.

With right sides facing, join shaped edges of right and left side head pieces from cast-on edges to last inc., then sew gusset between remainder of head side pieces, round rest of shaped edge, cast-off edge and down other side edge of each. Turn head right side out and stuff firmly. Sew head to body. Fold ears in half, right sides tog. and oversew side edges tog. Turn right side out and attach other edges to top of head. Sew eye patches to head, with W. yarn satin-stitch eye whites on patches, leaving a centre black part for pupils. With B., satin-stitch nose at point of head, then stemstitch mouth underneath (use the photograph on page 222 as a guide). Tie ribbon round neck.

Toy crocodile

(photographed in colour opposite)

MATERIALS

2 oz. Twilley's Bubbly (see note on wools and yarns, page 20) in green, 2 oz. in yellow, and 1 oz. in orange; one pair No. 10 knitting needles (see page 26); foam filling (washable) or kapok for stuffing; scraps of black and white felt.

MEASUREMENTS

13 in. long and $7\frac{1}{2}$ in. wide, including legs.

TENSION

5 sts. and 8 rows to 1 in. (see note on page 15).

ABBREVIATIONS

See page 26; G., green; Y., yellow; Or., Orange.

Note. *Yarn should be used double throughout.*

BODY

Back. With G., cast on 8 sts. Work in st.st., inc. 1 st. at each end of every alt. row until there are 26 sts. Cont. straight until work measures 9 in. Now work 2 sts. tog. at each end of next and every foll. 4th row until 2 sts. remain. Cast off.

Base. With Y., cast on 8 sts. and work in st.st., inc. 1 st. at each end of every alt. row until there are 20 sts. Cont. straight until work measures $8\frac{1}{2}$ in., then work 2 sts. tog. at each end of next and every foll. 6th row until 2 sts. remain. Cast off.

MOUTH

With Or., cast on 6 sts. and work in st.st., inc. 1 st. at each end of every alt. row until there are 22 sts. Cont. straight until work measures 4 in., ending with a p. row.

Next row: k.2, *k.2 tog., k.3; rep. from * to end: 18 sts.

Cont. straight until work measures $6\frac{1}{2}$ in., then work 2 sts. tog. at each end of next and every alt. row until 6 sts. remain. Cast off.

LEFT LEGS (make 2 in G. and 2 in Y.)

Cast on 6 sts. Work in st.st., inc. 1 st. at each end of 2nd and 3rd rows. Cont. straight until work measures 2 in., ending with a p. row.**

Next row: cast on 6 sts., k. to end.

Work 9 rows in st.st., beg. with a p. row. Now work 2 sts. tog. at end of next row and beg. of foll. row. Cast off.

RIGHT LEGS (make 2 in G. and 2 in Y.)

Work as Left Leg to **, but end with a k. row.

Next row: cast on 6 sts., p. to end.

Work 9 rows in st.st., beg. with a k. row. Now work 2 sts. tog. at end of next row and beg. of foll. row. Cast off.

Opposite, top: toy spaceman (page 230), Aladdin and Abanazar (page 226), crocodile. Bottom: a fashionable wardrobe of doll's clothes (see page 227)

TO COMPLETE

With right sides tog., backstitch one G. leg to one Y. leg, leaving short edge between cast-off sts. and 6 cast-on sts. open. Turn right side out. Rep. with other leg pieces. Place back and base tog., right sides facing. Place mouth between front (cast-on) ends, right sides facing, with wider end of mouth next to back. Backstitch tog., sewing mouth down back for 4 in. then up base for 4 in. Leaving 5 in. open on each side, sew rest of body tog. round tail.

Turn right side out and stuff with foam filling or kapok. Stuff legs, ladder-stitch openings. Sew one leg into body at each end of side opening, then sew remainder of opening. Rep. at other side. Cut four ½-in. strips of white felt 3 in. long, cut notches out of one long side like a saw. Sew one strip to each side of mouth for teeth. Cut 2 circles of white felt 1 in. in diameter and 2 circles of black felt ½ in. in diameter. Sew black circles on top of white, then sew white circles to top of crocodile, at "head" end, for eyes.

Aladdin and Abanazar
(photographed in colour on page 224)

MATERIALS

For Aladdin: 1 oz. Hayfield Gaylon Double Knitting (see note on wools and yarns, page 20) in black, 1 oz. in rust, 1 oz. in fawn and 1 oz. in orange; one pair No. 10 knitting needles plus a single No. 10 knitting needle (see page 26); foam filling (washable) or kapok for stuffing; oddment red yarn.
For Abanazar: 1 oz. Hayfield Gaylon Double Knitting (see note on wools and yarns, page 20) in red, oddment in each of black, fawn, yellow, purple and white; 1 ball Hayfield Jewel (see note on wools and yarns, page 20) in green and 1 ball in yellow; one pair No. 10 knitting needles (see page 26); foam filling (washable) or kapok for stuffing; red metallic thread.

MEASUREMENTS

Aladdin: 9 in. tall. Abanazar: 13 in.

TENSION

Double knitting: 6 sts. to 1 in. **Jewel:** 6½ sts. to 1 in. (see note on tension, page 15).

ABBREVIATIONS

See page 26; B., black; Rt., rust; F., fawn; Or., orange; R., red; Y., yellow; Pu., purple; W., white; G., green.

ALADDIN
FRONT BODY AND LEGS

Leg. With pair of needles and F., cast on 8 sts. and work 1¼ in. in garter st. Join B. and work 1¾ in. in garter st. Leave sts. on stitch holder. Work another leg in the same way.
Body. Next row: k. across sts. of second leg, then across sts. from stitch holder: 16 sts.
Work 1½ in. in garter st. Leave sts. on needle.
Tunic Flap. With Rt. and using third needle, cast on 16 sts. and work 2 in. in garter st.
Body. Place needle with tunic sts. in front of needle with body sts. on it and with Rt. k. 1 st. from each tog. to end of row: 16 sts. Cont. in garter st. for 2 in.**
Face. Join F. and work 1½ in. in garter st. Join B., and work ½ in. in garter st. Cast off.

BACK BODY AND LEGS

Work as Front Body to **. Join B. and work 2 in. in garter st. Cast off.

ARMS (make 2 alike)

With F., cast on 14 sts. and work 1½ in. in garter st. Join Rt. and work a further 1½ in. in garter st. Cast off.

HAT

With Or., cast on 80 sts. and k. 1 row.
1st row: k.4, k.2 tog., *k.8, k.2 tog.; rep. from * to last 4 sts., k.4: 72 sts.
2nd and alt. rows: k.
3rd row: k.4, k.2 tog., *k.7, k.2 tog.; rep. from * to last 3 sts., k.3.
5th row: k.3, k.2 tog., *k.6, k.2 tog.; rep. from * to last 3 sts., k.3.
7th row: k.3, k.2 tog., *k.5, k.2 tog.; rep. from * to last 2 sts., k.2.
9th row: k.2, k.2 tog., *k.4, k.2 tog.; rep. from * to last 2 sts., k.2.
11th row: k.2, k.2 tog., *k.3, k.2 tog.; rep. from * to last st., k.1.
13th row: k.1, k.2 tog., *k.2, k.2 tog.; rep. from * to last st., k.1.
15th row: *k.1, k.2 tog.; rep. from * to end.
16th row: *k.2 tog.; rep. from * to end.
Rep. last row once. Fasten off.

TO COMPLETE

Embroider features on F. face: with B. yarn work 2 straight stitches for each eye and with R. yarn work one straight stitch for mouth.
Place 2 body pieces tog., with right sides facing, then oversew seams tog., rounding corners at head

and feet and leaving tunic flap free and one side open. Turn right side out. Stuff head firmly with foam filling or kapok then run a thread round neck, pull tight and fasten securely.

Stuff legs and body and ladder-stitch opening. Sew top of tunic sides tog., leaving last 1 in. open. Fold arms in half lengthwise and oversew long edge and one short edge, rounding corners. Turn right side out, stuff and stitch opening. Attach to sides of body just below neck.

Join side seam of hat then sew hat to top of head, leaving a brim of about 1½ in.

ABANAZAR

FRONT AND BACK BODY AND LEGS (worked in one long piece)

Front Leg. With B., cast on 10 sts. and work 1 in. in garter st. Join W. and work ½ in. in garter st. Join R. and work 3 in. in garter st. Leave sts. on stitch holder.

Work another leg to match.

Front Body. Next row: k. across sts. of second leg, then across sts. from stitch holder: 20 sts.

Work 1 in. in garter st. Join Pu., and work 1 in. in garter st. Join R. and work 2½ in. in garter st.

Face. Join F., and work 1¼ in. in garter st.

Crown of Hat. Join Gaylon Y., and work 2½ in. in garter st.

Back of Head. Join B. and work 1¼ in. in garter st.

Back Body. Join R. and work 2½ in. in garter st. Join Pu. and work 1 in. in garter st. Join R. and work 1 in. in garter st.

Divide for Back Legs. Next row: k. 10 sts.; turn. Work on these 10 sts. only in garter st., first with R. for 3 in., then with W. for ½ in., then with B. for 1 in. Cast off. Rejoin R. yarn to remaining 10 sts. and work to match first back leg.

ARMS (make 2 alike)

With F., cast on 14 sts. and work ½ in. in garter st. Join R. and work 2½ in. in garter st. Cast off.

HAT BRIM

With Gaylon Y., cast on 40 sts. and k. 1 row.

1st row: k.2, inc. 1 st. in next st., *k.4, inc. 1 st. in next st.; rep. from * to last 2 sts., k.2: 48 sts.

2nd row: k.

3rd row: k.3, inc. 1 st. in next st., *k.5, inc. 1 st. in next st.; rep. from * to last 2 sts., k.2.

4th row: k.

5th row: k.4, inc. 1 st. in next st., *k.6, inc. 1 st. in next st.; rep. from * to last 2 sts., k.2.

6th row: k.

Cast off.

CLOAK

Note. *Use Y. and G. Jewel yarn tog. throughout.*

Back. With 1 strand Y. and 1 strand G., cast on 36 sts. and work 6½ in. in garter st.

Sleeves (make 2 alike). Cast on 10 sts. at beg. of next 2 rows, cont. in garter st. on these sts. for 1½ in.

Divide for Fronts. Next row: k.24, cast off 8 sts., k. to end.

Cont. in garter st. on last group of 24 sts. for 3 in., then cast off 10 sts. on sleeve side. Work on remaining 14 sts. in garter st. for 6½ in. Cast off. Rejoin yarn to remaining 24 sts. and complete to match first side.

TO COMPLETE

Embroider features on F. face: with B. yarn work two straight stitches for each eye, and one stitch for moustache, leaving long ends hanging at each side. With R. yarn, work one straight stitch for mouth below moustache.

Fold body in half, with right sides facing, then oversew seams tog., rounding corners at head and feet, and leaving one side open. Turn right side out. Stuff head firmly, then run a thread round neck and draw up tightly and fasten securely. Stuff legs and body and ladder-stitch opening.

Fold arms in half lengthwise, with right sides facing, and oversew long edge and one short edge, rounding corners. Turn to right side and stuff. Stitch up opening. Attach arms to sides of body just below neck.

Join hat brim in a circle, then sew to head round beg. of Y. crown. Turn brim up. Sew side and sleeve seams to cloak then attach to body round neck. Make a plait 7 in. long with three lengths B. yarn. Knot one end, and attach other end to middle of back of head. With metallic thread work herringbone-stitch around centre of Pu. waist.

Doll's clothes

(photographed in colour on page 224)

MATERIALS

For coat, hat and shoulder bag: 1 oz. Hayfield Double Knitting (see note on wools and yarns, page 20) in flecked black and white and an oddment of Hayfield 4-ply (see note on wools and yarns, page 26) in black; one pair No. 8 knitting needles (see page 26); 2 press studs.

For evening dress and cape: 1 oz. Hayfield Jewel

(see note on wools and yarns, page 20) in white and 1 oz. in gold; one pair each Nos. 6 and 10 knitting needles (see page 26); one crochet hook International Standard Size 2·50; shirring elastic.

For frilly dress: 1 oz. Hayfield 4-ply (see note on wools and yarns, page 20) in pink; one pair No. 10 knitting needles (see page 26); 1 press stud.

For swimsuit: 1 oz. Hayfield 4-ply (see note on wools and yarns, page 20) in white and an oddment in navy; one pair No. 10 knitting needles (see page 26); one crochet hook International Standard Size 2·50.

For midi-length suit: 1 oz. Hayfield 4-ply (see note on wools and yarns, page 20) in red; one pair No. 10 knitting needles (see page 26); shirring elastic; 3 press studs; oddment of red and white striped cotton (optional).

MEASUREMENTS
To fit a doll 12 in. high.

TENSION
Double knitting: 5½ sts. to 1 in. with No. 8 needles. **Jewel:** 6½ sts. to 1 in. with No. 10 needles. **4-ply:** 7 sts. to 1 in. with No. 10 needles (see note on tension, page 15).

ABBREVIATIONS
See page 26.

COAT, HAT AND SHOULDER BAG
COAT BACK
With flecked double knitting yarn, cast on 29 sts. Work 3 rows in moss st. (see page 23). Change to reversed st.st. (see page 23), beg. with a k. row, and work until Back measures 4¼ in., ending with a k. row.
Waist. Next row: p.1, *p.2 tog.; rep. from * to end. Work another 2½ in. in st.st.
Cast off 5 sts. at beg. of next 2 rows. Cast off.

COAT RIGHT FRONT
With flecked double knitting yarn, cast on 18 sts.
1st row: k.2, *k.1, p.1; rep. from * to end.
2nd row: *p.1, k.1; rep. from * to last 2 sts., k.2.
3rd row: as first row.
Still keeping the border of 2 sts. in garter st., change to reversed st.st., beg. with a k. row, and work until Front measures 4¼ in., ending with a k. row.
Waist. Next row: k.2, *p.2 tog.; rep. from * to end. Cont. straight for another 2¼ in. ending with a k. row. Cast off 5 sts. at beg. of next row. Cont. until work measures 2½ in. from waist.
Cast off.

COAT LEFT FRONT
Work as Right Front, with garter-st. border at other side and reversing shaping.

COAT COLLAR
Join Fronts to Back at shoulders. With right side of work facing, and with flecked double knitting yarn, pick up 14 sts. round neck and work 3 rows in st.st. inc. 1 st. at each end of each row. Cast off.

COAT SLEEVES (make 2 alike)
With right side of work facing and with flecked double knitting yarn, pick up 12 sts. from a point on Back ¾ in. below shoulder seam around armhole to matching point on Front. Work 2¼ in. in reversed st.st., then work 2 rows in moss st.
Cast off in moss st.

SHOULDER BAG
With 2 strands of black 4-ply yarn, cast on 7 sts. Work 14 rows in moss st. Cast off.

HAT
With 2 strands of black 4-ply yarn, cast on 31 sts. Work 6 rows in moss st., working 2 sts. tog. at end of last row.
Next row: *k.4, k.2 tog.; rep. from * to end.
Next row: p.
Next row: *k.3, k.2 tog.; rep. from * to end.
Next row: p.
Next row: *k.2, k.2 tog.; rep. from * to end.
Next row: p.
Next row: *k.1, k.2 tog.; rep. from * to end.
Next row: p.
Next row: *k.2 tog.; rep. from * to end.
Next row: p.3 tog., p.2 tog.
Thread yarn through sts. and fasten off.

TO COMPLETE
Coat. Join side and sleeve seams. Sew press studs to overlap of Fronts at waist and neck edge.

Shoulder Bag. Fold in half and join open edges. Make either a crochet ch. (see page 24) or plait 3 strands of yarn to a length of 8 in. Sew ends to each side of bag.
Note. *This shoulder bag piece may be made into a muff if preferred. Fold into a cylinder and join along edges. Complete as Bag.*

Hat. Sew side seam.

EVENING DRESS AND CAPE
DRESS FRONT AND BACK (2 pieces alike)
With No. 10 needles and 2 strands of white yarn, cast on 40 sts. Work 3 rows in st.st. (see page 23), beg. with a p. row.
Next (picot) row: k.1, *y.fwd., k.2 tog.; rep. from * to last st., k.1.
Cont. in st.st. until work measures 6¼ in. from picot row, ending with a p. row.
Waist. Next row: k.3 tog., *k.2 tog.; rep. from * to

last 3 sts., k.3 tog. Cont. in st.st. for another 1½ in., ending with a p. row, then work another picot row, omitting last st. Work 2 more rows, then cast off.

CAPE
With No. 6 needles and 2 strands of gold yarn cast on 64 sts.
1st row: k.2, *y.r.n., p.4 tog.; rep. from * to last 2 sts., k.2.
2nd row: k.2, *k.1, into next st. work k.1, p.1 and k.1; rep. from * to last 2 sts., k.2.
3rd row: k.
These 3 rows form patt. Cont. in patt. until work measures 6½ in. Cast off.
Edging. With crochet hook and 1 strand of yarn, and with right side facing, work down long edges in tr. and d.c. (see page 24) as follows: insert hook at right end of edge, 3 ch., 4 tr. into same place, 1 d.c. into next st., *5tr. into next st., 1 d.c. into next st.; rep. from * to end.

TO COMPLETE
Dress. Sew 2 pieces tog. along long edges. Sew hem at top and bottom. Run shirring elastic through waist and top. Make 2 lengths of crochet ch., each 2 in. long. Sew to Dress to form shoulder straps.
Cape. Make a crochet ch. 10½ in. long and thread it through holes in patt. 1½ in. down from one of the short edges to form tie at neck edge. Draw up and tie in a bow at front of neck.

FRILLY DRESS
BACK
With No. 10 needles and 4-ply yarn, cast on 32 sts. Work a picot row as given for Evening Dress. Now cont. in st.st. (see page 23), and when work measures 1 in. work 2 sts. tog. at each end of row. Then dec. in same way at ½-in. intervals until 18 sts. remain (4½ in.). Cont. straight until work measures 7 in. Cast off 6 sts. at beg. of next 2 rows.
Cast off.

FRONT
Work as Back for 4½ in.
Next row: k.8; turn.
Work on these sts. only, working 2 sts. tog. at inside edge at ½-in. intervals until 6 sts. remain.
Cont. straight until work measures 7 in. Cast off.
Rejoin yarn to remaining sts. and work to match first side.

SLEEVES (make 2 alike)
Join Front and Back at shoulders. With right side facing, pick up and k. 14 sts. round armhole (7 sts. each side of seam). Work 2¼ in. in st.st., ending with a p. row. Work a picot row as given for Evening Dress, then p. 1 more row.
Cast off.

FRILL
With crochet hook, work ch. (see page 24) approx. twice the length from hem of skirt to shoulder, round back of neck and down to waist.
Next row: 1 tr. into 3rd ch., 1 tr. into each ch. to end. Fasten off.

TO COMPLETE
Join sleeve and side seams and turn up hem and sleeve edges. Run a gathering thread through ch. edge of frill and draw it up to fit from hem of skirt to shoulder, round back of neck and down to waist. Stitch in place. Sew a press stud at base of front V.

SWIMSUIT
PANTS
With No. 10 needles and white cast on 16 sts. Work 2 rows in garter st. (see page 23). Change to st.st. (see page 23), beg. with a p. row, and work 4 rows. Cast off 3 sts. at beg. of next 2 rows then work 2 sts. tog. at each end of next and every alt. row until 4 sts. remain. Work 4 rows. Now inc. 1 st. at each end of every row until there are 10 sts. Cast off 3 sts. at beg. of next 2 rows. Work 3 rows in st.st. K. 1 row. Cast off in k.

TOP
Pick up centre 5 sts. from cast-off edge and work 3 rows in st.st. Inc. 1 st. at each end of every alt. row until there are 15 sts. Then work 2 sts. tog. at each end of every row until 9 sts. remain. Cast off.

TO COMPLETE
Join side seams of pants section. With crochet hook and blue yarn work d.c. (see page 26) all round top of pants section and top of suit. Make a crochet ch. and attach at sides to tie at back.

MIDI-LENGTH SUIT
SKIRT FRONT AND BACK (make 2 pieces alike)
With No. 10 needles cast on 33 sts. and work 4 rows in moss st. (see page 23). Change to st.st. (see page 23) and work until Skirt measures 1¼ in., ending with a p. row.
Next row: k.7, k.2 tog., k.1, k.2 tog., k.9, k.2 tog., k.1, k.2 tog., k. to end.
Work 1 in. in st.st., ending with a p. row.
Next row: k.6, k.2 tog., k.1, k.2 tog., k.7, k.2 tog., k.1, k.2 tog., k. to end.
Cont. to dec. in this way at 1-in. intervals until 4 dec. rows in all have been worked. Cont. straight until Skirt measures 4½ in., then work 1 row in k.1, p.1 rib. Cast off in rib.

JACKET BACK
Cast on 18 sts. and work 3 rows in moss st. Change to st.st. and work until Back measures 3½ in., ending

with a p. row. Cast off 6 sts. at beg. of next 2 rows. Cast off.

JACKET RIGHT FRONT
Cast on 11 sts. and work 3 rows in moss st.
Next row: moss st. 3, k. to end.
Next row: p. to last 3 sts., moss st. 3.
Cont. in st.st. with moss-st. border until work measures 3 in., ending with a p. row.
Next row: patt. 4 sts. and put on safety pin, patt. to end.
Work 2 sts. tog. at neck edge on next row, then cont. until work measures 3½ in.
Cast off.

JACKET LEFT FRONT
Work as Right Front, reversing shaping.

Toy spaceman
(photographed in colour on page 224)

MATERIALS
1 oz. Hayfield Gaylon Double Knitting (see note on wools and yarns, page 20) in black, 1 oz. in fawn and 1 oz. in cream; one pair No. 10 knitting needles (see page 26); foam filling (washable) or kapok for stuffing; scraps of black, white and orange felt; 9 in. by 4½ in. transparent film; short lengths of brown and red yarn and red thread.

MEASUREMENTS
12 in. high and 4 in. wide, approx.

TENSION
6 sts. to 1 in. (see note on tension, page 15).

ABBREVIATIONS
See page 26; B., black; F., fawn; C., cream.

FRONT AND BACK BODY AND LEGS (worked in one long piece)
Front Leg. With B., cast on 10 sts. and work 4½ in. in garter st. (see page 23). Break yarn and leave sts. on safety pin.
Work a second leg to match.
Front Body. Next row: k. across 10 sts. of second leg, then 10 sts. from safety pin.
Work a further 4½ in. in garter st.
Face. Join C. and work 2 in. in garter st.
Back Head and Body. Change to B. and work 7½ in. in garter st.
Divide for Back Legs. Next row: k.10; turn.
Work on these sts. only for 4½ in. in garter st. Cast off.
Rejoin yarn to remaining 10 sts. and work 4½ in. in

garter st.; cast off.

FRONT AND BACK OVERALLS (make 2 alike)
Leg. With F., cast on 10 sts. and k. 1 row. Work in garter st., inc. 1 st. in every st. on next row: 20 sts.
Cont. until work measures 3 in. then leave sts. on stitch holder.
Work a second leg to match.
Body. Next row: k. across 20 sts. of second leg then 20 sts. from stitch holder.
Work 1½ in. in garter st.
Next row: *k.2 tog.; rep. from * to end: 20 sts.
Work ½ in. in garter st.
Next row: inc. 1 st. in each of first 2 sts., * inc. 1 st. in next st., k.1; rep. from * to end: 31 sts.
Work 3 in. in garter st.
Next row: *k.2 tog.; rep. from * to last st., k.1. Cast off.

ARMS (make 2 alike)
With F., cast on 16 sts. and work 3 in. in garter st. Cast off.

NECKBAND
With F., cast on 40 sts. and work 1 in. in garter st. Cast off.

TO COMPLETE
Embroider features on cream face: with brown yarn stemstitch 2 eyebrows and satin-stitch 2 eyes underneath; with red yarn embroider 2 short vertical stitches for nose and stemstitch mouth. Fold over body, with right sides facing, then oversew seams tog., rounding corners at bottom of legs and sides

JACKET SLEEVES (make 2 alike)
Join Fronts to Back. With right side of work facing, pick up 14 sts. round armhole (7 sts. each side of shoulder seam). Work 2¼ in. in st.st. Work 1 row in moss st. Cast off in moss st.

TO COMPLETE
Skirt. Join side seams of skirt. Run shirring elastic through ribbing at waist.
Jacket. With right side of work facing, pick up sts. from safety pin on Right Front, pick up 19 sts. round neck and pick up sts. on safety pin on Left Front. Work 2 rows in moss st. Cast off in moss st. Join side and sleeve seams and sew press studs down moss-st. bands on Fronts.
If wished make a high-necked underblouse in striped cotton to put under suit jacket.

of head, and leaving one side open for stuffing. Turn right side out. Fold arms in half lengthwise, with right sides facing, then oversew long edge and one short edge, rounding corners. Turn right side out.

Stuff head with kapok to bottom of face, then run a thread round neck, pull up tightly and secure. Stuff legs, then centre of body, and ladder-stitch opening. With right sides facing, place overalls back and front tog. and oversew inside leg seams and side seams. Turn right side out and fit on spaceman, pinning at back and front of neck and round ankles. Hemstitch round ankles and neck. Stuff arms and ladder-stitch openings. Sew to sides of body about $\frac{3}{4}$ in. down from neck.

Fold transparent film into a cylinder and sew ends tog. Fold neckband in half lengthwise and fit one edge of cylinder into fold. Stitch along edges of neckband through film and both thicknesses of neckband with a red thread. Place cylinder and neckband over head and hemstitch fold of neckband to neck.

Cut a circle of black felt to fit top of cylinder and sew it to cylinder. Cut a piece of black felt 9 in. by 2½ in. and roll up tightly lengthwise. Secure edge, then place horizontally on top of back and stitch to back. Cut strips of orange felt ¼ in. wide — four 10 in. long, one 7 in. and two 6 in. Sew 7-in. strip round black felt at top of helmet. Attach ends of two 6-in. strips to centre of back of helmet, then bring down back of helmet and round black felt cylinder on back and stitch to cylinder. Sew two 10-in. strips at back waist, take over shoulders and sew to front waist; sew two to back waist, take between legs and sew to front waist. Cut a strip of black felt ¾ in. wide and 8 in. long and a strip of white felt ¼ in. wide and 8 in. long.

Put black felt strip round waist, covering ends of orange strips, and sew ends tog. Put white felt over black and join ends. Stitch waistband to body at centre front and centre back. Cut four circles of black felt ½ in. in diameter and 4 circles white felt ¼ in. in diameter. Sew one white circle to each black circle with a cross-stitch worked with black thread, then sew 2 black circles to right leg, 1 to left leg and 1 to left side of chest.

Chapter 9
For the Children to Make

Dish cloth

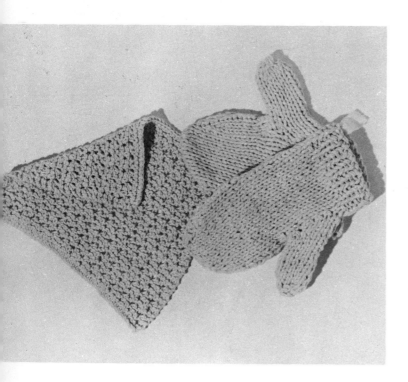

MATERIALS
2 oz. Twilley's D.42 or S.17 Knitting Cotton (see note on wools and yarns, page 20); one pair No. 6 knitting needles (see page 26).

MEASUREMENTS
12 in. square.

TENSION
8 sts. and $10\frac{1}{2}$ rows to 2 in. (see note on tension page 15).

ABBREVIATIONS
See page 26.

TO MAKE
Cast on 47 sts.
1st and 2nd rows: k.
3rd row: k.2, *y.fwd., k.2 tog., k.1; rep. from * to end.
Rep. last 3 rows until 21 rows of holes have been worked.
Next row: k.
Cast off.

Oven mitts
(photographed in black and white above)

MATERIALS
4 oz. Twilley's D.42 or S.17 Knitting Cotton (see note on wools and yarns, page 20); one pair No. 2 knitting needles (see page 26); $\frac{1}{2}$ yard white tape $\frac{5}{8}$ in. wide.

MEASUREMENTS
To fit an average-sized hand.

TENSION
7 sts. and 8 rows to 2 in. (see note on tension page 15).

ABBREVIATIONS
See page 26.

Note. *Use yarn double throughout.*

TO MAKE (2 alike)

With 2 strands of yarn, cast on 26 sts.

Work 6 rows in k.1, p.1 rib.

7th row: k.

8th row: p.

9th row: k.12, k. twice into next 2 sts., k.12.

10th and alt. rows: p.

11th row: k.12, k. twice into next st., k.2, k. twice into next st., k.12.

13th row: k.12, k. twice into next st., k.4, k. twice into next st., k.12.

15th row: k.

17th row: k.12, k. twice into next st., k.6, k. twice into next st., k.12.

19th row: k.22; turn.

20th row: cast on 2 sts., p.12 (including 2 cast-on sts.); turn.

Thumb. Work 8 rows in st.st. (1 row k., 1 row p.) on these 12 sts.

Next row: *k.1, k.2 tog.; rep. from * to end of row. Break yarn, thread through remaining 8 sts. and draw up tightly. Use yarn to sew edges of thumb tog. on the inside.

Palm. Next row: join yarn to inner edge of sts. on right-hand needle, pick up and k. 4 sts. from bottom of thumb, k. 12 sts. to end of row: 28 sts. on needle.

Work on these sts. in st.st. until work measures 3½ in. from first palm row.

Shape Top. 1st row: k.2 tog., k.9, k.2 tog., k.2, k.2 tog., k.9, k.2 tog.

2nd and alt. rows: p.

3rd row: k.2 tog., k.8, k.2 tog., k.2 tog., k.8, k.2 tog.

5th row: k.2 tog., k.6, k.2 tog., k.2 tog., k.6, k.2 tog.

7th row: *k.1, k.2 tog.; rep. from * to last st., k.1. Cast off.

TO COMPLETE

Oversew sides of glove tog. on the inside. Cut a 6 in. length of tape, fold in half, tuck short edges in and sew fold of short edges to inside of glove at the bottom of the seam edge.

Oven cloth

MATERIALS

4 oz. Twilley's D.42 or S.17 Knitting Cotton (see note on wools and yarns, page 20); one pair of No. 7 knitting needles (see page 26); 1 yard white tape 1 in. wide.

MEASUREMENTS

26 in. long and 7 in wide.

TENSION

5 sts. and 6 rows to 1 in. (see note on tension, page 15).

ABBREVIATIONS

See page 26.

TO MAKE

Cast on 36 sts.

1st row: k.

2nd row: p.

Rep. these 2 rows until work measures 38 in. Cast off.

TO COMPLETE

Fold each short end over 6 in. with right (smooth) sides inside. Oversew side edges tog., making a pocket at each end. Turn right side out. Bind each side between pockets with tape, hemstitching the tape firmly in place, tucking in short ends of tape and hemstitching them too. Fold remaining tape in half to

make a loop for hanging up, tuck in short ends and hemstitch fold of short ends to middle of one taped edge.

Hot water bottle cover

MATERIALS
3 oz. Sirdar Double Knitting (see note on wools and yarns, page 20) in main shade and 2 oz. in contrast; one pair No. 6 knitting needles (see page 26); 2 press studs.

MEASUREMENTS
9½ in. by 13 in. approx.

TENSION
4½ sts. to 1 in. (see note on tension, page 15).

ABBREVIATIONS
See page 26; M., main shade; C., contrast.

Note. *Use yarn double throughout.*

FRONT AND BACK (make 2 pieces alike)
With 2 strands M., cast on 44 sts. and work 3 rows in k.1, p.1 rib.
Next row: k.22; turn.
Work 5½ in. in st.st. (1 row k., 1 row p.) on these sts. only, ending with a p. row.
Join C. and work 5½ in. in st.st. Leave sts. on stitch holder. Rejoin C. to remaining 22 sts.
Work 5½ in. in st.st. on these sts., then join M. and work 5½ in. Break off yarn.
Next row: with M., k. across all 44 sts.
Work 3 rows in k.1, p.1 rib. Still working in rib, cast off 14 sts. at beg. of next 2 rows and then work 3 rows in rib on the remaining 16 sts. Cast off.

TO COMPLETE
Join the 2 sections of each piece down centre by oversewing on the wrong side. Join side seams in the same way. Join bottom seam (cast-on edges) leaving a 2-in. opening in middle for tab of bottle. Join top seam (cast-off edges) at sides for about 1 in., leaving rest open. Sew a press stud each side of "neck" of cover.

Rainbow cushion cover

MATERIALS
5 oz. Sirdar Double Knitting (see note on wools and yarns, page 20) in as many different colours as liked (left-over yarns can be used); one pair No. 8 knitting needles (see page 26); 4 press studs.

MEASUREMENTS
To fit a cushion 15 in. square.

TENSION
5½ sts. and 7½ rows to 1 in. (see note on tension, page 15).

ABBREVIATIONS
See page 26.

STRIPS (make 3 alike)
Cast on 28 sts. and work in st.st. (1 row k., 1 row p.) until work measures 31 in. Join a different colour as often as you like but always start new colour on a k. row. The cushion cover in the photograph changes colour at 2, 3 and 4-in. intervals. Cast off.

TO COMPLETE
Join the 3 strips together by oversewing 2 long edges tog. on the wrong side. Fold strips in half, with right sides tog. to form a square. Oversew side edges tog., then sew press studs to open edges, tops evenly spaced along one edge and bottoms to match on other. Turn cushion cover right side out. Using 6 strands of one colour or 2 strands each of 3 colours, make a plait long enough to go right round cover plus 16 in. Sew plait round three joined edges of cover, leaving a 2-in. loop free at corners, then sew along one open edge.
Carefully fit your cover over a 15in. square cushion. Fasten with press studs.

Tea cosy and matching egg cosy

MATERIALS
2 oz. Sirdar Double Knitting (see note on wools and yarns, page 20) in 1st colour and 2 oz. in 2nd colour; one pair No. 6 knitting needles (see page 26).

MEASUREMENTS
Stretches to fit most sizes of teapot.

TENSION
4½ sts. to 1 in. (see note on tension, page 15).

ABBREVIATIONS
See page 26.

Note. *Use yarn double throughout.*

TEA COSY
FRONT AND BACK (make 2 alike)
With 1 strand of 1st colour and 1 strand of 2nd colour, cast on 40 sts. and work 4 rows in garter st. (every row k.). Change to st.st. (1 row k., 1 row p.) and work 6 rows.
Next row: p.
Next row: k.
Rep. these 2 rows once. Now beg. with a k. row, work 6 rows in st.st.
These last 10 rows form patt. Keep working in patt. and cont. until work measures 4½ in.
Next row: working correct patt. row, patt. 4, *work 2 sts. tog., patt. 3; rep. from * to last 6 sts., work 2 sts. tog., patt. to end.
Work 7 more rows in patt.
Next row: *work 2 sts. tog., patt. 1; rep. from * to end.
Patt. 1 row.
Next row: *work 2 sts. tog.; rep. from * to end.
Cast off.

TO COMPLETE
Join 2 pieces by oversewing side and top seams tog. on inside; leave open from beg. of 2nd ridge to end of 3rd ridge on one side for teapot handle and from beg. of 2nd ridge to beg. of 3rd ridge on other side for spout. Make 2 pompons, one in 1st colour and one in 2nd, following instructions on page 82, and using card circles 2½ in. in diameter. Sew to top of tea cosy.

EGG COSY
TO MAKE
With 1 strand of 1st colour and 1 strand of 2nd colour, cast on 28 sts. and work 4 rows in garter st. (every row k.).

Change to st.st. (1 row k., 1 row p.) and work 12 rows.

Next row: *k.2 tog.; rep. from * to end.
Work 2 rows.

Next row: *p.2 tog.; rep. from * to end.
Thread yarn through remaining sts., draw up tightly and fasten off.

TO COMPLETE
Oversew side seam on inside. Make 2 pompons, one in 1st colour and one in 2nd, following instructions on page 82, and using card circles 1½ in. in diameter. Sew to top of egg cosy.

Striped scarf

MATERIALS
4 oz. Sirdar Double Knitting (see note on wools and yarns, page 20) in main shade, 2 oz. in 1st contrast shade and 2 oz. in 2nd contrast shade; one pair No. 9 knitting needles (see page 26); one crochet hook approx. International Standard Size 4·00.

MEASUREMENTS
45 in. long and 7 in. wide approx.

TENSION
6 sts. to 1 in. (see note on tension, page 15).

ABBREVIATIONS
See page 26; M., main shade; A., 1st contrast shade; B., 2nd contrast shade.

TO MAKE
With M. cast on 71 sts.
1st row: k.1, *k.1, p.1; rep. from * to end.
2nd row: k.1, *p.1, k.1; rep. from * to end.
Cont. working these 2 rows.
Work 26 rows in all with M. Break off M. and join A. Work 6 rows with A. Break off A. and join B. Work 10 rows with B. Break off B. and join A. Work 6 rows with A.
These 48 rows form patt. Rep. patt. 6 times, then work 26 rows with M. Cast off.

TO COMPLETE
Cut a number of 5-in. lengths in all 3 yarns. Take 2 lengths of M. and fold in half; take crochet hook and push it through end of one short edge of scarf, slip hook through looped end of yarn and pull this loop through. Slip ends of yarn through loop and pull up tightly. Rep. with A. yarn next to the first loop, then with B., then use each of 3 yarns in turn all along edge. Do the same at other short edge of scarf.

Mittens

MATERIALS
2 (2) oz. Sirdar Double Knitting (see note on wools and yarns, page 20); one pair No. 8 knitting needles (see page 26).

MEASUREMENTS
Width 3 (3½) in.; length 4¾ (5¾) in.

TENSION
6 sts. and 8 rows to 1 in. (see note on tension, page 15).

ABBREVIATIONS
See page 26.

TO MAKE (2 alike)
Cast on 38 (44) sts. and work 2 (2½) in. in k.1, p.1 rib, working twice into last st. of last row: 39 (45) sts.
Next row: k.17 (20), work twice into next st., k.3, work twice into next st., k. to end.
Next row: p.
Next row: k.
Next row: p.
Next row: k.17 (20), work twice into next st., k.5, work twice into next st., k.17 (20).
Next row: p.
Work 2 rows in st.st. (1 row k., 1 row p.).
Next row: k.26 (29), work twice into next st.; turn.
Next row: p.11, p. twice into next st.; turn.
Thumb. Work 10 (12) rows in st.st. on these 13 sts.
Next row: k.1, *k.2 tog.; rep. from * to end.
Next row: p.
Next row: k.1, *k.2 tog.; rep. from * to end. Break yarn, thread through sts., draw up and fasten off. Oversew edges of thumb tog. on inside. Turn thumb right side out.
Palm. Next row: join yarn to inner edge of sts. on right-hand needle, pick up and k.5 sts. from base of thumb, k. across remaining 16 (19) sts.: 37 (43) sts. on needle. Cont. in st.st. on these sts. until work measures 4 (5) in. from end of ribbing.
Next row: k.2 tog., k.2 tog., k.10 (13), k.2 tog., k.2 tog., k.1, k.2 tog., k.2 tog., k.10 (13), k.2 tog., k.2 tog.
Next row: p.

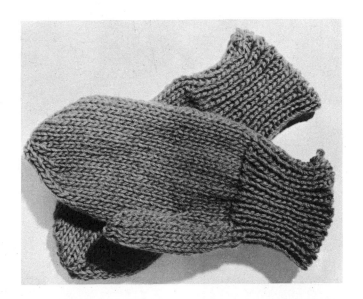

Next row: k.2 tog., k.2 tog., k.6 (9), k.2 tog., k.2 tog., k.1, k.2 tog., k.2 tog., k.6 (9), k.2 tog., k.2 tog.
Next row: p.
Next row: k.2 tog., k.2 tog., k.2 (5), k.2 tog., k.2 tog., k.1, k.2 tog., k.2 tog., k.2 (5), k.2 tog., k.2 tog.
Next row: p.
Cast off.

TO COMPLETE
Oversew side seams and along tops on the inside.

Angora bolero
(photographed in black and white on page 238)

MATERIALS
3 (3, 4, 4) balls (½-oz.) Paton's Fuzzy Wuzzy (see note on wools and yarns, page 20); one pair of No. 10 knitting needles (see page 26).

MEASUREMENTS
To fit chest size 22 (24, 26, 28) in.

TENSION
7 sts. and 9 rows to 1 in. (see note on tension, page 15).

ABBREVIATIONS
See page 26.

BACK
Cast on 78 (84, 92, 98) sts. and work 4 (5½, 6¾, 8) in. in st.st. (1 row k., 1 row p.) ending with a p. row.
Shape Armholes. Cast off 5 sts. at beg. of next 2 rows then work 2 sts. tog. at each end of every k. row until 66 (70, 74, 78) sts. remain. Cont. straight until armholes measure 5¼ (5½, 5¾, 6) in. from beg. of shaping, ending with a p. row.
Shape Shoulders. Cast off 10 sts. at beg. of next 2 rows and 9 (10, 10, 11) sts. at beg. of next 2 rows. Cast off remaining sts.

LEFT FRONT
Cast on 20 (24, 28, 32) sts. and work 4 (6, 6, 6) rows in st.st.
Shape Front Slope. Next row: k. to last st., k. twice into last st.
Cont. working twice into the last st. of every k. row until there are 30 (34, 38, 42) sts. Cont. straight until Front measures same as Back to beg. of armhole shaping, ending with a p. row.
Shape Armhole and Front Slope. Next row: cast off 5 sts., k. to last 2 sts., k.2 tog.
Now cont. to work 2 sts. tog. at beg. of every k. row for armhole shaping until 1 (3, 4, 5) such decs. have been made, and at the same time work 2 sts. tog. at front slope edge at ½-in. intervals until 19 (20, 20, 21)

sts. remain. Cont. straight until armhole measures the same as Back armhole to beg. of shoulder shaping, ending with a p. row.

Next row: cast off 10 sts., k. to end.
P. 1 row. Cast off.

RIGHT FRONT
Cast on 20 (24, 28, 32) sts. and work 4 (6, 6, 6) rows in st.st.

Shape Front Slope. Next row: k. twice into first st., k. to end.

Cont. working twice into the first st. of every k. row until there are 30 (34, 38, 42) sts. Cont. straight until Front measures same as Back to beg. of armhole shaping, ending with a p. row.

Shape Front Slope and Armhole. Next row: k.2 tog., k. to end.

Next row: cast off 5 sts., p. to end.

Now cont. to work 2 sts. tog. at end of every k. row for armhole shaping until 1 (3, 4, 5) such decs. have been made, and at the same time work 2 sts. tog. at front slope edge at ½-in. intervals until 19 (20, 20, 21) sts. remain. Cont. straight until armhole measures same as Back armhole to beg. of shoulder shaping, ending with a k. row.

Next row: cast off 10 sts., p. to end.
K.1 row. Cast off.

ARMBANDS (make 2 alike)
Cast on 7 sts. Work in k.1, p.1 rib until strip is long enough to go right round one armhole. Cast off.

EDGING
Cast on 7 sts. and work in k.1, p.1 rib until strip is long enough to go round lower edge of Back, up Front, round back of neck, and down other Front. Cast off.

TO COMPLETE
Join shoulder and side seams by backstitching them tog. on wrong side. Oversew edging to Bolero and armbands round armholes.

Index